THE PRINCE OF NAPLES

The true story of one boy's secret war on the Mafia

As told to

Hugh Gurney

First published in Great Britain in 2021 by Alpha4All Limited

Copyright © Alpha4All Limited

Cover images by Shutterstock.

Edited, designed and produced by Tandem Publishing
http://tandempublishing.yolasite.com/

An earlier version of part of this book was published in 2013 by Revolution Press under the title *The Prince of Naples: A True Story.*

ISBN: 978-1-9168833-0-7

10 9 8 7 6 5 4 3 2 1

A CIP catalogue record for this book is available from the British Library.

Printed and bound in Great Britain by CPI Group (UK) Ltd, Croydon CR0 4YY

A Note on the Text

I first met the Prince at a house party in a major European city. Two middle-aged ex-pats hanging out in a kitchen which neither of us called home. At the time I was teaching drama to young offenders in South London. On hearing this, the Prince's ears pricked up and he embarked on a nine-month crusade to persuade me to turn his 'early life story' into a book. Needless to say I found most of his story literally incredible, but the concrete and realistic emotion within his diaries convinced me.

Names, places and dates have been changed to protect the innocent.

For ease of understanding we quote currency in euro, even though the lira was the Italian currency of the 1980s.

– Hugh Gurney

'True patriotism hates injustice in its own land more than anywhere else ... the tyranny of the party that succeeds, by force or fraud, in carrying elections ... must be broken ... but [it is] our own fraud which frightens us, it is our own evil thoughts which madden us.'

– Cicero

THE FIRST COMMANDMENT

I was born near Naples at the foot of Vesuvius, the volcano which destroyed the ancient city of Pompeii. Legend has it that the people of Pompeii were so corrupt and debauched that God was left no choice but to send down his wrath upon them. He shouldn't have bothered because Naples, the modern city that came in its place, turned out even worse. As a teenage boy, my own eruptions were frequent, each bigger than the last. Just as it was at the end of Pompeii, innocent people's lives would be destroyed just so I could 'get' the bad guys. But like God, I really shouldn't have bothered.

I was a pretty boy with an unusual dose of curiosity and a high IQ: 163 when tested by Mensa. By the time I was two years old, I could not only speak but also read and write. Once, a teacher, annoyed by my arrogance, challenged me to read a paragraph of about 300 words, memorise it and recite in front of the class. Unfazed, I did as demanded, but then I also recited it backwards, from the last word to the first. I was only six years old but I didn't like being bullied. Unfortunately, my talents came without warnings or instructions. A rebellious personality like mine, in a city like Naples – it was an accident waiting to happen.

Most of my family had not even been to school so I was an amazement to them. Later, I became convinced I was adopted, but they never ceased worshipping me and my talents, and I loved it. My family was very average and very Catholic. I was neither, and I proved it with what I did.

During my early years, I spent the summers at my maternal grandparents' house up in the mountains outside Naples. Except for my Granddad, that side of the family were all as lovely, devout and law-abiding as my Mother. They all had an influence on me of some kind, but the strongest influence came from my Granddad. I loved him more than my own parents. Even now, I still pray to him before I fall asleep. He was incredibly charming and funny. Into his late fifties he rode a motorbike and dressed in the latest fashions. Without a single grey hair, he looked twenty years younger than he was.

He loved ladies, cigarettes and a drink or two. And he had a lot of spare time to indulge these 'hobbies' thanks to his cosy government job as a road inspector; knocking off at 1 p.m. every day. At the same time, he was a great family man. He would do anything for his wife, whom he loved dearly, for his children and, of course, for me, his eldest grandchild. Through sheer charm, he could get away with any practical joke, no matter how extreme. His real genius, though, lay with locks and safes: he was an ex-locksmith and still fully licensed.

From my earliest memories, my relationship with him was always special. I loved him with all my heart. Every summer, away from my beloved school-work, I learnt as much from him than I ever did from a book. It was practical stuff but, as long as I was learning new things, I was happy. I was fascinated by his ex-profession. Well, I didn't care much for locks *per se*, but the ability to open them without a key tantalised me. I was content to endure hours of patient practice while my Granddad lovingly shared his secrets. We spent days on end in a garage. He called it his workshop; I called it his laboratory. By three years old he had taught me how to break the combination on a safe. When he was at work, I carried on studying the material he left behind. By six years old I would venture alone to the library to find out more: stuff he didn't know, abòut ever-more complex security devices. When summer ended, I didn't want to go back to the horrible city. I didn't have the same freedom there and that frustrated me.

He would solve 'lock problems' for friends of friends in the village. As I grew older, he brought me in on the 'game'. Then he would let me do it on my own – supposedly to show off his grandson, but I think it was because he knew I was now better at it than him. To his credit, he shared the money he made with me. Never 50–50, of course, but I earned more in a day than most kids my age earned in a whole summer. I was like a child piano prodigy, only my fingers danced on dials not keys, but to these men, hearing a safe open was sweeter music than any concert.

With the money I financed another obsession: the need to look good by dressing sharply. Italy was the birthplace of what we now call 'designer fashion'. By the 80s, the Italians had taken this to the level of an Olympic sport. I couldn't tell you what makes it so addictive but I can tell you this: I was hooked; 100 per cent fashion victim. My friends and neighbours went to incredible lengths to wear the latest fashion, regardless of expense. Looking good became a social necessity. If you did not wear the right 'Names', you simply were not good enough. I could not let that happen. Money was tight at home but I found ever more elaborate ways to boost my wardrobe, and fuel my addiction. Everyone was at it but I stood out and this is how I first got my nickname.

In the south of Italy, nicknames are very common. They are not chosen but awarded. Often they are descriptors of physical or personality traits, usually with a big dollop of irony or sarcasm. In Naples, a nickname *is* your social name. Your real name becomes redundant. I was aloof, dressed elegantly, affected to speak a better quality of Italian than the neighbourhood accent and worst of all struggled to contain my obnoxious superiority, so mine was an obvious choice. From the age of seven, everyone, apart from close family, just called me 'Prince'. I loved it. Obviously it was sarcastic, referring to my peculiar mannerisms and personal delusions, but as I felt like a real Prince I liked it.

Unfortunately, it inflated my delusions rather than puncturing them. Like a real Prince, I felt I had a divine right to expect the best out of life, more so than those around me, which just isolated me even more. When I was strolling in the neighbourhood, if people looked me up and down in a way that was anything less than complimentary then I would think to myself:

'How dare you! I am the Prince here, and you are a nobody!'

One day, one of my aunts came to visit. She neglected to shower me with compliments on my dress sense. I gave her such an evil look that my Mother noticed. She waited until her sister had gone before mentioning it...

'Son, vanity is a sin! Never look at anyone like that again, do you understand?'

It fell on deaf ears; all I was worried about was how to expand my wardrobe, so that the next time even the most dowdy of aunts would take notice.

Being driven and ambitious I didn't mind putting pressure on myself but I resented being pushed around by anyone or anything else. If the system and society at large tried to bully me, that simply could not be allowed, but the key moment that shaped my life was not caused by humans, it was 100 per cent down to natural causes.

I was reading in my room when my Mother called me for dinner. I had spent the entire afternoon immersed in a great adventure from the past: Napoleon Bonaparte's extraordinary rise to power. My Mum had cooked fried chicken and chips, one of my favourites, but not even that alluring smell could drag me away from Old Boney's exploits. Then, my Father burst in.

'Son, I am not telling you twice. Get your ass over to the kitchen now or else!'

I hated it when my Father talked to me like that. I know 'or else' is just a figure of speech but to me it was just another form of bullying.

'OK, I am coming' I said, wishing I had said 'Vaffanculo!' but that would have made it worse, as it means f**k off. It didn't stop me hating him. I think I was the first to hate him, before he made other enemies. I put my books away sullenly and walked out.

My food was on the table in the usual spot; my Dad, the hypocrite, already re-installed on the sofa watching TV rather than at the dinner table; my baby brother sat in his high chair; and my Mother doing the washing up while she waited for my Father and I to take our seats. But as I sat down, the whole building started to shake. The kitchen light swung twice before going out. The dinner table started to dance. I did not understand what was going on but my Father did.

He scooped up my brother from his chair, grabbed my hand and together we ran for the door, with my Mother close behind. We bypassed the lift, into the stairwell and ran down the steps, two at a time. I was impressed with my Father's ability to leap down the steps while carrying my brother. My parents were running for their lives; jumping down the last few stairs in each flight was just a great game to me!

We emerged into the gardens, where our neighbours had already gathered. The men, including my Father, looked deeply shocked. The women and children around me were screaming and crying but I listened only to the sounds from further away: buildings crashing down, sirens and alarms. When the glass in the windows of our block finally gave way, the broken panes dropped majestically into the lawn a few metres away. This spectacle drew the most chilling screams. We could all imagine what that glass would have done to a human body. I thought about the buildings further away that were actually collapsing. I imagined someone being buried alive under the rubble of their own home. Unlike everyone else, I was not afraid. On the contrary, I loved it. Having spent my childhood reading about other people's adventures, I was finally living one of my own. The sense of danger made me feel more alive than I had ever felt before. From what I could see, others were not feeling the same way. It felt like I and only I had just discovered a new drug. In a flash, I had become an adrenaline junkie.

It was 1980, and the most powerful earthquake since Vesuvius exploded in AD 79 had just hit the Campania region of Naples. Thousands of buildings crumbled like sandcastles. Hundreds of people died, lives were shattered and those who survived were left with nothing. That episode changed Naples forever. Everyone, even those not directly affected by the ruins, would feel the pain. More than six million Neapolitans would be affected by the earthquake and its repercussions ... but in due course the entire country would feel the effects of my revenge.

All my family and friends survived. We also survived the aftershocks. The building we lived in did not collapse. It only cracked, then cracked again, and was finally declared unsafe. We had to move out. Out of sentimentality or self-pity, we assembled to watch it being demolished. When it came crashing down, it brought with it the dreams of my Father who had worked so hard to put us there in the first place. My reaction was more upbeat, I loved watching the way the explosions caused the block to collapse in on itself, leaving just a cloud of dust.

In those days, no one had home insurance, so we were left to fend for ourselves after begging meagre handouts from the State. It must have been difficult for my old man: a wife, a toddler (my three-year-old brother); a pain in the arse spoilt brat (me) and no place to call home. My Father was a very proud man. He could easily have taken us to live with the in-laws but he didn't want to look like a failure in their eyes. Instead, he accepted a unit in the emergency housing knocked up by the council. Even on day one, these temporary shacks were not fit for human habitation. My Father trusted that the State would soon re-house us. He was mistaken.

The moment my life really changed was when I walked through the aluminium doors of our new 'home'. My expensive wardrobe was gone, and with it my books and all my dreams. I felt empty, so empty that I didn't feel anything at all, just numbness. I couldn't believe that life could go so bad so quickly. My mind worked in a ghastly way: after composing myself after the initial shock, I simply reminded myself of how special I was and, therefore, that I would find a way out of this mess.

'Someone has to pay for this ... and he is not going to be me,' I promised.

I went to the council archives to research and study the causes of the disaster. The earthquake was a violent one but I soon figured out that its consequences were greatly magnified by poor quality construction: all made possible by illegal permits with false safety certificates. This conclusion was so simple, any child could've worked it out. The politicians and local building companies were in cahoots. The former had been corrupted by the latter to turn a blind eye. They had blood on their hands for those that died of disease from poor sanitation in the aftermath and worse still condemned three hundred thousand to a living hell while they enjoyed the hundreds of millions of euros they had effectively stolen.

'We've got a good legal case against those crooks. We should fight back against the system,' I said to anyone who would listen. Unfortunately, not only was this message being delivered by a child, it was also the sort of message that was totally alien to the good people of Naples. But nobody was going to do anything, let alone sue. I decided to sort this out myself.

Not bad for a birthday wish, wouldn't you say? Yes, it was my twelfth birthday: one I celebrated without a cake (my Mother had other priorities), without presents (my Father had no money to waste) and most hurtful of all no guests (I couldn't explain that). I started to suspect that one of my Granddad's crude theories was correct: being nice, respecting others, going to church and being a good citizen – none of these were worth it. People who had lived this way were now homeless. Those who hadn't lived in mansions and villas with beautiful cars parked in the driveway. Their biggest problem was whether to wear an Armani coat or a Versace. My coat was gone, together with my books and my life. My sanity might soon follow.

'I am going to get it all back, one way or another' I swore.

Life in the shanty-town, as I called it, was not worthy of a Prince. For example, bathing took two hours. We had to share the same bathroom with a dozen residents from four other units, one of which was home to a family of giants. These were not the friendly, docile creatures of fairy tales. The head of this family was a beast: twice the size of my Father. He left big black curly hairs in the bath. It looked like a thousand dead spiders. I called him 'The Spiderbeast', although not to his face of course. The morning queue for wash-block started at 5 a.m., and this was a Neapolitan queue, not a British one. The biggest and the strongest went first while the rest, including me, waited patiently if we did not want a beating. There was no feeling of 'we're in this together', no collective 'spirit of the Blitz', at least not at bath time.

Our family finances were under attack from all sides: from trivial issues, like having to re-buy cooking utensils, all the way to the serious; my Dad was signed off sick from work for three months on a reduced salary as he couldn't cope with the stress.

Money became so tight that all my savings were, understandably, confiscated for the good of the family.

Now that the Prince was wearing rags and smelt like a pig, I fell out of love with my nickname, but I never lost faith that I would love it again one day. Instead of calming down and accepting my lot, my anger went up a notch.

Under the Italian system, at twelve heading for thirteen I was about to finish the penultimate year of secondary school. I cared a lot about my studies, so doing well this year was very important to me. The shanty-town was two kilometres further away from my school than our old home. Just getting there each day was difficult and I had nowhere to do homework. On top of that, I was constantly teased about my fall from grace. The Prince tag had become a target for abuse. Hurtful though this was, I had the willpower to channel it into finding a way out of this mess. I virtually lived in the public library. When not doing homework, I threw myself into finding out all I could about construction and building safety. For months after that tragic day, all I did was study. My anger pushed me past the limits of what any healthy teenager should endure. I dreamt of becoming a lawyer and taking them all to court. In all my dreams the ending was the same: I won and they lost.

The day my Mum gave me the money for the ticket, I ran the five miles to the station and across the tracks to the other platform. I thought about keeping the money and running all the way. After the train, I had to take a bus. All told, it took about two hours. As soon as I sat down on the bus, I felt a huge relief: all of my problems vanished. People on the bus knew me and, more importantly, they loved me. When they called me Prince, they did it with respect, like they meant it. They liked my clean looks, my manners and my charm. People from the mountain were simple and yet they saw straight through you. They were not bothered about the clothes you wore. They didn't even know which brands were in fashion. The reception on the TV was so bad that they didn't watch it, so the media could not influence them. These were real people who did not need the comfort of brand names and consumerism. When I was with them I felt happy. I was deep in a daydream when the bus driver shouted to me that it was my stop. Time to shed the anger I had brought from the city and have fun.

Grandma greeted me with the usual enthusiasm: showering me with kisses; leaving saliva all over my face. It sounds disgusting but I loved the affection. My Granddad was not there to greet me, he was in bed. When I got to see him, he did not look right. He was pale and weak. He had lost those eyes of a squirrel that made me laugh so much. His body seemed to have shrunk too.

I asked him how he was, hoping he'd say, 'I'm all right, kiddo,' as usual.

'Not so good lately, but I'm just having some tests done, son. I've fallen for this beautiful nurse and I'm pretending to be sick to get her to come to see me. That is all it is! I'm only 61 years old. Young by today's standards: nothing to worry about,' he said, smiling to put a brave face on the pain. I knew that, in spite of his jokes, he was dying. It took all my strength to choke back my tears. I felt his love, as if my being there was more important than anything, including the fear for his own life. I felt a mix of joy and sadness: that special feeling that only ever lasts a brief moment.

Afterwards, I forced Grandma to tell me the truth. He had cancer of the liver from years of drinking. Apparently, the drinking had got much heavier in the last year. Only months later would I find out why.

I knew vaguely what cancer was but I still went to the small village library to find out all I could. No matter how many hours I spent there, my research only confirmed my worst fears. This was terrible timing; first a physical earthquake, now an emotional one. In the days that followed, when I saw him I played along, pretending to fall for his charm, forcing a smile on each occasion. 'Better 50 years as a lion than 100 as a sheep,' he said, adding 'Sometimes the spirit to survive is just too strong even when the body is weakened.'

Even if he didn't have cancer it seemed he couldn't think of anything worse than an extended old age, drugged and bedridden. But it was still sad to see him reduced to a sheep after being a lion so long.

That summer, we didn't do the usual safe-cracking. Instead, we spent a lot of time talking about his experiences and life in general. Knowing he was dying, he tried to teach me about life. He wanted to give me the benefit of his wisdom, to fast-track me into adulthood. This, of course, is impossible. If it weren't we would all do it and skip those terrible teenage years. Towards the end of the summer, the rest of the family had arrived, An endless procession of 'specialists' with briefcases came to examine him. So, I went to the public library, instead, to search yet again for a cure. I knew it was impossible. I felt lonely and powerless, daydreaming of a cure specifically for liver cancer. In my single-minded way, I didn't give a damn about lung cancer, bowel cancer or any other forms of the disease.

If I saw other kids having ice creams at the bar with their family or teenage boys chatting up girls in the summer heat then I felt a stabbing pain. I resented their happiness.

After four days of being kept from the old man, I woke up to an overcast sky. Summer in the mountains normally brought blue sky every day. Instead, it was hot and humid. I felt uncomfortable and fearful, and not just because of the pool of sweat I woke in. I went to the kitchen to get some breakfast. The whole family sat silently around the table. I knew what was happening but I still helped myself to a café-latte and some biscuits. Usually they were my favourites but they tasted awful. The family doctor was there too, casual in a white T-shirt and jeans but without the usual smile. He was a dear friend of my Granddad and the whole family, but his presence was a bad sign. Like my Granddad used to be, the doctor was a fine figure of a man in his late fifties, but today he looked like the Grim Reaper. My Mum and Grandma started tidying up; then my Dad got up to go out for a walk. Inevitably, and with a sense of dread on my part, the doctor stood up and came to sit with me.

'Hey there, how are you?' he said, acting as if nothing had happened. He was a bad actor. 'I want to see my Granddad. Now, please' I said, trying to hide my contempt.

He forgave my outburst with a grandfatherly smile, which just made it worse. The doctor was a good Granddad to his own family and he knew I loved my Granddad. What he did not know was the extent to which I lived *for* my Granddad. He was my life. I didn't care so much about the rest of my family. The feelings I should have had for my Father were transferred to my Granddad. I hated the doctor now. I wished he were dying. He did not matter. Before this little chat could go any further, before my worst fears could be made real, I stormed out. I was afraid to hear the truth. As a distraction, I went to the bathroom to comb my hair; I wanted to look my best. When I got out of the bathroom, the doctor was waiting for me. His worried look conveyed his compassion for my despair but I couldn't deal with it. I despised him even more.

'I want to do this on my own. Go back to the kitchen.'

He was shocked. The once lovely and chatty little boy from the city was now ordering him about like a battle-hardened soldier.

'I am here if you need me. OK?' he whispered.

I waved him aside and charged my cavalry up two flights of stairs, but as I put my hand on the door knob to my Granddad's room, I froze. At first, I couldn't find the strength to open it. When I finally went in, I looked down to avoid seeing him. When I turned round to close the door behind me, I exaggerated the movement, taking as long as possible, to delay the inevitable. Only then did I find the courage to face him. He was lying, apparently lifeless. But he wasn't dead yet. There was no colour anywhere: the sheet was white; his skin was grey and his hair was black. It was a shocking sight. His jet black hair no longer made him look young; it just looked out of place, like an unkempt wig thrown on for effect. Tubes were connecting his body to two bottles which hovered over his bed like vultures. He had withered to skin and bones. His eyes bulged out of his head. I felt myself withering in sympathy. Afraid to disturb, I approached his bed gently but he waved me forward with a frail hand anyway. When he spoke, it was so quiet that I had to strain to hear him.

'Kid, in life you have just two categories of people: those who shaft others and those who get shafted. Make sure you are on the right side,' he said bluntly.

11

He wasn't wasting energy on pleasantries!

This struck me as unusual for such a mild-mannered man, but he wasn't finished:

'I tried to do something with my life but I failed and now it is too late for me. I left nothing for my kids. I do not even own the house I will die in. Son, do not live how I have. Get what you are entitled to. Fight for what is yours. Do not fail like I have!'

A crude philosophy, but one that lured me in nonetheless. Exactly *what* I should fight for he did not say, but, given what was happening back in Naples, I had little doubt what he meant in practice.

For the rest of the year, whenever I was trying to get to sleep, that sentence would haunt me. I struggled to fault it. Black or white, rich or poor, stupid or clever, or however else you cared to divide the world up, no theory would be any better at distinguishing the happy from the unhappy as the 'mighty shafters' and their 'shafted' victims. These days, lots of self-help gurus proclaim 'don't be a victim', but few bother to add 'be a bully', and with good reason. I wanted there to be a more wholesome alternative but over time, as these words sunk in, they became my 'First Commandment': the foundation on which I would build a life of hateful revenge. Not for one second did my Granddad envisage what I would do next, but indirectly his words were responsible. I went into that room a boy and left a crusader. Two mornings later, at the end of August, I was woken very early by a scream. My Grandmother was crying so hard that you could've heard her from the next mountain. I already knew why, so I just got dressed as best I could and went to pay my last respects. I did not cry but my family did, in great quantity.

They should have cried for another reason: his passing had made me cold and unresponsive, my moral compass off-kilter. If I could not love him then I had no love left for anyone. I felt disgust for those around me who cried like little girls while we had to go back to the shanty-town and live like rats. At the funeral the priest preached 'forgiveness for all'. Those words were an insult rather than a comfort. I missed my Granddad like crazy. I wanted to hug him and ask him if the stuff spinning in my head was right or wrong but he was not there to answer. This is when I made up my mind that my anger was not misplaced and I had to do something more to get revenge. It was time to unleash my anger on the people I held responsible for our plight. My Granddad had helped me identify my target. I would make it my crusade to free all the victims from the tyranny of the bullies.

My Grandmother's mourning seemed to go on forever. She lost all the sparkle that had made her fun. I forgave her as Granddad had been her world and now her world was empty, but I still found it impossible to spend time with her. It was worse with my parents. Repressing their own grief, they couldn't deal with hers and so couldn't wait to see the back of her. As soon as the paperwork was done, off we went, back to our living hell in the shanty-town.

Just three months earlier, at the beginning of the summer, I had arrived full of hope and enthusiasm but now, travelling back, I was empty and angry. An unpleasant thought: I had not earned anything all summer, the locksmith work having dried up for obvious reasons. There was no money to reinstate my designer wardrobe. Very disappointing. I needed a plan to get me exactly what I wanted. The time had come for me to cash in on my talents and quash the pain in my heart. I didn't realise it then, but in order to take revenge on 'the shafters', to bully the bullies, I would have to become a bully myself. I was just a boy, but I had the anger of a man running through my veins.

The first day back at 'home' was cruel and depressing. It was dangerous outside on the streets and, even if my parents hadn't insisted on a curfew, I would probably have imposed it myself. So, at night I sat indoors, alone with my thoughts. Even in the bosom of my family, I was still lonely because there was no one inside that shack who I could discuss my angry dreams with.

The next day, I did what I always did: found refuge in my books. As the only solid part of my revenge plan was to sue those who put us in this situation, I borrowed engineering books from the library to better understand how the earthquake caused some buildings to collapse and not others. In the engineering aisles, I stumbled across a new and exciting collection of books. It was love at first sight. The 'Blast Engineering' sub-section was not as well stocked as the rest of engineering, but naturally it was a lot more alluring.

As I was preparing to start a new year at school, another piece of my Granddad's advice came back to me: 'Hang around with people better than you and pick up the bill.'

In Italy, like many countries, there are still classes; generally, the rich spend most of their time with other rich people, the well off with the well off, the poor with the poor and so on. I was classified as homeless, so I was beyond poor, at the very bottom of the social table. I have seen horses with nicer stables than ours.

If I was to follow my Granddad's advice, my very first task was simple: I would have to mingle with the rich and powerful. Even if I couldn't afford to pick up the bill, I would have to hide the fact I was homeless. With luck, I would be able to watch and learn from them.

'Time to go to church and make new friends,' I said to myself.

The second Saturday of September that year, I sought out the church in the wealthiest part of the city. The priest there was short, round and balding with bad teeth. He looked really odd. The church, on the other hand, was stunningly beautiful and as big as a cathedral. This was Naples' equivalent of Notre Dame and they had made the hunchback the priest. What had this Don Vincenzo creep done to get this gig? Luckily for me, I didn't have to like him; I only had to get him to like me. This was a role-play for which I rehearsed as hard as any professional actor.

When Anthony Hopkins created the infamous Hannibal Lecter, the way he spoke with a lick of the lips and a hissing 's' was considered genius. But he must have tried saying 'Clarisse' a million times in the mirror before he alighted on a way to send shivers down so many spines. It was with the same dedication that I prepared my speech for Don Vincenzo. After hours of practice and several strange looks from my school friends (I could not practice at home), I decided to aim for a combination of sincerity, vulnerability and zeal. I stood in front of the mirror and gave it my best shot.

'Signore Vincenzo, I don't know how to say this so I will just say it. I want to get closer to God. I feel that society is corrupting me. As an escape I have buried myself in my academic studies but it is not fulfilling me. There is still emptiness.'

At this point, I pause hold his gaze and then punch my heart for effect.

'Tell me, Don Vincenzo. Can you help me to get closer to God?'

A perfect mix of shy yet sincere: quite frightening really when you consider that I was not shy and certainly not sincere. When I said it for real, Don Vincenzo's eyes lit up and he stumbled to reply as if he, himself, was nervous.

'Well, you could, if you wish, be ... an altar boy ... only if your parents allow it, also.'

He already had two altar boys but I never considered those monkeys as competition. Don Vincenzo never stood a chance now that 'the Prince' was locked on to his target.

Despite the beauty of the church, it was little more than a comfortable social club for the rich and powerful. I was undercover and ready to observe my enemies in their own backyard. From then on my Sundays went the same way. They started at 9 a.m. with cleaning and tidying the sacristy. More often than not, there was an 'after mass' party. People brought aperitifs and food to share. Before the service, I would prepare the booths for the food and drinks. Then I would get dressed in my new white uniform and at 11 o'clock we went out on stage to perform. It was just like the theatre, only without the make-up. The real show, however, was afterwards in the sacristy.

During the first few Sundays, I felt very uncomfortable in the presence of these people, especially their children who all looked so perfect: well behaved and smiling. Unlike the residents of the shanty-town, they all seemed so carefree. I might have been the Prince but these guys were the real royalty of Naples. When they went to get bread, they didn't queue up to pay like the rest of us; they would collect their bread and pay whenever they wanted, if they paid at all. The parents were top doctors, judges, industrialists, politicians, professors. *La crème de la crème* of Naples was there. It was more of a networking event than any serious attempt to worship God. Some of them thought they *were* God: they often referred to the ordinary people of Naples as if they were no more than a herd of cattle. This annoyed me so much that I wanted to argue with them but I was here for a bigger prize. I had to keep my mouth shut and stick to just watching, or I would blow it on the first day.

If they found out just one detail of my shanty-town reality, I would be excommunicated in an instant. Making them think I was one of them was one big lie but, thanks to my clean diction and my rehearsed knowledge of some good topics for sophisticated conversation, I was confident I could handle it. If anyone asked an awkward question, I would distract them with a swift and charming change of subject. But only a madman would try and 'go the distance' without a well-rehearsed cover story. I invented a new address. My Father became an engineer and my Mum a doctor in a hospital in the nearby city of Salerno. To immediately bat away any detailed questions about my family's lack of history in Naples, I would say that my family had very recently relocated from Salerno. Naples is a big city; they would never find out the truth but to be sure I even changed my last name. I could claim that Granddad's words had inspired me but, in truth, the idea for this deceit was all my own. I can't fully explain why. I had no reason to think I was a good actor. More likely, I just liked to take a gamble.

Once you start lying, it is not easy to stop. You must have a good memory (which, thankfully, I had) but, more importantly, you must stay in character even when daydreaming (which I did a lot). Why was I doing this? A vague idea about researching the enemy, nothing more. I would get a couple of euros and some refreshments after the mass but in terms of tangible results it was never going to be worth the hassle. My gut instinct was to persevere. Like the lottery, you have to be in it to win it. I started to enjoy the relief from the shanty-town and maybe, subconsciously, I had meant it when I had asked Don Vincenzo for spiritual help.

After the initial powerful earthquake, the region experienced a series of aftershocks. Buildings that had survived the initial 'quake became unstable, so a whole new wave of families had to come and set up in the shanty-town. More and more units (they could not be called houses) were crammed in between the existing ones. If the shanty-town was a melting pot, then someone had just turned up the heat.

I came from a 'normal' family, just below the middle class. Before the earthquake, we had a nice apartment and my Dad had a decent job in a private telecommunications company. We didn't have money to waste but we were comfortable. My parents were polite, hard-working and law-abiding. Before the 'quake, all of our neighbours were similar: normal people with normal lives; but here in the shanty-town, normal people were in the minority. Most of the families were loud and uneducated, sold stolen goods in the street, paid no taxes, were quick to anger and sometimes violent. My Dad had worked all his life to give his children a better future. Now, destiny had put him back where he first started. No wonder he got depressed.

I'd never had a good relationship with my Father but strangely he was still one of my inspirations. You learn more from someone that makes mistakes than from someone who is capable and successful. My Dad's primary weakness was his vanity. It must have run in the family! He was tall and slim, with deep green eyes and lovely black hair that never seemed to move an inch. Despite his modest intelligence, his vanity gave him ambition. Just as he never stopped wanting more out of life, he never quite achieved it. This constant disappointment ate away at his confidence. His frustrations often erupted in bouts of violence and unpleasantness. In the shanty-town, he'd already had a few bust-ups with our new neighbours, leaving my Mum to clean up the mess. It was a losing battle to stay on good terms with the neighbours and, little by little, my Mum became isolated. At a time when she needed friends she had nobody, not even her family.

The atmosphere at home was tense at the best of times. I seemed to get instant-onset cabin-fever as soon as I walked in. When my Mum cooked inside the tiny 20-square-metre 'lodge', the smell that lingered quickly became unpleasant. We had no windows, so in wintertime, when we had to eat inside, our clothes had to be washed constantly to rid them of cooking smells. Playing in the street was not an option for me either, so I went to the library whenever I wasn't at school. After 6 p.m. when the public library closed, I had nowhere else to go. The kids in the area were very different from me. I spoke clean Italian and, as I acted with composure and class, I really stood out. My nickname didn't help. They were Italian chavs. If they went to school, it was only to keep the authorities off their backs. As soon as the law allowed, they would drop out and devote themselves to a life of petty crime. They were reasonably clean and well-dressed but either they or their clothes smelt strange. What really set them apart was the anger in their eyes and their lack of fear. To them death looked no worse than life. I did not like them, but I had to try to fit into their 'street league'. I could fight a few guys and, ideally, give them a good beating. Unfortunately, my natural strength was intelligence. It may have been natural for them to smash one another in the face, wrestle on the ground for hours and then go home bathed in blood, but I despised physical violence and I couldn't bear to see bruises on my beautiful face. They teased me endlessly but I never confronted them. I was afraid that if the situation escalated I would end up in hospital. Once again, I found the answers in my books...

Cicero, the famous Roman orator, once said: 'You can control a man with the strength of your body, but you can control the world with the strength of your tongue.' Unlike my Dad, who was making enemies everywhere, I needed a strategy to make the neighbourhood respect me and even work for me. What planet was I on? There was no chance of getting the respect of these vermin. Even if they weren't scum, no one likes a smart-ass, and I was a smart-ass.

The solution was staring me in the face. Nothing brings different people together better than a common enemy. If I could identify and promote a battle against someone we all hated, then I would have an army at my disposal. I had the weapons to achieve my revenge right on my doorstep. Like a lion tamer's first day on the job, I had to train them without them eating me first. It would be a long careful process. One day, I was woken by my Mum's screams:

'Oh my God! What's wrong with the fridge?'

My Dad wearily got up to have a look.

'The fridge *is* working. It's just we had another power cut last night. Try to salvage what you can,' he whispered, defeated.

'The milk is still good. At least we can have breakfast,' she said.

The milk was not good. Far from it. I had no choice; I still had to lump it down or my Dad would vent his anger on me. As I ate, I contemplated how days that start badly usually get worse. I was right because not only did the milk not taste good, but it gave me an immediate urge for the bathroom. I rushed out to the public toilets. Thankfully, the queue was not too long. *Only* three people were in front of me. I calculated ninety seconds per crap: a four and a half minute wait, all told. I reckoned I could hold on that long, just. After the longest five minutes of my life, it was my turn. I sprinted into the cubicle, slammed the door and was about to slide the lock when a massive, hairy hand bashed the door back in my face. Pain exploded in my nose making my eyes water. A hand grabbed my collar. Through the tears I could see that the big lump of man attached to the hand was the Spiderbeast. Resistance was futile. He tore my toilet paper from my hands, threw me on the floor outside, and in he went. The door slammed, the lock clicked and silence resumed as if nothing had happened. Despite the pain from my nose and the bruises on my ego, I still needed a shit.

I would not be able to hold it in much longer.

I heard giggling behind me, so I turned round.

'There are some bushes over there. I wish I could use them myself but my knees are not too good' said an old man behind me in the queue.

I couldn't wait a moment longer so I waddled over to the bushes, careful not to provoke my bowels any further. Once hurriedly installed behind the bush, I slipped my pants and underwear down. I held onto a branch from the bush while squatting so I could lean back and keep my anus aiming well away from my clothes. I was too busy concentrating on this balancing act to remember I had no toilet paper. The relief that followed was heavenly, but this just distracted me from noticing that my branch wasn't holding too well. When it finally broke, I lost my balance, landing squarely on my own dump. I wanted to cry. It is times like these that you really need a whole roll of toilet paper to clean up, but I had none. After using my hand and some dry soil to scrub up the best I could, I ran home to do it properly. Then it hit me: we didn't have a bathroom! I would have to wash my bottom, in full view of the whole family, in the same sink where my Mum washed food. So I just washed my hands, took my rucksack and went to school, my pants glued to my cheeks with excrement. I felt dirty for months but, worse than that, I felt violated. I blamed everyone, including the Government but, most of all, the Spider-beast for bullying me. I was in a frenzy of hatred. Someone once said: 'There is a fine line between genius and insanity.' Being a genius, I was more vulnerable and I would certainly go mad if this continued.

All day at school, I tried to calm down. I had just about managed it by the time I left the library, but it had taken all my strength. As I was trudging home, a few kids were having a kick about in the street on the outskirts of the shanty-town. I studied them warily, trying to suss out how much danger they posed. Then a car reversing out of a parking space gently nudged a moped parked next to it. The tiny Fiat didn't hit it hard enough to do any damage; at least none that I could see. Unfortunately for the family in the car, the kids playing football took a different view. Straight away, they stopped playing and surrounded the car. The smallest of them (why is it always the smallest?) went to the driver's window.

'You damaged my motor. You owe me money!' he screamed in high-pitched low-quality Italian.

The driver, a man in his early forties, looked like a member of the shanty-town's middle-class minority. He had his family with him: his wife and two young children.

'I just touched it. Piss off!' he replied.

Middle class or not, he was probably as angry and fed up with life in the shanty-town as the rest of us, but that response was not clever. The gang jumped on the roof of the car, screaming like furious monkeys. The roof started to cave in on the terrified family who were also screaming on the inside. One of the boys blocked the driver's door to stop him getting out, even though the father wisely showed no inclination of doing that! Normally when I get scared I can still function rationally – feel the fear, then do it anyway – but this time I was overwhelmed by the sheer scale of mindless violence. I still had a chance to run away while these feral kids enjoyed their carefree moment of madness, but I was frozen to the spot. I just couldn't bring myself to run, not even for my own life.

These animals kept at it until all the windows were shattered and the roof could not cave in any further. Still, I could not run. Then, in a flash, they woke up from their insanity. They looked around for any witnesses and saw me. The ring-leader approached, with the others close behind. He smiled a menacing fake smile.

'Hello mate. All right?' he whispered.

'You someone that minds his own business? Or you someone looking for some of that?' he added, pointing proudly at the smashed car.

A tiny mouthful of my own vomit arrived uninvited in my mouth. I gulped it back. He grabbed my jumper and threw me on the floor. My books flew all over the place. He took one and started to tear it apart.

'If you say a word to anyone about this, you will end up like this book. Y'get me?'

He lifted me up and pushed me away with enough force that I was already running when I hit the ground. I didn't turn back to get the rest of my books, I just kept on running 'til I got home. I got there early, so that didn't arouse any suspicion, but I was as white as a ghost and covered in mud, and that certainly did.

'Did you get in a fight?' my Dad screamed. I did not respond so he continued.

'If you did, you better have won! If you got beaten up, I will give you the rest. Do you understand?'

I didn't understand. No matter how much I tried to think how it could, it still made no sense. I had no energy left to puzzle over it. I just felt sick, so I skipped dinner and went to bed.

The next day, I woke up with a high temperature and the knowledge that my days in the shanty-town were numbered, regardless of whether I left on my own terms or in a coffin. If yesterday was anything to go by, it would be the latter. I tried to invoke a variety of supernatural powers to help me. I started with my grandfather's ghost and ended with the Devil himself, but none of them responded. In the end, I resorted to the only things that could save me: my imagination, willpower and resourcefulness. I still felt deeply violated. I was not hurt physically but I had been overpowered by a succession of bullies: the Spiderbeast; the neighbourhood kids and my own father. After three days of existential suffering, my fever broke and something magical happened. My soul cleansed itself. I brushed aside all those negative feelings, closed my eyes and I could see the way forward.

THE FIRST PLAN

Step One: Befriend Pasquale

Pasquale was the 15-year-old leader of the local gang of young criminals. A few months ago, when I first met him, I had said 'Hello' too casually, without proper respect. I got a black eye for my trouble, but at least now I knew the risks. He was only three years older than me but at six feet tall, with dark good looks, he seemed a lot more. His violent outbursts meant all the kids in the neighbourhood feared him. Very rarely did his victims fight back. Even those who fancied themselves as 'tasty' thought better of retaliation – Pasquale was an expert street fighter. But his reputation now preceded him so proper fights were now few and far between. Forced to use violence to solve his problems from an early age, now he knew how good he was at fighting. Everyone in the shanty-town was angry to some degree. I was, and if I'd had his skills I would have used them. But I didn't, so I needed him on my team.

Pasquale never smiled. Instead, he wore a permanent scowl. No ordinary one, this was the most menacing look. On the streets of the shanty-town, looks, attitude and reputation are everything. It didn't take much self-belief for Pasquale to be the hardest person in my school since he was the only 15-year-old in a school where everyone else was thirteen or younger.

For Pasquale, it was not Groundhog day; it was Groundhog year, and heading for Groundhog decade. In the past, his teachers had 'passed' him at the end of the year just to get rid of him but now he had a headmaster who did not bend the rules. Unless he studied, he would never leave school because in Italy at that time it was the law that you had to finish school with at least the basic secondary school diploma. On this point, I had heard his mother screaming at him in desperation. It was her dream for her boy to get some kind of qualification. It was understandable, given that his older sister who was still only 19 had a four-year-old child and his older brother was in jail for burglary. With the headmaster and his mother both steadfast, Pasquale could not just drop out. This was useful information in my quest to get close to him, but it was also a big warning to avoid him!

I thought I had an angle; even the worst gangsters loved their mothers so I figured Pasquale did too and would want to please her, if he could. I would give him the chance. Rudimentary research on my 'mark' revealed that his father was a scumbag who didn't give a damn about his son's education. He sold stolen goods to top up his winnings (or more likely losses) from playing cards at the bar and claiming disability benefits. Broken dysfunctional families seem to be on the rise everywhere these days, but in Naples they have always been popular. Maybe I was naive, but it made no sense to me for them to settle for so little in life. Pasquale might have picked on me for the way I dressed or spoke but, deep down, I reckon he envied me.

So, the first step in my plan was to befriend a bully, not to get revenge on one. I just had to find a way to make him feel comfortable around me. Then we could communicate and I could bring him round to my way of thinking. In the end, I would control him like a puppet and, with him, the rest of the gang and then the entire neighbourhood. Not bad for a first plan, huh?

If he got an inkling of my true intentions, even for a moment, then my life in the shanty-town would become unbearable. In the meantime, the next step was to get a sideways transfer to Pasquale's class. The trouble was the school year had already started and the people in the admin department were too lazy to do a mid-term transfer without a compelling reason. I had a compelling reason but...

It had to look like normal school business; like the transfer was not my idea. On the school notice board I checked out the list of all the students in Pasquale's class. Among the 24 students was a chap called Gianni, the headmaster's son. From what I knew of him he was a mild-mannered genuine nice guy, but he had no real friends either inside or outside of school. Plenty pretended to be his friend but only in the hope of receiving some favour from his father. Without their patronage, he was too nice to survive and would have been bullied out of the school a long time ago. Gianni's father was the kind of a man who had already kept an unruly pupil like Pasquale in his school for an extra two years, just on a matter of principle, so Gianni's false friends never stood a chance of getting any favours; but in Naples that is how people saw life. It's not what you know but who you know. Later in life, I discovered that this happens almost everywhere but it's much worse in Naples. Here the expectation of corruption was like a disease infecting everything.

Gianni was my passport to Pasquale.

Gianni, while not the brightest kid, was not totally stupid either. I am sure his bullshit detector had been honed from all the practice fending off would-be friends. Two days later, the school schedule was published on the school notice board. Everyone had to come to check it at some point. I waited there from the minute it was posted. After a very long hour, I was starting to think he would be the only child in the school who wouldn't come.

Of course, his Dad would tell him at home: Gianni didn't need to come. I was about to give up, and had completely stopped thinking about my *lines*, when he turned up, on his own. As he squinted at the gigantic board, I steeled myself. I stepped in and patted him on his shoulder.

'I was wondering if you could help me to read my schedule. I've lost my glasses and I can't see it properly,' I said.

'My name is Gianni. What's yours?' he replied. With such a terrible lisp that 'is' was pronounced 'iz'.

'My name iz Prinze.' Stupidly, I couldn't resist mimicking his lisp. That had to stop. And it did, from that moment on.

'That name is not up here,' he said as he pondered whether I too had a lisp or whether he should be offended.

'It's my nickname. That's my real name,' I said normally as I pointed at the list.

'How do you know, if you can't read it?' he said, looking genuinely confused.

I stared back, also confused. Was he onto me already? He was sharper than I was expecting.

'Jokez!' he said, giggling like a girl. Phew! Panic over. I smiled back limply. I guess he'd just got lucky and pricked my guilty conscience by accident.

He proceeded to read out my schedule slowly and deliberately, his lisp in overdrive. It was torture. When it was finally over we exchanged a polite 'Ciao' and I disappeared. The first tiny step of the first part of my very first plan was accomplished.

The next day, I stalked Gianni for over half an hour up and down the corridors before I managed to pretend to bump into him. We both said, 'Hello, how are you?' at the same time. I took a deep breath in readiness to let rip with my best pre-prepared banter when Giovanna, a girl from my class who I suspected had a crush on me, appeared hovering at my elbow. Had she been stalking me just as I had been stalking Gianni? I really liked her; the opportunity was too good to miss. I turned to look into her sweet face and big round eyes.

'Can't you see I'm busy with a very important friend,' I snapped.

She went bright red, looked like she was about to cry, turned tail and fled. I turned back to Gianni. He was initially shocked, then impressed. So was I, but I made sure I didn't show it. Shocked: that I could be so cruel. Impressed: that my self-control was getting better.

As I was chitchatting with Gianni, I pretended to hang on his every word in an effort to make him feel good about himself. He was a sensitive chap. Painful as it is to admit, Gianni and I had one thing in common: we were both nerds. The similarities ended there. When I could I looked good, dressed well, and it seemed at least one pretty schoolgirl had a crush on me. There was no evidence, one way or the other, to say whether half the girls in the school didn't fancy me. Giovanna was probably just the tip of the iceberg. That's just how I thought back then.

I'm not sure what the minimum IQ is to be a nerd, but Gianni wasn't even in the same ballpark as me. He could only dream of being clever enough to be a full-blown nerd.

'Show me a wannabe nerd and I will show you a loser!' I said to myself.

I didn't like him but what mattered was whether he liked me.

'I'm way good at literature but way bad at maths' he said.

'Why don't we team up? You teach me literature and I will help you in maths. Together, we can rule the world!' I said, feigning being struck by a brainwave.

The trick worked: he felt that someone was genuinely interested in him. We decided to get together that afternoon to help each other study. I did not tell him where I lived in order not to scare him off. People like him would not be seen dead in the shanty-town. Instead, he'd pick me up outside the school and we'd go to my place together.

As we strolled together through the shanty-town he must have thought it looked more like a refugee camp than a part of Naples. Well, if he did he would've been right: the shanty-town was a refugee camp. Fear, disgust and then pity etched themselves even deeper on his face as we passed the toilet block. The local women had started off with good intentions, organising a cleaning rota, but they had lost motivation once the kids had vandalised the facilities for the umpteenth time.

My shack must have been a sorry sight to someone who lived in a villa. His bedroom alone was probably bigger than the whole shack! He was used to feeling inferior but I had to make him feel sorry for me and, thus, superior. My ego didn't want anyone feeling sorry for me but I knew it would help the bonding process. The dark, manipulative side of my personality was cool and calculating. Ego and vanity would take a back seat to get the desired results.

Maths was second nature to me and, for the record, so was every other subject I took at school. I had recently read Machiavelli's *The Prince*, that famous handbook of political manipulation, because I really wanted to manipulate people. I certainly didn't need Gianni's help to understand literature; I fully understood what Machiavelli was on about.

In contrast, Gianni's mind couldn't really connect with maths. He subconsciously refused to learn it. A simple equation would generate an irrational phobia that shut his brain down. I did manage to hammer home a couple of useful tips before the end of the afternoon, for which he was grateful. He had a test at the end of that month and he had a lot of catching up to do. This was my opportunity to manipulate him to get what I wanted. As I was walking him back to his safe neighbourhood, I pretended to wrack my brain on how to help him but all the time I was wishing he would come up with the idea of having me moved to his class. The idea had to come from him so that his father would make it happen. We had reached the point in the road where it was time to part and he still hadn't suggested it.

'Why don't I get myself moved to your class?' he shouted in a eureka moment.

Nightmare. Not only would this not get me into Pasquale's class but, once Gianni was in my class, I would never be able to leave. My heart stopped. I had just felt the aching difference between having a plan and executing it. A plan, no matter how good it is, never goes to plan. I had to quickly throw cold water on this dangerous idea. The few seconds it took felt like an eternity.

'That's a great idea. Can we make it work? Surely the school won't move you so early in the term?' I ventured.

'I know people who have the power to make it happen.'

He still thought that I didn't know who he was. I had been very careful to keep it that way. I paused to construct my masterstroke response.

'Really? I am none too comfortable with such a dodgy deal ... Who are you? I thought you were my friend, not some gangster!' I said in my best outrage.

In Naples, accusing someone of being a gangster is almost a compliment. He lapped it up.

'Not that kind of dodgy, I am the son of the headmaster so it could be done by the morning' he said.

'Wow,' I exclaimed, 'I did not know that.'

'I know, I'll get my Dad to move you to my class. What do you think?' he blurted.

'Great idea. You bloody genius!' I exclaimed, almost gasping with relief.

Mission accomplished – one step closer to my target. Victory tasted so sweet that I hardly noticed the usual insults shouted by the other kids as I walked home: not because I was getting used to them, but because I knew that they would soon stop bothering me, forever.

I ate my dinner at home. It was the usual rubbish but my taste buds were alert for once. Suddenly, it tasted good.

That night, for the first time in ages, I fell asleep smiling. It was only a month and a bit since my Granddad's death but it felt like a lifetime. I was getting more manipulative by the day. That didn't taste so good, as the knowledge of what I had just done gnawed at my conscience. The days of me being genuine and nice were over. Innocence, once lost, cannot be reclaimed. On the other hand, bigger challenges lay ahead and, if I was to survive, I had to really toughen up.

In those days, school ran from Monday to Saturday, 8:30 a.m. to 1:30 p.m. On Friday it was Gianni's turn to stalk me around the school so he could accidentally-on-purpose meet me in the corridor. He was anxious to close the deal so he invited me to his place that afternoon where he would introduce me to his parents. It would have been a wonderful idea if only I had been dressed for the occasion. My wardrobe had been decimated by the earthquake. I used my best clothes only for church and special occasions, and at school scuffed around in the no-name rags my Mother had bought. I told him that I had to go home first: ostensibly for lunch and to tell my Mother where I would be. I rushed back home for a quick sandwich, washed as best I could and put on my Sunday best. My Mother was thrilled that I had such a high-class friend. Of course, she knew the headmaster's famous family only by reputation, but what a reputation! In fact, unless I had suddenly made friends with the president's son, I could not have done any better in her eyes. My Mum lived for her kids and one of them was going to visit the Naples equivalent of Beverly Hills.

From the moment I met Gianni outside the school, my performance started. Straight away, he noticed how I was dressed. He didn't take friends home very often, so he must've been happy

I wasn't in my usual rags. I was cool, good-looking and well dressed. More importantly, I was his friend, or so he thought. I don't know what my face looked like when I saw his house, but I felt my jaw drooping south. Then again, Gianni's jaw had hit the floor when he saw my place! The gates opened automatically into a driveway. Lovely trees lined the drive, guiding guests up to the entrance of the house where three expensive cars were parked. The big wooden front door was decorated with brass knobs. Even their kennel looked better than my place. This was not a typical headmaster's house. No employee of the State could afford such a palace, at least not if they were as straight as Gianni's father. Gianni's great-grandfather was the founder of one of Italy's biggest arms and munitions manufacturers. Gianni's father clearly didn't *need* to work, which is why as headmaster he was incorruptible. In Naples, that made him unique.

A beautifully dressed lady opened the door. Gianni's mother was by no means attractive, but the clothes and the expensive hair styling made her look pure Hollywood.

'So, you're a Prince, are you?'

I resented the sarcasm but reasoned she was just envious of my looks and academic reputation.

'Yes, madam' I said, smiling at full power. 'I lost my crown and jewels in the earthquake so the only gift I can offer you is my smile and a kiss' I added as I leant over, brushed her cheek, and made a 'mwaahh' sound.

She visibly relaxed. Her body language no longer tense, she was melting like butter, almost cooing as she ushered us into a grand living room. On the table was a plate of superb cakes. My eyes popped out of my head. Then she left us.

Finally alone with those cakes, I waited, out of politeness, for Gianni to pick the first one. It was excruciating staring at the cakes, tummy rumbling, while he swanned about the room as if eating a cake was the furthest thing from his mind. What was wrong with him? After what seemed like forever, I gave up and just took one. Oh my God!

I hadn't had a proper cake since the 'quake and I had never had any cake as good as these. When Gianni and I headed upstairs to his study, I took the rest of them with us on a big plate.

After our little treat, we got down to business. The little fatso had it all worked out: me staying for dinner; casually mentioning to his Dad how we were such good friends and that I was equally good at maths. Like me before him, he was hoping that his Dad would make the suggestion of us being in the same class. It seemed I wasn't the only schemer!

I had to sit still and listen to his endless nonsense about a poem he had once read once, just because it was now on my study list too. After a few minutes I wished I was back in the shanty-town.

All I wanted was revenge. All Gianni wanted was to be popular. It had become an obsession, which in turn fuelled his delusions. This was very uncomfortable as it is easier to manipulate other people than to manipulate your own feelings. Unfortunately, now I could do both.

'Do not look at the effect; look at the cause,' I said to myself.

After the torture of the mutual tutoring had ended, Gianni and I spent five minutes rehearsing his plan to get his Dad to move me to his class. It wasn't a lack of preparation that made me uncomfortable or even the unsophisticated plan; it was just the man himself: Gianni's father, the headmaster, was inscrutable. The only times I had seen him close up were when he handed over my results at the end of each year. He would say something like 'Good job, well done' but nothing more. Now I was in his house, eating his cakes and had just (air-)kissed his wife. This man represented the society and system I was dreaming of destroying. I didn't know him but I found myself despising him. Nonetheless, he was a clever guy; if I gave him even a hint of the real reasons for my discomfort he would read me like a book.

When we came down the long flight of stairs his wife was there watching TV. She turned to us.

'Would you like to join us for dinner?' she asked me.

Suddenly I had to react, think ahead. Dinner would finish at around 10 p.m. How to get home? It was too late to go home on my own through the shanty-town. I hesitated. She read my mind...

31

'My husband can drive you home if that's what is worrying you.' If he did, he might have his car stolen so that was out. There was no phone at my home with which to warn my Mother. She would be worried to death if I wasn't home in time for dinner. On the other hand, I did not want to miss an opportunity to move my plan forward or, indeed, to leave such beautiful surroundings. I wasn't just talking about the décor: winter was fast approaching, and we had no heating at home. Here I did not need to wear a jumper after dark, there was no stench of cooking, no tiptoeing around all the possessions crammed into a tiny space. I wanted to get the job done as soon as possible but, like Caesar, I had to 'retreat in order to win'. I reluctantly declined. I excused myself, fended off the insistent and prolonged pleas of Gianni, and left.

On the way back home I felt pretty sorry for myself, not because I was going back to the shanty-town but because I had blown a great opportunity.

My mood was so dark that it made my shack look even more depressing.

Sunday was supposed to be a day of rest, but not for me. I put on my other set of beautiful clothes, slicked my hair and slipped into the role of angelic altar boy. My Mother was terribly proud that I was going to church but couldn't understand why I went to one so far away that I had to take a bus. In a twisted version of the truth, I told her that it was because some of my friends went there. This calmed her fears. 'How gullible' I started to think, then caught myself and, in a rare moment of humanity, suddenly felt sorry for her.

On the way there, I reminded myself of all the lies I had told the previous week. I was hoping something good would happen. Good things happen in churches all the time but good for me would not be good for 'them'. That day in the House of God would be a milestone in my transformation into a fully functioning criminal.

The mass passed without incident. You didn't need to be a genius to help the priest with a routine that he had done a thousand times before. The real action began at the après-party. People had taken notice of me because of my posture, the way I conducted myself and, of course, my looks. I saw young girls looking at me and for a moment my vanity took over: it felt sweet.

I was serving orange juice and still enjoying the smiles from my new fan club when two glamorous couples approached.

'Hello, you're new here aren't you?' one of the wives asked.

It was a rhetorical question but I still nodded.

'What's your name?' another asked.

Still easy, so I told them. They introduced themselves warmly.

'Welcome to our church' the taller man said.

'So, where, do you live?' asked his high-cheek-boned wife.

'Oh, round here, in the area,' I said, turning red. My brain was working overtime and my legs had gone wobbly.

Two of them said 'Where?' at the same time.

Suddenly, I remembered that my Dad had a cousin living not too far away. Saved! But I didn't know the address. Not saved!

'Close to the shop in the corner, by the bank, in the tall building' I blurted. 'My parents are still looking for a flat and I am staying with an auntie for now.'

'What do your parents do?'

Phew! I knew that one. Panic over, I calmly replied with juicy elements from my cover story. Finally, my heart rate calmed. I felt pretty silly because, on reflection, they were neither overly inquisitive nor suspicious. They were just making casual conversation. When someone called them over they repeated their welcomes and moved on.

As soon as they were stuck into their new conversation I collapsed into a chair, my face bloodless and cold. I had almost been caught. I had made the same mistake that I had made the day before. Yet again I had failed to plan ahead. I hadn't learnt my lesson. Was I stupid enough to just sleepwalk into the next disaster? I promised myself I would not need another reminder. In the future I would plan for every eventuality. I couldn't continue to rely on the blind Goddess of Luck because one day she would desert me.

As trivial as this experience might sound, it was horrifying. As a kick-up-the-ass, it could not have come at a better time. I had become over-confident, feeling I could and would get away with anything. Before that day, I knew I had a brain. After it, I knew I would really have to use it to its full potential. My plans would inevitably get more complicated and dangerous but, before starting to make any new plan, I would remind myself of how I felt that day at the church. The process of using these memories to stimulate the motivation to work hard and plan for every eventuality would become my 'ritual'. We all have a personal ritual. To begin with, following it is a conscious choice, but eventually it becomes second nature. In the end, we stop moulding the ritual and we mould to the ritual. Mine would mould me into a criminal: one prepared to carry out ever more elaborate and dangerous plans.

My ritual would empower me to continue with my ambitious plans. That might sound like a blessing but it was a curse. Imagine if I had been caught: I would have been exposed as a liar. So what? I would simply have stopped going to that church. Maybe I would have laid my entire revenge plan to rest, thinking that it was doomed and that I was not up to the task. Would I have gone back to having normal dreams like everyone else? I wish I had stopped at this point but I will never know if a sharp humiliation in front of the entire church would have made a blind bit of difference. I did know that I was still in business ('Undercover Revenge Business' a.k.a. URB) and getting better at it all the time.

Later that week, Gianni invited me to his house to meet his father. This time, we would make sure we closed the class-transfer deal. Normally all I had to do was to get home from the library every day without getting beaten up; the prospect of dinner with Gianni's father was much more stressful. I knew I just had to relax and be charming but I was desperate to make him like me. Humans can smell desperation: they don't like it when people try too hard to be liked. Every two minutes throughout the excruciating meal I would get tense then command myself to relax. I had just forced myself into a relaxed phase and was really enjoying being relaxed when the big man turned to me...

'And so, young man, what have you learnt about literature from Gianni?'

I was so relaxed I almost told him the truth: 'Not a sausage!'

Instead, I regurgitated Gianni's useless critique of 'Tyger, Tyger', William Blake's famous poem. I won't bore you with the details but Gianni was certainly no tiger when it came to poetry and I didn't feel like one either after spouting it.

Gianni's father nodded throughout my spiel. He didn't seem impressed, but he didn't seem suspicious either. After all, he was probably well used to Gianni's nonsense theories by now, so he turned his laser gaze on Gianni.

'And what have you learnt about maths from your new friend?' So, it all came down to this, did it? I would not be judged by what I successfully taught the fool but, instead, by how well the fool could express what it was I taught him. I would happily take my chances with the former but the latter was a total lottery. Gianni took a deep breath. I tensed as if anticipating a train crash: some waffle about Pythagoras would impress no one, especially his Dad.

'My new friend has taught me the most important thing about maths,' Gianni declared.

'Ambitious start but the higher you fly, the further you fall,' I thought.

His father raised an eyebrow.

'No one isn't cut out for maths. It is just a matter of working hard and not giving up. Eventually it will come. He told me that not every subject is as easy, for me, as literature. In fact, our weaknesses are more worthy of attention than our strengths.'

Gianni stopped as if waiting for applause. His mother fidgeted. His father stared back implacably for a couple of seconds, then turned to face me.

'Quite the philosopher aren't you?' he said sceptically.

I was still wracking my brains for a witty riposte when the father burst out laughing. Gianni, his mother and I all joined in. Oh, how we laughed.

**

35

The shanty-town was getting busier by the day. New families were cutting trees down to make space for a few bricks and a tin roof. Our 'unit' looked like a castle in comparison. The streets got muddy when the autumn rain arrived, just as the cheap asphalt wore through. It was not easy for me to keep my chin up. As winter arrived, we found ourselves spending more time indoors. There was very little room for two adults, a kid and a baby that was always sick. I took refuge in my books. Until now, I had simply tried to repress my unhappy feelings but now I delved in with abandon, wallowing in the darkest of emotions.

Gianni's father organised my transfer in record time. I was in my new class being introduced by my new teacher the following Monday. If I had applied by the ordinary channels, I probably would have graduated before they got round to it. Life is so easy when you are part of the system.

The class was arranged in rows of desks, each seating two. Most desks had a pair of pupils seated there, and when I surveyed the class there were only a few spare seats. I searched the room. Gianni was, of course, sat alone. I made eye contact. His look implored me to sit next to him. Pasquale was not hard to spot. Even sitting, he towered above his younger classmates. He stared back menacingly. He was sat alone too; not surprising, given his reputation. I doubt he wanted to be friends with the rest of that class and it looked like the feeling was mutual. Obviously, no one in the class had read Machiavelli's famous line:

'Keep your friends close but your enemies closer.'

Or perhaps they just didn't have the guts to put the theory to the test, preferring an alternate theory:

'Only a madman sits closer than necessary to a wild beast.'

If you sat next to him, you might have to talk to him. I already knew from experience that if you said 'Hello' the wrong way you could piss him off, and as his neighbour you were always in range of his fists. I marched down the aisle. Gianni's big brown eyes stared at me. I stopped by the empty chair.

'Would you mind if I sat here?' I asked, my voice full of respect.

Pasquale looked up, surprised. He had seen me before when

he pestered me but thugs like him pestered so many people that I doubt he would have remembered. He nodded without giving it any thought. Then again, he didn't go in for much thinking. I, on the other hand, was doing nothing but thinking as I chose to sit down next to Pasquale, not Gianni. My grandfather's advice echoed:

'Live like a lion or survive like a sheep.'

Today, I had chosen to be a lion. Now I had to tame one. If I didn't get into Pasquale's good books quickly I would run the risk of being pigeon-holed as a smart-ass nerdy pipsqueak and lose my chance forever. So, even when I knew the answer to the teacher's questions, I broke the habit of a lifetime and just kept my mouth shut, biding my time. Believe me, that was difficult!

A week later, the effort paid off. It was maths test day. Everyone in the class was shit-scared: everyone except me. I saw it as more like doing a crossword while sat on the toilet. As the class waited for the teacher to arrive they indulged in pointless last-minute revision while I just daydreamed.

Gianni was sat across the aisle from me, sweating like a horse into his expensive pullover as he furiously scanned his notes. His newly acquired philosophy of hard work was not doing him much good.

'I will do your test for 50 euros,' I whispered in his ear.

'Please! Do it well and I'll give you 100!' he whispered back.

'Done,' I said.

On my other side sat Pasquale. I studied him closely: normally a risky thing to do, in case he saw you looking. Gone was the arrogance of his street persona. He couldn't rely on those muscles now. His eyes wandered, searching for a miracle cure to his ignorance. Desperate to finish the school year, sick of sharing his days with a bunch of 12-year-olds; when he was vulnerable he looked so sweet.

'*I'll* do your test,' I blurted.

He stared back, trying to suss me out.

'You taking the piss?' he said.

'Come on, I'm good at this, really good.'

'This a trick? I'll...' he said before I cheekily interrupted him.

'I know you'll kick my head in, but if Gianni trusts me enough to *pay* for my help, why wouldn't you?'

'I ain't gonna pay yer!'

'I know that too. It's free. What have you got to lose?'

He scowled, forced to think for a second. Then he nodded. He knew he was in last chance saloon.

We would soon be given a test paper, each with different questions, all of equal difficulty. This prevented us from cheating by simply copying each other's answers. We had two hours for the test, just about enough. They didn't think that cheating by doing two tests was a realistic threat. I had set myself the challenge to do three. All of a sudden, I felt the same anxiety that everyone else felt. I was not used to that kind of pressure, at least not at school.

'This could be a fun challenge,' I thought, before my new ritual, born out of the recent near miss at the church, kicked in...

'Don't get cocky; think how you are going to do this and plan for every eventuality,' I reminded myself.

First, I needed Gianni to pass me his test without him being noticed. As clumsy as he was, he would have been caught instantly and of the two of us, only I, the one not related to the headmaster, would have been expelled. And there would be life-threatening consequences when my Father found out. Second, I had to rush their tests but mine had to be perfect: I took pride in always scoring top marks. Third, I had to find a way to clearly write their answers on a separate sheet of paper and pass it back to them with enough time for them to copy it onto their answer sheet. I would have had no problems switching papers with Pasquale, as he was right next to me. However, after explaining it to both of them twice, I knew that if I failed it would be because of them, not me.

I took ten deep breaths to calm myself. I didn't just breathe, I thought about each breath, felt the hot warmth of the air as it came out of my mouth. I learnt this tip from one of my psychology books under the heading: 'How to dominate the flow of emotions to maximise performance.' These days it's called living in the moment.

'Please, Sir. Can I go to the toilet?' I shouted.

'If you must!' the teacher replied.

And with that, I was into action. As I stood up, I let my exam paper drift onto the floor. After a very quick visit, as I approached my desk I stumbled. I held on to Gianni's desk and took his exam paper down with my fall. While I was on the floor, I casually switched the two papers, giving Gianni mine and putting his on my desk. Sat in the corner, the teacher didn't have a good view and never noticed. I had to work out the answers on a separate sheet of paper, quickly enough so he would have time to copy them. His handwriting was just as abominable as he was, so I could not actually fill them in for him. I did it in record time. I kicked Gianni's chair. He got up and, in the process, threw my exam paper on the floor. I bent over in a flash and switched them again but, this time, his proposed answer sheet was carefully placed inside it. Gianni started to copy it as I started on Pasquale's paper. Pasquale was sat next to me so it was an easy swap. I probably should have just done his: I would have had more time.

In the end, I smashed all three papers. I could have scored 100 per cent on all of them but I made sure that Gianni would get about 70 per cent. Pasquale was trickier; 60 per cent was the pass mark but even 65 per cent would have looked too good for him so I had to aim for 61 per cent and hope I didn't hit 59!

With half an hour to spare I strutted out, head held high, like a prince.

THE ENEMY

Four days later, walking home from school, I had a terrible attack of déjà vu. A rough-looking boy lurched towards me. By the time I realised it was the ringleader of the gang of 'Hyenas' who had 'done' the car, it was too late to cross over. My heart was in my mouth. He looked at me menacingly and raised his arm. I flinched. What I thought was a punch coming my way morphed into a hard slap on the back. He laughed like a hyena at his silly trick; he even looked like a hyena but he was still just a scumbag. Even if he didn't punch me, it didn't mean he didn't want to. I was deciding how to deal with him when Pasquale's moped turned the corner. From fifty metres away I still recognised the big scar on his smiling face. He rode helmetless and his gold-toothed smile, wide and genuine, was directed at me, not the Hyena.

'Hey Prince, how are you?' Pasquale shouted above the whine of his two-stroke motor.

'Respect!' the Hyena said, hurriedly offering his hand to me in a clenched street greeting. He was in a rush to claim me, to compete with Pasquale, as if to say, 'He was my friend first.' I was a pawn in their power game, except the Hyena didn't even know what the game was. His animal cunning sensed the way the tide was going and went with it.

'Wanna lift home?' Pasquale enquired as he pulled up.

I climbed onto the bike. Now the Hyena and all the other rough kids of the shanty-town would know I was connected to Pasquale. Although Hyena-boy was stupid, he knew that I'd clocked his swift flip from foe to friend. On the street everything you did was for show. It was all one big show for me too, because I was undercover.

When Pasquale dropped me off after what would be the first of many lifts home from school, he kissed me on the cheek like a brother. For the first time since the earthquake, life was enjoyable. I'm sure Pasquale felt the same way. For the first time ever, he'd been congratulated by the teacher in front of everyone. It must have felt great. He liked the taste of victory, albeit from cheating, and he was hungry for more. He was desperate to pass that school year and graduate. I was his best chance. He would be putty in my hands. As I got off the bike I turned and held his gaze.

'I'll tutor you every day and next time you will pass the test on your own,' I said.

His big brown eyes widened in disbelief. I was playing with his mind. I had no doubt that he'd already pictured his mother watching him receive his diploma with a big smile on her face. No more bad letters, no more teachers sending the police to his house, and no more threats of expulsion. A new beginning would lead to a better life, a better job and a better house.

I could see that playing across his face when I made my offer and suddenly I realised we had something in common: we had both started out with the same dream of a good and successful life. Mine had morphed into a dream of revenge but I never stopped believing I would make it come true; but he had given up on his for so long that he had stopped dreaming altogether. A man without a dream is a man without a soul. By the simple act of cheating on his behalf, I had convinced him to believe in me. Now I had to get him to believe in himself. Until now, violence and crime were the only ways he knew how to get things done and make himself visible. He was not afraid of consequences: he had nothing to lose. A man with nothing to lose has no fear; he will kill, slash, rob and rape. That is how a criminal is made. I met a lot of people like Pasquale over the years and, apart from a few who were actually mad, they all came from the same beginnings as him. From then on, whenever I saw him I'd do my best to make him feel good about himself so that he would believe that he could do OK at school, just like everyone else. But I didn't really care about him or anyone. All that concerned me was how to manipulate the world to achieve my goals. I would feel ever more disgusted with myself. Pasquale would feel the opposite, growing to know that someone really did believe in him.

When I looked up to say goodbye, he was still smiling. For a moment, I forgot why I was doing all this. I felt normal again:

warm and giving. It only lasted until I went inside my shack.

My Mother was watching a tiny TV by her bed. A few feet away, hidden behind a makeshift curtain, was my bed. As soon as I sat on it, my thoughts went back to the bullies who kept us here: those same guys from the posh church. We were crammed into a hellhole while they were living it up on the money sent from the government and other European States for the reconstruction.

The next day at school Gianni gave me the 100 euros in return for his success in the maths test. He started to say thanks. A minute later he was still thanking me. I interrupted him with the same offer I had made to Pasquale, but with one important difference: Gianni would pay me 350 euros a month.

Pasquale would attend the same tutoring sessions, but for free. I wouldn't let him know that Gianni was paying me. To be seen regularly with him in the shanty-town would be payment enough. For the first session, I rode with Pasquale on his moped to Gianni's house. Gianni's mother's face was a grotesque sight when she first laid eyes on Pasquale. He looked a lot older than fifteen, with a large scar and a golden tooth decorating his face, while his body was tall and his posture intimidating, especially for a woman just over 5 feet tall. The closest she had come to someone like him before was watching a pirate movie. It was difficult for me to explain why this young criminal was on her doorstep. She was still speechless when Gianni and Pasquale went upstairs, so I ushered her into the kitchen as if I were the host. Thanks to the discipline of my 'ritual', I had planned for her reaction and was well prepared. I had memorised several books on the art of manipulation, including *De Oratore* by Cicero, the great Roman orator.

'How dare you bring that ... that "thing" into my house? I will call the police and have you both arrested. I thought you were a nice kid!' she screamed.

And that was just the beginning: the tirade got worse. Now was the big test. Could I successfully apply my new skills in psychology? Or were they just more useless theories clogging up my brain and slowing my instincts?

I listened carefully, keeping eye contact at all times, and then, once the adrenaline was in full flow, I shouted something completely irrelevant:

'What a lovely smell! Are you cooking chicken?'

The smell was obvious. She was baking a cake. Had I said, 'What kind of cake are you baking?' it would have made her more angry, realising I was just trying to change the subject. The smell was so unlike chicken that just mentioning chicken forced her to take a moment to think and try to make sense of it. The rational part of her brain kicked into action as she struggled to understand. Meanwhile, the adrenaline subsided.

'No, I am baking. Can't you smell it?' she explained patronisingly, suddenly calm.

My trick had worked.

'Ahhh, that is what it is. Well, it smells lovely.'

'Thank you,' she replied.

'Your son and I want to help this boy. He has had a bad start in life but we can be a positive influence. In return, Gianni will learn to interact with people like him. It will make him more rounded – might even toughen him up. I will take full responsibility for Pasquale's behaviour. You will be happy.'

It calmed her like a Jedi knight and with that I kissed her on the cheek and trotted upstairs to join the others. When it was ready, her freshly baked cake followed us upstairs, accompanied by a big smile.

Teaching those two boys felt like shouting at a deaf man. Hard work and perseverance were required. Mind you, it had its perks, too. As we toiled away in Gianni's father's study, we were surrounded by more than a thousand magnificent books and the finest furniture. The desk we worked on was mahogany and large enough for ten children to sit around. The chairs were like sitting on a cloud. The room was decorated with fine antiques and memorabilia from the couple's many trips to exotic destinations, giving it a mystical feel. It felt like heaven compared to the public library where I usually did my homework.

I would explain how to do a certain mathematical formula and then give them some time to do an exercise while I dived into the books on display. Reading the books was the best bit. Being the tutor of two dimwits held no joy; just a means to an end. When their time was up, I would reluctantly close whatever brilliant volume I had discovered and become their tutor once more, ready to listen and correct what they had done, and then set them a new exercise before reopening my book.

Whenever they worked hard, they made some progress, albeit slowly. For me, it was all about getting the chance to read beautiful manuscripts in luxurious surroundings. Forget the shabby public library with its worn out, obsolete books. Here, I had the very best at my disposal: brand new books still smelling of fresh paper. That gorgeous smell made learning feel sexy. Gianni's father clearly had a great passion for one subject above all: the majority of his books were on chemistry. I, too, had a weakness for it, fascinated as I was by any element of the periodic table that might react explosively. During these sessions I learnt more than Pasquale and Gianni did.

The father was a tall and stylish middle-aged guy. So far he had aged gracefully with never a grey hair out of place. His quiet distinguished air made him appear distant and even stuck up.

'Do not look at the effect; look at the cause. Find a common ground, establish a communication channel and make the subject yours, whoever he might be,' I instructed myself.

Unlike his wife, he was not very communicative or emotional so, for instance, when he saw Pasquale in his house he limited himself to a look of disapproval, nothing more. I judged him too clever for my usual tricks. I would have to think of something special for him.

Of all the chemistry books in that vast study, the ones which the headmaster read most often, the ones with little marks in them, the ones with more signs of wear, were the books about explosives. He had left one next to his engraved rocking chair which was full of notes, earmarks and highlights. He must have loved explosives. I tried to find out more about him from Gianni. It wasn't hard; like most sons, Gianni was proud of his father and boasted of his achievements. He had a very good engineering degree from a renowned university in the north of Italy. He had been in the military but left when he was passed over for promotion once too often. He was the second-in-line heir to a large munitions and weapons company, set up by his grandfather, which had grown enormous and now supplied artillery and explosives to governments all over the world. The business was now run by his older brother. Judging by his obsession with explosives, I am sure that he did not enjoy being left out of it. Suddenly I realised why the headmaster always seemed so ill at ease outside of the school. At school he was the big chief, the headmaster, and this strange feeling evaporated. But when he was not at school he must've felt frustrated and inferior, knowing that his father had chosen his brother over him to handle the business. Perhaps this had led to his obsession with explosives in later life, but I reckoned he had always been a pyromaniac from his early years. I was amused to imagine that such a mild-mannered man had a dark side.

I read and learned the chemical equations and combinations of explosives, both ancient and modern. I was like a child alone in a candy store. I fell in love with the theories that, when reproduced in a laboratory, could unleash the same destructive power as the earthquake that had ruined my life.

Although I knew a lot about Gianni's father, I hardly ever saw him as he would come home after we had already left. Still, his son was making huge strides, not only academically but also socially. One night we found ourselves laughing our heads off in the study. Some stupid childish joke had just set us off. When the laughter stopped I felt like I actually, genuinely, liked these two guys. No hidden agenda. Gianni's mother was more comfortable with us now. I had instructed Pasquale to be polite and cordial with her, so as not to scare her. She had replied in kind with lovely cakes at 4 p.m. and a beautifully cooked dinner after studying. To eat there was a dream come true. What had begun as a tedious task felt more and more like a blissful escape from the shanty-town. She was happy to describe me as a 'friend of Gianni' to any visitors. She also showered me with respect and gifts. She could see I was having a positive impact on her son. He was blossoming in every sense and she was grateful, as only a mother could be. She did not know that her son was paying me but she knew my situation at home so she would slip ten or twenty euros in my pocket from time to time, which I gladly accepted. In my first month of tutoring I made half my Dad's salary, ate like a king and read books the likes of which I could never have borrowed or afforded. That should have been enough.

I spent as little time as possible in the shack. With the money from the tutoring my wardrobe filled up again with clothes that were worthy of 'the Prince'. I even had money left over to join the local gym where I could shower away the stench of the shanty-town. When my parents questioned where all the stuff had come from, the answer was, for a change, the truth: 'Gianni gives them as presents in exchange for my tutorials.'

Better yet, Pasquale announced that he and I were 'cousins'. Now the local street kids not only had to leave me alone, but had to 'give me respect' whenever they saw me. Some of them went even further, saying good morning to my parents every day as well. Once in a while I even stopped for a chat, a few jokes and maybe to kick a football with them. Life felt good again. I'd had a taste of success and I *wanted* more.

After church, school and the sessions at Gianni's I only went home to sleep, but it was here where my one remaining problem lay. I was used to all that space in Gianni's house, whereas my little corner of the shack was barely big enough for my bed. It started to feel even smaller as I grew taller.

In three months, even after replenishing my wardrobe, I had managed to save 500 euros, which I hid behind my bed where Mum wouldn't find it. No one had built another shack directly behind ours, so I had an idea: I would build an extension. I wanted, and would have, my own separate room with my own set of keys. When I asked my Dad for permission, he just laughed. He didn't think I could do it so he said yes without giving it another thought. What he did not know was that I had read so many books on construction that I could have applied for an architect's licence. I had no problem with designing, planning, buying the materials and building the extension with my own window, my own door and smooth plastered walls. A willing workforce came from Pasquale's gang. They had experience working for local builders. Now it's called child exploitation but back then it was simply enterprising youth. They got paid and by the end of the autumn half-term holiday I had my own mini-palace. My Dad was laughing on the other side of his face now. Even my Mother was jealous. Reluctantly, but true to their word, they let me enjoy it alone without interfering. After all, I had just freed up a lot of space in the main shack so everyone was a winner. Those rascals in Pasquale's gang even knew how to tap into the electricity from the street lamps. My little electric heater would be on all the time in the coming winter, making my room the warmest in the neighbourhood. Last but not least, it helped me to meet and get to know more of the guys in Pasquale's gang. Even Pasquale didn't know where the money came from, but to have spare cash when everyone around me was poor made me look special. Even better, I had managed the project as a leader so they, Pasquale included, started to look up to me rather than down. I had built my own palace with my own money and my own people.

December came in all its winter glory and, like most kids my age, I was looking forward to Christmas. Even after my Granddad's death, we would spend the customary two-week holiday up in the hills with my Grandma, the one woman I loved more than my own mother. I was happy and cheerful again. I had rediscovered the bubbly personality that had first made me popular at school before the earthquake. Maybe it was because I was once again the best-dressed kid in town, but I was controlling my own destiny again and loving it.

Compared to their own dismal starting point, Gianni and Pasquale were doing fantastically well at school. They were also improving on other fronts. Gianni started to look cool and act pleasantly. Even Pasquale looked less like a criminal; instead, he looked like any other pupil, just bigger. Pasquale felt more at ease with our awkward fat friend too, although not enough to be seen in public with him as he had his own reputation to protect; it was enough to relax in his company when no one else could see him. One night after the usual tutorial, which had become by then more like a bit of fun than a job, the other two went upstairs to play computer games. I gently refused their invitation to join them, preferring to stay behind to drink from the study's many fountains of knowledge. Even in those days I despised computer games. I thought they would kill my brain. Since my brain cells were my passport to happiness I wanted to protect them.

I was so engrossed in some new theory of plastic explosive that I did not hear anyone enter, but I suddenly felt an uncomfortable presence. I turned around and suddenly the buttons of a very expensive cardigan were stuck up my nose.

'What are you doing?' Gianni's father whispered angrily.

He had come home early and, finding our study session was well underway, he had waited for us to finish. The sound of his son and Pasquale running upstairs prompted him to venture back into his own study. If he was a little displeased at finding me there then I, in turn, felt like a thief caught red-handed. A series of apparently illogical images flashed before my eyes and I knew then that I was turning into something that my Mother would not be proud of. There was a surge in brain cell activity, my muscles tensed and my pupils dilated. I was transported in an instant back to a well-rehearsed scene and, as I was, I went from being scared of him to a state of complete self-control. Aware of my new talents, nothing was beyond me anymore. I took a step back, so I could look up at his face, and composed my most sincere smile.

'I am enjoying this fabulous book, Sir!' I replied like a little soldier.

I had rehearsed the tone of that 'Sir' a thousand times and, judging by the plethora of military memorabilia on display, I had bet it would invoke fond memories of his military past. It did: he seemed to relax a fraction.

'I am very fond of chemistry and I could not resist this book,' I said to consolidate my advantage.

It was an audacious statement for a lowly pupil caught in the headmaster's study. Without batting an eyelid he took me up on the implied challenge, interrogating me mercilessly about the subject. I was faultless. He was shocked. He shifted tack again, treating me as if I were a peer instead of a pupil. The discussion went to the next level: the latest scientific developments in the world of explosives. After half an hour, he fell silent and relaxed, trance-like, in his chair.

Whatever it was he was thinking about, he appeared suddenly to reach a conclusion. He abruptly stood and beckoned me to follow him to the back of the room, where he opened a door. Curiosity easily overcame my fear that it contained a torture chamber for naughty boys.

'My son, Gianni, is not interested in this,' he said as we entered.

I may have been struck speechless by the gorgeous technology surrounding me but I, for one, was very much interested. It looked more like a professional laboratory than an amateur workshop. I asked him a thousand questions and he duly explained everything, happy to have found someone to share his passion. The way I saw it, when it came to chemistry I was the child prodigy that he wished Gianni had been: not such a wild theory, as every teacher loves an enthusiastic pupil and I played the role perfectly.

I could have stayed there for the rest of my life, and yet not have been satisfied, but it was time for me to go home. Pasquale had friends waiting for him, intent on hitting the street on a Saturday night. He had to go and he was my lift.

Nevertheless, the father insisted that I stay for dinner. I would stay overnight and he would call my parents to get their permission.

But we didn't have a phone.

He was not to be denied.

I asked Pasquale if he would tell my parents and come back for me early the following morning, as I had to help at the church with a mass of 'First Communions'.

To this day, I remember that evening with fondness. I simultaneously fed my twin appetites: fine food and explosives. It was worth the hassle of getting home. Shame I didn't feel the same way about church the next day. That felt really pointless.

I had been attending Sunday mass for nearly four months. That's

16 Sundays! I was giving up my only day off for the peanuts that ugly priest paid me; nothing compared to the money I was making off Gianni. I promised myself that, if Pasquale was late or didn't show up, I would blow it off and spend the day playing football with my new friends in the shanty-town. I felt like I was owed some rest and relaxation after my success with Gianni's father.

As fate had it, Pasquale came back for me at the agreed time. On the way, he quizzed me about why I went to church so far away. He may not have been clever but he was savvy enough to know that there was more to my attendance at church than faith in God. Unusually for me, I did not lie. I told him, straight up, that I was there to get to know the people who put us in the shanty-town so I could find a way to get revenge. I felt comfortable sharing my big secret with him for the simple reason that he was just as much a victim of them as I was. Anyway, wanting revenge was not a crime. Of course, just telling him like that was my way of asking him for help, to which he probably thought: 'You are just a kid, be a kid,' but he didn't say anything out of respect.

Later, when he dropped me off, he just said 'Good luck' with a cheeky smile.

I didn't blame him for having reservations about my little dream; I had them too.

'What the hell! I am here now – let me see the day through and then I will probably stop coming here,' I promised myself as he drove away.

Catholic First Communion at this particular church was one of *the* social events of the year in Naples, like 'Oscar Night' in Hollywood. Everyone came dressed like a million dollars and the place was packed. We had to introduce forty-five more kids to the path of Christianity where they would share, for the first time, the Blood and Body of Christ, a.k.a. some bread dipped in wine. Until then, I had never been very religious but all this fake 'churchianity' and 'religiosity', combined with the bigots who attended the whole shebang, made me even less interested. So many of the clientele, for that is what they were, were totally new to me. I had been there long enough to know who came regularly and who showed up once in a blue moon. This was the bluest of moons. They did what they had to do in the name of tradition. It meant nothing to them in terms of faith or spirituality, just an excuse for an expensive party. The richest would invite their friends and family to a restaurant for a big meal, sometimes with more than 300 guests and eight or nine courses. If you were not familiar with this custom, you might have thought it was a wedding. In fact, very few people ever have a wedding as fancy as the First Communion lavished on these kids.

Afterwards I was to serve the beverages so the priest briefed me about the important guests: details about who they were and their preferences for how they liked to be treated. He could have cut it short by saying they were *all* special and all had to be treated like royalty.

The après service refreshments were a lot more substantial than usual and, as a result, we would finish later. I had forgotten to tell my Mother that I wouldn't be back for Sunday lunch. She would be livid. As usual, I had no way to tell her. I was contemplating bailing out as soon as the service itself was over; but I didn't. All those well-dressed people and all those decorations smelt of money. Like a bloodhound on a trail, I had to follow. I was determined that my career as an altar boy would not be a waste of time. I could worry about my parents later.

It was clear, from both the way the priest described him to me and from the deference with which the other guests treated him as he took his seat for the service, that the most important guest at that charade was a certain large man, who I will call 'Bulldog'. This was not his real name but it's what he looked like: six foot four with a massive frame and a head so big it that looked like it weighed as much as his body. His head seemed to impair his ability to walk. He was totally bald with very expensive, thick-rimmed designer glasses, all wrapped up in an amazing suit. I knew all the details and prices for every fashion designer, which meant I knew this Zegna suit alone was worth over 5,000 euros.

I was sure he was the reason so many people in the shanty-town were living and suffering like animals; and if he wasn't then he certainly hadn't done much to stop it. He was the president of the Christian Democratic Party (CDP) of the Campania region, third in command of the Italian Parliament: one of the most influential politicians in Italy at the time. Don't be fooled by the name; his party had nothing to do with the Christian religion, nor with the good people who followed it. Worse, it had nothing to do with democracy. They rose to power in the fifties and stayed there, almost without a break, for the next forty-five years. They sucked the marrow out of Italy during the economic miracle of the sixties. They were associated with the Mafia, the Freemasons, the Red Brigade and any other bunch of evil Italians you care to mention. Some of it was urban myth but some of it was true. The shanty-town and its impoverished inhabitants were no myth. The CDP must have siphoned off the aid money given to Naples to rebuild after the earthquake, leaving the people to fend for themselves. My blood was starting to boil as I thought about him as the evil head (and it was a big fat hateful head) of the most evil organisa-tion. This story could only end one way. He was the ENEMY.

I composed myself during the service. Afterwards, with my tray of beverages, I waded into the crowd: deep undercover amongst the enemy. After mingling and handing out a few drinks, I took my half-empty tray and set up station. I chose a space between two circles of guests. One contained nobody of interest. The other contained Bulldog and some female companions. Like Sherlock Holmes, I studied them for clues. All the women around him lis-tened avidly with a certain awe so I deduced that none of them was his wife. I too was keen to hear what he was saying so I inched closer, straining my ears. I was picking up a word here and there but not enough for it to make sense. Then someone (I never found out who) barged into my back. A couple of glasses of orange juice started to tip off my tray. I steadied the tray with my supporting hand, which stopped one glass from spilling, but the other was already turning upside down in mid-air. The likely destination for the bright, caustic liquid was the white, silk-clad backside of one of the lady companions of Bulldog. I had a fraction of a second to react before the juice would be loose. Then nothing would prevent a hefty dry cleaning bill and, worse, the spotlight turning on me. With my free hand I batted the dropping glass and its contents into the gap between this group and the next circle of guests, where it hit the floor and smashed. A thin patch of juice spread across the floor. I could live with that. As I bent to pick up the broken glass I looked across at the woman in white. Her backside looked great but, more importantly, it was still 100 per cent white. It was a shame I could not say the same for her conscience, because if you were a friend of Bulldog then you were an enemy of mine.

'What have you done? You clumsy boy!' Don Vincenzo screamed from behind me.

'Someone nudged me,' I said as defiantly as I could for my meek altar boy act.

'Don't try to blame your ineptitude on others,' he said, wagging his finger at me.

'You will pay for that!' he added, pointing at the mess on the floor.

While Don Vincenzo fumed I simply bent down and continued picking up glass. Then I heard another voice that sent shivers down my spine. It was a voice I knew well enough.

'Don Vincenzo, don't be harsh on the boy. I saw what happened. It was not his fault. In fact, he acted valiantly to prevent it staining my companion's dress,' it said.

The voice was unmistakably Bulldog's.

'Oh Signore, is that so? Well, I am very sorry. I should not have jumped to any conclusions.'

'Humpf!' was all Bulldog could say.

When I was confident I had picked up all the glass I stood up. While the Hunchback showered Bulldog with his usual compliments, I gazed up at the throbbing jugular on Bulldog's massive neck. The priest continued, his oratory reaching a most disgustingly smarmy stage. So bad that I felt sorry for Bulldog having to endure it; no wonder his vein was throbbing. As for me, I was confused and deeply upset. I hated Bulldog and yet he had stuck up for me. Perhaps I was wrong about the guy; he seemed to be the only one here with a sense of justice and fairness. Perhaps I should stab that massive vein in his neck with a shard of broken glass before I actually started to like him.

'And what's your name, young man?' Bulldog asked, finally interrupting Don Vincenzo's endless compliments.

I didn't hear the question at first; my imagination was running wild. In less than 30 seconds I had killed him six more times in eight different ways. I didn't, of course, but just timidly gave my name with a forced smile. I was many things but I wasn't a killer. Besides, he would have swallowed me in one go with a head that big. He looked at me with what I took to be a hideously patronising smile.

'You're new to the congregation, aren't you?'

My little heart stopped. It sounded like the ultimate insult to me; I felt like I was about to burst into tears at such a routine question. My mouth went dry. My jaw locked.

To escape the excruciating pain, I just nodded.

It was my first encounter with him and I felt utterly defeated. I added this humiliation to my mental list of crimes that I swore he would pay for.

You only have to win the last battle to win the war. This was just the beginning.

Unaware of what was going through my mind, Bulldog introduced me to his ten-year-old daughter, Greta. She was the prettiest thing I had ever seen. She smiled so warmly that I calmed down in an instant. I think she had a crush on me. Or was it the other way round?

For my safety, my sanity and to avoid further emotional distractions I decided that from now on I would limit my contact with Bulldog to make sure he, or my anger, didn't wear me down. I needed to be fresh to face him. To that end, I set off to circle the room. There were other politicians there as well, all from the CDP and each of them, no doubt, sharing the ill-gotten pie. They were all worth observing, I suppose, but I wasn't really interested in these minions. The grey of politics was far from the pure logic of maths and chemistry that I knew and understood. I could never understand why my people chose to put these criminals in charge of our country. That was one of the many reasons why I chose to educate myself. The CDP's guys had done a great job of selling their lies to the people. If nothing else, I can learn how to sell lies too. I suddenly felt buoyed. I had caught first sight of a weakness in my enemy: the fondness for his daughter.

I changed focus once more. As I looked around, I noticed all the women. All were beautiful, their hair stylish, expensive dresses flowed over their figures and their jewellery was equally harmonious. I thought about my own mother and the other women I saw where I lived: all dressed in rags with hair like an overused broom. Even their wedding rings, although still gold, were dull. Almost twelve months in that hellhole had taken its toll on my Mum, robbing her of her vitality, which soon led to the loss of any remaining beauty. She was now one of the ugliest in the whole shanty-town. On the other hand, the ladies in the church looked and smelled sensational. The more I looked at them, the more beautiful they seemed. We only lived twenty kilometres apart and yet they were a different species. Even their kids looked stunning. The kids in my neighbourhood were shoeless and dirty. Go to the monkey enclosure at the zoo to get an idea of what their rotten smiles looked like.

My anger turned to despair. There was so much happiness on these faces and so much unhappiness where I lived. If I took my revenge I would simply spread the unhappiness virus, taking happiness away from the few who had it but with no guarantee that it would have a positive effect on anyone in the shanty-town. I started to wallow in self-pity. Normally, I would bypass a state of sadness and go straight to feeling angry or, at worst, disappointed. The downside is that you never live in the 'now', always dreaming of a better future but only once revenge has been served.

But I needed a constant stream of compensations and distractions:

Lost your beautiful wardrobe in an earthquake? Get some money and buy a better one.

Living in a shack? Build an extension.

Beaten up every day? Befriend the gang leader and get respect instead. Even my grandfather's death had not led to self-pity. I had loved him more than anyone; he was always in my heart and I still think about him every day. I was actually glad that he died like he did: better 50 years as a lion than 100 as a sheep. If I had managed to avoid self-pity after the most tragic event of my life, then I was not going to let Bulldog drive me to it.

But this time it was different. I couldn't see myself dealing with all this. I felt overwhelmed by the hopelessness of the situation. The cast of my nightmares was sat before me: the very people I held responsible for all my troubles. Maybe it was their sheer number, their polished looks or their happy and smiling faces but they started to look like a brick wall: each brick another perfect smiling face.

Resigned to my life of mediocrity and suffering, I continued to serve drinks on autopilot. My brain had gone on strike. With no new ideas, I was no longer sad; I just didn't care anymore.

'Whatever! So what?' I thought and followed it up with all the other clichéd excuses that losers and quitters use. When the beverages were all served and the party was winding down, I crumpled into my chair. My legs had joined the strike. If it had been a boxing match my trainer would have thrown in the towel.

Then one faint sound changed everything. This time it was not Bulldog's voice that surprised me. It may have been very faint but it was an old and dear friend. The sheer familiarity of this voice made me instantly forget all the negativity swirling inside me. It was music to my ears, but all that mattered was recognising it. The joy of the sound gave me enough energy to rack my brains one last time. Then, suddenly, I knew who it was. It was a Sargent & Greenleaf model 8400. Those dulcet tones were the clicks of the combination lock from the safe in the church's sacristy annex room. I hadn't seen the safe before because I never went in there and I had never heard it before because I was never sat close enough at the moment it was opened, but right now the priest was putting the donations away. The takings that day had surely set a record. I reckoned about 90 to 100 grand had just been given to the church. All those crooks were trying to buy their way into heaven. They stole in the millions but gave in the hundreds.

'Snap out of it, son,' my Granddad whispered in my ears, 'life is your oyster!'

After working with my Granddad for so many years, the sound of the first five or six clicks was enough for me to identify the make, model and year of production of any safe. No wonder he had shown me off to his friends like an exhibit in a Victorian freak show. I rarely disappointed my audience, getting it right 90 per cent of the time. Opening them up was even easier for me and on that score my success rate was 100 per cent.

Suddenly, a bad day became the greatest day. I had fulfilled the first rule of combat: know your enemy. I even knew where they lived; or, at least, I knew where I could find out. More importantly, I knew where the money was. That it was inside a safe in a locked room was the least of my concerns.

The priest gave me ten euros for my day's work. Plus, the finest ham sandwiches, the best cakes and other leftovers were all neatly bagged up for me to take home. I am not going to say that he had been unfair to me. No, he had been quite generous. It's not like I had ploughed a field. However, and I certainly didn't expect him to know this, people like me, they think differently. I believed I was entitled to a percentage of the takings because I was a key member of the 'show' we had just put on. I think one percent would be reasonable so forget ten euros; he should have given me at least nine hundred!

The emotional crash of earlier wasn't forgotten but I had no intention of quitting either.

'There is no chance, no destiny and no fate that can control or hinder the firm resolve of a determined soul.'

I took the ten-euro note and the bag of food and went home happy, but I was two hours late for my Mother and neither of these gifts would calm her. She was spitting fire!

The last day of school before the Christmas holidays. For the first time in his life, Pasquale was looking forward to his end-of-term report. On top of that, he was now like a brother to me. Despite the difference in our intellectual abilities, his being three years older and much more streetwise meant I could still respect him. More than respect, I actually enjoyed his company.

Gianni had also done well that term, although I'll never know how much was down to favouritism. After all, no teacher wanted to be the one who failed their boss's son. Nonetheless, he had improved a lot. I was warming to him too, but to a lesser extent. He was naive and childish but his constant generosity made an impact on my cold heart. His family felt strongly about me too. They invited me to their house for the 'lazt zupper before Chriztmaz', as Gianni put it. By now I was a regular guest at his father's laboratory. After we three lads had finished our homework, I would stay on in the lab as long as possible, not just as a test tube monkey; I added value with my input to his experiments. Quite often, I stayed over so I could work late in the lab. My Mum did not mind. She was thrilled. I took full advantage: my lean-to bedroom stood no comparison with the crisp sheets on the soft bed in their guest room.

While I planned out Gianni's revision for the holiday period, he told me about his family's plans for Christmas in Courmayeur, one of the most expensive skiing resorts in Italy. But I wasn't jealous, because I too was leaving the city to go somewhere special. I wouldn't have swapped with him for the world: I was dying to see my Grandma.

Gianni's father had given me a Christmas present of 400 euros in return for my help with his son. Between the two of them, I had received over a thousand euros and counting. Luckily for me, neither wanted the other to know that they were paying me. It's pretty disgusting: I was supposed to be his friend but rich people think they can buy anything. Nevertheless, I wasn't going to give the money back. To put it in context, my Dad earned only 690 euros that month as he spent more time in bed on sick leave than at work. To me it looked like all the money in the world and mentally I had already spent it on some nice additions to the Prince's wardrobe. As it was Christmas I even gave my Mum 150 euros, claiming the priest had given it to me. I didn't tell her that he would soon be giving me so much more!

Good times never last but I didn't care as I was ready for whatever fate had in store for me. This 'know-it-all' attitude was another nail in the coffin of the nice kid I used to be.

The car trip with my parents and kid brother to my Grandma's opened my eyes to how bad things were at home. I had been spending so much time at Gianni's and whenever I was at home I was so engrossed in my thoughts that I didn't pay attention. My Mother was on the verge of a nervous breakdown, my Dad now a shadow of his former self and my baby brother permanently sick with tonsillitis, bronchitis and whatever else kids get at that age.

My Dad was never at his best when we had to visit his mother-in-law but this time he had reason to fear it even more, as genuine criticism could and would be levelled at him. He was losing ground at work due to the amount of sick leave. Being stuck all day in a tiny shack is never good for the mental health of a grown man. My Mother had made no real friends in the shanty-town apart from one lady who occasionally popped in for a coffee. Both my parents were lonely, their paranoia insisting they kept 'those horrible neighbours' away. When my Dad could muster the strength, he would go down to the council and engage in fruitless protest about our 'imminent' relocation. Every time, he would came back a nervous wreck and take it out on my Mum. On a couple of occasions, when I was away at Gianni's, he had become violent and beat her. Selfishly, I saw only how it affected me, which was badly.

It's a sad state of affairs when a son can't look up to his father but I just didn't respect him anymore. It never occurred to me to try to walk a mile in his shoes.

In the two hours that it took us to get to my grandparents' village, I realised I would have to forget all my latest victories.

Resting on your laurels is for losers, if you'll excuse the contradiction. Manipulating Gianni, befriending Pasquale, the money earned from tutoring, my new room and my lavish wardrobe were all just stepping-stones to the big payback.

The love I felt for my Mum was real and I couldn't see her taking much more of this. In fact, I couldn't see my Father or my brother taking much more either. Before long, my parents would probably divorce or my brother catch pneumonia. I was running out of time to put things right before the damage would be irreparable. I had to find a way to get my family out of the shanty-town and into a proper house. The first thing that came to my mind was the sacristy with its inviting safe, all the beautiful money in it, possibly valuable documents and God knows what else. For a burglary like that, I had to up my game and plan every last detail.

In theory, I would have no problem opening that particular model of safe or the door to the room that protected it, but I needed the right tools and to get those you had to be a registered locksmith. It's not like going into a DIY shop and buying a hammer.

When we finally arrived at Grandma's house, I went straight down to the locksmith lab, or should I say the room it used to be in: it was stripped bare. My Nan, bless her, had sold the lot. I was devastated. All the instruments, tables and knives gone, its soul had been ripped out. Worse than that, the old cow had, in effect, sold off some of my most precious memories of my Granddad. It wasn't about the money; she wouldn't have got much so she probably did it just to try to move on. So I understood and I still loved her but that didn't stop me muttering 'You bitch' over and over as I cried for my Granddad and his ex-tools. Then I realised I didn't have time to feel sorry for myself.

Confucius said: 'If it is a problem, solve it. If you cannot solve it, it is not a problem, so do not worry about it.'

'So you've got no tools. Solve that, Mr Genius,' I said to myself like a madman.

For inspiration, I went back to the lab and rummaged through what little was left. Even though the lab was on the ground floor, right next to the front door, I was so deep in thought when the doorbell rang that I didn't hear it. My Mother, who was in the kitchen on the first floor, had to shout down to me:

'Are you deaf? Open the door will you?' She was hysterical but she didn't know I had a million dollar question to solve. My brain was still in full flow when I opened the door without even looking up.

'Who is it?' I barked.

When I did look up, I was face to face with my saviour: a five-foot tall, fat, bald man, about 55 years old.

Cocco, short for Francesco, was my Granddad's ex-colleague and best friend. He wasn't totally bald, he had a very thin string of hair plastered to his scalp that wriggled from one side of his head to the other, but he was most definitely short and overweight. He looked like an angel to me. He had clearly made an effort to dress up for his visit, but he shouldn't have bothered because it was an epic failure. He was wearing a faded leather jacket with a brand new pair of jeans and a scruffy pink shirt. I would not have been seen dead in any of those on their own, let alone in that combination. Still, by the standards of the village, he was smartly dressed. He seemed shocked to see me, which was surprising because he knew and liked me, and he must have known the family would come up from Naples for Christmas.

'Maybe those rumours that he is after my Grandma are true,' I reasoned privately.

Cocco was a genuine practising locksmith. He owned the very tools I needed and, in exchange for them, I would have sold my Grandma to him without another thought. He had been like a brother to my Granddad and, as he did not have grand-kids of his own, I felt that he also loved me like a grandson. I did not return his affection. I was not the typical kid that loved people easily but I had grown to like him, well ... tolerate him. It goes without saying that he had always been blown away by my natural ability with locks and safes. He had just lost his wife, a mere three months after my Granddad's death. His only child, Paolo, had never married. After suffering a terrible bout of meningitis as a kid, Paolo was permanently brain-damaged. I could see the loneliness in Cocco's

61

eyes. I knew it well. It was the same look as my Mum's.

On the doorstep, Cocco hugged and kissed me just like my Grandfather used to but this time I did not mind.

'Be my guest, but give me the damned tools!' I thought, but what I said was: 'Would you mind if I visited your workshop? It would remind me of my Granddad.'

He agreed to my request immediately, as if relieved. I liked him more already.

It was my first Christmas without my Granddad. I needed someone like Cocco as a Granddad substitute, not just for his tools. His lab was much more modern than my Granddad's, who had continued only as a hobby once the road inspector job came along. Cocco's workshop contained all the tools I could need: each the most advanced of their type. He even had a laser machine; in those days that was a rarity. Unfortunately for me, he was an honest man too. I could not see him understanding my plan to rob a church. So, I could not be straight with him about that. He lived too far from Naples for me to casually pop over and borrow a skeleton key and a stethoscope for the day. But borrow them I must.

That afternoon, we didn't get any locksmithing done; I just ate cakes and drooled over his instruments. I was no closer to thinking of a way to bring up my need for his tools but, luckily, he was keen for me to come back tomorrow so I could try again then.

He had a 'special job' for me: to open a very complex modern safe to which the owner had apparently forgotten the combination. I was no longer the gullible 12-year-old from last summer so I didn't believe him.

I certainly didn't think he was the honest man I had previously given him credit for. This was great news.

When I arrived the next day, there was a 4-ton safe in the middle of his lab that hadn't been there the night before.

'How did that get there?' was my first thought, but I didn't ask.

It was a *MANNINGER 568 85*, the Rolls-Royce of safes. Only a jeweller, or indeed a bank, would have the money or need for such security.

'Whose is it?' was my second question and it was even more pertinent, but still I didn't ask it.

As I ran my hand over the smooth metal surface, I started to think that Cocco was underestimating me. He must've thought I was too young to know the real world, that I was just some freak safe-cracking monkey. I was so fascinated by the challenge that I cast my suspicions aside: I was going to open that thing, no matter what.

'If it is man-made, it can be man-broken!' I shouted to myself like a Kamikaze.

It was silent when you turned the dial and built thicker than a tank. Dynamite would not make a scratch. I knew a bit about it but I needed to get to know the inner workings better so I sent Cocco off to the head office to get the manufacturer's instruction booklet. Only registered locksmiths had access to these; the Internet was not yet invented and you definitely couldn't borrow a copy from the library. The office was 40 miles away and would be closed over the whole Christmas holidays. If he couldn't get the manual today, I would be back in Naples before we even started. He dropped me straight back at my Nan's and was off, wasting no time on pleasantries and not wanting to bump into my family while he was *persona non grata*.

Whoever lugged all that metal halfway up a mountain must've been pretty desperate. How was it even unloaded from the truck? My suspicions became certainty: Cocco was either a thief or he was working for one.

Yup, my Nan's new suitor was a crook: music to my ears. You can't make a dodgy proposition to an honest man, but a dishonest man is a lot more malleable. By the time the old man came back with the manuals, I had planned what I would do. He honked his horn and I ran outside and jumped into the van. As we drove, I studied him in a new light. When you know what you are looking for and you look carefully, it is surprising how much a worried man gives away. I listened to his patronising gibberish, saying nothing. When we went back to his lab, I got down to work under his anxious gaze. He had good reason to be anxious; this safe was too modern and complex for him. I was his only chance and even then it was a long shot.

The instruction booklet alone ran to 58 pages. The lock mechanism was very complex and extremely quiet. Even with a stethoscope I could not hear a thing when I turned the dial. It was, quite simply, the best safe that money could buy at the time. Cracking it was verging on the impossible. Unfazed, I devoured the entire manual in two hours. Now I could picture the lock in my brain but, since I couldn't hear it or see it for real, I was not much closer to breaking it. I thought, 'I need something like an X-ray to see inside,' but an X-ray machine would cost more than the safe. X-rays are just one form of electromagnetic radiation; microwaves are similar but less powerful. Less powerful meant cheaper and easier to use. I had read about using microwaves for this kind of thing. I knew the theory. It's the same as radar (using radio waves) or sonar (using sound waves). In the case of sonar you fire off a beep, it hits the ocean floor and echoes back. The speed of sound in water is known so you just have to measure the time it takes from beep to echo and then you can calculate the depth. You could do the same with microwaves travelling through the metal of the safe. The only problem is that handling microwaves, although easier than X-rays, is a lot harder than making a few beep noises underwater! To make it easier, all I needed to do was detect when the combination lock was lined up with the tumbler and when it wasn't; I didn't need to know exactly how thick the metal was, just when it was thickest. This is because, no matter how complex a safe is, its mechanism is always based on a simple concept: it has some holes that you fill by slipping some cylinders into them. When you turn the combination, you put all the cylinders in the right place and you will have enough grip to open the door with the handle. Even the latest safes and locks now work under the same principle but they use a computerised combination which makes no sound when selecting the combination as it has no moving parts. Thankfully, this safe wasn't like that; it still had a big dial on the front like the ones in the movies. The combination code is usually written down as 12 left, 25 right, 13 left, 30 right, and so on. If you were doing it with a stethoscope you would start turning to the left, one notch at a time. You would listen each time for a different sound indicating that it was lining up. By the time you had turned 12 notches to the left you should hear a slight change in the sound it makes as it goes to the next notch. Then you turn to the right 25 notches and do it again. It's not like it suddenly goes 'click'. If it did, any dumbo could break it. From the outside the Manninger was silent but inside the combined depth of the metal, when the combination was 'lined up', would be greater: maybe only by a thousandth of an inch, not enough to see or touch, but enough for a microwave to take a few nanoseconds longer to penetrate and bounce back. That's the theory but I had never done anything like this before so I couldn't be sure.

I did not have a computer; I had a very basic electromagnetic gauge: a little black box with a basic digital readout. Cocco had bought the gadget out of pride, deluded into thinking all lock-smiths should have the latest technology but, if he was honest, he was never going to use it. Today was his chance to learn how but the only depth he would discover was the depth of his delusion. My plan was this: learn how to use the box; calibrate it; calculate as closely as possible the penetration levels; then use it, instead of a stethoscope, to detect the combination.

The whole afternoon went by in a flash just understanding the safe, its material and the structure of its locks. Then I had to understand the frequencies of radiation that the machine could emit and how fast they could travel in various metals. After that I went home but carried on working. I needed to calculate the microwave penetration times. The manual told me that the lock had seven cylinders. I needed to find all seven holes and then move the combination to slip all the cylinders into the right places. I stayed up all night calculating.

It is not my intention to train anyone on how to crack a safe but suffice to say that what I learnt would eventually put Manninger and a few others out of business.

I finished at 7 o'clock the following morning, just as my Grandma started making coffees and cakes for everyone. I drank plenty of espressos but I could not eat. Despite my lack of sleep I was still feeling confident about the challenge. I knew I would need some luck, as there were too many variables for me to control it all. Look at CERN: all the world's best physicists in one place and they still can't get their Large Hadron Collider to work on demand. It's as temperamental as a vintage car. However, I was an eternal optimist so I was already making plans for what I would do once I'd opened it.

The next morning was the 23rd of December. I had to get the job done today because on Christmas Eve the family's tolerance for my adventure would likely end and I could be stuck at Grandma's house until it was time to go back to Naples. I had too little time and no room for error. I asked for permission to spend the day with Cocco. He may not have been deemed a suitable companion for my Nan but he was, after all, like family and they were too busy squabbling with each other to worry about me. For once, I was happy to be ignored.

Cocco came fifteen minutes early. He didn't honk his horn, he just waited for me to notice he was there. He looked even more worried than before. Desperate for some peace of mind, the eager-to-please chitchat was gone, replaced by loads of questions about how I would open it. I wanted to calm him but I did not want to make false promises.

'Look, I have a good idea and I'll give it my best shot. Now, stop stressing me out!' I said. He wasn't happy but at least he shut up.

I spent the morning charting the metallic depths of the safe's lock. It was pure trial and error, like playing battleships. Luckily, it was always my turn to drop another depth charge. By 11 a.m., I was confident that I had plotted out the internals of the lock. After no sleep the night before, I was really tired.

At one point, I forgot to focus on staying awake and just found myself in a trance, staring at the safe hoping to discover some kind of supernatural X-ray vision.

Instead, I just had to keep on working; my calculations were perfect and I was detecting the holes whenever the cylinders lined up. However, lack of sleep exaggerates fear and tension, and I had to pause repeatedly to wipe my sweaty palms. I felt like a surgeon performing a heart transplant. The only difference was that, rather than having a nurse wiping my brow, I had an old man hanging over me like a vulture: huffing, puffing and sweating as well. There was one more crucial difference: no one was going to die if I screwed up. Or so I thought.

Just before lunch-time I was confident I was ready to open it. I had two jobs that day: the first was to open the safe; the second, and probably more difficult, was to get the truth out of the old man. To prepare for the second task, I needed some rest.

'I am making progress. I want to go home to eat and to get some sleep. I will come back here at 4 o'clock,' I told him.

He was shocked but, more than that, I saw fear in his eyes: not the usual anxiety but something deeper. I watched him slowly realise that he had no choice but to agree to my request. He reluctantly led me to his car. I smiled as I got in.

After lunch I had a nap, then went down to Granddad's empty workshop and rummaged around to find a heavy screwdriver and a pair of cable ties: the really thick zip-lock ones where, once you slip the cable into the latch and pull it through, it would hold two bears together. I put them safely in my pocket and sat on the sofa to wait for Cocco. Deep down, I knew something big was going to happen that would change my life forever. I might even die but the only thing for certain was that I was leaving the house as a schoolboy for the last time. I was like a boxer facing his career-defining fight: win, and life would never be the same; lose, and...

Losing didn't bear thinking about.

Shortly after 4 p.m. I was back in Cocco's lab, one by one turning the dial to line up the cylinders while triple-checking them with microwaves. This fiddly work took more than two hours. Finally, I reckoned I had finished. All I had to do was turn the handle and see if it opened but, instead...

'Can you fix me a sandwich and squeeze me some orange juice? I need to refuel!' I asked him. I was hungry but mostly I just wanted to get him out of the room.

'How far have you got?' Cocco asked anxiously.

'Going well but need to refuel for the final push. How about Parma ham with cheese?'

Off he went, happy that 'we' were making progress. He had no idea or he would have been livid. The kitchen was just above the laboratory so I could hear him moving around above me. I opened the lab door so I could hear the stairs. I put the cable ties and the screwdriver on a shelf opposite the door, ready for action.

Time to open her up. I just knew it would open. I knew when I pushed the handle it would move. The grip just felt right. The very moment I pushed it, my heart raced. No going back, life would be very different. One gentle stroke of the handle and the door swung freely. Open.

Inside, there were more than 20 different compartments, each covered by velvet cloths. I opened them one by one, straining my ears to listen for any sound of the old man on the stairs.

Even though I had tried to imagine what was in the safe, I still wasn't prepared for what I saw: bracelets; chains; brooches; rings and all kinds of jewellery, all crammed in so tightly that you couldn't see the bottom of the drawer. All the pieces were encrusted with diamonds, rubies or other gemstones: the entire stock of a decent jewellery shop. I guessed it was more than 20 million euros-worth. I never imagined I would come face to face with such wealth. It could have been 50 million but my brain stopped thinking straight whenever I tried to calculate an accurate estimate. A herd of elephants could have come down the stairs with my sandwich and I wouldn't have noticed, I was now so mesmerised by all that bling.

I was wallowing in greed and it felt good. They called me the Prince but this would make me the King. I could buy my family a hundred new homes, the best clothes, and the best of everything. I could've bought the whole city and rebuilt it! All my study of the properties of 'Au' (a.k.a. Gold) in the periodic table had never mentioned that humans could be intoxicated by it: I was drunk on gold.

I had my El Dorado moment but then my rational survival

instinct kicked in. I calmed myself with thoughts of all the wars fought over gold and diamonds. From pirates to genocides, religion may have been the excuse but greed was the real reason. All of a sudden, I felt afraid and uncomfortable.

In my heightened state, Cocco's steps on the stairs boomed like a jack-hammer.

I crept over and quietly pushed the door so it was ajar, then stood behind it with the screwdriver in my right hand. I was a good seven inches taller than him but a lot weaker. Even though I had never used violence as such, I had seen enough of it in the shanty-town that I thought I knew a move or two; I was confident rather than actually skilled.

As soon as he opened the door, I placed the screwdriver onto his lower skull and wrapped my left arm around his neck.

'Sit down and do what I tell you or you are dead! Place the tray on the table, pick up those cable ties, wrap them round your wrists and pull them tight with your teeth. Make sure I hear the latch click. No sudden moves, or you will be no more.'

The old man did not respond. I pushed the point of the screwdriver onto his skull so that blood oozed from the tip. Half an inch deeper and he would be dead. I saw the blood – good, I could decide his fate. A vision of my guardian angel, my Granddad, appeared to me. He disapproved. Now I was afraid; then ashamed. In one supreme effort, I clenched my jaw and just got on with it.

'I will kill you if I have to and I will enjoy it!' I promised.

He did not test my resolve. Once his wrists were tightly tied, he sat down calmly. I had seen some rope on the floor earlier and, to stabilise him further, I fashioned a noose around his neck and tied it off onto a water pipe running above the door. If he tried to get up, he would strangle himself.

As I walked around him, I kept a close watch. His eyes bulged at me in disbelief. I had the situation under control but my heart was beating so hard that I could hear it. I might've been more scared than he was. I sat down on a stool behind him, unable to look him in the eye.

'You are going to tell me everything; and you better tell me the truth, as I'm very disappointed in you!'

'If you want to kill me, go ahead. You would be doing me a favour!' he sobbed.

I threw the screwdriver onto the floor. I came round in front to face him. The sight of the defenceless old man's big brown eyes wet with tears brought me back down.

'OK, relax! No one is going to do you any harm, I promise you. I'm not a killer.'

I opened the safe for the second time and pointed.

'Now, tell me more about this.'

He watched in amazement as I opened and closed the different compartments.

He was whispering 'Mother of God!' over and over.

'Tell me, what is 20 million euros-worth of gold and jewels doing in your lab? I opened this thing – you owe me that much,' I said, firmly but courteously, and then gulped some orange juice for an urgent sugar injection.

I kept my eyes stuck on him. He sat silently for a minute but it felt a lot longer. As my patience was starting to run out, he opened his mouth.

'OK, I will tell you everything! Before I do, can you please untie my hands?'

I still did not trust him so I went upstairs to phone my Mum to tell her where I was. I'm not sure why I bothered; she already knew where I was. It was probably just to hear a comforting voice but it did serve as a reminder to him, if he needed it, that he couldn't hope to get away with harming me.

If he let me go, I had enough incriminating evidence to have a hold over him. All in all, he would never have harmed a fly, let alone a young boy, but the circumstances clouded my judgement. The whole thing felt surreal.

A law-abiding citizen would have called the police at once but the situation was now just too perfect to ruin it by calling the cops. And I was an accessory to whatever crime had taken place.

Could I trust him? Yes, based on his sobbing, so I untied him. Either that or he was a fantastic actor.

'I loved your Granddad like a brother. You of all people should know this. And you, you were like the grandson I never had, nor am likely to have. I can't believe you were so afraid of me you had to tie me up!'

'I'm sorry, okay? Get on with it.'

'Four years ago, your Granddad and I started a wine-making business. We put our life savings into a large piece of land next to the cemetery. We planted the grapes and did most of the work ourselves. We had both concluded that new lock technology had made us obsolete. We both liked wine and we knew how to make it. Unfortunately, we ran out of money before we had bought all the machinery we needed. Neither of us owned the houses we lived in so the banks wouldn't touch us. In the end, we had to go to a loan shark to borrow the 20,000 euros needed to stay in business. Two percent a week interest was quite a lot but we thought we would have been able to pay it back quickly once we sold the first harvest; but that year the weather was bad. The wine was bitter and we made much less than we expected. We carried on paying the interest out of what we earned doing our day-jobs for as long as we could but, inevitably, we fell behind. Now we owe 44 grand. If I do not pay, we are in trouble. These are not nice people. I only started this for my son, Paolo. I don't think he will be able to cope once I am gone. He is only partially handicapped, so they say he can work but no one will give him a job. I wanted to leave him a business he could live off. When the loan sharks offered me the job of cracking this safe I couldn't turn it down, especially as they promised to cancel the debt in return. I knew it would be illegal but I didn't expect this. I don't want to become a criminal but we needed to pay these animals back or...' he tailed off into sobs.

I seethed at the thought that, during all those summers spent opening safes, my beloved Granddad had used me just to pay interest to those scum. They had already repaid the original loan; the 44 thousand they owed was now just more interest on unpaid interest.

'Who is this person?' I asked.

'The Butcher', he whispered.

This time, I was not surprised at all. Everyone had heard of this guy but only by rumours of his reputation. He was supposed to be in his late 30s, young for a Mafia boss. He was not just a thug but an intelligent business-minded criminal. He had come up through the ranks of the organisation at such an amazing speed that he had started to worry and annoy the existing bosses. The loan sharking was really just an excuse to 'buy' property for peanuts. He would lend to desperate farmers, sure in the knowledge that they would fall behind on the outrageous interest. Then, as soon they did, he would repossess their land as if he were any other bank. He had applied the same principle to shops and other businesses, menacing his way to a large portfolio of enterprises across the region. He had thus laundered his way to a legitimate fortune. No wonder the other crime bosses were jealous.

I had not heard of any 20 million euro jewellery heists around Naples so I assumed the safe had been stolen up north, probably in Milan where Italy was at its wealthiest. The Butcher had had my Granddad and this fool Cocco by the balls so he had the whole set-up, ready for this kind of gig. Little did he know that those two old men were using a child to do their dirty work. I pitied my Mum: her son was only 12 years old and already working for the Mafia!

I had never dealt with these guys before but, from what had been said around the shanty-town, I had learnt quite a bit about how they operated. Once they get hold of you, they never let go and the debt is always on, no matter what the original agreement was. I was concerned that, even if they kept their word, they would come back later with more demands and, when Cocco was finally no use to them, they'd kill him.

So far during that Christmas holiday I had experienced guilt, greed, bloodlust and pity. Now I was getting to know real fear. When Cocco said 'we', he did not mean him and his son, he meant him and my Grandmother, as she would inherit her husband's debts. As this was a Mafia job, it meant her whole family, possibly even me, were in real danger just because of some interest. I had to think of a way out and quickly.

I had more than 20 million euros of gold in front of me. My initial reaction was a common one. I could nick a few bracelets and diamond rings, sell them on and buy my Mum the house she desperately needed. But what would happen as a consequence of this action? How did these guys trust this old man not to touch anything? Would they notice if 200 grands-worth of merchandise went missing? That would be less than one percent of the total value so it would be unlikely.

Okay, I'll do it. I'll skim our share off the top first, here, now. I was thinking fast. Too fast. I could have taken it this time and maybe got away with it but it's Russian roulette and eventually you lose. That is what happens to the average criminal stuck at the coalface with ruthless and much cleverer bosses above him. A gang of any calibre would never have pulled a job this big without knowing exactly what was in the safe. To take the risk and steal a safe they had to know what was in it. A professional thief would make sure they had an exact inventory. Why go to the considerable trouble (I still couldn't see how they got the safe into Cocco's lab) of a theft like this if the contents did not justify the risks. Also, they would need to create a pipeline of customers to sell the merchandise on to. An inventory would be invaluable for that too.

On the other hand, if I were to try to sell any of these items I would have to go to a fence: someone who probably already dealt with these guys. It would only be a matter of time before they found me out.

'There is a time for action and a time for inaction; the man who lives until 100 always chooses the right one.' I knew this but did Cocco?

All our lives depended on *his* dealings with them. Anything silly could get me and my family involved. I explained this to him but he didn't get it at first.

'How do you know for sure that they have an inventory?' he asked.

'I don't!' I replied, annoyed, 'But if they do and you touch something we're all dead. The upside is a few thousand euros – the downside death. The risks do not match the rewards, understand?'

'Yes, yes, I promise I won't touch a thing,' he mumbled back.

He was depressed about it all. Grandma was the only other person with whom he could share this burden. No wonder he visited her so much; there was a lot of stress to unload. No doubt, it was the same stress that killed his wife and drove my Granddad to suddenly increase his drinking, hastening his death. Cocco's wife was a churchgoer, a believer in God and the goodness of people. She would have been crushed by the consequences of her own husband's poor life choices.

I wearily put the Butcher in third place on my personal 'to-do' list, after the Bulldog and fixing the shanty-town.

'OK, I will help you. But from now on you work for me. Understood?'

'I will do anything you say,' he said, burying his head in his hands.

'I have to go – take me home,' I ordered. 'Call those bastards and get them to pick this stuff up as quickly as possible.'

I fixed him with a stare before I told him the important bit.

'Be relaxed and tell them that you will always be available if they need you. Moreover, tell them that you took nothing out of the safe and invite them to check their inventory in case they don't trust you.'

He looked back at me blankly.

'Come on! Repeat what I just said.'

We rehearsed it a few times until I was satisfied with his performance. It shouldn't have taken him so many goes to get it but he was in shock. Not just from a screwdriver in the neck, it must have been the climax of months of worrying.

'Come back here tomorrow at 10,' I commanded as I shut the car door later.

That night I couldn't fall asleep. There were far too many thoughts rumbling through my mind. I was still fixated with working out how they had even got the safe up the mountain. Despite everything else, my ego still had time to worry that someone was so much better than me and, as usual, I said to myself: 'Keep learning Prince. You are not the finished article yet!'

My ego amused me; I spent half my time keeping it in check and then, when I relaxed for a second, it crept up on me like bad grass. According to one of my psychology books, vanity and self-obsession are good for nothing and are only cause for unhappiness and underachievement.

Even after presenting them with an open safe, Cocco would still never be free of his debt. I was just hoping that they would let him live, for now. Only by making himself useful and available could he buy his short-term safety. Otherwise, he would be a loose end: a witness to their crime who must be silenced. If they thought they could use him again they would leave him alone. Assuming my Grandmother owed half of the amount that was being paid off from cracking the safe, then what now for her? Would they leave her alone? What else could they be after? The vineyard? The wine-making equipment? Surely they didn't have the time or the motivation for wine-making. I just had to hope I was right and that things would be OK. It wasn't like I could intervene and make a difference but I didn't believe in just hoping. You either made it happen or you sat back as life's suffering was inflicted upon you, either by accident or by design. What good was it to hope that these guys would forgive and forget? They never did either.

With all these thoughts circling in my head, I finally fell asleep. I dreamt I was an Edwardian aristocrat embarking on the *Titanic*. When I woke up, gasping to breathe in an icy sea, I expected the nightmare to be over; and it was but the reality was worse. I would prefer to take my chances in a lifeboat than try to outwit the Butcher and his mob. More people survived the *Titanic* than the Mafia. I realised what had been bothering me; I had not explicitly told Cocco not to mention me to the Mafia.

In his first sign of obedience to his new master, Cocco came to pick me up at the agreed time. I asked him to drive me to the vineyard. On the way he told me that the tough guys had come to collect the stolen goods. Apparently, they had declared the debt paid off and then wished him a happy Christmas. But, conveniently for them, they had left the empty safe behind. It would be impossible for us to move. Instead it would be a permanent scar in his workshop, a tattoo that broadcasts 'I am a criminal.'

'Yes, but what did they say about what I told you to say?' I asked, desperate to learn our fate.

'I told them word for word. And they said "Of course. If we need you, you will be our man. Look after yourself. You have done a great job." I am sorry for taking all the credit.'

'No apologies needed, believe me,' I spluttered.

And then I blurted, 'Promise never to tell them about me!'

'I would never do that to you,' he replied, offended.

The first thing on the agenda was to get rid of the safe. There was 30 years' jail time right there. The fact that the gold and jewels were gone would really annoy the prosecutor too, because it's not like you could divulge who had them; that would be like signing your own death warrant. To hide the safe, I explained how to use round table legs as rollers: a technique used by ancient Egyptians to move heavy stones. It would only get it as far as the corner of the room but, with a nice tablecloth on it and some decorations, nobody would ever bother with it. It couldn't stay bang in the middle of the workshop.

I was about to ask to borrow Cocco's locksmith instruments for my own little bit of safe-cracking when we arrived at the vineyard, so I decided to ask him later. I got out of the car and walked briskly past the bushes to see what was left of Cocco and Granddad's dream.

It was in a sorry state, mirroring Granddad's physical and mental state before departing this life. Their pathetic patch of land only had a vague resemblance to the surrounding well-manicured vineyards. There were still orderly rows of poles but nothing else. Weeds and bushes had taken over, corrupting the soil and everything else in sight.

I raised my eyes to the sky and silently promised: 'Granddad, I still love you. I will put this right one day, I give you my word,' and with that I turned to Cocco.

'I need to borrow your lab tools for a business idea.'

'What business?'

I was flat-footed. Although we had just shared in a criminal activity, there is a big difference between being forced into aiding a crime and stealing from a church entirely of your own volition. I was still struggling to think up a suitable lie when he broke the silence.

'It doesn't matter what you want them for as I cannot think of anybody more worthy to possess the tools of my life's vocation. You have saved my life and that of my son. I'm not retiring for another five years so my licence could come in handy for you to get more tools too. I am too old to be messing about with these modern things anyway. My eyes have gone and I can't hear the church bells, let alone the combination. The only thing I ask is, if those bastards ask me for another "favour", I will say yes but *you* will have to do it.'

He was a broken man. The little energy he had left should and would be reserved for his son. Until now he had always been ashamed of Paolo, foolishly half-believing the ignorant snipes of the villagers, but now his son was the only thing he had left to take care of. My gut instinct had been right from the start: I hadn't needed that screwdriver. He might have been a fool but he was a good man: a victim of events that had spiralled out of control.

For me, too, things had got out of control; the power of life and death over another human once experienced cannot easily be forgotten. My innocence was well and truly lost, forever.

All the time I had been thinking about this he had been waiting for my answer. He was staring at me on the verge of breaking down completely.

'Sorry. Yes. We have a deal. Not only that, I swear to you on my Grandfather's grave that should anything happen to you I will take care of both the vineyard and Paolo.'

He gently wrapped his large hand round my scrawny one and then, almost shyly, hugged me. As the hug developed I melted, responding with the same warmth. As he cried quietly so did I. It felt like I was hugging my Granddad who, despite his freshly discovered naughty secret, I still missed a lot. As always, the only feeling I could not control was love.

Three months later, Cocco did what he had promised and delivered all his equipment to a 'cave' near Naples. The whole set-up was worth a lot of money but, as most of these instruments would be impossible to obtain without a locksmith's licence, it was priceless. It gave me the power to achieve the impossible. After his last delivery of instruments, we never saw each other again.

He died three years later. I did not make it to the funeral. I never liked funerals; I always had better things to do. Apparently, his son cried next to his bed. Seeing that would have upset me. I didn't know how to react to such grief in others so I just steered clear.

I went to Cocco's lab some years later. The safe was still sat there, in the same corner of what was now just a garage, with the same tablecloth on it. I kept my promise, buying Paolo's share of the vineyard for much more than it was worth. Poor Paolo had little understanding of money; he did not even realise I was trying to help him. He just signed the papers as I had told him to, while calling me his little brother. Wary that some crook would soon part him from his new riches, I put the money into a trust that paid him a decent monthly income for the rest of his life.

Many years after that, I made the vineyard beautiful again. My grandfather was actually buried in the adjacent cemetery but I have always felt that his soul was somewhere in the vineyard. Now, more than 30 years later, when I drink the wine made from it I still think about him.

Call that a holiday? I was knackered. I should have been on a high after pulling off such a challenge. Instead, I just ran out of energy. Fighting my emotions all the time wasn't smart. It was a drain on precious resources. After the safe-cracking episode, I spent the rest of the holiday in front of the fire, feet up on the sofa, reading old Batman comics. I looked up from time to time to watch the flames flickering. I could watch fire all day long. What I did not like watching was my family imploding around me. I was upset at my brother's fragile state of health, upset at my Mother's constant depression and angry with my Dad for dealing with it by losing his temper so often. On top of that, it wound me up even more to think about how happy we were before the earthquake. Unless I mastered the art of self-control, one of these many emotions would come back and hijack this adventure.

That's if the Mafia didn't hijack it first. I couldn't get away from the fact that I was involved with them, even if only indirectly. In Naples, the Mafia was an integral part of the very system that I wanted to take on. If I pursued my revenge on the politicians then sooner or later I would cross swords with the Mafia again: and properly this time. Cocco had been able to insulate me but next time I might not be so lucky. I had to do something to protect myself. It would have to be radical or it wouldn't work. In this case, radical meant difficult.

Inspired by Batman, not his vehicles or the suit, for I had neither, the world would only ever see my squeaky clean teenage Bruce Wayne act; everything else would be hidden. If my enemies didn't know who I was, then they couldn't harm me but, more importantly, they wouldn't see me coming.

But I couldn't take them on alone. If my Granddad had still been alive he would have been cast perfectly as Batman's trusted butler. I would have to make do with Gianni and Pasquale as fat Robin and big Robin. Unlike Bruce Wayne, I wasn't a millionaire: I had the back end of a shack, a borrowed scooter and 500 euros. Forget the Batman analogy; I just needed a hideout, a trusted gang and money to finance operations. That was the extent of my strategy. As soon as school started, I would get to work on all three.

The first day back at school was nothing more than re-establishing a routine. I went back to teaching Gianni and Pasquale and helping Gianni's dad in his lab. I was looking forward to mass on Sunday as a chance to get more information for my revenge.

In winter, it is not easy for a child to get around Naples. My Mother wanted me back home at a reasonable time so I had to rely on Pasquale for lifts to Gianni's or school. I started to feel more and more trapped.

One thing that had miraculously improved over Christmas was my relationship with the rough boys in the neighbourhood. I was no longer just tolerated or grudgingly given respect. My 'connection' to Pasquale had gone up a notch and they had certainly noticed. They weren't suddenly best mates but I could actually talk to them without fear or discomfort. A collective bout of amnesia had also been needed to forget the bullying that had gone before and the holiday had provided the perfect opportunity.

Once I was back in the swing of things, I set out to find a base from which I could work and prepare my schemes. Like the 'Batcave', it needed to be hidden but with access to electricity, and large enough to house all of Cocco's instruments but small enough to be invisible.

'Maybe I could find something there...' I thought, looking at the imperious volcano from my shack.

I had made the lateral mental leap from the 'Batcave' to Vesuvius, but I didn't even have transport of my own to get up there and go looking, so recruiting my own gang was now priority number one.

Ockham, an English philosopher of the 14th century, said: 'Usually, the right answer is the most obvious one.'

Pasquale appreciated my superior academic skills and he treated me like a real brother. When he saw me with money he never tried to steal it or even demand that I buy him anything. He was grateful for what I was doing for him at school. I had got the best out of him by giving him belief. With my help, he now had a chance at a normal life, a normal job and a normal future away from prisons and police. He was fascinated by how much I knew about everything but, also, by how I controlled people around me. He saw for himself how I had brought Gianni's parents under my spell. Pasquale's mother loved me too, which helped me to feel more like family. One thing was for sure: if I needed someone to be my number two, I could not have found better. He was strong, brave, afraid of nothing, executed my instructions to the letter, never contradicted me, trusted me and I trusted him: the perfect choice.

Except it was not perfect. It was far from perfect. My relationship with him was built on the pretence that I was everything he was not. How could I break the news that behind my pretty face lurked a monster whose criminal pretensions dwarfed his? How to tell him that his dreams of a normal life were an illusion, that I had befriended him under false pretences not to deliver him from a life of crime, but to use him to start my own criminal gang? The only difference between us was the size of my ambition. Okay, so my revenge had a noble cause but that wouldn't help him to go straight.

In hindsight it sounds terrible but at the time I was as confident as ever that I could spin it into a positive light, especially if I broke it to him gently, in stages:

Stage one: show him that I was a leader in the real world outside of the classroom and that I could do the job of gang leader. The world is chock full of people who talk the talk but can't walk the walk. The shanty-town was worse than average, bursting with wannabe criminals. There would be no faster way to lose all credibility with him than to start blabbing on about the 'Batcave' and revenge on all the politicians of Naples. He would laugh in my face. Many others had already laughed in my face but they didn't matter; Pasquale mattered. I had spent months preparing the ground but I wasn't even halfway to getting my man. My relationship with him so far had been choreographed like a ballet. I never asked questions; I always listened carefully to him, never giving him advice or my point of view so as not to sound patronising or naive. Now, though, it was time to bond with him on a deeper level. Then he would see that, together, we could achieve anything. Like the generals of the past, I needed a resounding victory against the odds to earn the unwavering loyalty of my men.

This being Naples, it wouldn't be long before an opportunity arose for a wannabe criminal to show off his skills.

Two weeks after we had come back from the Christmas break, Pasquale seemed worried and angry on the way to school. Actually, now that I was paying attention, it was fair to say that something or someone was always bothering him, but he hadn't mentioned it at all so I didn't know the first detail. I was a relief from his daily struggles, not a confidant. He didn't see how I could help with his 'out of school activities'. This time, though, he looked more concerned and distant than ever. Could I exploit this? You betcha...

'I ain't coming to school tomorrow; got fings to do!' he said.

'Okay, can I help?' I replied, trying to sound humble and concerned.

'No!'

'I am here for you if you need me,' I replied timidly.

'You deaf?'

'Okay, okay, I hear you.'

I felt lonely going to school, and then to and from Gianni's, by foot and bus instead of the back of Pasquale's scooter. I missed getting rides everywhere but I missed his presence even more when walking round the shanty-town alone. Not everyone knew I was his friend so after dark, in badly lit areas, which was pretty much everywhere in the shanty-town, I felt uncomfortable and afraid. I had become so used to not worrying that I forgot how scary the shanty-town was. Rough-necked guys would look me up and down, deciding whether to rob me or just beat me up for fun. I stood out like a sore thumb with my clean-cut hair, expensive jumpers and elegant walk. Shitting my pants every time I went back home made me realise how much I needed Pasquale. After not having seen or heard from him in three days, I was threatened by some toughs on the way home. It was only luck they didn't beat me.

Pasquale's Mum was a typical shanty-town mother: bleached hair and sporting a boatload of fake gold on her large frame. When she opened the flimsy door to their shack she looked thrilled, welcoming me in with a huge smile and a bear hug.

'How are you, my son? What a pleasant surprise!' she exclaimed and, before I could respond, she continued, 'I really want to thank you for everything you're doing for Pasquale. Do you need anything?'

'Like what?' I replied, somewhat surprised as I hadn't brought my shopping list. I did need a new Benetton jumper – the rats had eaten a hole in mine – but that wasn't what she meant.

'Anything!' she insisted.

'I want you to give me your youngest son so I can corrupt him!' I thought, as I shook my head emphatically in response.

'Well, if you do, just ask – we consider you one of the family now,' she shouted.

'Yeah, a family of criminals, and that includes me,' I thought, as I stopped shaking my head and started nodding instead.

She might have looked fake because of the cheap bling but her feelings were true. She was not sophisticated or educated like the women from the church, but when she smiled at you knew she meant it. Why else would she show off those rotten teeth? Like any mother, she just wanted the best for her kids and, in her case, not getting it had left a lifetime of frustration etched on her face: not surprising when your eldest son is in prison, your only daughter got pregnant before she reached the age of consent and Pasquale, the youngest, can't graduate from school. I offered redemption. No wonder she was grateful.

I asked her straight up: 'What is going on with Pasquale? What is happening?'

'His boss owes him money but he ain't paying up. He has worked there for more than three months, on and off at the weekend, some nights and over the Christmas holidays. Each day he just sits in the restaurant waiting 'til he gets what he's owed. That's where he is now. He has to be careful though; the guy is connected!' she answered candidly, as if it were a relief to unburden herself.

Welcome to Naples, where even some minor league tourist restaurant was protected by the Big Boss, the head of the Camorra (the Neapolitan Mafia). Local businesses, mostly shops and restaurants, paid a monthly fee for protection against all evils, the worst of which was the Camorra itself. Once you were 'connected', you became untouchable by the local gangs or petty criminals. If you even tried to do anything to the owner of the restaurant, you would be invading the Camorra's territory. The penalty was death, no exceptions, and they'd probably make an example out of you to discourage others. Pasquale could do nothing but beg: a sorry state of affairs not just for Pasquale but also the whole city.

This was the opportunity I had been waiting for.

That night in bed I dreamt up a plan. I got up earlier than usual and went back to Pasquale's house before school. His Mum opened the door. When I asked for him she simply turned round and shouted crudely at him to get up. When he came to the door, he gave me an evil stare.

'You gotta death wish or somethin'?!' he barked. If his mother had not been there, he probably would have knocked my lights out and gone back to bed.

'It's okay. I'm not going to school either. In fact, I have a proposition for you. Come with me; I want to show you something. If you don't like it, you're welcome to beat me up. Interested?'

'No worries,' he said, 'I wanna murk somebody but iz not you. Okay, wait outside, I'll be ten.'

I asked him to take me by scooter to Vesuvius. The place was beautiful: lush and rich. Naples looked like a different city from there: the gulf; the closely built houses and buildings; the blue of the sea; all accompanied by the most gorgeous smells of lemons, oranges, vines and wild herbs. I held my head high like a Roman aristocrat as I walked through the natural splendour.

'I know your problem and I have a plan. I will get that piece of shit to pay you what he owes and teach him a lesson he will never forget,' I said, firmly.

'You crazy? He'll have you killed! Stick to yer books, Prince!'

He said 'Prince' but his tone said 'Idiot'. I had his attention but for all the wrong reasons so it wouldn't be for long.

'It might not look like it to you but we are in the same situation: victims of the same cruel destiny; thrown out of our homes by natural forces, yet kept in crap holes by unnatural forces. I cannot punish nature but I can certainly punish the system that keeps us down. I need your help,' I said, while his eyes widened in disbelief.

I was losing him.

'But first I need to show you that I am worthy of it.'

Then I paused as planned, hoping my hook would work.

'Go on,' he replied, less aggressively.

Maybe he had taken the bait.

'Okay. You used to work for La Trattoria which, if I am not mistaken, is the direct rival of Carlo's, run by the guy that owes you. You told me once that you get on quite well with the owner of La Trattoria, right? So go and pay him a visit! Have a nice coffee with him, ask how much it's worth if Carlo's, his only competitor in the street, were to be flattened by a natural disaster: a natural disaster of such force that it will take Carlo at least six months to rebuild and, in the meantime, La Trattoria would get all his business.'

Pasquale just stared at me, open-mouthed.

'How are we gonna do it? Besides, me and the owner, we get on, yeah, but he ain't exactly a friend. I dunno if I can trust him.'

'Friendship is a bond born out of a common interest, but it becomes a partnership if it is born out of a common enemy. You have an enemy in common that you both hate. Assure him that no one will ever find out and that it will look like an act of God. Then he will agree, I promise you,' I replied as my heart pumped faster than was healthy.

Pasquale didn't know whether to punch me or shake my hand.

I had touched a nerve. He wanted revenge. And he needed the money. What made this hard for him to digest was that he never expected someone like me to come up with such a plan. On the other hand, he knew deep down that if he didn't take his chance to stand up to Carlo now, then the rest of his life in Naples would soon become one long queue of people like Carlo waiting to mug him off. Freedom from that kind of repression is irresistible to a proud man. Pasquale was nothing if not proud.

'Okay, but you better deliver this act of God, Prince!'

'I will.'

To cap off a fine morning's work, as we rode down the mountainside I spotted an unfinished house between the thick bushes. As it was ideal for my base, I made a mental note of the location and blew it a kiss from the pillion seat.

After the earthquake I had read so many books about construction and architecture that I should have got a degree *honoris causa*. The original idea was to take the corrupt builders to court, but in Italian they say: 'Impara l'arte e mettila da parte' or 'Learn the skill and put it aside.' Now I would need that knowledge for a different reason.

I found the blueprints for the restaurant, without arousing suspicion, by pretending to be a student working on an assignment. All the restaurants in that area were built in the 60s. They all followed an engineering pattern fashionable at the time. Since then building codes had improved. If you tried to build them that way now, they wouldn't be permitted. At least not without a big bribe.

Carlo's restaurant had originally been a large single-storey building with a terrace on top. Carlo had built another large room on the first floor that covered more than 50 percent of the ground floor. This was done without official permission so, technically, it was illegal but, considering what they had got away with elsewhere in Naples, this was a paragon of good behaviour. The reason it had survived the quake had nothing to do with its construction quality: the ground was more solid here. This just added insult to injury: good taxpayers living in shacks; criminals, like Carlo, getting lucky. That made it personal.

After studying the blueprints, I saw the Achilles' heel: the gas pipes running through the building like copper wires in a blue cheese.

The next day, Pasquale dropped me off at school. I briefed him one last time before he drove off to La Trattoria. I didn't see him again until after school. When I did, he immediately told me what had happened. From the look on his face I could easily guess.

Ten minutes after he arrived at La Trattoria, Pasquale was drinking coffee with the owner. It is unusual for the ex-busboy to be able to do this on a busy working day, just as they are preparing to open for lunch, but there was something about his purposeful demeanour and mention of an 'interesting' proposition. After some small talk, he hit him with it.

'Boss, how much you pay me, if Carlo's gets its own earthquake? Be outta action fo' least six months while they rebuild it.'

The owner laughed ... but then saw that Pasquale was not laughing.

The owner pondered for a while.

Pasquale sat silent and poker-faced.

'Five grand?' the owner ventured.

If a hint of a smile appeared on Pasquale's face, he hid it quickly.

By the time he got to the end of telling me this story, Pasquale's golden tooth was sparkling in an ear-to-ear smile.

'Over to you, Prince,' Pasquale said as he dropped me off outside Gianni's.

He was staking his life on my ability to pull off this gig. Now he had five thousand reasons on top of staying alive to want me to succeed. Looking back on it, his faith was stupendous. My high IQ couldn't explain why he believed in me. Was it the blind faith of a desperate man or divine intervention? To me it felt more spiritual, rather than forced, and I was touched.

That night I tutored Gianni alone. Pasquale stayed clear, as I had delicate work to do at Gianni's. I wasn't concerned about tutoring Gianni; my focus lay only on his dad's lab. I was fascinated by the chemistry of explosives. The headmaster had left the military as a failure and similarly failed to get himself involved in the family arms business. The lab had everything needed to conduct experiments with explosives. The headmaster and I were searching for a new explosive. Our experiments had all been done using very small amounts, it was all just theoretical. However, along the way,

I had learnt how to make some very modern explosives which were proven to scale up. With access to enough materials, an actual bomb would be easy, if a little scary. Boom!

Even though it was a Saturday afternoon, Gianni's dad wasn't at home. He was still busy at school with the end-of-semester results. After my boring tutorial with Gianni, I went to the kitchen and showered his mother with the usual compliments; then I went to the lab. Gianni knew about the lab now, and that I helped his dad out in there, so I asked him to come with me, as I didn't want his mother getting suspicious. The poor kid had no clue what I was doing. He didn't like that place and hated anything to do with chemistry and his dad's obsession. He ventured into that dreaded room purely out of loyalty to me, bless him. As he watched me prepare a bunch of colourless liquids, he got more and more bored. None of them bubbled, boiled or oozed vapour like in the movies and, even more importantly, none of them exploded. Not yet anyway.

Officially, the end-of-semester results were due the following week. Inevitably, the headmaster would know the results already, especially his son's, and I'm sure he would have taken a passing interest in Pasquale's and mine. That I had done well was a given but Gianni's and Pasquale's results were less certain. I felt sure that Gianni had done well and that Pasquale would finally graduate, if only by the smallest of margins.

The phone rang, then stopped, so I assumed that Gianni's mother must have answered it. I was slowly mixing liquids when she burst in. Having never seen her in the lab before, she caught me by surprise. I must have jumped back three feet from a row of half-mixed TNT. We all could have died. I was shaken by that thought, when I should really have been shaken by my guilty conscience, but neither Gianni nor his Mum had any clue what I was doing or why it was so very wrong. Only his dad would have recognised that it was not part of some ongoing, shared experiment and that I had gone rogue.

'Your father is coming home early,' she said in an ecstatic mood. I instantly deduced that the phone call had been from her husband, that he had told her Gianni's exam results and that they had been good.

'Damn,' I thought, 'I won't be able to finish my bomb.'

She showered her son with praise and me too for helping him. She insisted that I join them for dinner, then stay over and go home in the morning. As tomorrow was Sunday and I had already warned my Mother of this likelihood, I bashfully accepted. You could say I had been confidently planning for this scenario ever since I had first seen the lab.

When he arrived, the father's smile was so wide he had a problem getting in the door. He laughed and joked all the way to the kitchen. At the dinner table, his wife lavished us with a feast. The happy headmaster made a speech congratulating both his son and me for our magnificent work. The mother planted a big kiss on my cheek. I just wanted dinner to end so they would go to bed and I could get on with my mission. I did my best to relax and enjoy the food. The wine, which Gianni and I were allowed to taste, certainly went well with the chicken. By 11 p.m., the parents had drunk two bottles of wine between them. I'd had no more than a few sips. It was all part of the plan. They got so tired, or horny, that they just got up and left, wishing me and Gianni a good night and congratulating us once more as they went upstairs. Gianni swiftly followed them, assuming I would find my own way to the guest room. As he went upstairs, I switched everything off as if I was coming too, then I snuck off to the kitchen and made myself an overflowing triple espresso. Ten minutes later, as I downed the last of my coffee, you could hear a pin drop. I thought of listening outside their rooms to make sure everyone was asleep but I decided that creeping around like that was more likely to wake them: 'Let sleeping dogs lie!'

Wired on caffeine, I was itching to get on with it.

Earlier that evening, I had mixed up the base ingredients for two different explosives: a weak one, just enough to burst three gas pipes in the central kitchen; and a second, stronger one containing phosphorous so flammable it could start a fire in an asbestos factory. This would go off 30 minutes after the first charge to ignite the gas that by then would have leaked into every part of the building, As a fail-safe it was powerful enough to bring down the whole building anyway, in case the gas explosion alone wasn't enough to break the foundations. They were both made from a base of nitroglycerine but I had to dose them very carefully to make sure the first one broke the pipes but didn't start a fire. If all that happened was a small fire to alert the fire brigade, then the damage would not be enough to close the restaurant for more than a week and, more importantly, the evidence of my bomb would not be destroyed. That would end badly for Pasquale and me. It would be just as bad if not enough gas leaked during the 30-minute time gap. Then, the building would pretty much be brought down by TNT alone. The investigator would not see enough evidence of a gas explosion and would conclude that it was foul play. Apart from losing out on the 5000-euro bounty, we would get caught and killed by the Camorra. They would find us easily. This had to be an act of God.

I worked as quickly as I could to bottle those lethal liquids, always careful not to bash them around. Gianni's father's chemicals were state of the art so the explosive I was able to create didn't have to be very big to pack the punch I required. He wouldn't even notice that such small quantities were missing. More of a problem were the timers. He had only seven. I needed two and enough wire to reach round the entire restaurant. One day he would notice they were missing but I had no choice.

It took ages to connect the bottles up to the timers. Every creak from the old house made me jump. If the headmaster came down for a midnight snack and popped in to the lab to check on some experiment that he was dreaming about, what would my cover story be? That I got thirsty and came down for a sip of nitro? I was gambling that, no matter how weak his bladder or how strong his munchies, he would last long enough for me to finish the bombs.

At 2 a.m., I swaddled the bottles in bubble-wrap with the timers and the wires on top and put everything in my rucksack. They couldn't explode without a spark of some sort, hence the timers, but you can never be 100 per cent sure. If they did explode, my parents would have had to gather me up with a teaspoon for the funeral. I don't know where I got the courage from; I wasn't even 13 yet.

I nestled the rucksack in the corner of the study and went to bed. At 6 a.m., I got up, left a thank-you note on the kitchen table and then crept downstairs with the rucksack and its precious cargo. I was crossing the hall like a burglar when the mother arrived. She was holding my note but smiling and babbling like she was still drunk. She hugged me disgustingly close and thanked me a few more times.

'Don't touch the bomb!' I nearly said, as I tried to wriggle free. I couldn't drag her with me so I just had to wait until she released me. As soon as she did, I abruptly turned and strode out the door. I was beyond caring about manners.

Normally, it took forty minutes to walk back to my shack. With that cargo, it took two hours!

In my room I had dug a little hole in the floor as somewhere to hide my money. I wasn't expecting burglars; it was to keep it safe from my parents, who would confiscate it for family expenses. The cavity was big enough that I could line it with a pillow at the bottom, put the rucksack on top and another pillow above it. Every time I had to handle the rucksack, I got more nervous. I kept telling myself that it wasn't going to go off by accident, only by design, but the stress was mounting. I would be a nervous wreck if I didn't detonate it soon, which, in turn, would bring a whole new type of stress. It was too late: in hindsight, the moment of my proposal to Pasquale had been my last chance to back out and survive.

At 9 a.m., as agreed, Pasquale blew the horn outside. Inside, I carefully fitted the cover over the secret cavity and its deadly contents. I told my Mum I was going to church and hopped onto the back of the moped.

Before church, I got Pasquale to take me via my auntie's flat so I could check up on my cover story. Had anyone from church been asking questions over Christmas? Altar boys are not normally subject to security vetting but I wanted to cover every angle and my auntie was chuffed to see me, as usual. Importantly, she had nothing unusual to report.

My little alarm clock was set for 12:45 a.m. Both my parents were heavy sleepers. Even so, I didn't let it ring – already awake with anticipation. Using a little reading torch, I got ready meticulously, like a ninja going into battle. I knew that after this, nothing would be the same. What I didn't know was that, from now on, every day would fill me with nervous energy. Imagine the same tension and anticipation all day every day. It'll eat you alive. I'm surprised more criminals don't get ulcers or die of heart attacks.

Pasquale was waiting for me on his moped as I crept out of my lean-to with the explosives in my rucksack.

'Ride as slowly as possible,' I ordered him, as I clambered on.

On the journey to Carlo's, I felt every bump, corner, acceleration and deceleration. Pasquale could not equate that tiny rucksack with the severity of my warnings about its dangers and, since the Sunday night traffic was non-existent, the temptation to go faster was too strong. I squeezed his arm like a lunatic to get him to slow down.

We drove into the alley round the back of the restaurant. Pasquale cut the engine. We were parked up behind the bins, which stood on a patch of greasy dark tarmac stained from the years of cooking fat. It was 1:45 a.m. As the last 'pop' of the scooter's motor faded everything was silent, including my internal dialogue. I got off, put the rucksack down and took a deep breath, then vomited. The rasping of my throat and then the splat of the sick smashing the ground echoed like a thunderclap. Normally I have a strong stomach but in my fragile state the smell of the bins must've triggered it. Pasquale looked concerned. I imagined he was having a few regrets. He knew I was clever but he must've wondered if I had the guts. He had guts in abundance. I just needed to borrow his. His worried glare gave me the kick up the ass I needed.

After the vomit, I felt calmer. It was time.

Pasquale had told me that the restaurant did not have an alarm; there was nothing to steal and nobody expected anyone to break in somewhere 'connected'. For someone of my talents, getting in was easy; the only lock I didn't pick was the padlock on the fridge in the kitchen: I wasn't hungry!

I started by carefully placing the tiny stage-one explosives next to the gas pipes running through to the dining room. The pipes were made of cheap alloy and easily accessible behind a wooden cover, which I unscrewed. I connected these charges to the wires and placed the detonator on the wall with some duct tape. Then, a lot more carefully, I placed the heavier ones next to the master walls of the restaurant and repeated the procedure. The detonators were so small that they would have been reduced to nothing and the glass of the bottles would mingle with the rest of the glass coming from the windows. I would leave no more than microscopic evidence. The original plan was to stay behind and observe the building from down the road, in case a busy-body did enter during that half-hour window. If they did, I would have to choose between watching them die or going in and disabling the bomb to save my conscience but, in that case, I would certainly be sacrificing my own life to the Camorra. Since this was a decision I didn't want to face, I took the coward's way out instead: just leave it to fate. The area was predominantly hotels and camp-sites which, in winter, were empty so I figured it would be okay. Even if someone heard the first explosion, there would be no signs of fire at that stage so no one would be able to tell where it came from. If they called the fire brigade and started searching the area, it would take way more than 30 minutes to find the source of the noise, unless they got (un)lucky and guessed right first time. Winning the lottery was more likely!

I set the timers on the detonators for 30 minutes and one hour respectively, re-closed the door behind me and climbed on the bike. I told Pasquale to ride without headlights. Normally riding pillion without lights at night is pretty scary but anything felt safe after riding with the bomb earlier; and riding away from a primed bomb is always a relief. The way back was downhill so we rolled agonisingly slowly for over a mile before we turned on the engine. The first detonator would go off while we were driving home but we would be in bed in time for the big show.

I was safely back in bed with ten minutes to go, counting every second and staring at my digital watch without blinking. The bang was so loud that my tiny window shook.

I did not know what to feel. Afraid, in case I had killed someone? Relieved, because I had pulled it off? Proud that I had punished injustice? In the end, I just felt guilty. I was sweating nervously and couldn't sleep. Was this success? Why had I lowered myself to such deeds? I wanted to show Pasquale how good I was in order to get him on my side and to punish a bad person but the real reason was to prove (to myself) that I could: pure egotism. I could've blown up my own family and I could yet be assassinated by the Camorra. Apart from bolstering my ego, what had I got in return? Some money from the owner of La Trattoria. A meagre reward and not yet guaranteed. It was suddenly all very depressing.

I immediately promised myself that if I got away with this then I would not blow anything else up. And if I got caught? A dead man has no need for such promises and I doubt I would end up pleading before a judge.

After three hours of tossing and turning, I couldn't even remember if I had slept or not. I must have been thinking a lot because suddenly I understood the cardinal rule of criminality: rewards and risks must balance. A successful criminal checks that the outcome of his crime will justify the risks of the operation and I hadn't done that. Buoyed by my enlightenment, I modified my promise: 'In future, I will blow something up only if the rewards justify the risk.'

The same rules apply in all areas of life: a person makes the biggest mistakes when their perceptions of risk are skewed by emotion. How many times have you heard 'It's not about the money, it's about the principle' as the justification for some pointless feud? I rest my case.

The following morning, everyone was talking about the explosion. I was very glad to hear that nobody was hurt and, with that news, my old bravado came flooding back. Suddenly, I was on top of the world. After Cocco's safe, I had pulled off an even tougher challenge. Granted, it was misguided but I had done it.

Here is my advice for anyone who dreams of blowing up someone else's building (and who among us hasn't?): Don't.

Early reports blamed a gas leak for the 'disaster'. My plan had worked magnificently. The rule of risk and reward applied to the council too; a full forensic investigation would have cost a fortune, so they sent a cheap incompetent to check it out. If he had known how to do his job properly, he might have found tiny traces of nitroglycerine. In Naples the Mafia frequently set off explosions but they used basic fertilizer-based bombs – easy to detect as they left large quantities of fertilizer all over the remains. In contrast, my device used such small amounts of high quality explosive that only a forensic expert would have been able to detect them. The owner was 'connected' so the council investigator had little reason to suspect foul play – if it weren't an accident then who would dare go up against the Camorra? It didn't occur to them that some invisible boy with revenge on his mind might try.

It looked like an accident so they declared it one.

After school, Pasquale and I rode past the scene of our crime. My jaw dropped when I saw what I had done: a pile of rubble was all that remained. I was about to pat myself on the back when I remembered that I had nothing to be proud of; I had not followed the rule of risk and reward.

Pasquale went to see La Trattoria's owner the following Friday afternoon. Before he left, I told him how to play it: 'Say nothing. Enter without being noisy or obtrusive but make sure he sees you. Then sit down in a quiet corner, and wait. Let him make the first move. Wait for him to come over and say or do something. If he does not come over within a reasonable time, say thirty minutes, then leave without a fuss. It is not like we have a legally binding contract but he might guess that his restaurant will get blown up next. Let him think it but don't say it, don't even hint at it.'

I waited for him outside my shack, ready to go to Gianni's for my usual tutorial when Pasquale came back, if he came back.

The minute he left I was already desperate for him to return so I could find out what happened. After 90 minutes I calculated that Pasquale should be back. After 2 hours I was getting really nervous.

Had they kidnapped him? What if the owner of La Trattoria had grassed him straight to the Camorra? What if, right now, he was being tortured by the Camorra to get him to give up the names of his accomplices? It never occurred to me to try to run away or hide. No; I was already mentally preparing a counter-attack on La Trattoria.

Every moped that passed by raised my hopes but each time they were dashed when I realised it wasn't Pasquale. After a while, whenever I heard a moped I no longer dared to hope but, unlike all the others, my hopes were not dashed this time.

Finally, after two and a quarter hours, a moped stopped by me in a cloud of two stroke fumes. Not wanting to tempt fate, I didn't look up at first but when I did Pasquale's face gave everything away: his smile was as bright as his gold tooth.

Apparently, the owner was ecstatic. Business had trebled in a few days. Admittedly it was low season but, with summer coming and his main competitor out of the way, things were looking very good. He gladly offered Pasquale a glass of wine, accompanied by an envelope. They pretended to discuss a possible busboy job for longer than necessary and then parted warmly.

Pasquale had not opened the envelope. He felt it had to be done together. It was thick and full of 100- and 500-euro notes: six grand, one more than agreed and a big sigh of relief. With that money, the man had shown us that he was in it with us. Unless he was tortured, he was unlikely to grass us up. If they were going to torture anyone, they would already have hooked the electrodes up to Pasquale's balls back at La Trattoria.

When we went into my room so he could count out the money he separated it 50-50 without being asked. That was a good sign. When he had finished, he handed me one pile and kept the other.

'You's a genius, Prince,' he said with solemn respect.

I put my share back on the bed slowly and deliberately, holding his stare.

'If we want to keep on doing this, we need two things: a reason and a plan. Do you want to follow me on my journey?' I said, suddenly quiet and serious.

He nodded as if hypnotised.

'We have been lucky. La Trattoria paid up without a fuss but too much was left to chance. We cannot rely on luck. We took a big risk for just 6,000 euros. Next time, if we take a big risk it is only for a big prize or, as a last resort, to save our necks by taking out an enemy.'

He nodded again, still in a trance.

'So, here is what we need to do: we take a grand each but we put the rest in the hole. Four thousand will be our working capital for future jobs. We have a lot of work to do!'

'As you say, Boss,' he whispered, swiftly handing me back his share of the money.

I gave him back 1,000 euros before hiding the rest in my (no longer) secret hole in my floor.

Pasquale kissed my right hand in the Neapolitan sign of respect. Like a medieval soldier being knighted he had 'knelt' before me to acknowledge my leadership.

Alone that night, I shouted, 'I am the Prince and I mean business!' as if to the whole of Naples.

I was certainly feeling good about myself, but someone once said:

'When you think you are immortal you will make the biggest mistake of your life.'

Would I heed that warning? I was still a few weeks away from my 13th birthday, so the odds were against it.

THE CAVE

As the weeks passed after the 'gas leak' the guilt grew until it dominated my every waking thought. I didn't care about the owner of the flattened restaurant, but I did care about his employees, now out of work in a city where jobs were hard to come by. I may have been an angry young man but I wasn't a rotten criminal and was determined not to become one. The Prince of Naples was supposed to be more like Robin Hood than Scarface, but wave after wave of guilt could not be repelled. Like the young child who wants to go on the most gut-churning ride in the theme park but freaks out the moment it starts, my brains had got me into this ride and now they couldn't handle the thrills. Kids are not supposed to do this kind of thing, so they don't need to know how to stop doing it, but I needed to know!

What I needed was someone I could talk to about all this, a friend who I could treat as an equal; instead I was alone with my thoughts and fears. In the end I came to a firm conclusion: you cannot think your way out of this, you must simply take decisive action (or inaction).

It had taken guts to embark on the mission but it took even more guts to suddenly abandon it. As soon as I took the decision to walk away from my revenge, immediately it just felt right.

I knew that I couldn't just magic away the knowledge that I had blown up a whole restaurant but, if I could just go back to the comfort of a normal routine, then slowly the memories of what I had done would fade.

As I became less engrossed in evil thoughts and the illegal activities they led to, I grew more observant of the world around. But even without a keen eye it was easy to see that our shack was not well insulated; winter temperatures in Naples can come down to freezing and my younger brother was always ill with bronchitis. I washed and slept at Gianni's so often that I had become oblivious to the hardships in the shack but now I felt ashamed that I didn't share them with my family.

My kid brother was not the only one who was permanently ill: a host of diseases were gripping the shanty-town and its fast-growing population. We were now more than 10,000 families crammed into an area that the government first designated for just over 2,000. Because the shacks were supposed to be 'only temporary accommodation', they were not equipped with toilets and there was no central sewage system. Water from our sinks went directly out onto the street, creating dirty puddles everywhere. We had to share a toilet and shower block with five times as many people as it was designed for. It was a cross between a festival camp-site and a concentration camp. Many, including my parents, tried to do as much as possible at home. Urinating and defecating, the simplest of basic needs, was now a complicated affair. We had to do 'it' in a container and dispose of 'it' only when no one was watching. Its content went nowhere else but in the streets. As old people could not perform such acrobatics, they used the public toilets but by now most of these were more than public, they were open air: their doors vandalised, broken or ripped off by angry kids and disgusted adults. Words cannot describe their smell. The cold of winter kept the flies at bay but the following summer we would surely be totally infested.

As the cracks kept appearing to condemn another tranche of apartment buildings, more unfortunate families had to move out and find shelter in empty schools, garages, unused government buildings and anywhere else they could find. The shanty-town did have its own municipal generator giving free electricity but it was hopelessly overworked. During surges in demand, power would fade for everybody: a classic 'brown-out'. Worse still, sometimes it would break down completely. These 'black-outs' could last a day or two while we waited for repairs to the generator; and they became serious, leaving people cold, unable to cook and able to live only by candlelight. Things were worse at the weekend when demand was highest and the repair team slowest, preferring to watch the football.

If the electricity supply was a problem, then I wouldn't know how to describe the water supply. The local council had finally declared the water (when it was running, of course) unsafe and hazardous to public health. All that excrement being poured everywhere had run down the hill and contaminated the local reservoir from which our drinking water was supplied. It would have cost a fortune to retrofit a sewage system for us, so they didn't. The memo they sent to notify the population of the dangers in the water was so riddled with complex medical terms that a large part of the population could not understand it. Moreover, as incredible as it might sound to you, the department in charge of the issue was full of employees who took their pay cheques but never, and I mean never, turned up for work. Most of the department's employees were affiliates of the Christian Democratic Party and their 'jobs' were the direct result of a massive network of cronyism. The water should have been declared unsafe three months earlier but the bureaucracy had done all it could to cover up this scandal. So they made a bad situation worse, condemning innocent people to drink the bad water for much longer than necessary.

We were children of a lesser god, a disposable part of the society who supposedly did not contribute. We were not doctors, judges, entrepreneurs, teachers or skilled labour. Most of us were petty thieves with no skills; some had difficulty signing their own names. Actually, the decision to ignore us was just an efficient state at work, pursuing the greater good of the greater number. You couldn't argue with their logic even as you were struck by their cold-heartedness.

We had no voice since no one was organised or articulate enough to express our anger in any concerted way, leaving it to the vandals and their random violence.

The rotten food in the street had attracted colonies of abandoned dogs, stray cats and rats of all sizes. All the nasty smells became so ingrained in our clothes that, no matter how often we washed ourselves or our clothes, we still carried a stench.

If this had been some banana republic in Central America then fair enough but, back then, Italy was part of the G7 nations with fashion and engineering industries that were the envy of the world. While the northern part of our famously boot-shaped country was swimming in money and luxury, living 'la dolce vita' (literally translated as the soft life), we, although just as Italian as they were, lived in what felt like a concentration camp. The authors of this injustice went every Sunday to 'my' church, where they probably prayed that we would all die as quickly as possible so they could enjoy the stolen reconstruction funds in peace.

Apart from rats and dogs, we had another unwelcome visitor that January: cholera struck the day before my 13th birthday. When I heard of the death of a local seven-year-old boy, I was immediately worried about my own kid brother. From the day we arrived in the shanty-town, I had been telling my Mum to boil all our water before using it, even if it was just to wash a tomato, but other residents didn't pay that kind of attention to their health. And if they didn't, no one else would.

The 'doctor', our local GP, was a fool: a man who, I am sure, had bought his degree rather than studying hard at university. He declared the poor boy's death 'due to natural causes', citing high fever, freezing conditions and poor nutrition. The fact that the child had suffered epic bouts of diarrhoea and was heavily dehydrated apparently didn't arouse any suspicion. After that untimely death, I thought about raising the issue with the local public health authority but, like all my rants against injustice, who would believe a teenager over a doctor.

Cholera was not the only killer: meningitis, tuberculosis and a host of others would condemn more than 500 people to an early grave before the year was out. None of this was reported. We were not interesting enough for the media to come and investigate in order to expose what was happening. Ignorance did the rest; the residents of our shanty-town just sat back and took it without any constructive protest. Even before the earthquake, they were used to being treated badly; they knew they were alone and when something else bad happened, like it always did, they just took it on the chin. When they demonstrated their anger it was never truly righteous; instead, they indulged in self-destructive behaviour, not so much a protest as a forlorn cry for help: vandalising their own neighbourhood; drug and alcohol abuse; mugging and petty thieving; literally and metaphorically shitting on their own doorstep. The most constructive thing any of the residents ever did was to attempt a more ambitious and lucrative burglary in a rich area of Naples well outside the shanty-town.

Whatever they were, they were my people. No matter how much I denied belonging there, in the eyes of the world I was expendable just like they were. But I was different: I had a good brain. I would keep sight of my only sensible cause: protecting my family's mental and physical well-being. On top of that, to protect my own sanity I had to stay retired and steer well clear of any thoughts of revenge on the guys at the top, the source of our problems.

The residents vented their anger like enraged primates whenever an establishment figure was brave enough to show his face. Police cars, government officials, the occasional journalist, doctors and even fire engines and ambulances could and would be stoned from a distance or, if they looked like easy prey, assaulted at close range. I saw a social worker chased out of her car with wooden clubs by a gang. The famous sense of 'diminished responsibility' made this look acceptable to those who you would consider normal and law-abiding. We hardly saw the police here. After a visiting priest was beaten so badly he had to go the hospital, it reached the stage that no one came anymore, not even when we begged.

There was a young guy who lived next to my shack. He was in his early thirties and I just knew him as 'the IT Guy', as he was working for a bank in their IT department. I befriended him so I could find out more about banking, accounts and computers, all of which seemed to be necessary skills if I were one day to construct my case against the authorities. My parents liked him too as he was a decent and hard-working man, unlike most of the scum in the area. His young and pregnant wife had recently become my Mother's only local friend. They had coffee together almost every afternoon, where they shared the pains of our daily struggle.

One night, when I was having a rare dinner at home with the parents, we heard a hard knock on our door. It was our gentle neighbour, the IT Guy. The man, tall and slightly overweight, was breathing so heavily he couldn't talk. Finally, he caught his breath enough to tell us that he had just run two kilometres to a pay phone and back to call an ambulance, as his wife had gone into labour prematurely. Apart from having two children herself, my Mum had no experience of these things but both my Mother and Father felt they just had to try and help. I went along but made my little brother stay behind. I should have stayed too but I was curious and my parents were too caught up in the emergency to worry about me.

The woman had ballooned to what looked like twice her normal size. She was sat on her bed with her legs wide open, trying to push the baby out. She was sweating and screaming at the top of her lungs while my Mother looked for clean towels and my Dad frantically boiled some water. I admired my parents that day; they rose to the challenge. I had not seen camaraderie and compassion like it in the shanty-town before. What really dug a hole in my heart, though, was to see the young husband rocking back and forth in his chair like a man possessed. He was holding a rosary in his hands, calling for a miracle. Unfortunately, the miracle never came and nor did the ambulance.

As the poor bloke was praying, his young wife went into a convulsion so powerful that she almost jumped out of the bed. My Dad, a very strong man, couldn't hold her down as she began vomiting repeatedly and violently.

Her death looked like a relief to me, as she must have been in excruciating pain. The IT Guy had just lost his wife and baby. My Dad was holding my Mum who was crying so hard she was having convulsions of her own. I found it so horrific it made me feel ill. No child should ever be exposed to a tragedy of that magnitude.

We had a new more urgent worry. The IT Guy was collapsed on the floor and no longer breathing properly. Despite being dizzy with nausea, I tried to assist him. When my Dad realised how bad a state the guy was in, he came to help. That day, my Dad was a real hero. He grabbed him, frogmarched him outside and stopped the first car that came by.

'Hospital, now!' he roared, without asking any polite questions of the driver, a poor electrician who lived across from us.

The electrician knew of my Dad's temper and dared not ask any questions. He had seen it all before and, although saddened, he was used to the routine of the shanty-town. From the back seat, I regularly reported on the state of the suffering young IT Guy. We drove to A&E as fast as possible. We risked killing everyone on board several times. Waving a white handkerchief out of the car window gave us no more than a false sense of security as we dodged dangerously through the traffic. When we got to the hospital, my Dad pulled the IT Guy out of the car and approached two men in hospital uniform standing outside by the entrance. He courteously but firmly shouted for them to fetch a stretcher but they did not move.

'Call the porters. We are nurses,' they replied.

My Dad's eyes flared with rage. He gently put the IT Guy down, then pinned both men against the wall they were leaning on.

'Now, you are porters. If you do not take this man to the right place, I will tear you apart like warm bread,' he said.

For once, his raging temper was useful. They immediately did as they were told.

My Dad stayed with our suffering friend all night, pacing around his bed as the doctors stabilised him with tranquillizers. I was taken home by the electrician, too dazed to even open my mouth. When I got home, my Mum did not look right either. She was still kissing and caressing the young wife's lifeless body, invoking various saints in a litany of prayers.

I was of a scientific mind. I did not believe in heaven or hell; my world did not allow for unproven theories. In the heat of the moment, though, I put aside my cynical observations and prayed with my Mum. The saving grace was at least my younger brother had avoided this horrible episode, for once.

The IT Guy survived that experience but he was now in what seemed to be a permanent state of shock. After he came out of hospital my Mum fed him every day. I gave him a grand to make sure his wife and baby had a proper funeral. He was too choked to talk properly but he was *compos mentis* enough to pass the money on to the priest and undertaker. I was choked too, and angry. In all the 'inactivity' since the gas leak, I had seen too much suffering. I wanted to get back on the revenge trail but somehow I still knew full well why I had quit and, thankfully, I had the strength of mind to stay out of it. I congratulated myself on this willpower, not once thinking it could be divine guidance. That, in turn, got me thinking; maybe I could do something useful to get my family out of harm's way without bombing the entire CDP and the Mafia or getting dragged into a life of crime and revenge. In life there is always a third way: a middle ground. I had no idea how dangerous such thoughts were. I didn't do 'middle ground'. I was an adrenaline junkie; one sniff of excitement and I would be up to my neck all over again.

To get my family out, I needed money. I calculated that it would take 10 years of tutoring Gianni to get the money for a deposit for a new family apartment, and only if I stopped buying any new designer clothes. Face it: that was not going to happen.

The next day, I got a letter from Cocco asking where I would like him to deliver his tools. If you took away the parts of his letter that said 'when can I give you my stuff?' or words to that effect phrased in about four different ways, then you weren't left with anything apart from hello and goodbye. He must've been very keen to get rid of it. Since I had also retired, I had stopped thinking about the tools, let alone where I would put them.

In my case, time clearly was a healer. In the three months since the 'gas leak' I had started to accept the constant guilt of being a 'bomber'. No matter how bad the crime, eventually the criminal takes it for granted. It was not so bad now that I had brainwashed myself into believing it really was a gas leak, like some perpetually 'innocent' criminals do. I was still determined not to get involved in a whole load of revenge but it occurred to me that the money in the church safe might be enough to buy a new home for Pasquale's family and mine. Now, I did need a 'Batcave' but only to store some tools, not as a base to attack all of Naples' corrupt politicians. That's what I told myself, anyway.

'Pasquale, we will have left here by the end of the year,' I promised.

He did not flinch; he just nodded with respect. He knew nothing was beyond me.

We went back to the lower slopes of Vesuvius to search for the unfinished building. It was well hidden by bushes but we found it eventually. It was worth it.

Construction work on our building had been aborted a few years earlier. Like many others scattered across the region, the original builder's idea had been to build just enough (foundations and a few walls) to qualify for a government grant to help him finish it. Then, instead of building it, he'd let his company go bankrupt after embezzling the grant, worth a lot more than what it had cost him so far. It was a common scam in a city where swindling was an art form.

In this case, the work had stopped at the ground-floor level. There were only gaps for windows, no door and no electricity: a skeleton of concrete blocks with no roof. Useless to us but for the large cellar, which, one day, would have been a three-car garage under the house. Unlike the ground floor, the basement didn't even have holes for windows but the floor above acted as a roof and it had a large entrance across the whole of one side, again with no doors. By walling up the open entrance, doing some interior decoration and adding air conditioning it would be perfect. I measured it up and started to imagine how it would look. Better yet, there was a lamppost half a mile away, which lit up the tourist path to the volcano. I could steal electricity from there.

I had a budget of three grand: the money left over from the 'gas leak' and the funeral. All I needed now were some workmen. Pasquale had some basic construction experience but I needed greater expertise. I couldn't just call a building company. I had the same dilemma that faced every James Bond villain before me, and even Batman himself: the only way to be sure my lair would stay secret was if all the workmen were fully committed to joining our gang, easier said than done, but for once it wasn't me who solved the problem.

Pasquale suggested the Spanish. The Spanish was the nickname for his older brother who had just come out of jail. The only problem I had with the Spanish, as I made clear to Pasquale, was whether he would accept my leadership. There was no room for a loose cannon.

'Would a 20-year-old man, with plenty of experience of life and crime on the street and, thus, a reputation to defend, listen to a nerd seven years his junior?'

'He'll get how good you is. An' why you does it – he'll follow you, jus' like me.'

'Look, all that revenge mission stuff is over. We build this place up, use it to store the tools, hit the church safe and use the money to get our families out. It's a one-time deal – remember that. Will he still join us?'

'If he's gonna break the law, he better do it with us, not them gangsters who left 'im to rot in prison. He'll be loyal, I promise you. An' he's a good builder!'

It sounded fine but I wasn't keen to be bounced into a decision just because I couldn't think of anyone else.

'Let me meet him,' I said. At this point, I honestly thought I would be meeting him to see if he was okay for the gang but the moment the words left my mouth I realised it was too late: the job offer was 'out there' and he would be interviewing me to see if he wanted to work for me. That scared me, and rightly so.

I was even more worried when I finally laid eyes on him for the first time. Nothing Pasquale had said could have prepared me for meeting the Spanish. So far, I had met streetwise kids capable of a bit of bullying plus the occasional punch-up. The Spanish's face told a very different story. Two large facial scars, one on each cheek, and some smaller ones scattered round his face immediately gave the impression he wasn't afraid of getting a few more in a fight. At 6 foot 4 inches he was even taller than his brother. With wide shoulders, powerful arms and long blond hair tied back he was Conan the Barbarian. His eyes were deep and empty.

I shivered in the company of a man I was sure was a killer. His short jail sentence meant only that he hadn't been successfully prosecuted for murder; it didn't mean he hadn't done it. And, if he hadn't killed anyone before, he looked supremely capable of correcting that. At 20 years old, there was still time to rack up a few killings. I didn't want him to start with me. I felt like the mouse in the story of the Gruffalo who could survive on his wits alone – as long as the Gruffalo didn't suddenly wise up.

After some very gruff small talk that would have made the Gruffalo seem clever, the Spanish just blurted it out.

'Okay. I join your gang?'

The tone of voice he used rose at the end like a question but the body language that accompanied it said that this was not an offer I could refuse. I did not want to get beaten up on the spot for offending him. But, even more importantly, now he knew about our gang I had to let him join just to keep it secret. It was too late.

'Great, you won't be disappointed,' I said, anxious to end this uncomfortable meeting.

'Good, coz I got a few scores to settle myself,' he replied menacingly, ending the 'interview' even more uncomfortably than it had started.

The words 'loose cannon' were written in neon lights. Rather than regrets, I just had to make sure he wasn't pointing at me when he went off.

I showed him the building plans for the cellar that would henceforth be known as 'the Cave'. We discussed the materials and budget. He took the money and stuffed it into a pocket. He frowned as he studied the plans silently, mouthing the words like a lunatic. 'It'll be two weeks,' he said, suddenly sounding a lot more professional.

I did not need to warn him about the need for secrecy as he was the most streetwise of us all but, more importantly, I didn't want to patronise him on his first day working for me. I know it's splitting hairs but, even though he was not as smart academically as Pasquale, he grasped practical matters very quickly: like a dog, a big Rottweiler.

Now the gang was officially three, I had to rely on them as well as myself. That was both a great opportunity and a big risk. But, since we would only be robbing the simple safe in the church and retiring once we had got our two families out of the shanty-town, it was mostly opportunity and not such a big risk, right?

The Spanish did a superb building job. By the middle of February, the Cave was ready with my empty lab in place, the ventilation properly installed, electricity and my office. We did not have furniture yet but we gathered a few bits and pieces from skips around the city to make it more comfortable for the time being. It was bare and minimal but it would do the job of housing the locksmith gear.

I called Cocco and he came to Naples the very next day to start dropping off his instruments and tools. It took him two trips to get it done. He could not wait to get rid of them.

'Maybe they are cursed...' Well, he didn't actually say it but I knew what he was thinking.

As I did not want to show Cocco the Cave, he had to drop them at a lock-up garage in the city and we then painstakingly transferred them by scooter. This was the riskiest part of the job; so many heavily laden trips could easily have aroused suspicion. We were careful to do it at different times of the day, by different routes and always checking we weren't being followed as we left the last village on the hillside below the Cave. I stayed in the Cave and carefully arranged each new batch of tools as they arrived. After seven days, the locksmith lab and the Cave were good to go. We had spent all the gang's funds. It was time to replenish them.

A couple of days later, the three of us went to church ... at one o'clock in the morning!

We were ready. I knew the makes and models of all the locks. I had the necessary skeleton keys. It was as simple as that: the church had no alarm. In those days, crooks had enough principles not to ply their trade on consecrated ground. As far as I was concerned, it had been 500 years since anything sacred had happened in there.

Standing outside, I composed myself by suppressing all emotions. If you can do this, then you can become a criminal; and if you can't then you don't stand a chance. Then I walked purposefully towards the church. I was totally decided; no hint of hesitation. I kept walking straight as the brothers took up their lookout positions. After I unlocked the first door with ease, I went in.

It was very dark inside: only a hint of light from the street came through the windows but I knew it very well and I went straight across to the sacristy. Inside it was even darker but I didn't notice as I headed directly to the safe. No sooner had I got the tools out than the safe was virtually cracked. I don't remember the details because I was so focused but opening it must have been child's play after Cocco's Manninger. Anyway, I put my hands inside and soon felt some big wads of cash. As I slid them out, I heard the rustle as they fell into my bag.

'I'll count it afterwards,' I said to myself.

Like a robot, I just stayed focused on filling the bag as fast I could and getting out of there. By the time I had slid the entire contents of the safe into my bag, it was stuffed full. I had taken all the money and all the documents. Veni, Vidi, Liberatus: Latin for I came, I saw, I liberated, in this case from its owner!

The only things I left behind were a few funny-shaped metal objects, which, in the dark, I thought were valuable church arte-facts. For all I knew they were worth more than the cash but they would be too dangerous to sell on and anyway I still had some principles. So did the boys outside. They were constantly making the sign of the cross and begging forgiveness under their breath. They did their job, even though they weren't happy about it. I had no such concerns. I knew where that money had come from and who had donated it. There was nothing sacred about it. The real shock from above came later.

Back in the Cave, we sorted through the spoils. All doubts about the wisdom of this job were obliterated when the final count came in: over 101,000 euros in cash. It was greeted with a loud cheer from the guys.

That was not all: there was a load of documents and a ledger. At first glance I couldn't make any sense of them but I figured they must be important or why store them in the safe. As an act of pure optimism, I showed the ledger to the Spanish. He recognised some of the names: local bookies run by the Camorra. My heart stopped. That was the clue I needed to unlock the ledger. The priest had being gambling with charity money. There was a church fund for a drug rehabilitation charity that had been attracting large donations. The ledger, if it was correct, listed over a million euros in bets.

So, the drug addicts of Naples who needed help were dying so the priest could indulge his love of the horses, unless it was just money laundering; maybe the corrupt politicians donated to the church with the intention that the priest would 'give' it to the Mafia via a legitimate bet. Was I adding two and two and getting five? I never liked Don Vincenzo but he was a priest and I expected more of him. I asked myself: 'Is there any decent human being in this godforsaken place?'

The Spanish wanted to kill the priest while he slept. Pasquale searched the lab for something sharp enough to do it. I was not immune. High on adrenaline from the robbery I agreed.

When I had planned the church robbery, I had seen it as low risk. Maybe there was a low risk of getting caught but I had not accounted for the massive risk that it might reignite my desire for revenge. It flooded over me.

'Gotcha!' Pasquale said as he found a knife in the toolbox.

'Gimme that!' yelled the Spanish as he grabbed it, 'I'm outta here!'

'Calm down! With our intelligence we can slowly and ruthlessly ruin their lives. We can inflict more pain that way. A quick pain-less death is too easy,' I said coldly. Fine words for a 13-year-old, but I needed to sound like a bad man to convince them!

'Now, both of you repeat this promise. From this place, we will change our lives and those of our people.'

Pasquale and the Spanish liked to let their anger flare up but they also liked the comfort of having a leader to follow rather than thinking for themselves. Immediately, Pasquale started reciting the promise. Before he had finished, the Spanish had joined in. Their chorus of approval was music to my ears.

It all started here in the Cave. The Spanish surrendered his doubts about serving under someone so much younger than him.

He knew I was right and cold-blooded revenge was now our gang's super-glue. The revenge mission was back on.

Like a bloodhound that caught a scent, I kept trying to make sense of the rest of those documents. I found several invoices paid by the church from various charitable funds to a company whose proprietor was Bulldog. I had neither accounting nor banking knowledge at the time but you didn't need to be an expert; the priest was helping Bulldog siphon off and then launder money stolen from the city's budget. I felt sick. We are talking about enough money to build all the apartments our people were so desperate for. Now I wanted to find a knife to kill Bulldog, but instead I just cried myself to sleep that night.

Bulldog was already our prime target, now only more so. Our revenge felt noble, I swore to unleash my talents on that god-forsaken city. I couldn't keep my secret anymore. I decided to put my cards on the table and just see what reaction I got from Pasquale and the Spanish. I explained the big plan: we would rob, expose and mortify the guilty parties and then use the money we stole to help those in need. We would have completed our mission only when all the new apartments for the residents of the shanty-town were built. We would succeed not because we were righteous crusaders but because no one would suspect three lowly youths.

After giving each gang member 3,000 euros, I declared the remaining 92,000 as working capital for our mission. They both hugged me. They were proud of the responsibility I was bestowing upon them. It was almost biblical: I would lead them to victory against the forces of evil ranged against us and our families. We slept on the floor of the Cave for a few hours.

The next day, on the way to school, my brain pored over the facts I had learnt the night before. Exactly who were the forces ranged against us and how would I defeat them? The three forces that dominated my city and, to an extent, the whole country were the 'Unholy Trinity' of the Camorra, the politicians and, last but certainly not least, the Roman Catholic Church. All entwined to benefit one another; they had been at it since the beginning of modern history, all jointly responsible and, therefore, as bad as each other. Everyone knows about the world-famous Italian Mafia. To a lesser extent, I suspect, most people have heard from time to time about corrupt Italian politicians but, given the power of the Church in Italy, I am genuinely surprised that so few have come to the conclusion that the Church, or at least their leaders, must be just as bad. So much bad stuff happens on their watch that they don't do enough to stop: they simply *must* be complicit. They can excuse it with pragmatism, 'better the devil you know', but it is not holy. It is not what God would have wanted. God probably didn't want me to go on a righteous crime spree either but that doesn't change the fact that corruption in Italy would be a fraction of what it is if the Church stood 100 per cent against it. Instead, they themselves have become corrupted by their own immense power in Italian society. Vesuvius would have to blow up big time to wipe out all the bad people in Italy rather than just one debauched ancient city. In the meantime, it was left to me to fix it!

It was a circle of conspiracy. The Camorra sponsored the campaigns of the politicians. Well-funded politicians usually win. The indebted politicians gave jobs to their cronies and used the apparatus of government to protect the Camorra. The Church and its hierarchy were, in effect, in partnership with the Camorra. They received many benefits: healthy donations and the Camorra's godfathers' promotion of the pseudo-Christian credo of 'turn the other cheek'. Both the Camorra and the Church wanted people unhappy, as they were fertile ground for their ideology and recruitment of new personnel. It was a well-oiled machine, which worked as smoothly as a Swiss watch. Ironically, Switzerland is one of the few places that isn't run like this. Go to most South American, Arab or African countries and the similarity to Naples will be staggering. Look at the IRA and now the Taliban. Any time an organised crime outfit can partner up with the dominant local religion, the resultant effect on society is remarkably similar. At 13 years old, I may not have been clued up enough to understand exactly how they did all this but already I could see a simple formula:

POLITICS + RELIGION + ORGANISED CRIME =
UNDISPUTED CONTROL over the suffering masses.

Despite the strength of the system aligned against me, I still felt confident. They would not expect us to attack. We would creep into their homes and their bank accounts, trick them into mistakes, disguise ourselves either as schoolboys (easy) or women (harder) and generally be as sneaky as possible. They would not think to look for us. And our lives could not be any worse. To calm my fears, 'What else can they do to me?' became my mantra.

Did I fear dying? Definitely, yes, but I would have preferred to die in a noble rebellion than of boredom or sickness in the shanty-town. Rebellion was my religion.

I couldn't sleep for hatred of the priest and Bulldog, and if I couldn't sleep then I didn't need to worry about the guilt I felt from the 'gas leak'. Now there was no reason to continue to obey the last of my self-imposed restrictions. Bombs would be back on the menu of sneaky weapons I could use against them. I started to build up the equipment at the Cave so that one day it could match Gianni's father's lab.

Three days after the church robbery, the aunt who I used as a cover story for my altar boy alter ego showed up unexpectedly at the shack. That got me worried.

'I've got some bad news,' she said.

I nearly shat myself. I felt my palms sweating but if retribution were to come for the recent robbery it would not arrive in the form of an old lady knocking politely on the door. The bad news was actually very good news from my point of view. The priest had just died of a heart attack. I had to try very hard not to snigger. Justice was being done again. There was a price to pay: I had become a killer, if only indirectly. Of course, it was his own conscience that had finally killed him: he couldn't face admitting to his congregation or his crooked allies what he had done with their money. The Mafia would've killed him when they found out and he knew it. Personally, I would have expected him to commit suicide but his dicky heart threw in the towel first. How convenient ... for him. Technically, he had escaped a horrible public scandal but he would get his just desserts in the next life, of that I was sure.

That night I slept just like a real baby, waking every hour. I didn't wake up crying but I wanted to. Whenever I felt guilty, I reminded myself that his death was a fair punishment for his sins. I wasn't exactly happy to have (indirectly) killed someone but when those bloodthirsty brothers, Pasquale and the Spanish, heard they danced like they were in a Bollywood movie!

Later on, I heard that the police were investigating. Usually when an old man dies of a heart attack, a doctor signs it off, end of story. His connections with the Camorra's bookies and Bulldog meant that I expected them to discreetly clean up his affairs.

Why attract attention by sending the police?

That bothered me. I went back over what I had done. I had left all the doors and the safe shut and locked, exactly as they were before our arrival at the church. The police couldn't know that a robbery had taken place the night before, as the only one aware of the exact contents of the safe was the priest himself. When they worked out that money was missing, they would surely assume that the priest had embezzled it and taken the knowledge to his grave. It was case closed. Bulldog would be none the wiser that we might come after him next. The whole affair had gone so well that I started to believe that someone up there was looking out for me.

'Maybe it's Granddad!' I thought.

It was time for me to relax and enjoy the fruits of our labour. I gave ten grand to the Spanish to turn the Cave into a palace. He bought a sofa, a TV, a video player, a fridge, and a few other mod cons. He brought back all the change down to the last penny with receipts for everything. Amazing, considering his past as a violent thief.

Thankfully, the IT Guy was now feeding himself and the whole trauma had only – outwardly at least – left him with a mild stutter which, annoying as it was, should be considered a blessing. He had taken a lot of time off as compassionate leave but as he wasn't a permanent employee his contract was not renewed. Then he was unable to pay his bills and soon his creditors were taking action. You'd think he'd have nothing to lose but life has a knack for kicking people when they were down.

I decided that, one day in the future, the IT Guy would join our gang. The brothers weren't happy about the idea but they didn't object. It was simply the right thing to do: an act of charity that would have its uses.

Almost every day someone knocked on our door with a funeral invitation for some poor resident of the shanty-town. I never went; I didn't like funerals. Neapolitans, however, felt otherwise and, if they could, always showed up.

At Pasquale's invitation, there was one local funeral that I did attend. It was for the parents of a friend of Pasquale and, in order not to offend him, I went along. It was a double-funeral, as both the man and his wife had died of cholera. They left behind an orphan. The boy was lucky. His blood type was AB, which confers automatic immunity to cholera, So he survived unscathed.

His nickname was the 'Cat'. At 17 he was not much more than five feet tall, skinny but very agile, and when insulted he would certainly defend himself. He went straight for the eyes, hence the name. I was never comfortable in his presence, as he had half-blinded more than one person in the past. Up until recently, his victims hadn't been the type to tell tales to the police, but since his parents' deaths he had become more violent. The previous week he had attacked a coroner's assistant in a petty argument. The assistant didn't lose his sight but he did tell the police.

At the funeral, I felt sorry for the Cat. He had lost all of his previous exuberant, if misguided, vitality. His eyes were fixed on his parents' coffins. During the memorial service, despite the occasion, the police came to arrest him for the attack. They took him away kicking and screaming. The police would normally have had trouble tracking him down, so they seized the opportunity of the funeral. Worried that the Cat would slip away at the end, they did not even have the decency to wait until after the burial. He was surely going to spend several months in a juvenile correction facility. As they took him away, people shouted and threw whatever they could at the police, who had turned up mob-handed in full riot gear, having taken the shanty-town's reputation for violence all too seriously.

All that to pick up a child no more than five feet tall.

Even this minor incident was designed to send a message from the authorities back to the residents of the shanty-town: 'Don't mess with us.'

Well, I was going to mess with them as best I could.

The jail where the Cat was going was one of the worst in the civilised world. I never understood why they called it a 'Rehabilitation Centre for Minors'. When minors went in, they were usually rebels without a cause: petty thieves, violent but never a danger to society. When they came out, after being raped by inmates and guards alike, and generally violated, they were prime candidates for recruitment by the Camorra. They would become cheap labour who would do just about anything for a few euros or a piece of bread.

Pasquale was very concerned for his small friend. He hadn't been inside that place but knew others who had. He was sure that, despite the Cat's vicious talents, his small size would mean he too would fall victim to the worst the place had to offer. It was X-rated stuff that a 13-year-old shouldn't have to concern himself with. I had heard enough. I had to intervene.

I instructed the Spanish to visit the Warden, a seemingly gentle, middle-aged guy, and offer him a bribe of 500 euros a week to preserve the anus of our friend. The high price was to ensure sufficient resources were allocated to allow constant supervision. The Warden's salary was probably no more than 2,000 euros a month at the time. It was ridiculous that he had to be paid any extra, let alone doubling his salary, just to protect one of his charges when that was his job anyway. The crooked Warden accepted the offer without haggling. He knew a good deal when he saw one. The Cat was grateful and so was Pasquale. The Spanish was proud of me for that gesture but that didn't stop him politely remonstrating: 'Prince, if we keep giving our dough away, we'll be left with nothing.'

'Plenty more where that came from, my strong and trusted friend,' I said as I raised my right hand royally and touched his biggest facial scar.

'As you wish, Boss,' he said, as he took my hand and kissed it.

THE GANG

The Spanish was right. We were spending money too fast and not getting any closer to re-housing our families. Just over a month since the church job and, between my donation to the IT Guy's wife's funeral, some smaller gifts to other neighbours, refurbishment of the Cave, plus the gang's payments, we were left with less than half what we had stolen. I wasn't worried; helping neighbours in need was a good cause and I was sure we could get our hands on more money just as soon as we needed to. In a city like Naples, I would never be short of ideas for the next job.

My criteria would be strict:

Firstly, that the rewards justified the risks.

Secondly, that it would punish the right people.

Thirdly, that the gang and I would emerge from the job stronger than we went in; typically, by stronger I meant richer.

Fourthly, if it was an audacious 'grand revenge', then we could do it regardless of the other criteria. This was really just for my ego's sake as the gang were already fully motivated.

Of all the bad guys on my radar, there was one obvious candidate for our next target: the president of the CDP. The man who was using the church to recycle and steal the community's money – the man I called Bulldog. For him, I needed an infallible plan. Infallible plans usually take longer to cook up, but a series of freaky coincidences really sped up the process.

My Dad worked in telecommunications for a private company that subcontracted work from the State-owned telecoms company, S.I.P. Telecommunications. We're not exactly talking 4G but back then new technologies were arriving all the time. My Dad's company had to keep its employees up to date and regularly forced them to take courses. Each course ended with a full-on exam. If you started to fail these then they would assume you were an 'old dog' who couldn't learn new tricks. Promotions and job opportunities would then slowly dry up until eventually you were on the scrapheap. At least that's how my terminally insecure

Dad saw it. So, when he signed on to the latest course out of desperation, he took home every relevant study book he could get his hands on, and quite a few irrelevant ones too.

When I saw his stack of thick books, my eyes lit up.

'Wow!' I said.

'Yeah, tonight I'm hitting the books, son', he replied excitedly, but his faux-enthusiasm didn't fool me.

Telecommunications fascinated me: not as much as bombs but it was up there with safe-cracking. I also knew telecoms skills would come in handy for the gang soon enough. Frequencies, phone boxes, radio signalling, radio-controlled systems and everything else that was hot in telecommunications was there in those books for me to learn. While supposedly helping my Dad with his studies, I taught myself how to tap a phone and how to make a phone call using someone else's line without being in their house. Remote phone line activated locks were covered too, which meant that, in theory, I could open a lock by tapping a phone line. I was the perfect student but what I planned to do with the knowledge was most definitely not!

Warmer weather came sooner than usual that year, particularly welcome to the people in the shanty-town. They say you can't polish a turd but it did look better when the sun was shining and you could smell the flowers more than the rotting food. Spring always brought out the best in me and, despite the shanty-town, I still found myself smiling, once in a while.

I went to church with renewed vigour and a very holy intention: to send Bulldog into such a spin that his big head would fall off his thick neck. I was a boy on a man's mission. Since the previous priest's death, the flock had been tended by a temporary substitute sent all the way from Rome. This week we welcomed our new permanent replacement. He was a nice-looking man in his late fifties, not aesthetically challenged like the old hunchback. I had learnt by now not to judge people by their appearances so, until he proved otherwise, he was as bad as the rest.

Step one: get Bulldog's address from the parishioners' files. It was unfortunate that this was not some secret file because, if it had been, it would have been in the haul from the safe and I would have it already. Normally, such information is kept in the office. A sneaky altar boy would have no trouble getting a peek but this very file had been taken away by the police after the ugly priest's death. I still wasn't fazed.

The church was packed to the rafters that day. The community had rallied to welcome the new priest. People who never came to the ordinary mass turned up enthusiastically. Surely they only came to cut a new deal with the new man. I checked out the audience, my eyes boring like X-rays into their souls to see what lay hidden behind those expensive clothes. I saw a very large, bald head reflecting the church candles: target acquired! After that, I never lost sight of Bulldog, waiting throughout the usual post-mass refreshments for my opportunity. He was surrounded by his cronies, in deep conversation, but probably wondering what the old priest had done with the contents of the safe. I'm sure he knew what had been in the safe but, equally, he could only conclude that the old hunchback had spent it. The documents from the safe would be more of a mystery but a dead man cannot be tortured to reveal the truth. Beyond that, no one else was suspected, least of all me.

I got close enough during the serving of refreshments to hear him discussing his upcoming re-election campaign. As sickening as it was that the church was used for this kind of business, it was not useful to my mission so, like a shark who smells blood behind him, I did an abrupt U-turn and swam off through the crowd to where his wife was entertaining some wealthy regulars. Even though her audience was made up entirely of women, she was flaunting her incredible beauty: waving her blonde hair, flashing the whitest smile I had ever seen with the biggest, bluest eyes south of Milan (women down in Naples were almost always dark-eyed). She spoke very softly and clearly, with a mannerism worthy of royalty; after all, she was the queen of Naples. I had grown up a lot recently but I was still more naive about women than most 13-year-olds; I could not understand what a woman of her calibre was doing with such an evil husband.

Was I just being an idealist or was I forming a crush on her? Either way, she was married to the enemy, which made her the enemy too.

'Oh, Serpent with breasts, restrain your wicked magic!' I shouted to myself, though it was me that needed restraint.

Once recovered from my hormonal moment, I listened carefully to what she was saying about a party they were having that evening to promote the CDP's candidates. This vulgar discussion plumbed new depths by focusing on what food she was preparing (i.e. having prepared) and how much she had been working for it (i.e. spending on it) rather than what the candidates' messages were. A light bulb went off in my head: my cue to act! I put on the biggest smile and walked casually over like the shark I imagined myself to be.

'Good afternoon, ladies. Have you enjoyed the service?' I said in my best Italian accent.

They all looked at me, surprised.

'I could not help overhearing about your party this afternoon. As you can see, I have plenty of experience in serving refreshments. I would be glad to offer my services for such an important event. If you need me, all you have to do is ask,' I said, as I looked straight into the eyes of my intended victim.

My charm struck like a bolt of lightning. The ladies around Mrs Bulldog fell silent on cue. They stared at me goggle-eyed, no doubt admiring me as if I were the entire Armani summer collection. I pretended to ignore them. Bulldog's wife did not rush to reply. I stood firm and still and we both let the moment last. Thoughts swirled inside me as I kept unflinching eye contact with my target:

'Does she fancy me? I think she does. Stay focused, Prince, or you will fail.'

One of the others, an older lady, broke the silence...

'What a nice young man. When I see you at the altar, I don't know whether to look at you or the priest.'

The other ladies burst into controlled laughter. Helped by a tide of implicit peer pressure, I would surely get my invitation if I waited just a little longer.

'The catering is already taken care of and in any case I would not dream of it,' the wife of my sworn enemy said.

'No way, I'm never wrong,' my ego replied in my head, but she wasn't finished.

'I couldn't have such a dashing young man serving cocktails. You will come as a guest. Here, let me write down the address. Come around sixish. Is that OK?'

'See? She's clearly besotted,' said my ego.

Actually, it was Greta, her ten-year-old daughter, who was besotted with me. I didn't notice she had joined the group until she started jumping up and down with joy on hearing her mother invite me.

Afterwards, I walked 500 metres round the corner to meet Pasquale. This was our regular trick to hide the fact that I wasn't coming from my aunt's. After lunch with my parents, Pasquale took me to the Cave where I washed as best I could. It wasn't as nice as showering at Gianni's but I made a decent fist of it and topped it off with a designer outfit paid for by the church safe. I looked the part and I knew it: and that gave me confidence, not that I needed it. While the rest of the gang watched a movie on the Cave's new VCR, I surveyed my tools.

Cocco had been true to his word. Every tool and device that he had acquired over more than 25 years in the locksmith trade was now mine. Some of these were still alien to me but, lined up next to all the many that I knew well, it made an impressive array of technology. Amongst all that beautiful kit, there was a particular instrument that I had seen my Granddad use but which I had not: a pocket-sized metal detector. I took it out, turned it on and tested it. When I ran it over the table, with a knife held underneath the wooden top, the light went from red to green.

Pasquale dropped me round the corner from Bulldog's villa. I strolled up the driveway to the 'Palace' and was greeted by Bulldog's wife, the 'Queen'. She welcomed me like one of the family, taking my hand and guiding me through the crowd. I looked longingly at the buffet table as we passed. Despite the wealth and beauty that surrounded me, for a hungry 13-year-old, this was where the real action was: stupendous food and fancy drinks served by impeccably dressed waiters. I retraced my steps to get stuck in as soon as it was polite. I had not felt this good in ages. I felt like a movie star. No one forced me to like it so much. I couldn't blame this on the wicked ways of the world. I was corrupted by my own greed.

As I chomped on my fifth crab and sun-dried tomato antipasto, Greta came to greet me joyously. Her crush on me was so obvious, I would have been embarrassed if I wasn't so cold-hearted. With her mother's blessing, she offered to show me around the house. As nasty as I had become by then, I still felt like the big bad wolf in 'Little Red Riding Hood' but there was no way I wasn't going to take advantage of an innocent kid for the sake of my mission. Of all the luck I've had so far, this was the best. I couldn't have just wandered around casing the joint with a portable metal detector. Call it beginner's luck but without several such lucky episodes at the beginning of my career, I, like any other would-be criminal, would've either given up or gone to jail. The reason I'm telling you my story at all is that, by a mixture of both good fortune and skill, I managed to get a long way before my first mishap.

The tour started in the gardens. At my subtle prompting we did a full 360-degree sweep of the house. Electronically activated gates opened onto the driveway, which led up to the front door. There was a pebbled path winding through the most beautiful garden I had ever seen. Gardeners must have been on call 24/7 to tend every blade of grass.

Inside the palace was a circular lounge the size of a basketball court, with beautiful paintings, a magnificent piano in the corner and Middle Eastern rugs gracing the immaculate marble floor. The kitchen was twice the size of my shack, equipped with all the modern cooking aids. Each room was spectacular in its own way, especially to someone who had been living in just 25 square metres for a year.

My grandfather was almost right when he said that people in life are divided into just two simple categories: 'He who shafts others and he who gets shafted; the bullies and the bullied.' I was dead set on creating a new category with me as the founding member: 'He who bullies the bullies and shafts those who have shafted others.'

Greta led me round the house like a professional tour guide in a real palace, explaining everything about each room as we went.

'She must have done this plenty of times,' I thought to myself. 'Maybe I will marry this young girl once she grows up and all of my problems will vanish like a shot!' Quickly followed by 'Never let emotions get in the way of rational thinking.' Anyway, I was already bored of the wall-to-wall splendour, even if she wasn't.

'And where is your father's study?' I asked brazenly.

'My father does not allow anyone in there.'

'Well, you and I are not just anyone, are we? And besides, I am a big fan of his work for our city. I want to see for myself where the great man works.'

'We'll have to go downstairs and ask him.'

'Your father is a great leader; he knows his mind and he will surely say no, so what's the point?' I said, smiling gently.

She looked shocked. I kept smiling.

'Either do it or don't but you don't always need permission, do you?' I said, as I stroked her hair. She blushed. She stared at me, then turned around and beckoned me to follow.

The study door was locked. She took a key from its hiding place under a flower bowl in the large hall. She must have spied her Dad hiding it there many times before. I got the feeling that even she had never been in there, which only boosted my curiosity.

'It will be our little secret,' she whispered with a cheeky smile.

'You bet.'

She opened the fabulous wood door, decorated with gold leaf and ancient designs, a work of art in itself, but nothing could have prepared me for what lay within.

I was no art expert; in fact, preferring the sciences I knew very little about it but I did have an eye for beauty and I was impressed. Most 13-year-old boys would've just pretended to be interested in the artwork while trying to kiss her but I really was interested in what was on the walls. My problem was not how to make a pass but how to keep her interested while I did some discreet browsing.

The room was stuffed with gaudy but expensive art. This was not the vulgar tat of a man with more money than taste; Bulldog had plenty of both. The desk looked like a French antique but in brand new condition. On one wall hung the art collection. On the entire opposite wall was a library of antique books. Behind the desk, magnificent French windows covered by luscious curtains topped it all off nicely. The study smelled like a flower shop and yet had an aura of power. I scanned the books. All the ancient tomes on politics and history were there: Cicero; Caesar; Machiavelli and many others whose efforts had turned politics into the fine art of deception and manipulation. These books were so rare that, if I had known a good fence, I could have stolen just a couple of them and still got rich. But I didn't know one so, instead, I turned my metal detector on.

While I spouted pseudo-intellectual nonsense about how marvellous the paintings were, I casually stroked them. It was a pathetic act worthy of Mr Bean. Even a 10-year-old would suss me out soon enough but I had little choice but to get on with it while she was still absorbed in telling me about the house: when they had moved in and how much time her father spent in that room, etc etc ... yawn ... yawn.

At first, my search was for the obvious hiding place, behind all the big paintings hung in pride of place in the centre of the main wall, but the light on the detector stayed stubbornly red. I had drawn a blank and was about to try the bookshelves on the other side of the room when I noticed one runty little painting which was hung so low it was almost touching the carpet. I bent down comically to examine it, peering at the illegible signature in the corner of the tiny painting.

'Oooh, is that a...? It can't be...' the light in my palm went green, 'Ah it is!'

'It is what?'

'It doesn't matter.'

'Doesn't it?'

'No, not now. Don't you think we should go back to the party?

Your mum will be worried about what you've done with me.'

'I don't need her permission either.'

'Too true,' I said absent-mindedly as I sauntered towards the door, cruelly ignoring her come-on. Inside I was jumping for joy.

As she relocked the study door after us, I said, 'That was marvellous. Thank you,' as if I had just kissed her.

Her father must've been a real art lover; he had chosen a spot for his safe where he could open it repeatedly without re-arranging any of the more spectacular works. The only drawback was that he had to get down on all fours to do it. I would soon have him begging on his knees too.

On the way to join the rest of the party in the garden I put my memory to work, mentally photographing every detail of the house. As we came down the stairs, I noticed a device flashing on the wall. I knew it was a motion detector for an alarm but I still asked Greta about it, just in case she could shed some light on it.

'My Dad sent all the way to Germany for it. It doesn't ring an alarm bell; it just calls directly to the security guards. They call us back and if we do not answer after five rings, the guards have to be here within a minute,' she proudly replied.

'How do you know so much about it?' I continued, eager to mine this golden seam.

'My Daddy keeps bragging about how much it costs and how effective it is. He wants to set up a business importing this thing and wants Mama to run it!'

As I stared at the motion detector high on the wall, I pondered how such a nice girl could have such a bad Dad. I carefully made a mental note of the manufacturer's logo proudly displayed on the bottom corner of the box before letting Greta lead me back into the garden.

The party was in full swing. I went straight to her mother.

'A beautiful and perfect house but it cannot hold a candle to such a beautiful hostess,' I said.

I nearly choked on my own cheesiness so I was surprised she didn't but, instead, she lapped it up, blushing like a teenager. Then she introduced me to some of her distinguished guests. As painful as it is for me to confess, I had a wonderful time engaged in spar-kling conversation, especially as I stuck to my specialist subjects: history, philosophy, oratory and mathematics. For the first time in the young life of the Prince I felt at home, surrounded by other royalty: the Prince-like people whose existence had hitherto been confined to my dreams. Instead of trying to beat them, I should consider joining them. Afterwards, I travelled home happy. It didn't last.

Pasquale picked me up afterwards at the agreed point, 400 metres away, at the agreed time. A serious riot had broken out in the shanty-town and we had to sleep in the Cave, as even he was worried about crossing the front line. At least he had thought to tell my Mum I was staying at Gianni's that evening so she had nothing to worry about. I, on the other hand, was worried to death about her. While I was proud of having a savvy partner, the thought of my family in danger brought me back to reality in an instant. The 'chip on my shoulder' that had gone missing at the party returned. I renewed my vows of vengeance.

As I travelled home from school the next day, the aftermath of the riot was clear to see but, to the observer who was unused to the normal state of the shanty-town, it probably seemed as if little had changed; there were just a few extra burnt-out cars and their embers were fresher.

That evening, after the usual homework session, I went back to the Cave for a meeting with the boys. It was time to get the plan up and running. The Spanish was respectfully hesitant and I, for once, was not 100 per cent confident. While it would qualify as a gesture of grand revenge, it certainly wasn't foolproof.

Bulldog lived in the best area of Naples. Its residents not only relied on the police but they also had a private security firm looking after their neighbourhood. The police would usually shout, 'Put your hands up!' But the private security guards would shoot first and ask questions later. Guess who owned this private army of guards? The Big Boss, the head of the Camorra looking after his interests as usual. The more I looked into it, the more this job seemed just too difficult. More research was needed.

When I was doing some telecoms study with my Dad one night, I came across the alarms section of a handbook. Bulldog's model was there. I casually asked my Dad if he had seen one installed before.

'I know it only by reputation. Not many people buy it. Probably because it costs 50 grand or something like that. Anyway, they say it's impregnable.'

You could have bought a nice house with that kind of money but that didn't stop Bulldog from getting the best. That was bad news. The good news was that whatever was in that safe would be worth stealing. The other good news was that my Dad had answered my question without hesitation. Clearly he had no suspicion of what I was up to.

I whispered, 'If it is man-made, it can be man-broken!' to myself.

Back at the Cave, I took stock of all my research. I mapped the layout of the house from memory as best I could. I had a copy of the council plans for the surrounding roads. According to the council, the street and houses on it were 12 years old. If the safe had been built at the same time as the house or before, then it wouldn't be a problem. That just left the alarm system and the people connected to it.

I knew roughly how the alarm worked. As for the people: I knew the security guards were not shot shy; I knew that the man I was about to upset would pursue me to the end. He would follow any clue I left, no matter how small, like a demon. I understood the impact it could have, not only on me and my boys, but also on my family. No wonder the Spanish was reluctant. Failure was not an option. My gut instinct was to stop – right now!

You should listen to your gut.

Then I thought about the shanty-town.

I jumped onto my desk, the better to address the gang, i.e. the two brothers.

'For the next three months, I will be doing homework!' I shouted as if it were the best news ever. It certainly confused the brothers. 'Yes boys. Three months. To do this job right will take time. In the meantime, I will have important assignments for each of you.'

They were still looking at me, only a little less confused.

'Are you with me?'

Comprehension dawned. Pasquale was the first to react. He put his hand out in the middle of the meeting.

'All for one!' he declared.

'And one for all!' the Spanish and I replied, adding our hands to his in a group handshake. A huddle cuddle is cheesy but effective so I joined in enthusiastically but in my head I was aloof. I saw this as just a primitive bonding exercise: necessary for my troops but it didn't fool me.

I was going to spend as long as it took studying everything I could about fifty grand's worth of German alarm systems and how they interacted with telephone networks. It had to be well explained somewhere in my Dad's books or how else could they be installed and later maintained?

As for my Dad, his exam was also three months away. This was a distraction I could have done without. I needed to focus on the Bulldog. So far, my Dad's progress was miserable. He was not going to pass at this rate. To add to the misery, he took out his frustration on my Mother with a succession of petty arguments that led to shouting matches. I would step up my efforts and coach him every night to pass his exam and, along the way, I would study alarm 'maintenance' so I could pass my own big test. Every night, for 90 days, I sat down with my Dad in our shack and we studied, hard. Unlike other fathers and sons, the traditional roles were reversed. We both knew it but we didn't talk about it, we just got on with it. First we would cover all the stuff he would need to know and then, when he was busy doing some practice questions, I would investigate the Bulldog's alarm system. It could have been a real bonding experience but it was the opposite. I never thought of him as the sharpest tool in the box but I had never imagined he would be quite so slow. *How could that man be my Dad?*

I grew to despise him beyond reason. So, the next time I was alone with my Mother, I dropped the big question:

'Am I adopted?' I asked as sweetly as I could.

'No, son, why do you ask?'

'Well, do you think I could have been swapped at the hospital?'

'No, I never let you out of my sight.'

'Is Dad my Dad?'

I got a slap for an answer. When my Mother slapped, it was hard across the ears. Upset with herself for losing her temper, she stormed off to her bed and turned on the TV. As she channel hopped frantically, punching the buttons on the remote, I had a flash of genius: a vision in my head. Triggered by my still ringing ears, I literally saw the frequencies flowing out of the remote and into the television. Proof, if any were needed, that fate had already decided my destiny.

'Plip – plip' is a familiar noise now because every car has central locking, but back then only expensive cars and important buildings, like Bulldog's villa, had remotely activated locks. They all worked the same way: the remote control transmits a certain frequency of infrared to the decoder on the door which receives it. The gate's mini-computer converts the signal into a digital (i.e. binary) code which, if correct, tells the lock to open, close or activate etc. If I could just find a way to record the frequencies being sent, I could copy the keys to anything: a big 'if' back then.

After some lengthy research, I found a German manufacturer who sold stuff through a surveillance/anti-surveillance shop in West Berlin: basically, a 'spy' shop. The kit they sold would satisfy the dreams of any geek. According to the catalogue, 'Qualified Security Consultants' could purchase a clunky black box that did just what I needed – receive an infrared signal, record it and re-transmit it. If you could get your hands on one then it was perfectly legal to own; what you did with it was your business. Twenty years later, every car thief had one. A few years after that, the car manufacturers started making the codes harder to break by changing the frequency every time you 'plipped'. Before that slap, I was an expert in locks and keys; soon after, I became an expert in decoding remote alarms.

He wasn't a genius but the IT Guy was a thoughtful man and he certainly wasn't one of the enemy. Actually, he was one of the nicest human beings you will ever meet: too nice. If you kicked him in the head, he'd be worried about your foot. Normally he would've called the police if he you told him about a scheme like mine but something had snapped inside him, and I don't mean his new stutter. He was broken: no longer afraid of dying because he felt dead already. What struck me most was his lack of bitterness towards society. He lost his wife and his baby because of the way the State mistreated the shanty-town but he never once expressed any anger or resentment – the feelings that were slowly strangling my soul. One day, I was talking to him and I just came out and told him about my mission. I'm not sure why; as I expected, he took it all at face value, nodding placidly. By the end of our chat, he had joined the gang. He had nothing to lose and nothing else to do. I don't know if I did it out of pity for him or to bring someone more intellectual in. He would certainly be useful for my research; he had the right kind of brain and lots of spare time. I felt ashamed to corrupt someone so innocent with my illegal plans but I went with my gut feeling. Apart from his mental abilities, emotionally he would bring some balance to the gang: the rest of us were so full of venom. The Spanish wasn't concerned that we would be corrupting him. Instead, he worried that 'Mr Nice Guy' wasn't cut out for such an evil mission and would be a liability: someone who would surely let us down under pressure.

'He needs an income to live on, to pay his daily expenses. I just feel he will be an important member of our gang', was the best I could muster to persuade them.

In the end, both brothers backed down just because I was the boss. I allocated our new recruit a wage of 1,500 euros a month plus a split from any jobs we pulled off. I'm not sure he was listening to that part; he cared more for belonging to a group than for the money. For once, it just felt right to follow my heart.

I had all the elements of a plan to burgle Bulldog ready in my head and I was confident it would work. I just needed to get the necessary tools.

First I needed to break into the master telephone connection box for Bulldog's house. To do that, I had to buy some very specialist equipment, again from a company in Germany. Like most specialist equipment, not just anyone could buy it; you had to be qualified. I bought a computer and a printer for the Cave. With it, we created some fake letterhead for a well-known telecoms company, a competitor of the one my Dad worked for. We sent the orders to Germany, with an imaginary branch office as the delivery address, which was actually the IT Guy's shack. They replied with an invoice demanding payment. Because we didn't have a bank account, the Spanish took a train ride north across Europe to pick it up and pay in cash. It would have looked pretty fishy: a young man, with a scar on his face, buying something for a major Italian telecoms company with cash but, luckily, the left hand didn't know what the right was doing. The order was already approved so the lowly clerk in the parts department just handed it over. Being German he probably didn't even pocket the cash!

I also needed to buy some instruments from Turin and this time the IT Guy and the Spanish went there to get them for me.

Having planned how to deal with the alarms and locks that stood in our way, the private security forces that guarded Bulldog's neighbourhood became my main concern. With a good decoy plan to distract them our robbery would be so much easier. For the decoy I planned to use a bomb: my specialty. However, the bomb itself couldn't be anything too specialist; it had to be the same sort of basic set-up that the Mafia commonly used so it couldn't be traced. Instead of mimicking a gas leak explosion, this time I had to successfully mimic a Mafia 'turf war' attack.

To create even a basic bomb, I needed some very specialised chemicals. To get those chemicals you had to register your name and address and, unless you checked out 100 per cent, the supplier would report you to the authorities. There was only a small chance of this happening in a city like ours but, as we were risking our family's lives as well as our own, I could not leave such an important factor to chance. So, how could I get the chemicals? Gianni's father was the only source I knew: he was indispensable. Since I couldn't recruit my headmaster, I would have to recruit his son. This was a problem in itself, as I really didn't like Gianni. I thought him weak and spoilt. You simply don't choose people you don't like to join your gang; it goes against human nature. In addition, he and his family represented the very system that I wanted to destroy. In short, he just wasn't one of us. The gang and I wrestled with this conundrum.

'Get over it! The mission is the only thing that matters,' I said, to end what was turning into a very heavy discussion – we had no other option.

Gianni, being Gianni, would always be the weakest link in any plan unfortunate enough to include him. But, having convinced ourselves to allow him on board, Pasquale and I now had to convince him to join us. Incredibly, though we would be risking our lives on this job, I was more uncomfortable trying to recruit Gianni than robbing Bulldog.

Over the following days, at the end of the homework sessions at Gianni's when I should have rushed home to help my Dad, I tried to get him to paint a mental picture of all those heroes and martyrs who had fought for a democratic world, racial equality and freedom of speech. Over the course of four days, I instigated in him the desire to be someone who makes a difference. Pasquale, present at most of my speeches, was very impressed by my persuasive power. It was working better on my streetwise friend than on the son of a wealthy headmaster, who was a proving a tougher nut to crack. Even though he scarcely realised it, he benefitted immensely from his social status. I hoped the comparison with the aristocrats who fought for the abolition of slavery was not so far-fetched.

Finally, when I thought he was ripe, I laid my cards on the table and told him straight about my plans, my gang and the Cave.

'Will you help us?' I asked.

I remained silent as he contemplated my outrageous gambit.

I hoped he felt like a young idealistic knight invited by King Arthur to join the Round Table, but maybe he just felt like crying to his mother.

'It will be my honour to serve such an important cause. I might be a lucky kid in these surroundings but I have always felt my mission lay elsewhere,' he replied, so softly he was almost sobbing.

He would have gone on but I was so annoyed with the buzzing of his lisp that I gave him a fearsome bear hug.

'Urgh,' was all he could say as his breath left him.

'Okay, okay, you are one of us!' I said with relief.

The line-up with which I planned to change the world was: me, the Prince, delusional but clever; the Spanish and Pasquale, the muscles with no brains; the IT Guy, banking and computing knowledge but no spirit; and finally Gianni, the ... well ... forget it! He brought next to nothing himself but he had access to his Dad's credit card and that was crucial.

To his credit, Gianni, who I considered the least of our team, pulled off the hardest task. He successfully used his Dad's credit card to order the chemicals we needed. His Dad was a regular at this supplier and they accepted his order over the phone. Moreover, he was ordering chemicals so regularly that he didn't pay attention to what arrived each day. Still, Gianni did a super job disguising his voice as his father's on the phone and then getting up early for a week and making sure he was the first to meet the postman at the door.

Pasquale ferried the canisters over to the Cave. When I had finished mixing them they were a good basic explosive and, importantly, could no longer be traced to the specific chemicals that 'Gianni's father' had 'ordered.'

Bulldog's last big speech before the elections was now only a few weeks away. He would be out that night, for sure, and for a few other events before that. As soon as we were ready, we would take the opportunity the run-up to the election gave us. It would be our 'D-Day' or, as I called it, Bulldog-Day.

In the meantime, I still had to pass my end-of-year exams. That wouldn't be too hard. Getting Pasquale through the school year would be harder. Getting my Dad through his telecoms exam would be the hardest, even for a genius like me, but do it I must as it was vital for the health and stability of my family. His confidence in passing the exam decreased daily. As it did, my Dad became more and more difficult to deal with. I did not care about him but I was concerned about him taking his frustration out on my

Mother while my impressionable little brother would be forced to absorb the tension in the air.

Gianni and Pasquale passed with the results I expected and I did so well that I was put forward to continue my studies at a special school for gifted children; but all I could think about was what was happening this week, not next year!

All the equipment for Bulldog-Day was ready in the Cave and the plan had been rehearsed many times over with the boys. I had so much on my plate that something was bound to go wrong, and that something was my Father – or my *Mother's husband* as I called him.

Whoever he was, he was not ready and he knew it. Worse, he was a nervous wreck who couldn't sleep: another handicap. The only sane conclusion was for me to take the test on his behalf. I tried to tell him this but he wouldn't listen. It seemed I would have to let him do it his way and fail. We would all suffer for it.

I hadn't given up on helping him but it would have to be behind his back. I decided to see what the opportunities were for me to cheat on his behalf. There were so many candidates for this particular exam that it was set using five different papers: a new one each day from Monday to Friday so that they could stagger the candidates. It took place in one of the university buildings in Naples. Before I could devise a plan, I needed to see how they managed it. My Dad was due to take his paper on the Wednesday so I had a chance to observe the sessions on Monday and Tuesday.

The exam room was more like an open plan office than the usual school exams I was used to. It had more windows than walls and more steel than cement, which gave me the opportunity to watch from outside. As I stood in the corridor watching, an attractive young female admin assistant approached me.

'Can I help you?'

'I'm just waiting for my uncle while he takes the test.'

It was only half a lie.

'Really?'

She didn't believe me.

'Yes,' I insisted.

Luckily, she just gave up. She could see I was a child and thought what harm could I do.

They had four hours, with no break, to answer 250 multiple choice questions and they were watched constantly by twelve supervisors. The employees had to sit down at precisely 8.45 a.m. Once the doors were shut, they admitted no late-comers. I observed a few late arrivals on the Monday morning who took badly to being rejected, responding with foul-mouthed insults. The supervisors had to call security to expel them. I guess word got around because only one poor soul was late on Tuesday. He cut a dejected figure as he walked out. It made me think of how my Dad would feel if he failed. His dejection would soon turn to anger and, with a temper like his, who knew what the consequences would be. Supposing a candidate arrived on time, he then had to produce his passport and a work badge. The supervisor would check them both, make sure he was the rightful owner and only then would he put the exam paper face down in front of him. They were very swift in distributing the papers but on the Monday the exam didn't start until 9.15 a.m. because of the commotion caused by the late arrivals.

They were constantly supervised. Even if they went to the toilet they were escorted. It was all looking a bit tricky until I spotted that the supervisors had some spare exam papers on their desk. That pile, or just one of its constituents, would be my target.

On Monday night at dinner my Dad was a shadow of the prick he usually was. He did not say a single word; too busy wallowing in his own despair even before he had taken the exam. If he failed several exams and then actually got fired, that would be the time for despair! He could already taste his failure rather than the food he was eating. I despised him for his defeatist attitude. I never gave up even when the odds were stacked against me.

My Mum was the important one in all this. The loyal wife suffered along with her husband throughout this difficult period. I had to put a stop to her pain.

The next day, my Dad took the day off and did some frantic last-minute revision: the typical last resort of the no-hoper. I went to speak to him and found him with his thick head buried in those equally thick books. I wanted to kick some sense into that same head but I knew such an attitude was bound to fail.

'Dad, I have the solution to your problem. Tomorrow, I will also do the exam. I will give you the answers. You will pass. It's going to be OK,' I said charmingly, as if I was talking to someone at church as part of my altar boy act.

He looked at me, dumbstruck.

'Tomorrow morning just before it starts, there will be some rowdy visitors to the hall who will cause a disturbance, a decoy, while they steal a copy of your exam paper for me to complete. Do not be distracted. Simply do nothing – do not fill in your paper, not even your name, as we don't want two papers with your name on them getting into the system.'

'How will I get the answers from you?'

'Trust me when I give you my word that I will and before it is too late. Trust me.'

He looked sceptically at me.

'Don't worry, I can do that test in half the time.'

'Don't worry? Worrying is all I've been doing!'

He couldn't control his temper at the best of times. He looked like he was about to hit me when a timid knock on our aluminium door interrupted his anger. Right on schedule, it was the IT Guy. I had invited him as I figured he alone could be sure to calm my Dad. The bond the pair had established during the days at the hospital was special. Upon seeing the IT Guy, even my Dad realised life could have been a lot worse.

'I a-am h-here to-to h-help, p-p-please,' the IT Guy said politely as he sat down.

As the IT Guy's voice stuttered into life, my Dad's stubborn streak finally relented.

The next morning, I was ready for action: I had a copy of my Dad's passport, his work badge number and a black pen, the only ink colour allowed for the test. All I needed was the exam paper. At 7 a.m., my Father, the Spanish and I all got in the IT Guy's car to go and get one!

'God, please give me a miracle,' my Dad prayed out loud nervously as we drove.

'The miracle is sitting right behind you, dickhead!' I felt like shouting at him from the back seat.

At 8:45 a.m., my Dad took his seat in the hall. His denim jacket had only the last button done up. It billowed open and would allow anyone to shove in an exam paper if they came within reach.

At 8:52 a.m., the Spanish and the IT Guy barged into the session, claiming to be late arrivals. The IT Guy stood directly behind the Spanish so that they all focused on the roughneck. The Spanish then kicked off like a spectacular firework. Bang! Unlike all the other late-comers who slowly got angry as the full impact of being late dawned on them, by which time the security guards were on the scene, the Spanish went totally ballistic at the first mention of refusal. The dozen supervisors and the invigilator were caught by surprise. They were not trained to deal with this and were not 'up' for it either. The Spanish didn't need any training to play his role to perfection. He kicked over tables and chairs and ran amok screaming about what he would do to their families. It took all 13 of the supervisors just to try to corral this wild stallion; they had no chance of holding him down so the best they could do was to perpetually chase him round the room lest his berserk antics turned into a one-man riot. Meanwhile, the IT Guy calmly picked up a sheaf of five spare exam papers. As soon as the security guards arrived, the IT Guy winked at the Spanish who immediately calmed down. They both agreed to leave, although the Spanish threw back a few final screamed obscenities to keep up the pretence.

I watched it unfold like a silent movie through the big glass windows, then swiftly made my way back to the planned rendezvous at the car. The pair arrived seconds later smiling broadly under the influence of a heady mix of adrenaline and relief. I didn't want to break it to them but this was just the easy bit.

I went to the university library for the next stage: also easy. In order to avoid discrepancies, I filled in the whole paper including my Dad's details, personal information and signature, then

139

smashed the test in less than two hours.

Then for the hard part: to get it back to my Dad before he had a heart attack. The completed paper was stowed inside my blazer as I strode down the corridor towards the exam room. Looking good meant feeling good but that day my distinctive looks worked against me. The female admin assistant outside the hall recognised me.

'Back again? Can I help you?' she said jokingly.

'It's my Dad's turn in the torture room today but I need to get some keys from him,' I replied, trying to stay jokey while my palms went from dry to sweaty in a flash.

'Tell me who it is and I'll get them from him, you wait here.'

She didn't believe me before and she didn't believe me now, so she called my bluff very effectively. It was too late, far too late for any more lies. I told her my Dad's name dolefully and the do-gooder went off on her errand while I called her a few choice names under my breath. It was not her fault. It was my fault for not disguising myself better between my visits.

This was not just an unexpected glitch; this was dismal failure, albeit flattering in the sense that she had remembered me. My vanity wanted me to be noticed but I learnt the hard way the importance of being invisible on the job. I was screwed: I had just over an hour to deliver the paper to my Dad and I had blown my cover.

When she returned, she made a great show of kindness while she gave me those keys and then insisted on escorting me out of the building. With no contingency plan, I had to meekly comply. My mind was racing but to her I must have appeared to be just upset.

'Well, at least you get to go home tonight,' she said gamely.

'Aren't you going home?' I responded, playing along almost on autopilot.

'No. We'll be in here all night marking the tests.'

Suddenly I was alert and listening. She had given me a glint of hope and, to me, it sparkled like gold dust.

'What time do you finish?'

'Are you asking me out?'

I stared hard at her.

'No, I just want to know what time you finish!' I said, adding, 'It's a simple question. Answer it, bitch!' But only in my head.

'11 p.m. even if we haven't finished.'

This was more than gold dust...

'Do you expect to finish by then?'

'No. We'll carry on tomorrow.'

It was the mother lode.

'Great, would you like me to ask you out?'

'No. You're half my age!'

'OK, ciao!' I blew her a kiss.

I was ecstatic as I walked out into the street. Looking back, I think that maybe she was hoping I really would ask her out but, although I looked a lot older than my age, I was still too young to understand those kinds of 'no means yes' games girls like to play. To my young mind she just seemed confused. The cause of my excitement was not the flirtation but the information gained. Now I knew that the exam papers were kept in that building overnight for the following morning to be marked. I had from 11:15 p.m. until early morning to find them and add my Father's paper. Unfortunately, there were so many offices dotted around that building, all under lock and key, that it would have taken me all night or even all week to search them all.

By now, my Dad must've pulled all his hair out as I had told him not to write anything on the papers at all, not even his name. When he came back home that night he would want to kill me but I was only concerned with how to fix the exam, not how to fix my Dad's angry mood so, instead of going home to soothe him, I went to the Cave to think.

I had it in mind just to blow up the building that night and annul the whole exam. It was a big building, much larger than Carlo's restaurant, so I would need every last shred of the explosives Gianni and I had carefully accumulated: vital ingredients for the plan I had been hatching for robbing Bulldog. Using so many explosives just to get my Father off the hook was like using a sledgehammer to crack a nut and Bulldog-Day was only three days away so there was not enough time to replace them.

I didn't want to cross my own gang but I didn't feel like I had a choice. After all, these guys were really just strangers who I was paying to help me. They were not as clever as me and, in my opinion, I was just carrying them whereas my Dad was family. Blood may well be thicker than water but it still didn't feel right. Taking out Bulldog was 100 per cent gang business. I did not think it moral to use the explosives allocated for our mission for personal reasons. It would compromise my relationship with people who, so far, had proven very loyal to me.

I paid a visit to the local council as I continued to ponder my dilemma. I requested the blueprints for the university hall and several other buildings, posing as an engineering student just in case the clerk was checking – as if! They never checked anything there, even when they were supposed to. Living in a city full of people who were all corrupt, incompetent or lazy had its advantages.

Anyway, now I had the blueprints. Then I did what I always do when in a tight situation: batten down the hatches to study the data and solve it on my own. When the chips were down I didn't like to rely on other people with all the risk that entailed. Deep down, I don't think I truly trusted the gang. I was the Prince and, despite their loyalty, their skills were not in my league. I conveniently ignored the fact that it was me who had just messed up, not them. So, despite the fact I had a whole team waiting and wanting to help me, I kept quiet about my dilemma and went into 'lone wolf' mode.

I packed a rucksack full of everything I would need, including a selection of lock-picking tools and the all-important completed exam paper; then I went back to the university. Even though it only had one storey, it was a very large building. As darkness fell, it looked even more intimidating than it did during the day. The doors to the public closed at 6 p.m. The last students and staff were just leaving as I slipped in through the main doors at 5:55!

I found the cleaner's cupboard, which I had earmarked on the blueprint as my hideout, easily. Its door was around the corner of an L-shaped corridor, allowing me to take my time picking the lock without a high risk of being seen. Safely hidden inside, I used my torch to study the blueprints once again. There were over 100 offices around the edge of the building. Any one of them could have been where the exam papers were stored overnight. My plan was to come out at 11:15 p.m., when the building would be empty, and search room by room. I had time on my hands so I memorised the blueprint: there were 107 rooms that I had to break into, check their contents for signs of exam papers or marking activity, and then lock up again. At 2.5 minutes per room, it would take four hours to do the whole place. With an average amount of luck, I would only have to check half of them before I hit pay dirt. With terrible luck, I wouldn't find it until the 107th room, in which case timing would be very tight. By 8:30 p.m. I was as prepared as I ever would be so I tried to hunker down but sleep evaded me.

It was excruciating waiting for 11:15 p.m. but it was even worse when I allowed my mind to stray and think about my Dad. He was the elephant in the room and it was a very small room. I could imagine him in vivid detail fretting as the minutes ticked down at the end of the exam, knowing he had been let down by his son. In my rush to get back to the university and solve this without sharing it with the gang, I had forgotten to tell Pasquale or the IT Guy to get in touch with him and put his mind at ease. I was doing all this to help him and my family but in the short term I had surely made all their lives worse. I shuddered at my premonition in which I came home to find my Mother and brother beaten to death by my Father who had gone rogue. When I got beyond the fear of him, I actually felt sorry for him. How did he feel after handing in a blank paper, not knowing how it would end? All he would have felt is total and utter humiliation: not only because he knew he wasn't clever enough to do the test but because his son, if that's what I was, had let him down when it mattered most. It is easy to see with hindsight how badly I had lost sight of my real goal; instead of doing the best for my family, it had become purely about my ego. I just couldn't accept my own failure: that I was not the all-powerful Prince but a human being. In life, it is better to be honourable than successful but I was too young to know that.

I did know that right now the dark, hard and cramped janitor's cupboard was vastly more comfortable than going home to face my Dad.

Finally, 11:15 p.m. came and my torture ended. Aided by the torch, I started my task and that took my mind away from my worries. The first few locks were easy and the rooms were empty. Whenever a lock was sticky and took more than 60 seconds to pick, it triggered an instant stab of regret that I was having to do this at all.

By 3 a.m. I was hungry, thirsty and tired. I had been going for nearly four hours and I had only done 74 rooms. Not one of them was the treasure trove of exam papers, waiting for me to slip my Dad's perfect paper into the pile. I figured I needed one more hour.

By 4 a.m. I had checked all 107 rooms. Somewhere along the way I had opened the right room but failed to recognise it. To go back and check again more thoroughly would take too long. In my rush I had screwed up, again. What were the exam markers going to do? Leave all the papers out with a big sign saying 'Insert false papers here'? No; they would have locked them in a filing cabinet. I hadn't had time to open every locked cabinet I had encountered.

Now it was too late. It was time for Plan B. Plan B was for desperate fools. Plan B only existed because I felt this task was so important for my family's health that it was worth going beyond reason. I knew my loyalty should be to the gang but I was scared of my Dad and, in particular, what would happen to our family if he failed. I steeled myself against my own gut instinct and opened my rucksack. From it I took out four packs of explosive. It made me nauseous: knowing I was doing the wrong thing by the gang and about to destroy a perfectly good public building. I couldn't help myself; I was chained to my destiny like an out of control train that can only go where the track leads it. At some point the next morning, a worker or a student would arrive in the building. This being lazy Naples, I figured 5 a.m. was plenty safe so I had 30 minutes to set the charges and 30 minutes to escape. The exam hall and its surrounding offices had to be dust by 5 a.m.

Currently, it was only detached from the main university building. This meant it had its own water supply but it had no gas pipes so this time I needed all the civil engineering expertise I could muster. I would put the four charges, each with its own detonator, in each corner of the building so it would come down evenly. As the building was flat and long, about 55 by 35 metres, the easiest way to wire it up was to place the timer in the centre of the building with wires out to each of the detonators and explosive pairs. The exact centre of the building was in the middle of the big exam hall. I rolled some wire out to each corner, placed the explosives and then marched back to the central hall to do it again. Finally, I found myself in the centre of the hall, hunched over the wires and a clock timer. It was a nightmare getting the wires laid without getting them tangled and even then it looked more like a spider's web than a professional bomb. I was still confident I would pull it off. I was about to set the timer for a 30-minute delay and then flee when I heard a door clang and what sounded like a muffled footstep. What or who was it? Could it really be the janitor starting work at 4:28 a.m.? If it was, then he must be dodgy: here to steal a bulk load of toilet rolls rather than to do any legit work. Undone by a toilet roll thief – just my luck!

Or maybe it was another would-be exam cheat. Either way, I wasn't going to hang around and get caught. If I didn't blow up the building this would go down as my first proper failure but getting caught in there with a load of explosives would be an even bigger failure: one on a scale so bad, I couldn't comprehend it.

I did what I had to do. I turned out my torch immediately, then reached out in the dark and grabbed my rucksack, which by now only contained locksmith tools and a useless exam paper. I wanted to take the timer with me too; it was the most valuable part of the bomb-making kit and it was right there for me to salvage if I just disconnected it from its web of wires. On the other hand, I hadn't given up on my mission yet. If this sound proved to be a false alarm then leaving it connected meant I could easily come back and set it. Abort or pause? That was all I could think about as I crept to the side of the room, inching past exam desks in the dark. Who was I kidding? There was no way I could continue the mission now. Even with only a 1 per cent chance of someone else being in the building, I didn't have the guts to 'push the button' anymore. I couldn't take the risk that I would end up with blood on my hands: even the blood of a bent janitor. Time to make a tactical retreat. I quickly went through a mental list of the evidence I would be leaving behind. I was wearing latex gloves so no fingerprints but there would be four loads of pre-mixed explosive and some basic detonators: not stuff you could buy in the supermarket but not unique to me either and, in mixed form, unrecognisable from what 'Gianni's father' had purchased. That just left the timing clock that I had stolen from Gianni's father's lab. The headmaster could've touched it himself in the past. Had I wiped it? Yes but wiping is not an exact science; his fingerprints could still be on it. If he had registered his purchase, then the police might contact him as part of their routine inquiries. Then he would notice some of his timers were missing and the fingerprints would confirm it. Once he had bought them off I would be the prime suspect. I couldn't leave the bloody timer.

I walked back into the middle of the room, feeling my way along the edge of the exam desks. I tripped on one of my wires and pushed a table hard enough that its folding legs collapsed. It slammed down. I froze.

Hearing nothing more, I moved on. I found the timer, quickly unscrewed the wires and stowed it in my sack. I retraced my steps back to the door at the perimeter of the grand hall and then out into the corridor. I inched along the walls of the corridor until I found a fire exit. I was sure it would be alarmed. I had a choice: exit here and risk setting it off or go all the way round to a main door, have to pick the lock to get out and risk meeting the janitor heaving off his cargo of toilet rolls. I breathed a sigh of resignation mixed with relief and then pushed the door open and strode out into the street, which was just as empty and quiet as inside. I was already doubting myself. Since that first noise I hadn't seen or heard anybody. Maybe I had imagined it. Spooked by a non-existent janitor: that really would have been pathetic. It was too late; tonight's mission was aborted and the vital explosives sacrificed.

It was too early to go to school and I certainly didn't want to go home so I walked across town for 30 minutes to kill time until the buses started. I caught the first bus towards Vesuvius and walked the last kilometre to the Cave. Luckily, the Cave was empty, as I really didn't feel like being social. I just wanted to curl up in a ball and feel sorry for myself.

To put myself out of my misery, I tried to fall asleep on the sofa. I lay there remembering the episode in the church when I had felt defeated and dejected. I remembered promising never to feel down again, which gave me the willpower to push back against the tide of feelings of failure.

I woke up at 3 p.m. Gianni, the IT Guy and the two brothers were ribbing each other and laughing. I felt embarrassed that I was about to ruin such a pleasant atmosphere.

'Guys, we have a problem. Actually, I have a problem. A personal problem which now affects us all,' I shouted.

Although they hadn't seen me wake up they knew full well I was there on the sofa and yet they still jumped like they'd seen a ghost.

'I have cheated you. I took all our explosives that were for the Bulldog job and instead used them to try to help my Dad. He really needed my help or our family would collapse. If he fails his exam, he'll take it out on my Mum. And me. He'll beat us both.'

'Oh yeah? We didn't hear no bang,' Pasquale said.

'It gets worse. I took the explosives to blow up the building and annul his exam but I had to abort. The janitor arrived early. So, I haven't helped my Dad and I had to leave the explosives behind. I have lost them all with only three days to go.'

I had never been so honest in my life with anybody, let alone guys like these who I considered beneath me.

'I promise we will find another way.'

The boys looked at each other in clear discomfort. I had put them 'on the spot'.

'Family comes first. Do "da plan" later,' Pasquale said.

'I acted without permission; will you forgive me?'

Pasquale looked at the others, then at me. He could see my deep distress.

'You done what you had to do, Prince. One of us in a mess, all of us in a mess!'

'Wweee will worry abbbout tttthe Bbbbulldog-day later. Wwe are wwwith you, Bbbboss!' the IT Guy said, his stutter getting worse with the emotion.

'All for one and one for all!' shouted the Spanish.

They huddled together and put their hands one on top of the other, then waited for me to join in. I did.

'All for one and one for all!' Gianni, IT Guy, Pasquale, the Spanish and I shouted with gusto.

It is many teenagers' dream to have their own gang and now I had one. I was blown away, overcome with emotion. That group handshake bonding ritual, which I had previously dismissed, now meant something tangible.

'Won't the police find the explosives?' IT Guy asked.

The IT Guy certainly knew how to bring someone back down to earth but, this time, he was right: there were some details worth worrying about.

'Yes, but I mixed it so it won't match anything Gianni supplied for us. They won't be able to trace it to anybody in particular – it will just look like the Mafia.'

'Or the Red Brigades!' Gianni blurted out, like he was going to wet his pants at the thought. In his dreams, Gianni was now a genuine revolutionary. I was about to shout him down by explaining that Naples University was a Communist hotbed already so it wouldn't exactly be a priority for a hit from the Red Brigade. Then I remembered that I had recruited him on the basis that the gang were revolutionaries, not greedy criminals.

So I just said 'Yeah, or the Red Brigade' and let him enjoy his thrill.

I understood how lucky I was to have those guys with me and how close we had become. There had never been an argument about money, no dispute of my command and they were always ready to rescue and protect me if needed. I had judged them too quickly. If we were to be a team, we each had to be different. I couldn't expect them to provide the brains. That was my job. If anything, they would have been entitled to hold this episode against me down the line if anything went wrong but they never did.

I slept at the Cave that night. I told myself it was because I was very tired but really it was because I was too scared to face my Dad. Like a coward, I got the IT Guy to pass a message to my Mother that I was all right. On Friday, I went to school where I spent the day worried I would be suddenly arrested. I kept thinking I had made a mistake: left a fingerprint on the wrapper of the explosives from before I donned gloves or some other clue I hadn't remembered. That uncertainty scared me but when I thought about my Dad, I got really scared. Whichever way I looked at it, he would be mad as a snake when I saw him. At least his paper was blank; with luck, he would be put down as a 'no-show' rather a 'fail', which meant I might yet get a chance to help him if I wasn't in jail.

No news was good news. The TV was most definitely not awash with reports of unexploded bombs. The Spanish told me that he hadn't heard any rumours of an attempted attack on the university. We will never know for sure but the best explanation was that 'my' janitor did exist and was so dodgy that he sold the explosives he found to the Mafia, rather than telling the police. Only in Naples!

On Friday evening, buoyed by the lack of bad news, I came home to face the music. My Dad was there. So sure was I that he would hit me that just seeing him made me flinch. I must've jumped back two feet. He just stared at me. Then he hit me.

I didn't like him. I don't think he liked me. I had begun really not to like him before he hit me but this punch certainly wasn't going to help us get on. That I felt guilty for letting him down softened the blow, like I deserved it. In typical fashion, I repressed all the feelings of humiliation that would normally accompany such an act. In fact, I felt more pain from my own sense of failure than from 'that punch'. Life at home hadn't been fun and carefree for a long time but now I knew it would never be so again. I was worried for my Mum. The sooner I got my whole family out of the shanty-town, the better.

Ironically, it felt like I had lost a father but gained a whole new family: The Gang.

It was a warm and sticky morning when I woke up in my make-shift bed at the Cave. I felt uncomfortable and dirty. Even though it was only 8 a.m., the air conditioning unit was already on maximum, and struggling, but at least the Cave had air con, unlike my 'home' in the shanty-town. Since being hit by my Dad, what I called 'the Punch', I had more or less moved out to the Cave but that day I didn't feel at home there either.

I thought a good shower might help, so I decided to travel all the way down the mountain into Naples to Gianni's to get one. But the problem was not the dirt on my skin – the fear of failure was getting to me as Bulldog-Day loomed.

I had a clear plan and I was about to share it with the boys. I had a very short window to get it done and no room for error: Bulldog would be out campaigning every night this week but, once the polls opened on Friday, it was quite likely he would suddenly stay in every night to rest. Politicians, especially the corrupt ones, are at their most vulnerable just before an election. This week was my chance to act.

Moreover, Bulldog's ghastly features (massive head, ludicrous comb-over, thick rimmed glasses and even thicker neck) had been a constant companion in my nightmares for the last four months. I couldn't wait any longer; we had to be ready to go into his house on Sunday. I wasn't a common thief: I was inspired by the evidence I had found in the church safe and was hoping there would be more like that in his safe. In short, I didn't just want to steal his money: I wanted to destroy him. My obsession had reached fever pitch and would drive me insane if I didn't act. We would do it on Sunday.

Bulldog lived, along with most of Naples' rich and powerful citizens, in an exclusive neighbourhood where the picturesque roads intertwined with plenty of blind alleys, cul-de-sacs and crescents, connected to the rest of Naples by just two roads. Even though they were all public roads, the two routes in and out each had a guarded checkpoint. The zealous security guards scrutinised everyone who came in. If you looked suspicious, then you would be watched like a hawk until you left. On a normal day, you had two guards on each entrance plus many more on patrol within, communicating via walkie-talkie. This week, with many of the residents attending campaign parties, they would surely lay on extra guards to protect the empty properties. I had planned a decoy bomb to distract the guards but I had wasted my 'firepower' for that option.

Only one robbery had taken place in Bulldog's area in over nine years. The two thieves involved both got themselves shot and then arrested: one died of his wounds; the other was beaten to death in prison while awaiting trial. Such a low level of burglary was unheard of anywhere in Italy, especially in Naples where stealing was more popular than football.

How do you get five guys, of different shapes and sizes, riding two mopeds and a motorbike, through the checkpoint without being noticed? I wrestled with this seemingly impossible problem all the way to Gianni's. To make my day worse, when I arrived at Gianni's his mother was cleaning the guest room, the one I used to shower.

'You can use my room if you want,' Gianni said.

I was so deep in thought that I didn't hear him but Pasquale did.

'Hey, do you want to use my room?' Gianni tried again.

Still no response.

Pasquale's big hands grabbed my shoulders and shook me.

'Wake up, Boss! What's your problem?'

'What?' I said, finally waking from my daydream.

'Why don't you use my room to shower and change?'

'Oh, okay,' I replied, still in a daze.

Just as my mind finally tired of worrying about getting past the guards, I started wondering about something else: I had been going to that house for more than 10 months but I had never been in Gianni's room. Why was that?

Gianni and Pasquale went off to the living room to play computer games, leaving me alone with a fresh towel. To repay his kindness (and satisfy my burning curiosity), I crudely and cruelly invaded his privacy. In my extensive snooping round his bedroom, I found several very small mannequin dolls. Such were their precision you could not call them toys. Each had a different hair style and make up; each dressed for a different glamorous occasion; many wore miniature jewels.

My conclusion: Gianni was also dressed up; a girl dressed up as a boy! Of course he wasn't really – he was gay. Looking back, it's surprising I hadn't worked it out before. The term gaydar hadn't even been invented yet but clearly mine was no good. Then again, I was only 13. What was not surprising was that he had kept his sexual orientation a secret...

Gianni's father was ex-military, old-fashioned, a headmaster and a male chauvinist: he never let his wife express an opinion except to agree with him. So, Gianni and I had one thing in common: we both differed vastly from our fathers.

'His apple has fallen even further from the tree than mine. Actually, so far away that the tree was no longer visible from the apple!' I giggled to myself.

I laughed about it like any schoolboy would have back then but then I asked myself some serious questions. Why can't he express his real nature? Why does he have to conform to someone else's idea of normal? Why can't he be free to be whoever he wants to be?

One by one, those hard questions pounded at my young heart. So, after all, Gianni was one of us. Even he, born into money and a life made easy by his social status, was effectively being bullied by society into being something that he was not.

Despite my initial amusement, I had the good sense not to spread the joke around. That would not have done my mission any favours. The other boys would have been merciless. In Naples at that time, coming out was not an option. It was rumoured that a local father had killed his own son rather than face the shame of his son's homosexuality becoming public. The mere fact that this rumour existed shows how most people felt. I told myself that I was open-minded. If people were nice and respectful, then they could come in every colour and shape and I would accept them. Still, I couldn't help giggling about it once more. As I showered, I kept picturing the horror on his father's face if he were to find out. Despite my massive IQ, I still had a childish sense of humour.

As Bill Conti's *Rocky* theme tune played in my head, my shower revitalised me. Stallone's famous movie had become an instant hit at the Cave. We had worn the videotape out in two weeks from watching it so much. The underdog 'bum' lived in a rundown ware-house not dissimilar to our ramshackle Cave. And he took his fight all the way to the Heavyweight Championship of the World. We felt it wasn't just about boxing: it was about people like us, inspired to fight all the way against the odds. The Cave was already a shrine to Rocky: film posters, old boxing gloves (not Rocky's!) and even a dented trophy were glorious decorations on our windowless walls.

That theme tune had an incredible effect, charging me up from head to toe. The electricity affected my brain the most, generating vision after vision in my mind's eye. Like a super computer left to solve a problem on its own, all I had to do was to wait for my brain to spit out the answer. And then it came. Suddenly I knew how the gang would get past the guards.

I got dressed and rushed downstairs to find Gianni and Pasquale.

'All of us. To the Cave!' I screamed.

Pasquale had to make two trips: one for me and the other for Gianni. Then, he had to fetch the others. Nowadays, one Facebook post, 'meet at the Cave in 1 hour,' would be enough but back then we had no choice but to do it the hard way.

When Pasquale went to fetch the IT Guy and the Spanish, he left Gianni and me alone.

'I know about your hobby,' I said.

He looked shocked.

'Yes, sorry, I snooped in your room. Look, I don't know what sexual inclination you have but you are still a good friend and the gang needs you, now more than ever, okay?' I said.

He nodded tentatively.

'But it would be better to keep this a secret between us. Don't be ashamed. In fact, your skills are going to be vital in the next operation.'

By using the words 'your skills' I had contrived an outrageous euphemism for his sexuality but, for now, I just wanted to make my life easy by avoiding the issue and the conflict it could bring. To convince him, I spelt out in detail his role in our upcoming operation: how he could finally become a vital member of the team in his own right and not just a proxy for his father's credit card.

'No problem, darling!' he said in an unmistakably camp tone.

'But we can only be friends. Nothing else. You know what I mean?' I said, hoping to end the topic.

'I know but I will be hoping you change your mind' he replied with a wink.

'Yeurrgggh!' I thought.

To prepare for that famous Sunday, the day I called 'Bulldog-Day', I had to:

Steal a big expensive car;

Find out what the code was for the alarm at Bulldog's house;

Programme a remote control to open Bulldog's electronic gates;

And buy some climbing gear – hooks and ropes.

Most important was decoding Bulldog's unbreakable alarm. I studied this particular alarm over and over and only spotted one weakness. Every time you turned the alarm on, you had to type in the code on the mini-keypad. So far, so normal but, because this alarm was permanently connected to the security firm, the codes being typed in not only went into the alarm but echoed down the phone line too.

I borrowed my Dad's overall, badge and tools. The Spanish stole a white van. We printed some big letters in the same style as the telecoms company and stuck them to its flanks.

The IT Guy, playing the role of my supervisor, drove the van and me to Bulldog's area. In those days, all the landlines went through a local junction box before joining the national phone network. As we cruised around, aided by the plans I had borrowed from City

Hall, we spotted the box that served Bulldog's villa and pulled over.

Unless someone looked very closely, we would appear to be a legitimate maintenance team. As I knelt to open the box, I reflected that it would be very bad luck if a real telecoms van were to show up at this moment. Those thoughts vanished as I was confronted by the web of wires inside. The mass of lines were organised into numbered bunches. I had found Bulldog's phone number at the church, despite the polie raid, so I quickly identified his home phone line. The dedicated line for his alarm would be in the same bunch of wires. Unless all his neighbours had alarms like his, the rest of the lines in the bunch would be normal home phone lines. The odd one out would be Bulldog's alarm. I hooked my Dad's equipment up and, one by one, called each phone line in the bunch. If a human answered I quickly hung up without even saying 'wrong number', marked the wire with chalk and moved to the next line in the bunch. If it rang like a normal phone or was engaged then I also moved on but didn't chalk it up, as it was still a 'maybe'. If it answered with a mechanical beep or silence then I stopped calling. Then I waited a minute. The IT Guy was on 'lookout' with binoculars in our van. If he saw a security van on the move at faster than the usual patrol speed then it meant one of three things: a real burglary was taking place nearby (as I explained before this was highly unlikely); they were coming to get us (in which case we were in big trouble); or, the third option, I had triggered the alarm and the security guards were responding within 60 seconds just as Greta had claimed they would. After I'd 'done' nearly half the lines in the bunch, I got what I thought might be a 'hit' and gave a thumbs up to the IT Guy. He raised his binoculars to his eyes and scanned the roads around us.

'Vehicle approaching', he called down to me.

I jumped up to join him in the cab.

As the van approached you did not need binoculars to see it so I calmly prised the binoculars from his tight grasp.

'Get ready for a fast getaway,' I said.

The IT Guy flashed a worried look at me.

'Don't worry, I'm confident they're not here for us,' I added.

He didn't look consoled.

The van sped past, its gruesome occupants uninterested in us. I, of course, was now very interested in them. I followed them with the binoculars as their van wound its way up the hill and into the drive of a big villa: one which I instantly recognised. It was Bulldog's. I jumped down from the van and connected my decoder to the freshly identified 'alarm line'. The trap was set so we left.

The next day we all had different jobs to do:

The Spanish had to find at least three expensive cars and secretly stick an infrasound receiver underneath each of them. I decided on three rather than one to hedge my bets, as I needed the owner of at least one of these cars to turn his alarm and central locking on and off via remote control sometime in the next 12 hours. Once the owner plipped the alarm, the receiver would register the signal and, after a little work on my part, I would literally have the keys to their car.

Pasquale had to go 35 miles by scooter to buy some specialist climbing gear.

Gianni had to turn me into a woman. He prepared a dress, a wig, some balloons for breasts. I didn't like being the one who had to cross dress but, due to my hairless face and clean features, I was the best candidate and it was my fault we were doing it this way in the first place, having lost the explosive intended for the original decoy plan.

Later that afternoon, Gianni, the least likely of us to stand out, had to walk past Bulldog's house and place an infrasound receiver device on the electronic gates. The device was the same as the ones installed underneath the cars. When Bulldog opened the gates via his remote control, it would register its signal and, again after a bit of work, I would have the 'key' to his gate.

The next day, the Spanish picked up the receivers from under the cars. Gianni did the same for the one by the gates. The IT Guy and I picked up the decoder from the phone junction box. It had kept track of all the traffic on that line, which turned out to be just the same two codes repeated in alternating order. I was expecting just one code but then I realised the 'ON' – activate code and the 'OFF' – deactivate code weren't necessarily the same. Most people would set them to be the same for an easy life, but Bulldog wasn't most people. Either way, I didn't know which was which. I was annoyed that I hadn't anticipated this. As I wrote down the codes, I remembered that when I watched the security van visit them for the false alarm, I had seen three cars parked in front of the garage in the drive of the villa. If I was sure of this memory, then I could be 99.9 per cent certain that someone was in the house when I first attached the decoder, which meant the alarm was off when I first tapped the line. Which meant the first code in my recorded sequence would be the 'ON' code. I would use the second code to turn the alarm off when we broke in.

We stripped the old telecoms logos off the van. The Spanish then parked it back where he stole it, except he moved it a few hundred yards so that, when it was found, the police would think that the owner had drunkenly forgotten where he'd parked it.

After packing a full day's work into just a morning, we met up back at the Cave. From there, it took me another afternoon of work to break the algorithms and to learn the frequencies for the three cars and the gate. Now I had the code to Bulldog's alarm, the remote control signal for his gates and the keys to our new car.

When the Spanish, Pasquale and I went to collect one of the cars, all three of us had to perch on Pasquale's tiny moped. For this reason, we chose the nearest car of the three.

The remote 'plipped' and the little red alarm light went off but the doors didn't open. I had incompletely decoded the frequencies. It seemed that this one needed two signals, one to 'do' the alarm and one to 'do' the central locking.

We drove to the next nearest car. The owner had moved his car from the street onto his drive since the Spanish had tagged it. We 'plipped' the alarm and the doors unlocked themselves with a click but then we aborted. We decided it was parked too close to the house for comfort, since the Spanish still had to hotwire it.

The third car was parked in a safer position (for us not the owner). The 'plip' worked. The Spanish got in and cracked open the plastic casing around the ignition to expose the wires while Pasquale kept 'lookout'. The car started first time: it was a new Mercedes-Benz after all. As the Spanish drove off, Pasquale and I followed sedately on the scooter. Our first successful infrared car theft. If they were all this easy it would not be our last.

Back at the Cave, all that was left to do was to tie the Spanish to the underneath of the Merc. We tried to do what Robert De Niro did in *Cape Fear*, when he tied himself to the exhaust pipe underneath the car. I'll say this: it looked easier in the movie. After a bit of experimenting, we managed to attach him in what seemed like a secure fashion.

'Okay. You're on!' I exclaimed.

'No way's you lot driving me like this,' the Spanish shouted from under the car.

'Is good enuff,' Pasquale replied.

'Shut up! My feet is too close to the exhaust pipe! It gets hot, innit?'

'You got thick boots. You wreck 'em, I'll buy you new ones with my share,' Pasquale retorted.

'What about it snaps off? Do *you* wanna get you face blasted off then run over? Coz I don't!'

'Whas-da-matter? Scared, big bruv?'

'Vaffanculo!'

I had to find a way to charmingly interrupt the sibling rivalry before it got violent.

'We are running short of time. Okay, we put it to the vote. What do you think Gianni?' I asked cheekily.

Gianni squirmed as I put him on the spot. I guess he wanted to say something witty to make the others laugh but he was too scared of the Spanish to say anything remotely close to the bone so a joke eluded him.

'Don't worry, I'm kidding! Spanish are you happy with this?' I asked.

The Spanish grimaced as he shook his head.

'Get him off and try again,' I commanded.

After a lot more experiments and yet more adjustments, the

Spanish finally said he was ready and at 10 o'clock on Sunday night the show went live. I was the 'belle of the ball': Gianni had gathered the best dress, wig and make-up from his mother's wardrobe. He even had the cheek to put me in a skirt, exactly what I had told him not to do. He must have got off on it. The others certainly did.

'Is yer punishment for leaving behind dem bombs, Boss!' Pasquale said poker-faced.

'What happened to all that "All for one" stuff?' I replied laughing.

The IT Guy was wearing his best suit but it was still the biggest disappointment to me of the day, so far.

'Is that the best one you got? We have got to do something about that, brother! Your first bonus will be spent on a Zegna,' I said, both appalled and tasting victory.

Luckily Gianni didn't have to dress up, he just had to play himself because he already fitted the profile of the son of wealthy homeowner but, to spite him, I ordered him to suck a lollipop for show.

We got into the car and the IT Guy connected the ignition wires. No sooner had the car fired up than the Spanish was shouting again from under the car. I froze. Had the exhaust burnt him already?

'All for one!' he shouted.

This time we heard him.

'And one for all!' we shouted back.

The gang was already like a family to me but now the gang had to pretend to be a real family: the IT Guy as father, me as wife, Gianni as the son, Pasquale as the 'body in the trunk' and Spanish as the illegal immigrant underneath: a typical Naples family!

We sang, as we drove. Was it bravado or gallows humour? Whichever it was, considering that we were about to seriously upset one of the most powerful and cruel men in Italy, risking our lives in the process, we were amazingly relaxed at this point. You had to be crazy to do what we were doing and, for us, acting crazy was the only way of escaping this fact.

As we approached the checkpoint, we felt a knocking under the car. We pulled over where we could not be seen by the guards. I got out. On inspection, one of the hooks with which the Spanish was holding himself to the car had broken: he was hanging by only his left arm, his right useless as the only thing he could grab hold of was a hot exhaust pipe. Strong as he was, his arm would soon give out if we carried on like that. I was prepared this time. I brought out a roll of boxer's hand bandage. I wrapped his spare hand so he could hold the hot pipe without burning his hand.

'Just like Rocky,' I said, trying to encourage him.

It would protect him from the heat long enough to get us through the last couple of miles but would still require a lot more brute strength and stamina from the Spanish compared to the hook he had started with; but both he and we had no choice. I checked Pasquale had not suffocated yet in the trunk and set off for the final stint.

As we went through the checkpoint, I commanded my 'family' to lower the windows. It was a warmish summer night and we wanted the guards to see who was in the car. They had no reason to stop us and we wanted them to ignore us just as they would any other respectable family visiting the neighbourhood.

And they did but not before one of the guards looked at me with unconstrained lust, literally undressing me with his eyes. If he really had X-ray vision, he wouldn't have been very happy with what he saw under my blouse. Even at 13 and having little experience of these things it was a disgusting moment. Ordinarily, this would have been a useful educational experience: all young men, as they enter puberty, should be made to dress up and look cute in drag with fake breasts just to see how the other half lives but right now I was more worried about the Spanish, who still had to hold on for another mile.

Having finished his lollipop, Gianni was now eating his fingers as we finally approached the villa. Still, the Spanish valiantly held on. Just as we pulled up in front of the gates, a loud crack came from under the car and the exhaust note got much louder and deeper. The weight of the Spanish had broken the exhaust pipe. To our sensitive ears, the Mercedes' unsilenced engine now sounded like a shotgun going off every time it turned over. 'Loud pipes save lives' is a favourite refrain of Hells Angels but, in this case, loud pipes would attract the wrong kind of attention and only hasten our death. The IT Guy ripped the ignition wires apart, the engine fired one last bang and died. Then the IT Guy farted. Actually, it smelt worse than that.

'Have you shit yourself?' I asked.

He nodded matter-of-factly.

Luckily, Gianni and I kept it together: it didn't turn into a laughing fit. We all waited silently as the Spanish crawled out from under the car. We could hardly see him in the dark so no one else could either. I flashed at the gates with the remote control and they opened. The Spanish continued crawling all the way through the gates and only stood up when out of sight from the road. The IT Guy released the brake and the car rolled down through the gates with the lights and engine off. The gates closed automatically behind us. The slope of the drive took us almost all the way to the front door, finally crunching to a stop in the deep gravel just a few metres short. We waited a couple of seconds for the Spanish to catch up. When he arrived, he caught wind of the IT Guy and grimaced. He must have thought the garden had just been fertilised. To avoid any further embarrassment for the IT Guy, I told the Spanish to open the trunk and check on his brother. I picked the lock on the front door and entered alone. As we had rehearsed, the others stood by the car ready for an emergency getaway.

I had both the codes to the alarm in my bra and all my fingers crossed but now was no time for doubting whether I had chosen the right code. According to the manual for the German alarm, as soon as the light started to flash I had 20 seconds to deactivate it. I knew that if I got the code wrong, the phone would ring and the guards would expect verbal confirmation from Bulldog or his family. Then I suddenly realised that the day I watched the 'false alarm' the entire family must have been out, not in as I had supposed, otherwise they would have answered the phone and the security van would not have bothered to carry out a visual check. The three cars that I had seen in the drive meant only that the whole family had been picked up, perhaps by an official CDP limo.

If so, this meant the first code I had found on the decoder would have been the 'OFF' code not the 'ON'. Under pressure my thoughts started to get muddled. I desperately wanted to take time to think it through but there was no time. I decided there and then to swap codes. I entered the six numbers of the code I now believed to be the 'OFF' code. It took forever as my hand was shaking but I knew I had to be slow and careful, as a typing mistake would be just as bad as the wrong code. Bingo! The light turned green. It probably took no more than 10 seconds but it felt like a lifetime.

I beckoned to the guys, watching avidly from their posts by the car. I just had time to check each was wearing gloves before they piled in, hurrying to carry out their allotted tasks. Even though the brothers were the only ones of us who had police fingerprint records, it didn't hurt to be careful. Too late, I realised I had foolishly forgotten my own gloves. My fingerprints were already all over the alarm keypad. Luckily, I had never, to my knowledge, had my prints recorded; I had to make sure it stayed that way.

I directed the boys to the rooms I considered most interesting but I had to send the IT Guy to the bathroom to take care of his little accident. Then I went straight to Bulldog's studio. I promised myself to 'do' only the safe, as I fought the temptation to steal one of those rare books. It took me just five minutes to crack the safe using only a stethoscope. If my Granddad was watching, and I hoped he wasn't, he would at least have been proud my technique.

Each of us had brought a rucksack and all of them had been filled to the brim in just under 10 minutes. In the safe, I found large amounts of cash, documents of all sorts and more than 20 videotapes.

'Babies, you are going straight into our collection at the Cave!' I said naively, not asking myself: 'Who keeps their favourite family movies in a secret safe?'

It was 11:30 p.m.; Bulldog's meeting was due to finish at midnight but, given the arrogance of those politicians, they would probably be celebrating long into the night even though the polls would not be open for four days. The brothers wanted to stay on and steal more stuff since we had only taken a fraction of what was available but I did not want take any more risks.

As we exited the house and the guys saw our car, they felt a collective shock of despair remembering that the car was now too loud to be useful.

'The car is buggered. How do we get out of here with all the gear?' the IT Guy blurted as he went into another panic attack. The brothers had never been happy letting the IT Guy into the gang in the first place, thinking he would crack under pressure. He was our driver: all our eggs were in his basket and he was cracking up before our very eyes. When you are under that kind of pressure, it is not easy to think straight. It is congenital: some have 'it' and some, like the IT Guy, do not. Gianni probably didn't have 'it' either but, as he never fully grasped the gravity of what he was doing, he didn't feel the pressure. For him, it was more like a movie than real life. The two brothers, immune to pressure from years on the streets, certainly had 'it'.

I, myself, had a sudden urge to burst into tears and scream for my Mum. Instead, I took a deep breath, wiped my hands on my shirt and went to Plan B.

'Follow me,' I said as I marched away to my left.

I had rehearsed the gig in my head many times before: I needed a solution for every eventuality, one I could use in the heat of the action without having to think. I knew that Bulldog owned at least three cars. I had made the fair assumption that at least one of them would be here in the garage. While in the house earlier, I had searched the hallway for car keys and found some. So, to the relief of everyone, I marched the gang over to the garage to the left of the drive and was able to open up a Rolls-Royce with blacked out privacy windows using its rightful key. I wasn't sure why Bulldog had not used this beast for his evening out – maybe he didn't want to look too flash just ahead of the election – but at least my gang would finally look the part.

There was already a buoyant, almost casual optimism as we loaded the full rucksacks into the trunk.

'Keep your eyes wide open. The gig is not over yet!' I said, just as Gianni jauntily heaved his bag over the sill of the trunk.

Unfortunately he had hold of the wrong end and the jewels spewed out into the gravel. Contained in a bag they are easy to handle but, mixed with gravel, jewels are a nightmare.

'Leave them!' I shouted as the others frantically plucked at the lost jewels like hens pecking at seeds in the yard.

'But Boss...' Pasquale really couldn't bear to see such gems wasted. They did indeed look gorgeous sparkling amongst the dull gravel.

'Just leave them!'

'Yes Boss.'

We stuffed the trunk with some expensive rugs from the house to prevent the bags from rattling. The two brothers got in the back with Gianni and curled up on the floor under a blanket stolen from the sofa. Gianni sat in the middle as the IT Guy drove us back up the drive. As we approached the gates at the top of the drive I 'plipped' at them. After what seemed like a big delay, they started to open. By then, my heart (and probably everyone else's) was pumping at a million miles an hour. I had a map open over my skirt with planned escape routes plotted in case we got into a chase. We were fully exposed; if we got stopped and searched now, the car and its contents were enough to get us killed. The security guards would shoot us and then call the police. Our corpses would be identified and then Bulldog would send heavies round to our families and decapitate them. Or something like that!

The IT Guy was not just a mess in his underwear: he was a mess mentally too. He couldn't talk and so I wasn't sure if he could hear me.

'Slow down. Give them a gentle beep. But do not open the window!' I said as we approached the guards.

He looked blankly at me.

'The rich have air con so they never open the window,' I shouted in an effort to explain but it was worse than that: he was in a sort of fear-driven trance.

The unsuspecting guards stepped into the road trying to have a look at who was inside this magnificent car. The IT Guy tightened his grip on the wheel and just stared ahead as if he was going to run them down but at the last moment he slowed down to walking pace, allowing them to get even closer. The big face and leering smile of the one who 'undressed' me earlier filled the view through my window. Still dressed as a woman, I tried to smile despite my nausea. I should have given him the finger because they couldn't see anything through the privacy glass. I reached across the IT Guy, beeped the horn, the guards stepped back and we accelerated away.

All the way to the Cave we kept looking over our shoulders. When we reached the turn-off towards Vesuvius the brothers sat up out of hiding. We had almost made it but now it was time for the scary part: we turned off the headlights to drive up the mountain where the road had a sheer drop on one side. Thank heavens for the full moon. The low stone walls at the edge wouldn't stop much: a Rolls-Royce at full speed wouldn't stand a chance. Luckily, we weren't at full speed and we weren't a coach laden with gold either. This was going to be no repeat of the ending of the original *Italian Job*. At crawling speed it seemed to take us forever to reach the Cave.

Once inside, with all the bags laid out on the floor, we collapsed with relief. We were exhausted, physically and emotionally. We were speechless, unable even to celebrate for the first 20 minutes. A further 10 minutes later and we started emptying out the bags...

In my bag, I had gathered more than 300 grand in cash, reams of assorted documents and 20 or so videotapes. That was nothing! With the contents of all the other bags it looked like Aladdin's cave. The floor was strewn with artefacts of gold and silver. We were struck speechless once again by the beauty in front of us: bracelets; pearls; necklaces; tiaras; watches; tie pins; cuff-links. The guys broke into a chant:

'The Prince! The Prince! You are the best!'

'No, you are!' I replied humbly.

There were hugs, high fives and tears all round as the relief exploded into joyous celebration.

I counted the money again, then took 50,000 euros off the top of the pile and handed out a meaty 10 grand wedge to each gang member. No one objected, except Gianni who point-blank refused his share. He was not in this for the money but for the cause and the camaraderie: just to be loved by someone. We insisted on him taking his share but…

'Earmark the money for me. I will take it if and when I need it. Besides, I do not want my Dad to catch me with all that cash, it might get us all in trouble!'

'Fair enough. The money's yours, nobody will touch it, I promise you,' was all I could say, as I put his 10 'thou' next to a pile of 250 more in my office.

That boy never stopped surprising me but I had no time to worry about him as a new and terrible thought overcame me: by now every gangster, policeman, priest and whoever else Bulldog had in his pocket was looking for that car and for those who had taken it. It was so flashy and unusual that, if we drove it anywhere, we would be seen, which would rapidly lead to a painful death. Only one solution: the car had to stay where it was. I used one of my lab instruments to thoroughly check it for radio transmission signals. This was twenty years before the invention of car 'tracker' devices but I didn't want to take any chances. We covered it with bushes and branches but we were still very concerned. In daylight it would still be visible and that would be a death sentence. We might as well have had a nuclear bomb in the driveway. Once again, my planning hadn't been perfect; I made a mistake by taking such an obvious car. We should have turned the house upside down to find keys for one of Bulldog's less ostentatious vehicles.

Luckily, the moon was still shining like an arc light and we were all still high on adrenaline, as we needed to be 'up' for what we had to do next. We took the car apart, from the interiors to the wheels, leaving only the chassis. The interiors went to decorate the Cave and taking the wheels off lowered the car enough for us to hide it better. Gianni, who turned out to be an excellent gardener, filled it with mud, dug up some bushy shrubs and replanted them inside it.

'The most expensive flowerpot ever!' he said, as he added some flowers on top.

It took us late into the night to do it and our only reward was some distinctive lounge furniture and four large round rubbery coffee tables but we were alive and full of hope to remain that way tomorrow. We had one last sarcastic grappa toast to Bulldog's health and then went to sleep.

I woke to the sound of birds chirping outside. Immediately, I knew it was time for us to leave the Cave. During the day a few people would travel up Vesuvius and, even though we were off their beaten track, there was still a chance of bumping into someone who could give us away. Instead, I wanted us to show our faces around the neighbourhood to prevent suspicion.

I was learning that this is the hardest part of a criminal life. No matter how successful the job is, once you have done it you are always looking over your shoulder. You wouldn't do the job in the first place if you thought you would be caught but, even if everything goes to plan, you will have to live with a sense of uneasiness whenever there is a knock on your door, the phone rings or someone simply calls you over unexpectedly. It might look like a small price to pay but it is not. If you wish to know how I felt without subjecting yourself to my ordeals, try getting on a train without a ticket. You will find your heart beating faster every time the train stops. Everyone will look like a ticket inspector. You will be so anxious to get to your destination that the journey will last forever. When your life is at stake rather than a penalty fare it gets much worse. From that day on I lived with a sense of impending doom.

Naples was changed by the earthquake and not just from the architectural point of view. It had created a big opportunity for the Camorra to expand. Now there was another upheaval going on. What I did to Bulldog was much more than robbing his house. I invaded 'their' territory, challenging them in a way that nobody had even dreamt of before. All the security hurdles I had evaded to rob him would be nothing compared to their new *security* arrangements. They would be much more careful in future not to get robbed. But some things about how they operated would not change, they believed the best form of security was to preserve their reputation. My existence could not be tolerated.

THE REAL REVENGE

At once guilty, scared and yet proud of my goal, I decided to let the gang desert the Cave and go into Naples without me. I still had a mission to accomplish; I could feel guilty later. I spent the rest of the morning enjoying the views of Vesuvius as a distraction from dwelling on my new destiny. Restless, I went back into the Cave and sat on my Rolls-Royce throne. All those shiny valuables were still spread around the floor in front of me. Far from lifting my mood, they worsened it. This was no ordinary Monday morning blues.

While in town, the Spanish would visit the Rehab Centre for Minors to give the Warden his monthly pay-off for the benefit of the Cat but, before he did anything at all, he had to go and get me a coffee and croissants: I was starving!

I now had six new files of documents: over a thousand pages. Potentially a bigger prize than the money. As I waited for a much needed injection of sugar, I rummaged through the files. Initially overwhelmed, I methodically sorted them into piles: one for invoices; one for bank statements; one for faxes; one for contacts, names, addresses and phone numbers. It was all alien to me: banks I had never heard of and places far away. I just knew there had to be something that Bulldog was hiding or why else store it in a safe. I needed to read them again and carefully compare them to the haul from the church. To really put them to work for our cause, I had to discover the secret they contained before the election.

As soon as the Spanish came back with my breakfast, I sent him away to bring the IT Guy straight back to the Cave. The IT Guy's knowledge of banking computer systems might be able to decipher that mumbo jumbo.

It took me and the IT Guy the best part of the day to make sense of all the information: payments back and forth between different companies; equally large amounts being wired from one account to another within a company; invoices (possibly fake) and offshore banks (mainly based in Lugano, Switzerland). He was not in the gang by chance but I never dreamt that the IT Guy's skills would prove so vital. It looked like the CDP had stolen almost all the money sent by the European Community as their contribution to the reconstruction of Naples. It had been redirected using a web of false invoices to companies in Switzerland for work that had never taken place. We reckoned Bulldog had stashed at least 60 million euros in various Swiss bank accounts. The money siphoning system he had created was so vast that the total figure could easily have been higher but we just got tired of working it all out. Recently, I had been emotionally up and down like a yo-yo: one minute repentant, the next hell-bent on revenge, but for the rest of that day I was firmly in the revenge camp. I had just taken 300 grand but now I had 200 times the motivation to go after our next target: all the rest of Bulldog's stolen money. While he had that much money still left, our recent blow would feel like little more than a scratch.

Despite my uncomfortable home life, I thought it best to show my face in the shanty-town for once. At home that night, I was so engrossed in my thoughts that I didn't even notice my parents arguing. I went to sleep with just one thing on my mind: what Bulldog had done to my family and neighbours and what I would do to him. Luckily I was tired or I wouldn't have been able to sleep.

The IT Guy wanted to copy all the key incriminating documents and then hand them over to both the press and the police. In theory, Bulldog could not buy off the police if the newspapers wrote about it at the same time. In practice, it wouldn't work. Even if we got past the twin obstacles of a corrupt police and a cowed press, and it landed in the hands of an honest prosecutor (which was a big if), they would have gone to court, sat in front of a judge, arguments, counter-arguments, judgements, appeals, counter-appeals ... it could take years while our families and friends slowly rotted.

I needed a much faster fix. According to Machiavelli, it was better to control an enemy than destroy him. The downside of that was if Bulldog played ball then I wouldn't get to destroy him. I wanted to 'win' by getting the shanty-town re-housed but, in the interests of justice, I very much wanted Bulldog to 'lose'. Destroying him personally had become an obsession and it was not just me; Pasquale and the Spanish shared my anger.

No matter how good your ammunition, a successful blackmail depends on a fine balance between threat and demands. Go in too hard and Bulldog would be so demoralised he might simply go for broke and call your bluff. Then we'd be back to where we started, forced to rely on the authorities to expose him. Go in too gently and the threat may not be perceived as credible.

The practicalities of blackmail are also a nightmare: how to tell him without being seen? If he found out who I was, he would simply take my family hostage, force me to back down and then kill them anyway.

I was spinning in circles. Maybe the IT Guy was right: just send it all to the press and wash my hands of it. In search of an answer, I took another look at the materials: the documents were so alien to me that they swam before my eyes. At least I got my answer; it was obvious that it would take an educated and patient guy to go through them all and actually understand them. Busy reporters at the newspapers probably received so much junk from conspiracy theorists that this stuff would just end up filed in the bin as well. Moreover, I wasn't sure I could find a journalist who couldn't be bought and was willing to take on a suicide mission; this scoop came with a Mafia death warrant. Bulldog would simply laugh in my face. He might have been worthless in my eyes but you did not get to where he was unless you were supremely clever.

'Never underestimate your enemy,' Sun Tzu said.

So it had to be blackmail but I wasn't sure I could pull it off. Once again, something terrible had to happen to break the impasse.

When the gang, except Gianni, met up back at the Cave, I immediately suggested a tea break: a few cakes and a relaxing video on the TV. Maybe a good movie would inspire me just like *Rocky* did. But it couldn't be *Rocky*; we'd all seen it far too many times!

In fact, we had watched all our tapes too many times so Pasquale fetched the movies I had stolen from Bulldog. We reclined on our Rolls-Royce chairs and got stuck into the cakes and sodas as Pasquale slipped a cassette into the VCR and pressed play. Five minutes later, the same cakes were spat or vomited on the floor. The cakes, the best Naples had to offer, were not the cause of our sickness: it was what was on the tape.

After five minutes of collective paralysis, Pasquale stopped the tape. It took another thirty for the IT Guy to recompose himself. I had to lie down, I felt so sickened by what I had seen. I might have had a vast knowledge of science and psychology but I only knew about sexual intercourse in theory; nothing could have prepared a 13-year-old kid for the after-effects of seeing that depravity... I was so heavily traumatised from witnessing grown men abusing children our age and younger that Pasquale, who himself was also affected, had to literally pick me up, drag me outside and put me onto his moped. He had to constantly check all the way that I hadn't fallen off. For the first time in ages, I needed a hug from my Mum and when Pasquale finally got me home, she hugged me instinctively, realising I was in emotional pain, even though she hadn't a clue what it was. Pasquale stayed with me while the two older guys fast-forwarded through the whole collection. It was a dirty job but we had to identify all the perpetrators on the tape, other than the Bulldog of course.

My appetite had only just returned by dinnertime; I wanted to eat with my family so I put the mission on hold. If I took any decisions in this state of mind I would only regret them. At the dinner table, the bosom of my family looked different. Things just didn't feel the same anymore. I couldn't even look at my little brother. All these years later, I still can't believe the level of inhumanity to which mankind could stoop and, worse, I can't erase those images from my memory.

No matter how I felt, I still had a job to do. Something good had come out of something terrible: the blackmail plan had transformed from difficult to quite straightforward. The tapes were the key. He would do anything to keep them secret because if they went public no one could save him. My mission was now a crusade on behalf of all the victims of this abuse.

Pasquale took me back to the Cave at 10 p.m. I was worried

about the two older gang members who had sacrificed what was left of their innocence for the mission. The look in their eyes and their reluctance to make any eye contact at all said it all.

'Did you watch all the tapes?'

They shook their heads, slowly like a couple of zombies.

'How many did you watch?'

The IT Guy just looked at the floor. They had been struck dumb just like real zombies. Until the Spanish broke the silence...

'Not even half of dem but that was too many, way too many. Sorry. Prince, you must get a plan; make them pay,' he said, towering over me with his fists clenched.

I looked up to see something that I never imagined: a man who had been in jail for GBH, a man who had already dealt with the worst in life, was crying in front of me, a kid half his size. Those gentle tears rolling down his scarred face were the tears of my people, the tears of a generation abused in many ways, the tears of someone who could not deal with what he had seen. I felt that those tears were washing over me in a magical baptism, investing me with a supreme force, demanding that I use my talents to avenge those sins, but I couldn't reply to my friend in need; instead, I just turned my back and disappeared into my office.

'Your people await you!' The Spanish shouted after me.

If there was a time to prove that I was a worthy leader of my pack, this was it. The gang waited patiently while I sat in my office planning a counter-attack. No words were spoken; the whole Cave had become my sanctuary. After half an hour, I emerged.

'Fetch me a bastard dog from the neighbourhood and bring it back here in your car,' I told the IT Guy, 'While you are at it, beg, borrow or steal everything on this list.'

I handed him a list and a wad of cash. The list said:

A tape recorder with tape and batteries; a megaphone; 50 metres of loudspeaker cable; a pair of binoculars; some rope and five tough old bicycles.

'What are they for?' the IT Guy asked.

'I'll tell you later but know this: we need silent transport, no squeaky bikes. The rope is just to tie the bikes to your car!'

'And to tie up the dog!' the IT Guy added.

He didn't like dogs at the best of times and the strays in the shanty-town were a vicious bunch but this task was a relief after watching those tapes so he didn't complain further.

I turned to Pasquale, 'Go to the supermarket and buy half a kilo of steak. The tastiest stuff they have,' I ordered.

'We want revenge, not a barbecue!'

'Just get it and put it in the fridge to keep it fresh for when we need it,' I told him, not adding that when we eventually did need it, our lives would depend on it.

The Spanish and I stayed behind. He drew a map of the foot-hills of Vesuvius from memory. No one knew it better than the Spanish. Then I said, 'Go to Salerno and post this,' and gave him a letter addressed to Bulldog.

It said: *We have the documents, we have the tapes and we have your destiny in our hands. Come to meet us (see map overleaf) tonight at 9 p.m. Come alone. Any attempts to have the meeting watched will be futile. You would need a helicopter!*

On the other side was the Spanish's map of the mountainside, which I had copied out left-handed.

At lunch on Wednesday, the gang was joined by our newest team member. Having been starved for 24 hours now, the stray dog cried to be fed as he watched us tuck in: cruel but necessary.

We rehearsed our moves and then got into position on the mountainside 90 minutes before Bulldog was due to show. 9 p.m. approached and we started to get nervous. We knew all along one mistake would be fatal, so we should have been nervous from the get-go but, as the minutes ticked down, I worried that he had come even earlier than us and was already watching the 'watchers'.

When a large Range Rover with privacy glass throughout lumbered into view I dismissed my latest fear but the fact that I had never seen this car before in his drive got me suspicious all over again. It was the perfect car to hide a small private army. Assuming it contained at least the Bulldog, I watched it closely through my new binoculars but I couldn't make out if anyone else was hiding inside.

When it finally stopped, almost exactly at the point required of them by my map, I unleashed the dog and it immediately ran like the wind over to the Range Rover. Actually, it ran directly to a large steak hidden in the bush next to it. This morning, before the note had even been delivered, I had dragged the meat all the way from our hiding place to that very bush. The dog wore a big message tag on his neck: 'READ ME'. As the dog scoffed, Bulldog got out of his car and tore the message off.

'He looks a little upset,' I whispered, which made me and the guys smile for a second but then everyone, especially me, went straight back to being tense. The meat had worked. We were nearly a kilometre away and there were no helicopters and no suspicious 'ramblers'. Then again, the first we'd know if we had messed up would be when a bullet entered our skulls. I had told the rest of the guys that it would have been safer if they didn't come but they had invoked the, now familiar, 'all for one' deal. Plus, they wanted to see Bulldog squirm just as much as I did.

The dog's message read:

Take your jacket off. Display your hands clearly. Make sure that your friends do not get out of the car or you are all dead. Go up the hill and follow the signs.

After reading the message again and sweating some more, Bulldog elaborately pretended to put his jacket back in the car. He fooled no one; he was surely briefing his men because he certainly hadn't brought his wife!

It took that fat pervert no more than 15 minutes to follow our signs up to his next message but it felt much longer.

I had placed a bottle of water in the centre of a clearing that was the final stop on his climb. The gang were hidden behind thick bushes. We could see him but he couldn't see us. When he received his next message he was so startled, he nearly tripped over the water bottle; he was not expecting it to be verbal.

'You are welcome to the water, if you wish,' my voice boomed out of a low-fi speaker. I had connected the microphone of a battery-powered loudhailer down a long wire to the now separate speaker. This would disguise my location and my voice somewhat.

To be sure, I deliberately lowered my tone to a false tenor. It must've sounded very strange but that was the point. Judging by the speed he drank the water, he was very thirsty after his exertions. A bit of hospitality never hurts and, after all, he was in my kingdom now.

He spun around in the centre of the clearing, straining to locate his tormentors. He couldn't so instead he started to wander away from the centre spot.

'Stay where you are. Or we will kill you!' I boomed at him once more.

Pasquale cocked a toy gun for effect.

Bulldog's ludicrous comb-over was blown away by the breeze, leaving just a one-sided streak of hair down to his left shoulder. It looked wrong but, then again, he was wrong to his very core. Breathing heavily, he looked like evil personified as his nostrils flared.

'I know who you are and you better give me back what is mine!' he roared.

I paused for 10 seconds.

'Are you done getting angry?'

I paused again for effect before pressing the button on the mouthpiece again.

'You don't know anything about me but I know who you are, or should I say what you are!'

'Give it all back, we can forget the whole thing. I will make you all rich beyond your wildest dreams!' he said, softening his tone considerably.

After having tried the aggressive gangster part of his personality, he reverted to the sweet-talking politician.

'Enough. You have stolen the money from the reconstructions of projects 165, 187 and 194. The funds are in a trading company in Switzerland ready to be put to use. Tomorrow at the conference, I want you to announce that reconstruction work will begin as soon as possible. Be as detailed as you can. You must convince me and all of Naples that you mean it, that it will happen. If you do not, your life will be over. What would your wife's face look like when she sees, for herself, your exploits? And your daughter?'

That totally silenced him so I carried on in a slow, solemn tone:

'I have no interest in destroying you while you still serve the people but if you lose the election, resign or otherwise fail to persuade your colleagues to carry out the reconstruction then, be warned, you will no longer be useful to me and you will suffer the consequences.'

'How can I trust you?' he replied.

He made a good job of sounding confident but I could hear an undertone of defeat.

'You have no choice! Do what I tell you and it will all go away, I promise you,' I encouraged. He looked stunned.

'Just re-house those poor people: all of them. Be quick, no more delays. You will have to work as hard as you ever have to push this through fast enough.'

Now he looked truly beaten. Such a previously powerful man reduced to a wreck. I was worried I had overplayed my hand and he would feel he couldn't please me.

'Follow my instructions to the letter and you will satisfy me. Listen carefully...'

I laid the microphone next to a tape recorder loaded with a speech I had prepared earlier. I put an elastic band on the microphone's 'on' button and pressed play on the tape recorder. I'm sure he never listened so intently in his life. The message went on for several minutes at full volume, explaining to him the details of how the announcement should be delivered. Meanwhile, we slipped into the woods walking carefully at first, then briskly to cover a half a kilometre through thick brush to our hidden push-bikes.

We were safely back at the Cave before the Bulldog could have even run back to his car. Being so unfit, I would be surprised if he did more than a light downhill jog. We timed it so he would return to the car as twilight ended and it became fully dark. He would have no choice but to go home and fret. He would want to know who his blackmailer was but he couldn't so much as search the hillside until tomorrow. In the meantime, he would have to think about all the people he knew who hated him. A man like him would have a long list of enemies to work through. Even if he wrote them down, I doubt he would ever get as far as me: 'the altar boy who he once patronised'.

The beneficiaries of the blackmail were the families in the shanty-town. He would focus on looking for those residents who stood to gain the most from our demands but he would find only one truth: they all needed a new home. The shanty-town currently housed a few paid-up Communists who had spoken out against the CDP. Maybe they would get on to his list but, in the end, pretty much everyone in the shanty-town would be suspected before a bunch of kids like us.

We were well and truly invisible to all conventional forms of investigation but, if he rejected normal forms of investigation and just conducted a massive physical search of the entire hillside in ever increasing circles, then he would find the Cave, the jewels and us (assuming we hung around – a search like that couldn't catch us by surprise). Dangerous (for us) as this option was, I was confident he wouldn't bother.

I would be very surprised if he didn't just take the easy option and simply do as he was told. He would see it as good politics to go along with my demands.

The blackmail had him in checkmate but a man like him, the most connected in Naples, was still going to be spitting mad at being dictated to. I bet no one outside of the Camorra had ever told him what to do before. If he made the necessary public promises before the election, my blackmail threat would hang over him to make sure he stuck to them afterwards when, like most politicians, he would be under immense lobbying pressure to backslide.

We had seized our golden chance. The boys, including Gianni, were ecstatic. Sure we had nailed one of the most despicable human beings in Italian history, we finally indulged in endless hugs and high fives. At the time, Italy had last won the World Cup in 1938, before our time, but our celebration was as spirited as if we had just won it. A couple of short years later in 1982, Italy won it for real!

I couldn't properly join in the celebration because, as soon as my brain was no longer distracted from working on the gig, it flipped straight back to those horrible images, making me deeply nauseous. Thankfully, Gianni had not seen them; otherwise we would have been clearing up even more vomit at the Cave.

Our work done, we split up and went back to our homes to act normal.

After such an intense few days, I didn't venture back out until Friday, the eve of the election. I felt compelled to attend the CDP party conference to witness first-hand Bulldog's speech. I dressed slicker and smarter than ever before and did my hair like I was going to a wedding.

I was expecting butterflies in my stomach but instead I felt no emotion at all. Maybe I was drained but it was a bad sign that I was suddenly so hardened. I was wandering around the hall, looking for a comfortable spot to watch my sworn enemy finally submit, when I heard a faint voice calling my name. At first I couldn't recognise it. I turned 360 degrees scanning the crowd. Seeing no one I knew, I started to think I was imagining it. Worse than having no emotions, I was finally going mad just as I had predicted when I first arrived in the shanty-town. Then I caught sight of Greta. Incredibly, the young daughter of Bulldog had spotted me in the massive crowd and it was her shouting ceaselessly to attract my attention. I was relieved that I wasn't insane but then I realised that she was calling me over and, for once, I didn't know what to do. Run? Blank her? Luckily, I didn't overthink it; I just let my instincts take over and acted natural. I liked her; it was not her fault her father was evil. I went over and greeted her warmly like it was nothing. Then her mother showed up; she was ecstatic to see me too, hugging me like I was a long-lost member of the family. It was all a bit much so I just went with it in a daze as they led me through the crowd.

So, ironically, I got to watch Bulldog's speech from a VIP seat next to his beloved family. He announced the new building projects in grand style. His speech was bound to go down well in front of the party faithful but, when he surprised the crowd by announcing all the juicy details of the earthquake reconstruction projects, he suddenly got a standing ovation. That left me with mixed feelings. I had never planned for him to stand to gain in our 'deal'.

Like the master of politics that he was, he'd made a virtue of necessity.

I nearly broke into tears at news of my victory but had to suppress them for fear of giving myself away. When I got home I finally allowed myself to cry, never knowing if my tears were made of anger, satisfaction or just sadness at how bad some people were.

Immediately after the conference, I sent Bulldog a list of the most urgent cases to be re-housed as a priority because not even three freshly 'thawed' projects would be sufficient to re-house all those who had eventually been made homeless by the earthquake. I did not want me or my boys left out. The gang chose the people on the list together, dishing out happiness in direct correlation to their suffering in the shanty-town. In compiling the list I was careful not to allow a pattern, based on our connections or friendships, to form in case it could be analysed to finger us. Still, it was not easy to leave people out: we felt like Schindler writing his famous list. In the end, it grew to a thousand names: our families would be a drop in the ocean. The Spanish, as usual, had to carry out the boring but necessary long-distance trek to post it from Rome.

The day after the conference, I felt depressed. I was still confident that Bulldog would honour his promise. He knew the blackmail would never go away unless he found me first, which he wouldn't, but I did not feel completely satisfied either. Something was bothering me. Frustratingly, I did not know what.

THE AFTERMATH

I was growing tired, not just of the heat but the pressure of being a wanted criminal (even though they had no idea it was me).

Bulldog had brought to bear all the powers at his disposal to find out who had come into possession, not only of his money and jewels, but also of those sensitive documents and tapes. Police, tough guys and priests – the 'Unholy Trinity' at its best – were all asking questions regarding the robbery. These forces were scouring the city, to the point of questioning people in the streets whether they might have seen or heard anything that would lead to the capture of 'those criminals'.

It was a full-on man-hunt but they didn't have a clue where to start. Yet. Bulldog's car was still outside the Cave. Okay, it was covered up with plants and only the chassis remained but, with a little digging, it would soon be obvious it was his car. Passers-by were a remote possibility as the Cave was located so far from the main path up the mountain but it was still a risk that I didn't like living with. We had a death sentence on our doorstep.

Like professional killers hiding the body, the Spanish and Pasquale cut the chassis apart with a borrowed angle grinder. Equally professional, they disposed of that amazing car in tiny pieces scattered in different dumpsters all over the region, not just Naples. They were as careful as possible, always doing it during the graveyard shift: 3 a.m. to 4 a.m. With a really obvious part like the famous Rolls-Royce grille, the Spanish personally took it to a town 40 miles away to dump it. He wore two pairs of gloves, knowing that leaving a single fingerprint on that grille would have had the same effect as touching deadly poison.

We dug a hole 100 metres behind the Cave and buried our safe containing all the money, tapes, documents and jewels. I even moved all my potentially incriminating bomb-making books to the same hiding place.

With the Rolls gone and the booty hidden, it felt like our death warrant had been, at least partially, lifted. Meanwhile, Bulldog and his CDP were busy kick-starting the rebuilding projects. Day by day, the need for us to re-enter the 'game' was receding. I felt like I could retire from crime, go back to school and start to rebuild the normal life that I dreamt of.

Before I knew it, September came and, with it, a letter of invitation to the school Gianni's father had recommended me to. It wasn't just any school; it was a special grammar school set up by Mussolini's fascist regime in the 40s to give the brightest of the poor a chance in life. Showing that letter to my family induced an attack of euphoria.

They all proclaimed it 'the most prestigious institution in the country!'

And maybe it was: to be accepted, I had to sit an entrance exam, for which my preparation was not ideal as I still had a lot on my mind.

A famous Neapolitan philosopher once said: 'The exams in life never stop.'

Inevitably, it wasn't as simple as Gianni's father just helping me out for no return: there was a hidden agenda. Gianni was going there too. It was never said but my job would be to get him through it. I was not pleased. I had pushed the limits of what was possible just to get that boy through high school. It would be monumental to get him through a further five years of yet more complex studies.

Gianni had no place being there: he was not special, he was below average at best, but I didn't blame him for a second. He would have preferred Art School but lacked the force of personality to stand up for what he wanted. The pressure to conform to his parents' dreams must have been immense. Bullying, in a million different formats, was endemic in my world.

It was left to me to confront that pyromaniac a.k.a. Gianni's father. When I finally did speak to the big man in his study, I could only say this:

'I know what your game is. I'm grateful for the recommendation and I know how much Gianni's education means to you but don't think I'm happy about this. Not one bit!'

'How much do you want this time?' he replied, neither angry nor repentant.

It was as if he were merely bored by the topic, while I was disgusted that, even in the upper crust of Naples' society, corruption started at school.

As a retired criminal always on the verge of a relapse, what I needed now was a calming educational experience. The next five years could be that, but not with Gianni attached to me like a ball and chain. Perversely, he was my only true friend at the new school because I couldn't stand the idea of conforming to the preppy norms in order to be accepted into one of the many cliques. Consequently, I had no protection from the abuses of the teachers. I could have called in the Spanish or literally blown my tormentors into next week but, as I wanted to keep that part of my life separate and gain respectability, neither was an option. Equally, I had no intention of sitting back and just taking abuse so it all added to my determination to smash the whole system!

I sat the 'entry test' for the special school. Based on a variety of subjects (geography, history, maths and literature), it was designed to select the best. What bothered me the most was not the questions – they were easy – it was the other students. They were dripping in wealth: designer clothes; Swiss watches and perfectly coiffed hair. I was jealous of their wardrobes but disgusted at the same time. Just 14 years old and yet they wore the equivalent of my Dad's monthly salary just to sit an exam. They were not the children of the poor being given a chance; they were the offspring of the upper-middle class who paid the bribes needed to get a top-class education on the cheap.

'La *crème de la crème* of Naples: rich and thick,' I called them.

The Christian Democratic Party had won the election by a landslide. Being the dominant party, they would have won it anyway but their victory margin was, no doubt, boosted by Bulldog's reconstruction promises. Maybe that was what annoyed me the most: enforcing our blackmail demands had turned out to be a win-win, when I had always intended for him to be a big loser. He had come out smelling of roses and that bothered me. He and I certainly had unfinished business but it was something else entirely that really started to unsettle me. I began to realise the vast size of my enemy. The documents, the tapes and the CDP conference all meant one thing: Bulldog did not act alone. Bringing him down would not achieve my mission. The system upon which our society was built would swiftly find another even more ruthless and resilient leader. The documents in my possession showed that behind that fat pervert there was an evil and sophisticated organisation much bigger than even the visible face of the 'sistema' (slang for the way the Camorra had always run things on the street).

Despite my realisation, I felt no desire to quit. I was aware that my body had been weakened by all the stresses and that now was a good time to lie low so I took a few days off. I told Pasquale and Gianni to do the same. That left the Spanish and the IT Guy, the older members of the gang, to finish going through all Bulldog's tapes: all of them this time. It would not surprise me if some more CDP candidates, ones that I had met at the party conference the week before, were featured.

I gave the Spanish and IT Guy simple instructions: just write down the names with a brief note of their on-screen crimes and, when the list was complete, show it only to me, no one else. This was volatile information; in the wrong hands it could cause unpredictable reactions. Even though they were grown men and knew from before what to expect, it still unsettled them. They did a good job of handling it, knowing they were protecting the younger members of the gang. However, the results of their task would have a major impact on us all.

My Dad's exam had been rescheduled for that week but this time I simply got the IT Guy to bribe a clerk with many times his salary (about 30,000 euros) to give me the exam paper a day early. I was in no mood to waste any more energy on that particular issue. Now that money was no object, I used it to free up precious time for my crusade. It goes without saying but this time my Dad walked in with the answers already in his pocket. Consequently, life in the family-shack got a lot more tolerable but, after basking in the glory for a few days, I went back up to the Cave with the intention of pretty much living there for the rest of the summer holidays. I was looking forward to it. It would be fun, watching movies and just hanging out with the gang, although Gianni couldn't be with us as he had to go away on holiday with his family.

When I got to the Cave, to my absolute horror I saw the video recorder had been smashed. The Spanish was stalking the room like a caged animal. Then he punched the wall.

'I touched that scum; even shook his hand,' the Spanish shouted as he examined the damage the wall had done to his right hand, ignoring the hole in his own plasterwork.

The IT Guy looked on forlornly but Pasquale was showing signs of being infected by the same madness. I had made self-control my number one rule but it was not easy for the hot-headed Pasquale to follow my example and this time he had good reason to be upset. The Spanish was usually a cool customer; it took a lot for him to lose his temper although, deep down, he was as angry as the rest of us but when he blew his cool, he really let rip. The 'him' that the Spanish was referring to when he punched the wall was the Cat's warden, who he had recognised from the tapes. Like all of us he was already appalled by them but now it had become personal; when you know that someone you have been seeing every month is abusing the juveniles around him, it would make anyone lose it. The Cat was not a friend of mine but he was like a brother to Pasquale. By this virtue alone, he was one of us. The Spanish had been visiting the Cat regularly at the same time as paying off the warden and so he was also familiar with some of the other inmates: inmates whose faces he also saw among the victims on the tapes. Some of the guards were at it too. An ugly picture was now clear: those perverts at the prison, led by the warden, were running a paedophile ring using the young inmates.

Pasquale and I did not know any of the victims personally but the Spanish did, and that was enough. When riled he was a force of nature. He demanded that I use the gang's money to buy some guns and to kill them all. For a second, I agreed with him. The only reason we didn't was because I didn't know where to buy guns.

As the anger subsided, I brought the gang round to discussing other plans for punishment. When they tired of fantasising, I finally opened my mouth:

'Revenge is a dish best served cold! Proper planning is the only option. First, get the Cat out of there. No more money to that depraved bastard either. Once the Cat is out we will hit them one by one and, in the end, the whole evil system will collapse all by itself!'

Quite a speech: I even believed it myself at the time. The normal balance of only two hotheads in a gang of five had been swiftly overturned. The trouble was that I was not thinking straight either and what I thought was proper planning was anything but. With Gianni away, three angry young men could not be restrained by the sensible IT Guy.

Nonetheless, I had taken my eye off the ball, and now I was about to break my cardinal rule: maintain self-control and invisibility at all times. As the leader, I take full responsibility for the consequences.

The end of June brought a massive heat wave. The Cave was like an oven, unbearable during the day. We met up at night to plan together. Then, during the day, we each applied ourselves to our individual assignments.

The IT Guy bought a safe for the Cave and some locks for the doors. Not exactly Fort Knox but better than leaving it wide open, as we had until then.

The Spanish stalked the warden to find out where he lived and what his routine was. 'Get to know your target as well as you possibly can,' I told him.

Pasquale and I rode around with the moped to check out the homes of those guards implicated by the tapes.

The intensity of our workload had suddenly gone beyond what we did even to prepare for Bulldog-Day.

The warden was the first on our list and the hardest to get at. He lived in a block of apartments with his sick mother, who never left the house for a second. Apartment blocks were the hardest for me to break into unseen, the only way in being via the balcony or a window and only at night. The warden lived on the 16th floor!

Apart from the IT Guy, we had no patience and no intention of waiting to come up with the perfect plan so I went for the quickest option: blackmail. After all, it had worked on Bulldog.

We bought a professional broadcast quality video recorder: one capable of freezing images to be printed out. We then sent the pictures to the warden, demanding the release of all the victims we could identify and, of course, mixed into the list, the Cat's real name. Looking back, I can't fully explain the sloppiness. Collective loss of discipline was the major factor caused by tapes hijacking our emotions but I should still have thought more than once before acting; but at the time I thought nothing of it!

The Spanish went to visit a distant cousin of the Cat's parents. This man, called Roberto, was the closest living relative of the Cat so he could put himself forward as guardian. Roberto was a nasty piece of work but he had a large family and was poor so we had an angle on him. We reckoned without Roberto's own animal cunning: he could sense how much the Cat meant to us and demanded three grand in return for pretending to take the Cat under his guardianship. Even though the Spanish told him this simple gesture would prevent the Cat from being sent to a foster home where the raping and filming would continue, Roberto insisted on being paid just to sign a piece of paper. He had seven children of his own and no money for them either, so we were doing him a favour and, as the money was stolen anyway, we just paid up.

Two days after the warden had received his letter, Roberto was at the gates of the prison filling in the forms and getting custody of the Cat. The warden was acting quickly to protect his reputation. Roberto took the Cat home to meet with the Spanish, where he paid the remaining 50 per cent of the bribe. With his own guardianship papers under his arm, the Cat left on the back of the Spanish's bike, never to return to this bit of his 'family'.

We, on the other hand, welcomed the Cat like one of our own. At first, surprised to see me in charge, he was too wary to say anything. Understandable, considering that the last time he saw me, before he was jailed, I was the neighbourhood nerd. Of course, once the brothers had told him the details, he accepted my leadership immediately and thanked me (and the gang) profusely for all we had done: and we had done a lot!

When I knew the Cat before, I was intimidated by his violent outbursts and was never at ease in his presence. Now he was transformed: sweet, polite and respectful. He owed us and he knew it. Nevertheless, he genuinely embraced our mission, putting his services at our disposal.

The boy, orphaned by cholera, was only 15 years old; he had no place to live and only us who cared about him. I decreed he would live in the shanty-town with the IT Guy. For him it would feel like a holiday camp and the IT Guy would look after him like a big brother.

His presence added a new enthusiasm to the team, who were still traumatised by those horrible images. He was small but very agile and complemented our strengths extremely well. Moreover, he had an explosive personality, with a ready-made joke for every occasion. He quickly became an equally important member of our gang: a breath of fresh air at a moment when we desperately needed one. I gave the new arrival a couple of grand to buy himself a new wardrobe and settle in with the IT Guy.

Then we got back to work:

I told the brothers and the Cat to gather as much information as possible about any politician mentioned in the documents. That proved to be quite a job as we had only the names. Their faces were splashed all over the place on posters and billboards but, beyond that, we could hardly go around asking for information. Primarily, I wanted their addresses, and we got a few just by stalking them, but it would take forever to find them all this way. Including the warden and some of his guards, I had more than 60 people on our 'to-do' list. The gang and I were almost intoxicated on our own cocktail of revenge and revolutionary fervour. It was clouding our judgement but one thing was clear: the mission meant making sure everyone on the list suffered, one way or another.

Excuse me, 60 people? Serious mission creep is what it was. Were we going mad?

Despite this, while the brothers and the Cat were out stalking, the IT Guy and I knuckled down for a week buried in the documents. Thanks mainly to the IT Guy, we managed to get our heads round the next level of detail about how the scam worked: a vicious circle of fake owners of fake companies; fake Italian bank accounts; real Swiss bank accounts with no name and real companies based in Switzerland. I might have made it sound easy but, believe me, it was not. It was designed to be impenetrable. The IT Guy's banking experience was gained only in Italy so the thing that really stumped us was the Swiss side of the scam. We knew a lot about how the money got out of Italy but less about how we could find it and get it back, as we had little idea about the Swiss system, especially the world of private (i.e. secret) banking.

My favourite quote was 'Keep your friends close but your enemies closer,' which is why, during the whole summer, I still went to church 'religiously'. However, I understood that, in order for me to be even closer to my enemies, I had to open a new front in our battle. Time for a vacation: Switzerland, here we come!

I told my parents I would spend a month on holiday with Gianni's family. My Dad was so happy, having passed his exam, that he would not have cared if I told him I was moving to the Moon.

The gang came on the road trip, including the Cat but without Gianni, who really was on holiday with his family. It was wonderful to swap the shanty-town for a place of unsurpassed beauty, if only temporarily. Most of the gang had neither passports nor ID cards, so only the Spanish and the IT Guy could actually cross the border during the day. So, we stayed in a wonderful hotel on the Italian side of the border. At night though, the border guards literally knocked off and we could all go and visit the Ticino region at will to admire the wonderful scenery and check out those famous banks: some so bent they made Italian crooks look like legitimate businessmen.

I will tell you about our trip another time but suffice it to say we spent 100,000 euros in a month. We had a good time but not 100 grand's worth of good time as we spent 85,000 buying a business: a tired old shop in Lugano called The Trading Post, bought for cash from a dodgy man who was very keen to sell. It had a small flat above it so if any of us wanted to go and work there we could instantly justify a Swiss visa. It was the perfect bolthole, if we needed it, and a channel into Switzerland. Where we could go looking for the stolen reconstruction funds as well.

After having spent a month in the most beautiful region of Switzerland, coming back to the shanty-town was a shock to all of us. Inebriated by all that beauty, wealth and class, we were still daydreaming about it a month later!

The month after our Swiss trip was August, when the Cave was hotter at night than during the day. We invested in a more powerful air conditioning system so we could continue working there. The 300-grand cash haul from Bulldog was disappearing fast. I'd be studying all over again in the autumn when, if I focused on my studies, as I intended to, I would no longer have spare time for illegal fund-raising.

In August, Naples is absolutely dead. In those days, most people took the whole month off on holiday; the city became a ghost town. You wouldn't expect the residents of the shanty-town to have the money for a holiday but, nonetheless, even here it was a lot quieter than usual. It gave me the opportunity to reflect and watch the world around me. Even though my quality of life had greatly improved, I still had every intention of ripping that city to shreds; my desire to get my hands on all the embezzled reconstruction funds started to burn white hot. The best way to destroy

Bulldog was to steal it all back: this wasn't just anger, it was a practical solution to all my life's goals...

I promised myself I would feel no guilt this time: it wouldn't really be stealing if we used it for rebuilding Naples. And it would be easier to recycle it, as it was already non-declared and off the radar. If the authorities hadn't noticed it go missing so far, they wouldn't be able to suddenly start tracking it if I redirected it elsewhere!

Once those who knew about the stolen money, from corrupt officials to the big bosses of the Mafia, found out it was gone, they would turn on Bulldog and accuse him of betrayal, destroying him more efficiently than I ever could. It would be a most elegant revenge.

And, if Bulldog failed to keep the CDP on track for long enough to re-house every last resident of the shanty-town, then I would need this money in reserve to rebuild the extra houses.

Actually, pulling it off looked very ambitious, if not impossible. However, during my holiday in the Ticino region of Switzerland I had learnt enough about how Swiss bank accounts worked and it had given me some ideas. More determined than ever to do something spectacular, I went to the Cave on my own, closed my eyes and started to put a plan together. As my head was spinning with all the many ways I could do it, I found myself planning for something else entirely: the end of my career as a conventional thief.

After recently spending so many evenings lounging by the pool of a Swiss hotel with its integral cocktail bar, surrounded by men in suits and glamorous women, I had fallen in love with being respectable. I lived with guilt every day and was always half-expecting to be caught. But now I dreamt with childlike confidence that, at some point in the future, all that would be gone and life would be normal again. I had every intention of progressing with my education and eventually getting a good job, a salary and a career. I was not worried for myself; I was worried about some of the gang. Gianni, with his parents' wealth and influence, would be fine but I wasn't at all sure about what the future held for the other four if I just gave up being a criminal and the gang lost its leader overnight:

IT Guy: bankrupt and without a job.

The brothers: no education and very few skills between them.

The Cat: orphaned, without even a place of his own to live.

Without a steady income for the rest of their lives, they would slip back to where they came from. I had to find a way to get revenge but also to permanently sort out the boys' future. I had a lot of work still to do.

My family were finally re-housed in a beautiful new apartment complex with private gardens and individual garages. The Spanish, his brother and their long-suffering mother had to wait just another month for their new home. The IT Guy (and his house guest – the Cat) moved in three months later. By then, all of the 1,000 nominated families had left the shanty-town. I remembered fondly how we had all chosen them for the original list together nearly a year earlier but I was moved beyond words by seeing my Mum discover her new home, seeing my Dad finally get his own garage, and my neighbours walking through the gates as if they were going through the gates of heaven. For the families who got out, the day was marred only by the fact that so many of their old neighbours were still stuck in the shanty-town.

I loved finding things out. I preferred learning to burglary, blackmail and blowing things up. It didn't matter to me that I was way ahead of everyone else in my class, as long as I was free to suck up knowledge like a sponge. But that summer, two years after Bulldog-Day, as much as I tried I couldn't concentrate on my school-work. After living so long with violence, threat and danger, going back to normal life wasn't easy.

I'd got a whole city of people out of shit-hole shanty-towns and into real homes. Still, I didn't see myself as the saviour of the world or some kind of Robin Hood. Why? I could have given it all away but I didn't. I kept over seven million euros. Way more than I stole from Bulldog. Most of it generated on the back of stealing stuff in Italy and selling it in Switzerland. Back then that was an astonishing amount of money. That kind of money changes you.

It was time to get out while I was ahead. I wanted to enjoy the riches, my new house, my parents and my kid brother. I wanted to make new friends. So I swore I'd forget about stealing, blowing things up and all the rest. I promised myself no more crime.

No More Crime.

Months of sitting in an airless classroom full of normal kids, learning at their pace, left me wrestling my own eyelids. Keeping them open was impossible. I was buried alive. What's more, my teacher was a spiteful and abusive little man who could have learned more from me than I could ever learn from him.

'Are you listening "Prince"?' he asked, sarcastic emphasis on my name. The other kids laughed. I drew my attention away from the syrupy sunshine back into the hell of the sweaty classroom.

I'd been 'The Prince' since I was seven years old because of my haughty attitude. I was obsessed with my appearance and designer clothes. The name stuck even after I'd grown out of all that. In some ways I liked it because, deep down, I still felt I was better than everyone else.

I couldn't show it though. And I couldn't let anyone know about the money I'd stolen. At school, I had to play the part of the poor thug in a world full of rich kids wearing Swiss watches and perfectly coiffed hair. So, the name 'the Prince' had become ironic. It was a constant reminder of my low status at school. Even as the kids lower than me in both intelligence and riches laughed at my expense, I was forced to laugh with them.

As the laughter subsided and the teacher droned on, my gaze drifted back to the window. I was looking in the direction of the sports yard that would have been chequered with shadowy diamond shapes made by the sun shining through the fence, but I couldn't see it. I was hatching a plan to steal the teacher's car and laugh at him as he walked to school.

No More Crime.

I glanced at the clock in the hope that the lesson was over and couldn't believe it was only a few minutes since I last looked. It felt like hours. I'd fought corrupt politicians and the most dangerous crime syndicate in Europe, but fighting to stay awake in the classroom that term was the hardest battle. Was it possible for time to go backwards?

To have retired from a life of crime was a bizarre claim for a 15-year-old, I know, and it wasn't entirely true. While other kids were playing football, I was still getting a little criminal adrenaline fix to get me through.

I was spending weekends with Pasquale and Gianni at the Cave. We were in the incredible position of being able to listen in to phone calls made by the mob. I'd tapped their phones when we'd robbed them and every call was recorded onto a tape machine in the Cave. We'd sit back and enjoy listening while eating a bag of crisps and drinking soda, just as if we were at the movies.

I smiled to myself as I thought of those tapes. When the school bell finally rang, I sprinted to freedom. I ran down the corridors, bumping into and pushing through the hordes of 'rich but thick' kids as they filed out of open classroom doors to clog up the arteries of this supposedly special school. It was the end of term. Summer holidays. Outside, I mounted my brand-new Vespa and headed for the hills.

I strolled into the Cave, confident Pasquale or Gianni would already be inside. I was soon relaxing on the leather sofa made from the back seats of the Rolls-Royce. I put my feet up and munched a packet of crisps with my headphones on. The three of us were listening in to phone calls made by crooks, corrupt politicians, industrialists and bishops. Tomorrow we were all off on holiday to Switzerland to see the rest of the gang.

They ran a slick operation up there on my behalf, ringing stolen cars and fencing the jewels and gold we'd stolen. Although we had eight million euros in our own secret account, we couldn't spend it until it had been laundered. It had taken us a year to launder only 500k. I wanted to do it faster so I decided this would be a working holiday, the only kind of holiday I enjoyed.

For Pasquale, this trip was his vacation. Gianni's suffocating, over-protective family finally allowed him to go on holiday by himself.

The dream of the holiday in Lugano had kept me going through the whole school term. It kept me awake that night. The next day, after the plane landed in Switzerland, it made me run like a child through customs and out into the Lugano airport arrivals lounge.

I left the others behind. Even after the independent life I'd carved out for myself back home, arriving in a different country unaccompanied by adults made me feel joyfully grown up. Once past customs, I made straight for a blonde woman. Looks-wise, she wouldn't have stood out, except that she was wearing jeans, a T-shirt and the hat from a chauffeur's uniform. And she was holding a hand-written sign saying: 'HRH'.

'The Prince?' she asked. I nodded. She picked up my bags, despite my protests that I could carry them myself, and led me through the airport to a limousine. People started thinking I was part of some royal family. 'I'm not really a driver,' she said. 'They made me wear this. They thought it was funny.'

'OK. I get it,' I said.

'Your Dad is in the car,' she said, opening the door.

The Spanish, Pasquale's older brother, ex-con and gang member, spread his 6ft 4in frame across the back seat. 'Hello Dad,' I said without humour. He grinned at me, stretching the scar on his cheek, then shoved over so I could get in.

'Good to see you, Son.' he said.

I grinned at him and, if you can imagine it's possible to grin in a serious way, then that's the look I gave him. 'Yes, I'm sick of dressing like a schoolboy,' I said, looking down at my 'disguise' with distaste. In Lugano, I could be free to dress how I liked and be who I wanted to be. I wanted to look old enough to pass for at least five years older. I couldn't wait to change into the designer suit I had packed in my luggage, and my new 1,000-euro buckskin shoes.

I tried not to let the Spanish's presumptive behaviour bother me but, secretly, I didn't find it funny that he'd told the chauffeur I was his son, even as a joke. Yes, I knew she was Blondie, the Spanish's girlfriend, but last time I met her she had been the plain-looking girl on the other side of a crowded bar. I had ordered the reluctant Spanish to seduce her for information about the Swiss banking system and now she was acting like she was my step-mother! Then again, I couldn't blame him for following orders too well, could I?

'How much does she know?' I asked the Spanish, watching her closing the trunk on my luggage and making her way to the driver's seat.

'Don't worry. We haven't told Blondie the half of it. She knows we have a leader but nothing about him. She doesn't really think you're my son, though. She thinks you're some other relative coming for your vacation.' Shit, so it wasn't a joke – it was a cover story.

Then Blondie got into the front seat, shot me a look through the rear view mirror and said: 'You'd better put your seat belt on, kid.' I ignored her order and pressed a button on the armrest that controlled the glass partition between the driver and the back of the car. She held my gaze as I looked her straight in the eye with the most stony-faced expression I could manage, while the sound-proof glass slowly rose between us.

'Where are the others?' the Spanish asked.

'They're coming. I left them squabbling over their luggage,' I said.

Pasquale and the others appeared ahead of us, tumbling out of the automatic doors, dragging their luggage and looking lost. Minutes later we were all gathered in the limo, which hardly made a hum as we sped off into town. I soon forgot Blondie. The atmosphere in the back of the car was full of holiday spirit. I felt free for the first time in a long time and we laughed all the way to The Trading Post, the shop we'd set up to launder the money we'd stolen.

'We've done a magnificent job with the shop,' said the Spanish as we pulled up. 'It's looking like a real enterprise.'

Inside was IT Guy and I was glad to see him. He was the oldest in the gang and, apart from me, the most intelligent. He was also one of the nicest human beings I'd ever met. I'd saved his life by letting him join our gang so he looked up to me. For me, he was almost a father figure. He shook my hand at first but, as if he couldn't resist, pulled me into a bear hug and then held me at arm's length to look at me with a kind of fatherly pride in his eyes. 'Look at you, Prince. It's good to see you.'

The Spanish popped the cork on a bottle of 200-euro Champagne and I looked around the room to see that everyone was there. The whole gang back together again.

Gianni, the lisping runt of the litter.

Pasquale, the tough-guy street fighter.

The Spanish, Pasquale's even tougher brother.

The Cat, a little guy with a joke for every occasion.

IT Guy, educated, gentle and intelligent.

And me, the Prince, the leader, the God, the brains of the operation.

'To the future,' said Pasquale, raising his glass.

Blondie glared at me as I stood in my kids' clothes. I looked back at her and downed a glass of Champagne in one go.

'To the future,' we all said together.

I'd been doing a lot of thinking about the future on the flight over, as it happens. I'd been working out how we could launder more of our eight million euros and how we could make the shop into a larger business.

I washed and changed into clothes I felt more comfortable in and gelled my hair. We drank more Champagne and ate dinner in the restaurant next door to the shop. We talked about everything except what we had come here for. I had a lot to say but I kept it to myself for a while. We were celebrating and I didn't want to ruin the atmosphere by 'talking shop', but I was also aware that Blondie thought I was just some kid, some schoolboy relative of the 'grown-ups'. I wanted to keep that going for a while. I played up to it. I asked the waiter for a straw to drink my Champagne through. This got me the desired look of puzzlement and disapproval from Blondie, but it backfired because the guys thought it was a great idea and they all asked for one. I thought about asking Pasquale to cut my steak up but decided that might be going too far. Then I got bored of the game. Besides, I had business to discuss. Time to drop the school-kid disguise. Time to get down to business.

The conversation was buzzing; everyone was high on success and Champagne, as well as being on holiday. I tapped my glass with a fork to get everyone's attention. Serious now, I sat in expectation as the voices died down and everyone willingly and happily turned to me to listen. I glanced at Blondie and felt satisfied at her puzzled expression, then chastised myself for my immature need to shock and focused on what I wanted to say.

'We have a lot of cash,' I said to the hushed table, 'and that's a risk for us. We don't want to attract attention. So I think we should spend some of it, but keep the rest. And we'll make sure that what we do spend – we make it work for us. We need to create an asset: not any asset but a money laundering asset, and I think the best thing to do is to buy this restaurant.'

Blondie laughed and then went quiet when everyone looked at her without smiling.

'Good idea,' said IT Guy.

'Can I be the chef?' shouted Gianni, who loved to cook. I was pleased he suggested this, as his talent in the kitchen had been part of my idea.

'Yes,' I said and watched a grin take over his whole, stupid face. 'We can use some of the money to promote the restaurant by channelling the cash through it.' This was an accounting trick commonly used in Naples since restaurants, especially the cheap ones, are always cash businesses.

We discussed the plan into the night. We planned to hire good people from Naples. We'd bring the best food from Italy, with the cash always coming from the Swiss account; even the refurbishment of the restaurant would be paid for in cash. All this allowed us to borrow very little from the bank and, as we had small interest to repay, we could charge reasonable prices for a great meal.

Even if we traded at a loss for a while, we would have built a great brand. We'd give value for money, pay the loan back quickly and get our money back through the growth of the business. And we could create fictitious customers to launder a ton of cash, too.

The idea went down a storm with the guys, always shocked by my inventiveness (but not as shocked as Blondie, who sat listening quietly). I felt like one of those guys in suits who hung around Lugano talking business while sipping Champagne.

In the end, the Spanish had the decency to confirm to Blondie that I was indeed their boss, if she hadn't guessed already, but he didn't tell her any more about the gang or my place in it. While it took her a little time and maybe a little wine, she eventually began to chip in with ideas about how we could make the shop into a larger business. She turned out to have a more than adequate business brain and I could see she would be an asset to us.

While the others were laughing at something Gianni had said that was probably not meant to be funny, I turned to Blondie. I caught her eye, raised my Champagne glass and gave her a wink, then my best smile. She laughed and shook her head, then gave me a beaming smile back while raising her own glass. At the same time, we both took a 10-euro swig of fizzing golden nectar.

Those first few days in Lugano were exciting. I loved the change of scenery and the open life of luxury. I loved not having to hide or pretend to be a normal kid. Lugano was perfect: the Monte Carlo of Switzerland, home of the Italian-speaking, yacht owning mega-rich. You couldn't walk down a Lugano street without bumping into a Hollywood movie star and this is where 'the Prince' came into his own. I was a long way from that filthy shanty-town.

I was standing on Lake Lugano's crescent-shaped waterfront with Gianni, reluctantly having allowed him to tag along. He hung around me, his perpetual idiotic grin showing his million teeth, as he scratched the scaly patch of lizard skin he'd had on his elbow ever since I'd known him. I stood away, ignoring him as I surveyed the luxurious scene and watched girls as they passed by. I was considering getting a water taxi to Gandria but in the end I just stared out at the sunlight glittering on the water. I felt clean. Everything here seemed to be scrubbed and fresh.

When we came here on our first ever trip to Lugano, right after Bulldog-Day, we'd been shocked by this sparkling place. The sudden change from our crowded, dirty living conditions had left us awestruck and we were inebriated by the beauty, the wealth and class. Overexcited by it all, I'd strutted around like a celebrity – like I owned the city – dressed as a prince should dress, pretending to be older than I was. I drank alcohol and mingled with people who thought I was in my 20s. I had basked in our success, spending the money we'd 'earned' from robbing and blackmailing the Bulldog. We'd stayed for a whole month. I remember thinking it would last forever.

It didn't. And when we returned to Naples it was a trauma. Back to the shack, the rats and the grime. Even now, with my family re-housed, I could feel the anger boiling inside, and I couldn't let anyone see it. It was a long shot that anyone would guess what

I'd been up to, but it was always a risk. I didn't know who was in the Bulldog's pocket. The rich continued as before. Their houses were renovated, their swimming pools increased in number, their rooms filled with antiques and paintings; our world had been reduced to living in sheds with corrugated tin roofs like ovens in the summer and freezers in the winter.

They'd stolen millions and millions in earthquake aid money. I'd managed to get some of it back from Bulldog, but the rest was still being openly rubbed in our faces as new electronic security gates, new swimming pools built especially for their kids and bigger, shinier cars.

After I'd uncovered the Bulldog's evil paedophile ring and blackmailed him into funding new apartments for the city, he had put everything in his power into finding out who this new enemy was. Police, tough guys and priests were all on the lookout, asking questions, searching for me. Bulldog had activated all the powers he had to find out who had come into possession not only of his money and jewels but also his documents and taped conversations. They were scouring the city, relentlessly asking anyone in the streets who might have seen or heard anything that would lead to the capture of 'The Criminals', as we were called.

The effort of pretending to be what I most definitely was not was exhausting. From the way I dressed to the way I spoke and what I said, I had to perform, to create a whole convincing character as far from reality as I could imagine. It was excruciating and the only time I could be myself was in secret, in the Cave, with the members of my gang.

One Saturday afternoon, after dispelling some of my rage with the adrenaline of riding through Naples at life-threatening speed, Gianni and I went to church. We hadn't turned to God or gone there to pray for forgiveness; we went to help the priest collect money for the church funds. We usually went on a Sunday because we knew it was the only place we could mix with the people who lived in the grand mansions behind those gates, the people who had our aid money. We had a list of 21 addresses stolen from

Bulldog's safe: his accomplices, the people who had the rest of the aid money. It was at church where we could connect the list of addresses with names and faces.

The priest stood by the altar. His jowly face usually glowed pale and always looked somehow slightly damp but today it shone strangely red and green from the reflection of the sunlight through the stained glass window. He was gazing miserably around what had in the recent past been an elegant interior that could match up to any church in Naples. The beautiful marble and stone figures of saints that had watched over the congregation for a hundred years were gone and the church was dotted with empty plinths whose only job now was each to mark a two-metre space along the outer edges of the pews. The priest's predecessor had gambled them away, sold them to pay off his poker debts, along with the rest of what they'd had in the coffers. The priest dreamed of reinstating the saints, which now most likely stood in great big dining halls in grand mansions who knows where.

'We can help, Father,' we said. 'We can collect money on your behalf. We will give up our afternoons after school and go round to anyone you think would donate to get this place befitting the glory of God once again.'

He looked from Gianni's face to mine slowly, with hope and pride in his eyes. Gianni and I tried to appear earnest, standing with our backs straight and looking him in the eye. I had instructed Gianni, who had difficulty interacting with anyone outside his family or the gang, to maintain steady eye contact with the priest and not to stammer or to scratch. In the end we'd decided I would do all the talking. The priest trusted us; after all, we'd been working on him for quite some time. He didn't hesitate. He led us into the vestry and handed us a sheet of paper containing a list of parishioners' names and addresses – the area's wealthiest residents. Those who could afford to give to the church (or those who wanted to be seen giving to the church).

'God is on our side after all,' I said to Gianni as we ran down the steps outside. I was already hatching our plan, imagining complex alarm systems and dreaming of ways to get around them.

The list contained the details of some 60 people. Many of them I knew I could connect with the names on Bulldog's list: the politicians, councillors and police that had left us living in dust.

Twenty-one of the names on that document were listed as the Bulldog's corrupt accomplices. They were the richest and most powerful, and all publicly prominent with key jobs in government. Bulldog's documents reported that they each had more than three well-paid jobs that were used as a way to justify their sudden income jump: fictitious jobs to cover a very real and solid fortune.

Over the following few weeks, Gianni and I completed several rounds of the parish, visiting all 60 of the names on the list. When the time came to turn to the twenty-one, we chose the richest and the easiest first and visited them several times. Their wives would let us in and give us lots of money for the church along with cakes, drinks and sweets. They mostly spoke to me while Gianni shuffled his feet, saying thank you too many times, wide-eyed and wide-grinned. When they did address him, they spoke too loudly and too slowly.

We pretended to be in awe of the splendour of their houses and none of them could resist showing off so they gave us, the underprivileged kids from the poor side of town, guided tours of their grand houses.

'And this is the games room.'

'This fountain is made of the finest Italian marble.'

'This is an original painting by a famous French artist; it's worth a hell of a lot of money.'

'This is my husband's collection of 18th-century duelling pistols.'

'Mind that vase, it's more than 300 years old.'

We thanked them gratefully for their generosity. All the while I was collecting data, getting to know them and the layouts of their properties. By the time we decided we were ready, we knew exactly how to enter and get out of every single villa.

We gave all of the donations directly to the priest and each time the pride and admiration shining from his eyes increased.

The Grim Reaper had swept away entire families in the shanty-town, and the feeling of frustration that bit ferociously at my insides had grown to an almost unbearable level. I'd seen enough of their boastful displays of gaudy and unnecessary excess to give me the final push to begin our real work. Gianni, for all his faults, was so efficient at carrying out technical instructions he was almost robotic. He would watch me go through a sequence only once and then copy it as if he'd been doing it all his life. He had no idea of the reasons why he was doing anything, of course, but he could be relied on to repeat what he'd been told to do without fault. So I sent him around all the houses we had targeted after teaching him how to place a low-frequency recorder next to electronic gates. Hardly anyone noticed him, and those who did just smiled and waved. 'There's that poor retarded boy. What a shame.'

When Gianni had finished we had the remote control set up to access every one of the residences without being noticed or making any noise.

I had drawn a blueprint of every house we had targeted and I was rehearsing in my head what I was about to do in each one of them. On our initial charity collection round, one of the wives had told me they would be spending December in a ski resort in the north of Italy and the house was ideal from a security system point of view. This would be our first target. It was the house with a unicorn.

THE UNICORN HOUSE

The people who lived in the grand villas just saw us as kids collecting money for the church – good kids, but stupid kids with kids' brains. They offered us lemonade and cakes and made sure we didn't break anything or touch anything with our sticky little kids' hands. They couldn't have made a bigger mistake.

On the day we broke into the Unicorn house, everyone had been a little nervous but excited. We were in the Cave and Pasquale was sitting by me, listening to my every word.

'We have exactly 40 minutes to get in there, do what we have to do and get out again,' I said, holding up a small electronic alarm decoder. 'I'd like to introduce you to the Infrared Sonic Disrupter.' Blank looks all round. 'Okay, I like to call it "The Silencer". This will deactivate a burglar alarm for 40 minutes. After that, the battery will run out and if we're still in there the alarm will go off and we'll get caught.'

Gianni looked scared. Pasquale grinned. His gold tooth glinted and the scar on his cheek contracted. 'Plenty of time,' he said, looking relaxed and taking the device gently out of my hands to examine it. 'This little thing can really deactivate an alarm?' he asked.

'Yes,' I said. The gang had seen my inventive devices before but they were surprised every time I came up with something new. 'The time constrictions come from the frequency generator,' I explained. 'It emanates a high frequency that covers up the alarm system, giving the impression to the alarm that the house is empty. Unfortunately, as I said it gives us only 40 minutes' grace. After that, with the battery dead, the alarm will sense people in the house and go off.'

'It's so small,' said the Spanish as he leaned in to take a look and went to poke his over-sized finger into an open circuit on the device. Pasquale quickly pulled it out of his reach, smacking his brother's hand away, which started a wrestling match as the Spanish tried to get the device off him.

'Stop!' I ordered, attempting to take the silencer off Pasquale. 'Do you want to break it? If you break it we're out of business right now.' They gave up the device immediately, of course, but they carried on their fight. Pasquale had his brother in a head-lock and was pretending to punch him in the face, his fist just stopping before impact. Good job because even though the Spanish was 6ft 4ins tall, with large shoulders and powerful arms and had learned to fight in prison, one punch from Pasquale's giant hands could have spread his nose across his face.

'OK, guys, calm it down,' I said. 'We've got work to do.'

'Yes, Boss,' Pasquale said, releasing his brother's head and standing to attention, like a soldier ordered by his superior officer. The Spanish's lank blond hair looked messy which irritated me almost as much as Gianni, standing there looking camp, one hand on his hip, the other hanging in the air, useless apart from when he occasionally used it to scratch himself.

'This is going to be a breeze,' said Pasquale.

I knew he was right. I nodded in agreement. All muscles with no brains, I never got tired of Pasquale's devotion. I looked around at the rest of the gang to be sure they were all listening. IT Guy looked expectant but his eyes, as usual, were dead; the Spanish and the Cat were always primed with adrenaline and ready for anything. And Gianni, well ... forget it! He had his uses but he irritated me, a lot.

After going over the blueprint once more, I was satisfied everyone knew the layout of the house. We had rehearsed so many times and we each knew our role. We drove in full daylight to the Unicorn house in a white van we'd stolen the day before and hidden under the bushes near the Cave. The Spanish drove and the rest of us hid in the back in primed silence. At the ornate iron gates, we used the electronic remote to open them. It worked faultlessly, of course, and they swept open, inviting us in. I could tell that the Spanish's heart was in his mouth as he pulled the van forward up the winding tree-lined driveway.

When parked outside the front, the house and the van were out of view of the road because of the thick bushes and trees populating the garden. One by one, we jumped out onto the gravel with both feet. The guys were pumped with adrenaline. Their premature celebration, silent cheers, fists punching the air and wide grins made me nervous.

I led the way in through the front door. The locks were easy for me. The guys watched with admiration and awe as I easily dealt with each lock and opened the door with a gentle push. We were in. The Spanish stayed outside with the van to keep a lookout and to be ready if we needed a quick getaway. The rest of us went into the house. The Cat scoured each room and the IT Guy went off to find the phones while Pasquale, Gianni and I made our way to the study where we knew the safe was kept.

As soon as I'd entered the great hallway with the double sweeping marble staircases (the same marble the unicorn was made of) I was filled with hate for the people who lived here, and especially the woman who had given us a tour when we'd come collecting money for the church. As I looked around at the familiar furnishings and paintings hanging on the walls, I remembered her over-lipsticked mouth twisting in disgust at Gianni, telling him to mind the vase that was more than 300 years old. The urge to smash it was overwhelming. I resisted.

Entering the vast kitchen, I remembered the last time I'd been in that room. The bleached blonde, over-coiffed, over-painted woman, who had managed to serve us refreshments, show us around the house and give us money, all without ever lowering her snooty nose or directly looking at us, had asked me without any real interest, purely to break an awkward silence: 'So, child, what do you want to be when you leave school?'

'I want to be an astronaut,' I'd said, enthusiastically, deliberately childishly. She had raised her eyebrows and smirked at my stupidity. I looked at her crooked, smug mouth and then at the rest of her. I tried to imagine my poor mother carrying buckets of water and scrubbing the floor of our tin shack wearing the same pale pink linen pants suit, her plain face painted in all that make-up, her hair dyed blonde and set in the same stiff, unmoveable helmet shape as this woman's.

And then Gianni, his mouth full of cake, had dissolved my disturbing fantasy by coming out with: 'I want to be a dancer.' I nearly choked on my lemonade. The Unicorn house woman looked directly at us both for the first time, her eyebrows raised in surprise. Then her eyes cast down to Gianni's chubby little 14-year-old body and back up to his cake-smeared face. He put his cake down, stood and executed a perfect pirouette on his absurdly tiny feet. It was surprisingly dainty and graceful. I was as shocked as she was. Her expression was unforgettable. Her eyes were wide and her mouth opened in a perfect red 'o', as if to say something, but no words came out. Immediately she composed herself, regaining her superiority, her nose taking its previous snooty position in the air, her eyes once again diverted. She said, a little too sharply: 'Well, perhaps you should eat fewer slices of cake,' and started removing the plates from the table, taking my unfinished glass of lemonade right out of my hand and turning her back on us. It was, evidently, time to go.

I smirked at the memory of it as I made my way through the kitchen to the study, glancing at Gianni now. He was sweating and his little tiny feet were stumbling over themselves with no hint of the dancer's daintiness displayed before. I felt what was almost a sense of fondness for him. Despite his faults, he entertained us all by being unintentionally funny. I nearly laughed out loud as I imagined him in a tutu, like the hippo out of Disney's *Fantasia*. But when I reached the study and saw the safe, my focus returned, laser-like, onto the job I'd rehearsed in my mind so many times over the past months that I felt a strange sense of déjà vu.

It took me 10 minutes to crack the safe. I silently thanked my Granddad, the locksmith, for all he had taught me. Even though my knowledge and skill had quickly surpassed his, he was still the reason I was who I was. Pasquale gasped as I pulled the safe door open to reveal four stacks of used notes bound in elastic bands. There must have been 100,000 euros in there, and lying beside them an open box filled with gold jewellery studded with glittering gems. A wide bracelet with at least 10 rows of beautifully cut, glittering diamonds was laid out across the front as if someone had just taken it off. It was calling out to me: 'Snatch me, snatch me.'

But instead of grabbing the bracelet, stuffing it in my pocket and legging it out of there like I wanted to, I asked Pasquale for the notebook and pencil and he dutifully passed them to me. I roughly sketched a diagram of how the contents were laid out inside the safe, noting as well as I could the exact position of each item. Then I passed the notebook back to Pasquale, whose hands were shaking, I swear. I looked up at him and he wasn't looking at me, he was looking at the cash and the jewellery with greed in his eyes. 'No,' I said. 'Don't even think about it.' But I shared his temptation and I had to exercise more willpower than I'd anticipated. Not because I wanted the diamonds and the money, well, not entirely, but because I wanted to hurt the snooty lipsticked woman by taking her precious bracelet.

I carefully, with gloved hands, removed each item and reached into the back of the safe where there was a plastic office file box stuffed with papers and documents. I took it to the big desk and laid the papers out on top, took out my camera and snapped each one. When the film was finished I took another one out of my pocket and loaded it up, repeating until all of the documents were photographed. There was no time to read them, but I knew in my heart we had found what we came for. I put each document back into the file exactly as I'd found it. Then I placed all the items, the money and the jewels back according to the sketch I'd made and finally laid out the bracelet, clasp to the left, just as it had been.

The Cat and IT Guy appeared on schedule, just as I was closing the safe and setting the dial back to point to the same position where we'd found it.

'Three minutes to go, Boss,' IT Guy stammered.

I looked at him with a question in my eyes, and he nodded. He had fulfilled his mission and expertly tapped every phone in the house. With two minutes before the alarms would sense our presence and go off, we ran through the Unicorn house out to the waiting van with no 'swag bags', no jewellery and no money. Our gloved hands were as empty as when we'd arrived.

We drove out of the gates 39 minutes and 30 seconds after we drove in and the alarms remained silent. We were also silent as the van made its way up the hill to the Cave. I knew the guys felt depressed as the adrenaline high left them. Their mood wasn't helped by the fact that we'd had to leave all that money and jewellery behind, but I felt the opposite. I knew what I had in my camera was far more valuable than those trinkets and I felt exhilarated. They didn't understand and didn't have the imagination to foresee the consequences of what we'd just accomplished, but they trusted me and they'd watched me prepare for this for a full year.

I had been looking for something far more valuable to all of us than money or gold and diamond jewellery. Now we had photographic copies of the first set of documents. I had in my pocket the start of a game that I enjoyed playing, a game with an ending that would finally satisfy my hunger for revenge.

The corrupt politicians, councillors and mobsters felt secure with all their secret documents locked away in their safes but they were far from it. In the 40 days that followed our 'robbery' of the Unicorn house, we repeated the same activity in nearly all of the houses on the list. We waited until they were empty – most were away on vacation – then we blocked the alarms, went in, photographed their documents and left without leaving any indication we'd been there, leaving everything exactly as it was.

I developed each of the rolls of film myself and when I'd finished I spent hour upon hour poring over them, searching. I knew exactly what I was looking for: evidence of the stolen earthquake aid money stashed in Swiss accounts. And I found it – along with all of the names of their accounts, their account numbers and passwords. When I had them all collected and ready I scoured the documents again to find signatures and I stayed up night after night practicing all of them until I had each one perfect and feeling as natural as if I were writing my own name.

Swiss banks never communicated with the customers by phone (to preserve their secrecy) and only by fax if it was extremely urgent. If I knew all their passwords and faked their signatures, I could move money around at will, just like Bulldog had done when he stole the money in the first place. All I did was reverse the process. In a month of relative quiet, like August, it was easy to bring the money back to Italy directly to the Naples Council, or the Office For Reconstruction to be exact.

Pasquale worked there and had told me which accounts it should be sent to so that it could be rubber stamped by Rome and (re)allocated legitimately to the rightful housing project.

This was the reason I got him the job in the right department at the council. His place of work was the office where it all started and, with his help, it had taken me no time to make my way to the right places to get the procedure up and running. Once I got all the information about the accounts in Switzerland, I prepared all the faxes, signed them myself with the respective signatures and started to send them to Rome, where the central office authorised the transactions. Once the money was moved from Switzerland to the housing project account where it belonged, the clerks in various government bodies in Rome just sent the faxes to the building company to get the work started. I knew if I could get all that done by the time those crooks came back from their expensive vacations, it would be too late for them to reverse the process.

Because we left everything untouched, my victims had no idea what was going on.

With all the faxes prepared, the Minister in Rome approved all the housing projects; everything looked correct and all the building work had now been paid for. In a month, we stole in excess of 130 million euros and redirected most of it to the earthquake victims' re-housing project. It was simply beautiful...

The mob had been able to 'steal' the money without ever stealing it, technically, in the first place. The original theft of the money by the corrupt politician members of the mob had just slowed the flow of the funds to such an extent that years would go by. They'd make sure the costing, planning and progress of the building work was so slow that the clerk in charge would retire or change department, more files would open on new projects and more urgent items would replace the old ones. Over time, the projects the money had been meant for would be forgotten. In other words, they just kept the funds until the slow Italian bureaucracy had messed its own records up. They 'borrowed' the money and waited: as simple as that. If one of the clerks noticed any missing money and kicked up a fuss they'd throw a few grand his way or send a written apology or a good excuse, which bought them extra time. In the case of the rebuilding of Naples, this meant years. They would have kept the money forever and then spent it at their leisure once they were confident the whole thing had been erased by time and red tape.

There wasn't any news announcement after we redirected the money back to where it had been supposed to go, since nobody knew what had happened and everything looked so ordinary that the work started without major fuss or fanfare. It felt like – it was – a major victory. All the people in the shanty-town, together with another 14,000 families scattered everywhere else, would be re-housed.

During the rest of the summer, Gianni and I still visited the villas on Saturday afternoons, and sometimes after school, to collect for the church. Keeping our faces straight was somewhat harder than before, however, and I had a particularly hard time playing the school-kid in front of the Unicorn house woman because when I looked at her snooty face I was filled with joy at the pain she was going to feel when she found out she wasn't going to be able to buy as many cans of hairspray or diamond bracelets any more.

Revenge was well and truly in place and, when we'd completed everything and the summer came to an end, I called the gang together in the Cave and revealed to them that they were millionaires. I had skimmed off eight million euros for the gang. I had shared it equally between us, deposited in numbered accounts in Lugano. 'For rainy days,' I said.

We'd jumped around the Cave punching the air, punching each other, unable to contain our excitement. We felt indestructible, unchallenged and powerful. It was that afternoon that we made plans for our holiday to Lugano.

'Put your dancing shoes on, Gianni,' I said to his idiotic grinning face, 'you shall go to the ball.'

After those 'robberies', where we took nothing while taking everything, I should have been on top of the world. And for those first few days of our holiday in Lugano I was. I was still strutting around like the place like a celebrity. Okay, so I enjoyed the respect I had from the gang, but this was far worse, I was basically getting high on my own sense of importance.

Then, that day on the waterfront with Gianni, thinking back over how I had come to be living in such luxury and decadence, something changed. One moment I was high on life, excited about the day's potential and feeling the power of having so many choices available to me and then, in a split second, the world became flat and grey because of just one thought.

Gianni tried to make a joke about our elevation from school-kids to playboy millionaires: 'We can't get in a taxi. We're famous movie stars. We must have our own yacht.'

I looked away from his spraying mouth to gaze out at the luxury mansions floating gracefully on the lake and I considered the fact that I could have my own yacht, like Gianni said, if I wanted one. That was the moment, standing on the waterfront, when I realised I had everything.

'It's not enough,' I thought.

One thought, just three words, had the power to change my whole world. The novelty of Lugano fell away and I felt something sink in my chest. Just like that, in this glittering place, I was right back in the grip of the same yawning boredom that had engulfed me at school.

That night I struggled to get to sleep and I had a nightmare. I was running from the mob. They were coming for me and for my family. I was hiding with my Mum, my Dad and my little brother in a cellar and we had to keep quiet as the armed gangsters' footsteps pounded back and forth on the wooden trap door above us. My little brother sneezed and I put my hand over his mouth. There was a silence above that lasted a long time. I knew they'd heard and the trap door swung open and their guns came into view. Then I woke up, horrified, gasping for breath and covered in sweat.

It was a free fall into misery from then on; the days that followed were as much torture as the months I'd spent suffocating in school. Surrounded by glitz and glamour though I was, nothing pleased me. Dissatisfaction ate away and I became desperate for relief. And I found it. The descent into darkness was unstoppable: as inevitable as an alcoholic downing a bottle of vodka offered to him after months of being forced into abstinence.

I fought it, of course. I didn't just deteriorate there and then. The intelligent, rational part of me wanted to enjoy living the rich life I'd always dreamed of before the earthquake. I was always so calculating, so careful not to let my emotions get the better of me. But I was sick and tired of watching every step I made; I wanted to let it all out, let it spin out of control. The only way I could get the fix I needed was to stop analysing everything, to stop being aware. So I blocked out my logical thinking and shut my eyes to it. I started to be more irrational and impulsive, doing whatever I felt like and saying whatever I wanted. I had bottled up my emotions for two years and, at the end of the day, I was still a kid.

Back at the house the gang arranged to meet in the restaurant at 7 p.m. for dinner. I said: 'I'll meet you there,' and went off to my room. I knew I wasn't going to turn up. And it would be that way from then on for the rest of the vacation. I was acting up. I'd make more plans with them, for dinner or a trip somewhere, and then I just wouldn't go. I became inconsiderate, arrogant and cocky. I was a pain in the ass.

The only time I did turn up was whenever we went to the casino in Lugano for a few drinks and some food. I was blown away by the atmosphere. My need for excitement, for risk of some sort, was so acute that it wasn't long before being blown away turned into being sucked in. I had a lot of money in my pocket and, with the way I was dressed and the way I was so confident and arrogant, who the fuck could have guessed that I was 15? I bought a fake ID card and decided to take up gambling.

That first time we went, I stacked up the chips on the roulette table and, with a gin on the rocks and my slick hair and sharp suit, I felt like I was Al Pacino in *Scarface*. I slid 1,000 euros-worth of chips over to number 13. The IT Guy sucked in his breath and Pasquale gasped. No one bets on 13.

To be fair, the IT Guy had a right to worry because I'd borrowed the 1,000 euros from him. But the wheel stopped spinning and the ball was sitting in slot 13. I had won.

I felt invincible. I placed my next bet on number 7, another number we considered unlucky, smiling at the IT Guy, who folded up the newspaper he'd been reading, gave me a look of pure misery and walked away. I won again – and the next game and the next. I was flying high.

The first time I lost I couldn't believe it. I'd convinced myself I could overcome the odds of the casino with my mathematical skills, but from then on I kept on losing, of course. The house always wins. I was so drunk on the adrenaline and the need to fill the empty hole in my gut that, towards the end of my holiday, I was spending the whole night at the casino.

Before I knew it, I had lost more than 150 grand.

The boys weren't happy about me spending money in the casino, especially as I kept borrowing from them, but they didn't dare say a thing. Nonetheless, I had the money to make good on my losses and the guys knew that. Still, it didn't help; more than what I'd lost, what the gang really didn't like was the way I was behaving. I was getting more cocky and irresponsible every day. By the time my vacation came to an end, the guys were glad to see the back of me. I'd become impossible. On the day I left to return to Naples, I could tell by their faces that they were worried about me but I didn't care. All I cared about by then was the money I'd lost and my head was busy calculating how I could get it back.

My share of the money in the Cave had disappeared in my gambling losses and I had no way to take money out of Switzerland safely. I was a millionaire, I felt like a millionaire but I had no money available. Back in Naples, frustrated, I started to steal cars. I cut deals with a few dodgy mechanics in the area and they would order cars for me to steal and deliver to them. Then I'd spend the income from that every Saturday night by gambling in dodgy places run by the local crooks. I always came out cleaned out. Illegally gained, illegally lost. My school-kid disguise was slipping and I exposed my real character too often and to far too many members of the network of Naples criminals to be comfortable with what I was doing, but even this risk was a buzz.

I was breaking every rule that had made me and my gang a roaring success and I still felt neither danger nor fear. I was getting deeper and deeper in it and losing what had made me invincible: my invisibility.

Pasquale wasted his breath for weeks in trying to talk me out of being that monster, especially because I was mingling with unsavoury characters more and more. I was attracting attention from all kinds of sharks, as I seemed to have limitless amounts of money to gamble. It was only a matter of time before things got out of hand. It was lucky that I didn't have full access to the money in Switzerland, as now IT Guy was using it to expand the business, or I would have lost that too!

I was getting sloppy at school. I stopped going to church and went to the Cave only when I had no more money to gamble. I counted almost 150 cars that I'd stolen in eight months and I had nothing to show for it. That was incredible for someone like me. I lost in excess of five hundred thousand euros in less than a year.

I was chasing highs that could never satisfy me as much as when we were planning and robbing the villas. I was hungry for more revenge, more action, more planning, more anything other than just day-to-day living. Not even money could satisfy my hunger.

My fixes were gambling, stealing cars and listening to the taped conversations from the bugs we'd planted in the villas we'd robbed, in that order. All the time I was listening to those tapes, I was forming more plans in my head, searching for something to latch on to that would lift me out of my boredom: a thread, a lead.

I found the thread of something both interesting and disturbing on the tapes so I started bugging more and more people, unravelling a real network of crooks that spanned from our industrialists to the bishops (yes, the Church!) and to the new upcoming force of the underworld, the head of a large section of the Camorra – the Butcher.

As the list of bugged people grew, I was amazed by the calibre of the individuals I was listening to on those tapes: members of the Church; politicians from all parties; entrepreneurs; celebrities – the best Italy had to offer! Their illegal activities were jaw-dropping. Trafficking, pornography, child abuse – all of the vilest crimes you can think of were being discussed during those calls and I could hear all of it. I wasn't exactly pure as the driven snow myself when it came to crimes, I know, but theirs were stomach-churning.

It made it even worse to see them in public, humbly accepting thanks for rebuilding the city, knowing that inside they were seething with anger and humiliation.

One name kept being repeated more and more often. I kept picking up references to someone they called 'The big guy'. I started to link the pieces together and realised they were talking about the 'Big Boss', the local number one gangster and head of the most powerful criminal family this side of the Atlantic.

I began to realise, from the jigsaw of phone calls, that they blamed their missing money on the Big Boss. They thought it was him who had taken their money! While this made me feel relieved and safer, I was seething inside. I knew I couldn't ever take public credit for what I'd done but it felt like I had the credit when they blamed a mystery criminal. I felt like a masked comic book hero – I was Superman. It was like a punch in the face to realise someone else, someone undeserving, had the recognition that was most definitely mine!

After listening to endless hours of recordings, I knew that the inevitable was about to happen; the corrupt politicians wanted blood for all the money that was stolen away from them and, as they had placed the blame squarely on the Big Boss, it would be all-out war. The Big Boss benefitted financially from my actions as he controlled, directly or indirectly, most of the companies instructed by Rome to carry out the reconstructions. Moreover, the economy of the city as a whole had been growing as a consequence of all that money pouring in, again increasing the bottom line of the local Mafia. From a logical point of view, it made sense that those crooks blamed the gangster for everything: the jobs were carried out in an amazingly professional manner and he was the one who profited the most. The reigning political party felt betrayed and they started talking about recruiting the Butcher to replace the Big Boss. This would have unleashed a war of epic proportions on the whole south of Italy, with hundreds if not thousands of people left for dead as a consequence. I was amazed by their behaviour and by the nonchalance with which those people were negotiating the lives of so many, the very same citizens of a so-called republic that had put them in a position of power in the first place. I never sensed an ounce of remorse in their tone of voice, not once. They wanted someone to pay and they did not care that their revenge would come with a cost.

Despite my vivid imaginings of what it might come to, I had to play the life of a normal boy, a good student with nothing to fear. I thought that if I kept up appearances I'd be OK and, over time, the whole thing would go away.

When June came, Pasquale insisted on taking me back to Switzerland as he was genuinely concerned and wanted to get me out of there. I had not done so well at school for the first time in my life, but even that didn't bother me. My addictive personality was now in full control of my rationality and I had no way to reset.

I was 16 years and 6 months old. I had stolen in excess of 140 million euros, more than 300 cars, more than 1.5 million euros of jewels and I had got away with it. I had built my own gang, a successful business in Lugano (with their help, of course), got all my boys a job and re-housed more than 4,000 families by then, with another 16,000 flats on the way. So what if I had lost more than half a million euros gambling: no one's perfect! Or at least that was what I kept repeating to myself.

In Lugano, the guys physically blocked my route to the casino if they could and tried to brainwash me to quit gambling whenever they couldn't. I was very proud of them but very ashamed of myself: they had done everything I had asked them to do, to the letter, but now I was the one letting them down. I decided things had to change and, in order to keep away from temptation, I went straight back to spend the rest of the summer with my Grandma, mind fully focused on keeping away from cards and illegal joints.

I was struggling to contain an unstable personality. The life of a normal teenager was no longer for me. I could not relax around people of my own age. Paranoid? No, I had every reason to be worried.

I rewound to the moment we got the Cat out of prison. The letter to the warden had been anonymous ... but it might as well have had my signature on it.

ENCOUNTER WITH DEATH

One night, in a bar that had become my regular haunt, I ordered a whisky to quell the grogginess of the previous beers. In between the bottles of spirits on the shelf, there was a plastic statue of the Madonna watching over me. She was radiating an electric holy glow from her batteries. The bartender planted the whisky on the counter without looking at me (he'd never looked at me). He took my money and turned away. I raised my glass to his back and then to the Madonna. I downed it, then asked for another beer.

I liked this place but not because of the decor. It was because no one cared that I was under-age. The other customers were older working men who drank a lot and smoked. I don't know if they knew I was only 16, but no one mentioned it, except to call me 'Kid'. I also liked the small-stakes card games some of the regulars played. Feeling guilty about my promise to the gang I told myself I wasn't gambling, just playing a game or two.

I stood by one of the tables, watching them play. One of the men looked at me, said: 'OK, Kid,' and kicked a chair out. I sat down on it and joined the game. The first few hands I won some pocket change, a few euros, then I lost and lost again. I quit before I was cleaned out and went to play the video game on the console in the corner. I congratulated myself on my restraint. This time I wouldn't repeat my huge gambling losses.

It was a whole a year since we broke into anywhere and it felt like nothing had happened. Not since we re-stole the 130 million anyway. If I compared myself to other kids, I could have fitted a whole normal kid's lifetime into that one year. Gambling, alcohol, criminal connections, a secret hideaway, a gang. And we stole from the most dangerous criminals in Italy. And not forgetting the riches! We had eight million euros! Without the shadow of my addiction to adrenaline, I'd have seen that the year had contained several lifetimes' worth of events: extraordinary lives at that. Such was my mental state at the time, though, that none of it registered. I felt trapped. It seemed like time was flowing backward, torturing me with the slow agony of boredom. I couldn't even be myself with the gang anymore, not even in private in the Cave. I'd promised them, sworn to them on my honour, that I'd stopped gambling. Lies upon lies fuelled the fire that drove me towards the only release I could find – drinking and gambling in secret.

Aliens made of pixels stomped across the screen of the video console like marching soldiers. I fired laser beams up at them, blasting them out of existence one by one. But more kept on coming. I was, as always, determined to win so I didn't let up. I shot them all until I reached a level that had the little monsters moving across the screen at such high speed I had to give it all my focus. The bar and all the noise of the drinking, talking men disappeared. All I cared about was winning.

Then, through the concentration, a voice seemed to come from somewhere inside the back of my head. I ignored it, feeling annoyed. It was far away, like when my Mother tried to wake me up for school. Then a tap on my shoulder jolted me back into the room. I looked around, startled, angry. I was on for my highest-score and the interruption made me lose a life.

'Hey, Kid, you want a game of cards?' The trance broke. I was surprised that the guy calling me 'Kid' was, in fact, about the same age as me – but at least a foot taller. He was skinny, though his clothes didn't hang off him. He wore skin-tight jeans, which only highlighted the lanky body and big head. A giant head in fact, topped with a thick thatch of sand-coloured upward-growing hair dense as cat fur. He'd had it cut so it spiked up all over. He looked like a broom.

I looked him up and down, craning my neck to stare up rudely at the top of his spiky brush head. Then I smiled, shrugged and nodded. I followed the Broom to a table. We sat; he gave me a pack of cards to deal, leaned back and lit a cigarette. His confidence and the ease with which he moved made him seem much older. He gestured to the bartender with two fingers and a single glance, barely shifting his gaze from me and the cards. Two beers were brought to our table. I'd never seen the guy come from behind the bar to serve a table before.

'So they tell me you're called the Prince,' he said.

'Yep,' I said. 'Who's they?'

He answered by sweeping his eyes across the room and gesturing with his hand to the men sitting at the scattered tables around us. His cigarette was still resting in his mouth. His eyebrows raised as if I'd asked him something stupid, as if who 'they' were was obvious.

'You from around here?' I asked.

'Are you?' I had the feeling he already knew, which should have made me feel uncomfortable but I was drunk.

'Yep,' I said again and dealt the cards between us.

He handed me a cigarette, dragged on his own and picked up his pack. He shuffled with an ease and flow that gave away his familiarity with cards. I started to get nervous about losing even more money.

'Why did you pick me for a game?' I asked, suspecting 'they' had told him I was an easy target because I lost more often than I won.

'I thought it would be good to play someone my own age for a change,' he said, 'instead of all these old guys who whinge about their nagging wives or their bad backs.'

He sounded friendly. I relaxed a bit but still suspected I was dealing with a card shark about to have me for lunch. We played the game and chatted about the joys of under-age drinking. We had a laugh that no one ever asked for proof of age. We discussed mopeds, football and girls. I told him about the 'rich but thick' kids at my school and how I didn't fit in. I told him how I resented the rich people who lived in the villas and how I thought our politicians were corrupt. And I talked about my family, the filth we had lived in at the shack, and my little brother.

My alcohol-addled brain, our regular bursts of laughter and the joy of gambling with someone intelligent meant I ignored the warning signs: how he chatted easily with me without ever saying anything revealing about himself. I let it pass when he always answered a question with a question. I was also thrown by the surprise I felt when I started winning; it was too easy. Still,

I let that pass me by in favour of the buzz I got from outsmarting someone smart. I was also impressed by the respect he received from the usually surly bar staff.

I won the game. I slid the little pile of money from the centre of the table towards me, smiling.

'Another game?' I asked, hoping.

'Nah,' he said and laughed. 'You've taken everything I have.' He stood and turned his pockets inside out. 'Good game though. Next time.' He slapped me on the shoulder as he left. I stashed the money in my pockets and ordered another drink, making my way back to the Space Invaders. I'd had a good night and I felt high on the relief from boredom, the illusion of pleasure from absent pain.

A couple of months went by and I started to make a regular habit of having a few games a week with the Broom. He was unique. He was the only person I could enjoy gambling with. The rest of my gang thought I had quit and I didn't know anyone else my age I could trust. Even though we were spending quite a lot of time together, I knew little about him. I wasn't bothered that he was adept at dodging my occasional questions. Looking back, I'm sure he already knew everything about me before we met.

One night, a friend of the Broom's called Elvis turned up and asked to join us for a few hands. He was older, in his 30s. He had a ponytail so neat it was like a girl's and he wore an expensive leather jacket. He told me he was studying law at university and we chatted a bit about the inefficient legal system in Italy. I liked him. I felt comfortable with him. He came back the following week and I had made him feel comfortable with me, too: enough to make me a proposition. He invited me to an out-of-town poker session. The stakes, he said, were 'much more interesting'.

I missed the adrenaline from real gambling so I agreed.

Elvis told me the game was at a house 25 miles away in a place I didn't know well. It wasn't a rough area but anywhere away from your own manor had its dangers. People like me would never venture out without a good reason or a chaperone. It was a farming area, away from the hustle and bustle of the city, and the people were peasants so I didn't see any threat. The truth is the thrill of gambling was such a strong lure I'd have gone anywhere with him!

'How much to sit down at the table?' I asked.

He looked me hard in the eye for a beat, then hit me with it: 'Five grand minimum.'

That got me interested. There were still no alarm bells but there should have been. How could he have had any idea that a teenage kid like me would be able to raise five thousand euros?

The gambling monster was back and I was once again blind to the potential consequences of my actions.

It was the first weekend of December when I jumped on my Vespa and made my way to this place. I was so excited about the game. The house was beyond the Neapolitan suburbs. It was isolated, right in the middle of farmers' fields with no neighbours. I didn't think: 'No one to hear you scream.' But if I'd been watching myself in a movie, I would have.

The lights on the ground floor of the large ramshackle house were on and as soon as I rang the bell the door opened. The Broom and Elvis invited me into a big hallway. A brown toddler, naked apart from a filthy nappy, trundled along the stone floor on a plastic tractor. There was also a beautiful woman dressed in bright colours with yards of skirts. She looked at me with suspicion, swept the child up in her arms and said with a heavy accent: 'Come Chiki.' They both disappeared into a doorway. The Broom and Elvis led me to another room, where they greeted me with a whisky and soda. Four men in their thirties or forties were sitting around a table. They were dark-skinned with black eyes, wearing either vests or shirts open to reveal vests. They all had tattoos of roses, birds, and scrolls with words I didn't recognise. They wore big gold watches and rings. One, the oldest going by his grey beard and moustache, wore a cheap trilby made from straw. His face was like a goat's; his eyes were so wide apart I wondered if they worked independently of each other. His field of vision must have been 360 degrees. His name was Stevo. He gestured with his hand for me to sit, trailing a cloud of smoke from his cigar.

Sitting opposite me was a bald giant with a thick moustache

and tattooed arms. He was like a nightclub bouncer only more menacing. His eyes locked onto me, filled with suspicion.

'This is Boldo,' said Elvis, friendly and reassuring. 'Don't mind him. He's like that with everyone.'

I sat down in the chair between two empty chairs, comforted by the fact that the Broom and Elvis would have to sit next to me like some sort of protection. Pali, to the right, was tiny, about five four. I could tell he was the type of guy whose height meant he'd had to compensate by becoming as ferocious as a terrier. His teeth were rotten, his voice was high pitched and his words tripped out as fast as he could think of them. He sounded like a cartoon character. He was talking nonstop and laughing with the guy next to him, Emilian. Emilian was the only clean-shaven man there but the rest of him was so hairy he probably had to shave to avoid being mistaken for a gorilla. Fur almost totally obscured his tattoos. He had on a gold chain with what I thought was a Saint Christopher pendant but I wasn't sure since it only occasionally glinted through the thick forest. Neither Pali nor Emilian looked at me when Elvis introduced us. They just carried on talking and laughing. I couldn't understand what they said as their dialect was so strong (I wasn't even sure it was Italian). I had the feeling it was me they were laughing at.

By now I had worked out I was amongst gypsies. This didn't scare me. I had some sympathy with them as I knew a lot about their history. They'd been ostracised, tortured and killed in their millions. Being from a poor family myself, I felt a kinship with the Roma, especially since I lived in a shanty-town not so different from their camps. I knew they had to put up with suspicion, rejection and victimisation from the police. Even the Mafia wouldn't deal with them. But despite my political correctness, in this room, with these gypsies, I felt uneasy.

I didn't have much time to think further about their Roma origins. I stopped worrying about the menacing stares. The game started and excitement took over.

The cards were dealt and my surroundings disappeared, as I focused all my energy on my laser-like analysis of their poker faces and tells. I went into the same trance as I did on the Space Invader game, winning my only goal. Hours went by but it felt like only a few moments. All of my problems dissolved away, except just the one – I was losing.

At one point I noticed the Broom had gone. He'd said he was going for a toilet break and he hadn't returned. Elvis had disappeared, too, leaving me alone with the zoo animals. I couldn't communicate with them. Even after listening to their dialect for hours, I was still struggling to understand. When they made a joke with each other, I was not laughing. I was completely cut off from their conversation. I was not comfortable in their company but I was so engrossed in the game that I ignored everything else. After the small whisky I only drank water, so I can't blame it on being drunk, but by midnight I was down a staggering amount.

They had a borrowing facility and, when you had run out of chips, you could ask for some more. I did this 15 times. Yes, 15. Each time the Goat smiled and said: 'You good for it, Kid?'

All I had to do was nod and he would throw me another chip.

I knew I was going deeper and deeper but I hadn't realised how much. Fifteen times five plus the five I'd come with, added up to 80 grand in the hole. I guess I was already used to losing that kind of money back in Lugano, knowing I had millions stashed nearby to back me up. Although I still had those millions, they were a lot further away. I was thinking about how I could get the money to them when what I should have been thinking about was how they knew I could pay that kind of money back.

When the game was over, my total loss was 85,000 euros. I didn't flinch, I said: 'I will get your money by the end of the month, before the New Year.' The Giant got up from the table and his shadow engulfed me. He leaned in and said: 'By then you will owe 100 grand, including interest. You better pay.'

I said: 'I will be back here with 100 grand; you have my word on it. Give me some time to put it together.'

Fixing me with his black eyes he replied in no more than a whisper: 'You better.'

I was riding back home on my Vespa, dreaming up a way to get hold of the money without the boys finding out about my gambling when a car came speeding up behind me. Its headlights grew so fast in my mirror that I thought it must be a drunk driver. I slowed down and drove close to the edge of the bushes that lined the road to let it by. But the old Fiat 127 didn't overtake. It cut across me and pulled over, braking hard. If I hadn't done the same I'd have smashed into it.

I was still getting my breath back from the scare of the near crash when the Giant got out of the car and walked towards me. I felt a cold, hard fear run through my body and I wanted to run but my legs seemed disconnected from my brain. I thought I was in for a beating and imagined them finding my bloody body at the side of the road and my Mother crying. But instead of beating me up the Giant pulled out a revolver and put it to my head. I could feel the barrel pressing agonisingly hard into the skin of my forehead.

I thought I knew fear. Nothing I had done before had ever felt like this. I was numb. I couldn't feel anything at all. I had both feet on the ground and my hands on the Vespa but I wasn't in my body. I was beside myself looking on. I could barely see the Giant in the dark but there was another person there, a teenage boy who looked like me having a gun held to his head. But as the boy didn't feel like me, I couldn't be sure it was me. Beyond that I had stopped functioning altogether as that animal glared into my face so close I would have felt his breath if I'd been in my body.

'If you do not pay, next time I will pull the trigger,' he said. Then he lowered the gun, strolled away, got in his car and drove off.

It had lasted no more than 30 seconds but it felt like much longer. The experience was so intense that the memory would still fill me with fear even after 20 years. I now know what it feels like when you're about to die.

After the car disappeared, I was frozen. My knuckles were white as I gripped the Vespa's handlebars. Unable to move, I might as well have been dead for real.

Finally, I had enough energy to get off my Vespa and throw myself on the ground. I vomited everything I had inside me, and more. It had been 3 a.m. when I left the poker table and I was still by the roadside when the sun came out. I must have been there, paralysed, for over 2 hours.

I lay at the roadside with the sun coming up feeling thankful I had survived. If I'd known who I was dealing with, I'd have begged the Giant to pull the trigger.

I don't remember most of the journey home. I have only vague impressions of having to fight overwhelming resistance. I had to drag the power up from some deep place inside just to get on my Vespa and navigate the journey back through the countryside to the city. The urge to lie down at the side of the road and sleep was so strong that each tiny decision took superhuman effort: stand up; get on the bike; turn on the ignition; raise my eyes to the road; drive forward; keep my balance; turn a corner. Finally the resistance disappeared and I went into autopilot. Somehow my body knew what to do even though my mind wasn't present to give orders. I still marvel at how my body worked independently from my brain.

I do remember looking up at the sky: a bright and clear Sunday morning. Not seeing the beauty in my surroundings, I looked only inwards at my anger. Rage had risen up into my throat as I drove along those country roads, separated from my body, looking out across the fields like I was on a day trip. My mind wasn't stable and I couldn't hang on to the anger as it slipped away back to numbness and nothingness. The rest of the way home I think I was asleep, although I can't have been.

The next thing I knew, I was lying in bed. My Mother was there and a doctor was trying to bring me back to consciousness. I tried to pull myself up through what felt like thick brown earth, as if I was buried, but the effort needed was too much. Then I was burning. I saw a bright light and I thought I was dead. Maybe I had been shot in the head. Then I thought it was sunlight and that I hadn't made it home from the countryside. I was filled with terror that I had been hallucinating when I'd seen my Mother, the doctor and my bed, and in reality I was still lying in a ditch somewhere, dying.

The bright light, however, wasn't the sun; it was a torch. The doctor was just trying to get a reaction from my pupil. I had a temperature of over 41 degrees and I was delirious. I could only form impressions of the doctor, the room, Gianni's concerned face, the light of the torch. I wasn't sure where I was. I stayed in that state for days.

When I did eventually wake up I had only a vague recollection of the previous week. I managed to sit up in bed and eat. I had no idea if I'd eaten anything before that or how I'd gone to the bathroom and I didn't want to know. But now, I urgently needed to pee. I hauled myself up out of the bed: Frankenstein's monster lumbering across the floor, slowly, too weak to prevent my feet from dragging on the linoleum. In the bathroom I looked at myself in the mirror and in the middle of my forehead was a perfect red circle, like someone had marked me with a cattle branding iron. It was where the barrel of the gun had been jammed into my forehead. My own personal stigmata.

Gianni was there again, smiling, glad to see me awake. I was probably still delirious because I felt such warm feelings for him. My friendship with Gianni had always been driven by self-interest and revenge. He had irritated me and I'd been embarrassed to be seen with him, disgusted by his tiny feet, his stammering lisp, his stupidity, and his eating habits which drove me wild. I'd say I felt nothing for him, but the truth is I hadn't really thought about him at all. The possibility that he had grown on me, until now, had passed me by. He was a real friend and I felt fond of him. He could have lectured me about my gambling, for not having kept my promise. He should have been angry at me for putting the whole gang at risk. But he didn't and he wasn't. He just took my hand and told me he was my friend and he was there with me. I wanted to cry. I wanted to apologise. I did neither. I looked at his stupid big round face and listened to his familiar, faltering, unintentionally funny, pleasingly pointless conversation.

He came every day to see me and it was all I looked forward to – that and my little brother playing in my room and my Mother clucking around me, tucking me in and stroking my hair. Gianni's presence chased away the monsters that had entered my mind, through a gateway that had opened when that gun pressed against my head. When I had enough strength to speak full sentences I told him what had happened that night. He didn't say anything; he just listened.

After I shared my ordeal with Gianni, I felt less frightened, as if passing it to him had decreased its volume. When he left, I felt well enough to get up and have dinner with my family.

'Hello Boney,' said my kid brother, grinning from the table. I made a face at him as my Mother guided me into our living room, not quite helping me to walk but fussing around me in case I should fall.

'Hey Kid,' I said. 'You've got food in your teeth.' He hadn't and he knew it. He put the fingers of both hands in his mouth and stretched his lips out to reveal all of his teeth and gums to me, his little kid version of giving me the finger. I pretended to be disgusted. My father said: 'Stop messing around and eat.'

As I sat eating, talking to my family and, to my surprise, laughing, I felt so cared for and loved I wanted to stay in that womb-like convalescence forever. But I knew I couldn't. My kid brother called me Boney. I'd lost more than 6kg, so I had to spend another week in bed to build my strength back up. Tormented by what had happened, the slowly fading red circle on my forehead reminding me that time was running out.

On my last day in bed, Gianni brought Pasquale with him when he came to visit me. Unlike Gianni, Pasquale wasn't bringing me grapes and get-well cards, and he wasn't sitting by my bed holding my hand. He was wired and agitated, pacing the room with his fists clenched so that his knuckles were white. This wasn't the Pasquale I'd come to know, the guy with the responsible job and a stake in a thriving business. This was the tough and violent street kid I'd recruited years before. I could see the old rage re-awakened. And what he told me put an end to any kind of comfort I'd been feeling.

'We found out who your gambling pals were,' he said without looking at me. 'Only the Royal family.'

The flash of shame I felt for letting them all down was wiped out and I was propelled into a whole new world of horror. I was in debt to the Gypsy equivalent of the Mafia, who held power over their area by threats and violence. Stories of their vengeance were plenty and widespread and their methods were inhuman. In Naples, the Royal family of Gypsies was everyone's worst nightmare. No one, not even the Camorra, got involved with them. One thing was now clear: even if I had paid them the 100 grand owed, it wouldn't have been the end of it. If I'd known the Broom was a Royal Gypsy, I would have stayed well clear of him. Obviously.

'Once you're involved with this family, you know they're impossible to get rid of, right?' said Pasquale.

I nodded.

'They will pursue you in a terrible way,' he went on.

'Alright, I get it,' I said, trying to think through the bombardment of thoughts and fear.

'I'm going to get a bunch of guys together and sort this out,' Pasquale said.

'No,' I said. 'It was my fault. I promised to give up gambling. I wasn't cheated. I lost fair and square. So, technically, I do owe them that money. Let me just pay them and then we'll see what happens.'

'They'll never stop. Those guys are like the plague. You know it,' he said, looking directly at me for the first time.

'Let's just pay them and see,' I insisted. 'We will deal with their shit when it floats to the surface, yes?'

He stared at me for a long time then said: 'OK.' I could see his jaw twitching.

The revelation ended my convalescence and I got out of bed as soon as Pasquale had gone. I told Gianni my plans and swore him to secrecy. I got dressed and packed a bag with enough to last me a few days.

'What are you doing?' said my Mother. 'Where do you think you're going with that?' She pointed to my bag.

'I'm feeling much better and I just want to get up,' I lied. 'Gianni's asked me to go stay at his for a few days. I've got to catch up on my school-work.'

I saw her relax. 'Oh, OK. That will probably do you good, but don't do too much. I know what you're like when you push yourself too hard and you've been very sick. And you shouldn't be carrying that heavy bag.'

I handed the bag to Gianni. He wasn't expecting it to be so heavy.

'OK, Mother, I won't work too hard,' I said. I kissed her on the forehead, playfully punched my kid brother in the arm, ruffled his hair and we walked out the door.

I didn't go to Gianni's house. I went straight to the train station to buy a ticket to Lugano.

On the train, I kept myself busy trying to chat up girls. I had twelve hours of attempting to get phone numbers and thinking, trying to convince myself that once I paid these guys off, this problem would go away for good. I calculated that my share of the Swiss account now stood at more than 850 grand. I still had my share of the Swiss business to come my way when I reached 18 so, all in all, I could proudly say that, barring any more incidents like this, I would still have plenty of money left over.

The fear started to subside and I was in a good mood. I had learned my lessons. I genuinely thought I'd had enough of gambling and that I'd never be tempted to do it again.

When we crossed over the border, the beauty of Switzerland flooded my senses. Christmas time was now everywhere in all its glory and the weather was cold, fresh and crisp. Lugano glittered like a Christmas tree all year round, but I swear that from the train window it now looked like a million diamonds. For a moment I felt such pure happiness that I thought my heart would burst.

As the train approached my final destination, I watched the throng of people waiting on the platform. So different from Naples – all stylish and polished, all loaded down with Christmas shopping. Then I saw IT Guy. I was confused. What was he doing there? No one but Gianni knew I was coming. Maybe it wasn't him. Maybe it was just someone who looked like him. But it was him and he was staring right at me, obviously waiting for me, and the expression on his face swept aside the happiness in my chest and thumped in its place a heavy and leaden dread.

As soon as I was off the train, IT Guy took my bags, grabbed me by the arm and marched me to his car. He didn't even say hello, just: 'Come with me. We have no time.'

'Where are we going?' I asked, not wanting to know, knowing it was going to be something bad, something terrible.

'Your brother has had an accident. He's been taken to the hospital in Naples. We are going straight back to Naples.' That sentence was enough to crash my world. The next, ripped it apart. 'To the Cardarelli.'

The Cardarelli was not our local hospital but the general hospital in Naples. An ambulance would take a patient there only when the local hospital was deemed inadequate. Straight away that meant it was serious.

'What happened?' I asked him, stunned.

'I'm not sure, I just got the message to bring you back.'

For the next seven hours, IT Guy drove pedal to metal through the dark. During those hours in the fast lane, I felt I was getting smaller and smaller.

When we arrived at the hospital at around 7.30 that Sunday morning, the atmosphere between IT Guy and me was as sombre as if someone had just died. We'd hardly exchanged a word during the whole trip and I was in absolute panic, but nothing would have prepared me for what I was going to see.

As soon as I mentioned my little brother's name, the receptionist at the hospital offered no resistance and we were escorted by a nurse to where he and my family were staying, against all policies of the hospital. Normally, visitors were not allowed in at that time in the morning but, worryingly, they were making an exception for me. Everything, from the face of the receptionist to the concerned look of the nurse, contributed to my quickly growing state of anxiety. My heart was beating so quickly I had barely enough energy to spare to follow the brisk pace of the nurse leading us to where my baby brother was staying. IT Guy, despite being tired from a very long journey through the night, followed us without a whisper. When we arrived at a grey door in what looked like a very silent ward, the nurse, who so far had said nothing, said: 'Do not make a sound, do you understand?'

237

She gently opened the door and I saw my Mum leaning on a bed with her knees on the floor and my Dad looking at me with very tired eyes. His eyes were not only tired but also full of rage. Lying in that white bed was my younger brother, with tubes coming out of every orifice of his body and a machine indicating his heart rate. The beep was so gentle you could hardly hear it and the big grey door, closing behind us, felt like a metal prison gate being shut. The handle made such a noise that it echoed through the whole ward of the hospital. We were in the Resuscitation Ward, where they take the comatose and the patients within an inch of their lives.

Something was going on that I didn't understand. I was ready to have my Mother crying on my shoulder and I felt the rare urge to hug my Father in support; my instinct was to support my parents and to be supported by them through our family tragedy. But the IT Guy went over to my Dad, shook hands with him and gently caressed him on the shoulder, using the same care you would use when patting a dangerous animal. He whispered something in his ear and they both quietly left. Neither of them looked at me. I felt like a ghost. I was so shaken by what I was seeing, I couldn't process anything and I started to feel convinced I was dreaming. The same strange disassociated feeling of the night with the gun to my head took me over and I started to think once more that I was actually lying in a ditch out in the countryside and the past weeks had all been a dream.

I stood by my brother's bedside. The poor kid was so covered in bandages that you could hardly see his beautiful face. My Mum was quietly crying, repeating prayers. Without looking at me, she whispered: 'Look what they have done to him, look!' She buried her face in her hands again and carried on praying and crying quietly.

'They?' I said. Something unthinkable bubbled up and broke through the surface into my mind but I used all of my strength to shove it back down again.

Attached to the bed, at very end, I found the medical cards containing the endless list of injuries to my brother. Halfway through reading the long list, I dropped to the floor, banging my head against the chair. Not even that noise distracted my Mum from whatever she was doing. I sank down and lay with my cheek against the cold hospital floor. I knew they had done this. The Royal family had done this to my kid brother. I felt like I had died.

A big ugly judge was reading my kid brother's medical card. He was shouting: 'Permanent damage to his right eye,' and I felt a dagger going through my heart, 'Permanent damage to his left leg,' and another dagger ... I woke up. I didn't know where I was. Then I saw I had a drip attached to my arm. I was in a hospital bed.

I was still barely functioning or aware of what was really happening when I heard Pasquale whispering: 'Welcome back, Prince. Good to see you again, mate.' I felt his tears rolling down his cheeks and onto my hand. It was all too easy to sense his joy and relief that I had come back from a coma. Once again, the warmth I received from a friend gave me a new lease of life.

As soon as I felt able to speak, I asked: 'What happened?'

'You collapsed. You've been out for two days,' he said.

'My brother?' I asked.

'He's still in a bad way. But he'll be going home soon.' I could tell Pasquale was lying to protect me but I was too tired to argue. He then kissed my hand and told me to go to sleep again and that everything would be OK. It worked, as I went back to sleep with a little smile on my face.

A few hours later, I was properly woken by a doctor checking me out. He was happy with the way I was responding to the treatment. I was to have real food at meal times. I still didn't really know which way was up but I felt my strength slowly coming back.

The next day, after eating a few solid meals, I had the whole gang around me during visiting hours. Everyone was trying to crack a joke or to chitchat to me to see what condition I was in. But I could tell it felt unnatural.

'What the hell is going on? Someone tell me or...' I exploded.

They all looked at me like rabbits in the headlights about to be run down. Then they looked at each other. Pasquale being a bit of hard nut didn't give anything away but Gianni's look at Pasquale gave me a hint he had the answer. I stared at him hard until he gave in.

'Sorry Boss, but I better tell you,' he said. 'You'd find out in the end, I guess. It was me and the Spanish what done the Royal family,' he said.

'"Done them"? What do you mean "done them"?' I asked, incredulous.

'Yeah we done 'em good, they won't never be coming back at you!'

You can't just 'do' people. They grow back like weeds stronger and thicker than before. I knew that and they knew it too.

'Why did you do it?' I shot back.

'I got previous with them. So has the Spanish,' Pasquale responded.

I looked at the Spanish. His face was set pretty stern but he didn't try to deny his involvement.

'It was time they got it and now we got money,' Pasquale continued.

'How much did it cost? Who did you use?'

'Good guys. All reliable. Only cost 100 grand. Bargain. All out of my share.'

'So you just upped and did it because suddenly you could afford it?'

'Well, no, mostly because I was angry 'cause of what they did to you. I said to myself … this is what I said…' he was warming to his story now, caught up in the original emotion, no longer wary of my reaction.

'"I will get a bunch of guys together and smash those peasants to bits." That's what I said to myself. And when I say stuff like that, it gets done. You knows that.'

'I do now. Who else knows about this?'

'Just the guys what done it…' He was about to add an 'and' then stopped.

'And?' I said it for him.

'I may have mentioned it down the bar.'

I forget what I said – definitely a swear word, repeated.

I was in shock. 'It was them, wasn't it? They did that to my brother.'

Pasquale didn't say anything. He just looked at the floor. Then he answered my question by whispering: 'They beat him to a pulp. Twenty-seven bones in his body broken. They completely destroyed his eye, Prince.'

Pasquale paused about to cry. 'And it's all my fault.'

Then the Spanish said: 'No, Pasquale, I am also to blame because I was in on it; I helped recruit for you. I was as much a part of it as you.'

'We all were,' said the Cat.

'Except Gianni,' said the Spanish. 'We didn't involve him.'

'And IT Guy was in Switzerland' Pasquale sobbed. I had never heard him cry and it was a horrible wailing – like an old woman and not at all like any sound I could have imagined him making.

'He's got damage to his skull and spine that the doctors say could lead to brain damage and perambulation problems.' Snot came out of his nose as he tried to suppress a sob.

I should have cried, too, but I didn't. I wanted to smash everything; turn the bed over, throw the chairs through the window and then fall on my knees and howl like a wolf. But I couldn't because of the drip in my arm.

I felt the veins throbbing in my head and neck and a flash of pain. Then the tears came. Tears were appropriate for physical pain but too trivial a response for what had happened to my brother.

So – mystery solved. The gang had taken it upon themselves to get the Royal family off my back once and for all. And like all such violent deeds it had simply and directly led to more violence, this time against my little brother. The most innocent of bystanders.

I knew that what had happened to my brother was all Pasquale's fault. I should have been very angry with him but perversely it provided relief from my own tremendous guilt. He had done something which I had only dreamt of doing after spending the night in a ditch in the countryside. I had a grudging respect for him and since he had owned up straight away it helped me to accept it in some way.

'We need you back chief. Take control of the gang and lead us from here or we're all dead,' the Spanish said.

I couldn't argue with that; if we pulled any more vigilante nonsense the whole gang would be out in the open without any allies or protection, and in Naples death soon followed. I knew if I didn't do something, the next visit to my little brother and the rest of my family would be much worse.

Action of some sort was urgent but right then I was just a kid in hospital with tubes in my arm and I had no idea what to do. Despite everything, they still believed in me and in my ability to solve this by producing a miracle. Now I was both fuelled and felled by a mixture of regret, anger and the need for revenge.

What happened to my kid brother was just a calling card from our enemies. The card simply said: 'Come out and play, you bastard!'

Pasquale reckoned that the whole affair with the gypsies was a set-up and that someone knew that we were behind the reconstructions, the funds stolen and everything else we had done in the previous years. I tended to agree. But why were we still alive? One, they were not 100 per cent sure and two, if it was us, we had to pay them back before we died. Or so I speculated.

We talked about ifs and buts and, when the nurse came to drag them away as visiting hours ended, I made them a promise: 'We did it once – we will do it again.' I held out my fist in front of me and said: 'All for one...' and, like the musketeers, they all put their hands on mine and shouted: 'And one for all!' I then ordered: 'Leave me alone now.'

As soon as they had left, I went to sleep and didn't wake up until the middle of the night. First, I went back to the simple solution: blaming Pasquale directly for my brother's injuries. Then I blamed the rest of the gang. Then I blamed that damned Royal family. Then I blamed all of them together, then Pasquale again. This game of 'spin the bottle' went on for a while. When I finally woke properly, the bottle had stopped and it was pointing directly at me.

I was the only one that could be blamed for what had happened to my kid brother. I had ignored the warnings and dived right into gambling with the Broom and Elvis, even when I knew something was not right and could tell they knew more about me than they should have. I was the one who let this happen because of my own addiction to danger and the thrill of gambling. Pasquale and the gang had been acting to protect me after I had broken my promises, risking their safety and putting all of us in danger.

I cried with shame until it was light. Then I wiped my tears away and wandered down the mostly deserted corridors of the hospital. When I walked into my brother's room, my Mum was rocking herself back and forth on a chair in the corner, clutching a crucifix. She saw me enter but she didn't say anything; she just kept on praying. My Dad was by my brother's bedside. He looked just as bad as my Mum but he immediately took me out of earshot into the corridor to give me the details of my brother's condition, pretty much unchanged and still bad. Then he told me about the police, who had been there several times to take statements from my Mum, Dad and the doctors but were as baffled as everyone else. Who would do such a thing to a lovely kid? Even doctors and nurses were angered; no one could believe it. My Dad talked in a whisper and not because he was concerned about other patients sleeping. The whole accident had robbed him of all his physical and mental strength. He couldn't even look at me anymore; when he spoke to me, he looked down at the floor.

I listened to what my Dad said and gave him a hug, trying to encourage him. He barely acknowledged me and he left me there, standing outside in the corridors, without even saying goodbye: he went straight to his other son, the one who needed him most. I didn't blame him.

I went back to my room and sat on my bed, analysing all the data in my head and trying to make sense of it all. There was one thing I was missing but I couldn't see it. Sitting there, feeling shame on top of the acute pain and responsibility for my kid brother. It was like my kid brother had been a major organ – my heart probably – that I'd carried on the outside of my body, open and vulnerable, and they'd taken it and destroyed it as easily as crushing a fly.

Then it hit me... How exactly had the Broom and the Royal family known I had enough money for a high stakes game? And what else did they know about me?

There was an answer to this question and I wanted to know but at the same time the bigger picture started to creep in. Meeting me in the bar, getting to know me, enticing me to a big game, all of it had to have been planned from the start. Why? This family, the Broom, Elvis, they weren't connected in any way to Bulldog, the reconstruction of Naples or the money we stole and there's no way they'd be concerned with me or my actions.

Come on Prince – some piece of the jigsaw, some obvious piece is missing and you're just being too concussed or too stupid to see it. It was there, knocking on my skull trying to come in, but I was pretending I wasn't home because there was no way I wanted to open that door and face that spine-chilling fact. I started to cry again as I gave up the struggle against the all-encompassing enormity of the truth and its terrifying consequences: someone who was connected to what we did had paid the family to get involved. A power higher up was pulling their strings. I shuddered as I considered that this whole line of events leading to the attack could have been just the beginning: a message to me saying, 'We know who you are and what you've done.'

In the cold light of morning I reflected on what my gang of so-called friends had actually done.

I was not there but from what Pasquale had told me it sounded like a massacre. The gang of gypsies had been no more than thirty guys between the ages of 16 and 60. My gang had reduced their caravans to ashes.

Pasquale had just gone through what I had with gambling, but he was addicted to violence and risk; this revenge attack on the gypsies was an excuse to unleash all the frustrations he had kept in check while he was at work in a suit. I didn't blame him anymore, even though he'd lied, because the whole thing was my own fault. I had started it. I had tried to remind him to keep his violent rage in check but, then again, who was I to give anyone advice about rage and revenge?

I suddenly knew my kid brother's attack would have happened even if I hadn't owed that family any money or if Pasquale hadn't battled with them. Even though they were evil, violent and lethal, they were nothing compared to the beast we had awakened when we robbed and blackmailed the Camorra.

I said out loud to myself: 'And now they know who we are.'

Or at least they suspected us. And in their book that is enough to kill and maim.

When the guys all piled into my hospital room later that day, I was more open with them than I had been in a long time. I told them we were exposed. I knew we needed to work things out so we could keep ourselves alive. Hell, probably the only reason we weren't all dead right now was that they must have wanted us to pay them back before they killed us.

'We've made some mistakes, Boss,' said the Spanish. 'Left ourselves wide open.'

It's always the little actions that don't mean anything at the time that have the biggest impact on your life. When the Cat had been in prison we knew he'd be in danger, so we'd paid the warden to keep him safe. The Spanish had been our contact with the warden. Then we'd robbed Bulldog's place and found tapes of Bulldog, the prison warden and others abusing kids – the sickest thing we'd ever seen. We sent the warden copies of the tapes to blackmail him into releasing the Cat.

'The warden knew you,' I said to the Spanish, 'and that you had an investment in the Cat's safety and so it wouldn't have taken many brain cells to deduce that you were probably something to do with the blackmail as well.'

Pasquale cut in: 'The warden probably went straight to his fellow paedophile, Bulldog, with the tapes and, as the tapes were taken directly from the safe in his study, they'd easily have worked out the Spanish also had to be involved in the robbery.'

Pasquale became so agitated, he had to stand up just to burn the energy it gave him.

'It's gotta be obvious the Spanish was involved in both the

robbery and the blackmail. All the prison warden and the Bulldog would have to do would be to have a conversation, make some connections and they could easily piece the jigsaw together. Then all they'd have to do is find the Spanish,' Pasquale said.

'I know,' I said. 'I've been going over it for hours. I don't know how they've made the connection between the Spanish and me or the rest of us, unless they've been watching us. But I can see now that we've been discovered.'

I looked away and said quietly to myself: 'I should have been more careful.

'We have one hope,' I said. 'Look at us! Two school-kids, three street urchins and an accountant. They must think we're the hired help. If they thought we were the top of the deck we'd already be dead.'

All of this, the Royal family, the gun against my head, my brother: they were simply flexing their muscles and their end game was to scare us into coughing up the names of who had really done the job. There was one big reason I felt confident that they would never imagine we were the main guys responsible: I was still alive. Even if they thought we were somehow connected to the Bulldog's blackmail in some shape or form, their own pride would make it impossible to consider they'd been beaten by a bunch of kids and losers. In their paranoid criminal minds, we could only be working for a rival who had commissioned the job.

One name kept coming up in my head, one I'd heard being discussed over and over on the tapes. It was a powerful newcomer to the corruption that ruled over the city, a new Camorra boss: the Butcher.

'How can I take him on, what do I have on him?' I kept asking myself. The only good news was I was no longer afraid or emotional. I was as cool as I used to be. I had my power back. When I felt like that, I could have taken on the world on my own and believed I would win. So, as I had done in the past, I closed my eyes and started to put a plan together.

As the gang left, the Spanish turned to me again and said:

'Prince, we need you back. Come back, chief, to the way you used to be or we're all dead!'

I smiled at him and said: 'The Prince is back!'

The next day, I was discharged from the hospital along with a list of lifestyle recommendations like 'reduce stress' and 'stick to a healthy diet'. How do you reduce stress when every gangster in town wants to kill you? The belief I'd been exposed made me hyper-vigilant and I could sense the electricity running through my core. I'd jump at the slightest noise.

On top of that, I had my school-work to worry about. It might seem odd in the face of death, but I was very concerned about how my life would turn out if I didn't get all the academic accolades my IQ deserved. I still had to pass my exams, even without any time for revision. I'd have to aim for B grades instead of the usual straight As.

My Mum spent all of her time with my kid brother so I had to do my own cooking, cleaning and the rest. Her cooking wasn't known as the healthy option. Mine was worse: a lot worse. I had fish fingers and oven chips for Christmas dinner. It's no wonder I've hated Christmas ever since.

Three days after I left hospital I was back at the Cave, the only place I felt safe. It was like old times: Saturday mornings at the Cave, all the gang together. Crammed into my office between the thousands of tapes, we were united again as the *Rocky* soundtrack blared. The threat brought us somehow closer; if it hadn't been for the fear and the grief and guilt over my kid brother – a suffocating darkness that wouldn't leave me alone – I'd have really enjoyed myself, laughing and messing about between listening to those tapes from the phone taps.

Our job was to go through everything we had and work out how to stay alive. We came up with plan after plan, calculating pros and cons, discussing possibilities and rejecting ones that didn't work – which was all of them – especially the ones that led to us all being slaughtered.

Of course, right from the beginning, we had considered giving the paedophile tapes used to blackmail Bulldog to the press. We'd have liked nothing better than to expose the evil bastards, but that plan always ended in our demise. You'd think that to expose such sick corruption would cause an uproar big enough to bring down the whole system, but no publication or journalist in his right mind would have dared to print or report it. The Camorra were far too powerful. Whoever published that article would be printing his own obituary. Journalists had been killed for far less. Also, it would have taken years for the justice system to catch up with these crooks and by then they would be living in luxury on exotic beaches. In the meantime, we'd have been killed. Of that I am sure.

Every plan we had seemed to end in us dying.

I knew I'd let the gang down and I needed to say something so I said this: 'Just by showing up today, you've proved to be more than friends to me. I let you down. I was your leader but I didn't behave like it. I put your lives and the lives of your loved ones at risk. So, I'd understand if you walk out of that door and never want to see me again. It will be harder without you but, even on my own, I will win this. No matter what, you will always be like brothers to me.'

Simplistic and cheesy but sincere. Still, I thought to myself, 'If I were them, I'd just run away. Leave him in the lurch. His mess, his problem.'

But they weren't like me. This wasn't like before, when they were little more than penniless street urchins. Now they had a lot to lose: a successful Swiss business; money; jobs and a great future. Still, they turned up with the same attitude as when they had nothing. The boys were flabbergasted as they looked at each other, unsure how to react. It seemed like an eternity until...

'We got into this together. We'll get out of it together,' Pasquale said.

To my relief, the rest of the gang nodded in agreement.

'You might have dug the first hole, Prince, but I sure made it deeper,' added Pasquale.

The Cat obviously felt he had to join the confession game when he said, 'I'm responsible for giving away the identity of the gang because you had to get me out of jail.'

Gianni said nothing as he really did have nothing to confess but his eyes said it all: he would fight to the death for us; he was probably grateful to the whole gang just for giving meaning to an otherwise rubbish life.

I started to believe that we would find a way out of this mess.

That week I didn't visit my brother at the hospital. My mere presence seemed to unsettle my family.

Our family home had become a lonely place for me without the noise of my kid brother and the warmth and smell of my Mum's cooking. It made me even more determined not just to survive but to win. If only I could come up with a plan.

The next Saturday at the Cave it was straight down to business. First thing on the agenda was to get our families out of Naples, well, mine and those of the two brothers, Pasquale and the Spanish. Hopefully, Gianni's family weren't in any danger, and the IT Guy and the Cat had no families.

The first job went to IT Guy, as he was the only one who had the maturity and respectability to pull it off. He had to arrange for my kid brother to be moved to a private clinic in Turin. Easy enough but the tricky bit was to cover up who was paying for it. The ruse was that he would offer to pay for the private clinic with his own money as a thank-you for my family's help during his own troubles, when his wife and kid died. The private clinic would cost more than five grand a week but money was not a problem. I had to arrange for my Dad's job suddenly to be transferred to Turin so he would happily let his son be moved there. After a week of poking my nose around at his work and a very generous tip to the Naples office manager, in the region of 35 thousand euros, I thought I'd pulled it off.

Then came a tense wait to see if I was right.

Two weeks later, when my Dad got the news of his new job up north, I knew I'd done it. My poor Father, engrossed in my brother's state of health, didn't even question why he was asked to move office. But it made simple the job of persuading my parents to accept such a generous offer from their former neighbour. After initial rejection they inevitably accepted. Even someone so stubborn and full of pride as my Dad saw sense. To be fair, his stubborn streak wasn't a patch on what it had been. It was as if it had been ground down by the terrible events.

Four weeks in and it was done. My family had escaped from Naples. I stayed behind on the pretext I had to finish my school year, which was only made possible when Gianni persuaded his mother and father to step in and promise to keep an eye on me. Gianni's dad, the wily old headmaster, needed me to stay in Naples to keep his son on track academically. He knew that without me his bill for special tutors would skyrocket and there'd be no guarantee of success. We had never spoken about it but he seemed to sense that the Prince's help came with the cast-iron guarantee that I would do whatever it took to achieve what I'd promised.

It was a lot easier to get Pasquale's family to leave Naples. According to the Spanish it went like this:

'Would you like to leave Naples, ma?'

'Yes!'

'Then come to Lugano and help with my business.'

'OK.'

There was only one decision-maker in that family, and his mother was only too happy to put that horrible city behind her. Job done – again.

Those of us who remained in Naples – me and Gianni at school and Pasquale in the public works department – kept a very low profile, only meeting secretly at the Cave to review tapes, but we felt calmer.

I was sure nothing would happen now, at least not for a while. I reckoned the incident with the Royal family and my brother was just a provocation, nothing more. After all, if it were a simple case of the Royal family wanting their money back, they would have killed me long before now (after having made sure they got the money back first of course). Whoever had hired them thought we'd been involved as some low-level minions: that we just worked for someone big. They needed us alive to lead them to our big backers. This suited me because we could bide our time and, while my enemies underestimated me, I had an unfair advantage:

as long as we kept ourselves out of sight, they would be waiting a long time for our Mr Big to reveal himself. That was my theory anyway.

When all the fuss of moving our families out of Naples had died down, we were left with the job we had all been trying to avoid thinking about: the plan that would save our lives. I had moments where things seemed so normal, like when I was worrying about my school-work and planning for my exams, or riding my Vespa too fast through the streets. It was at these times when part of me wondered if I was just being paranoid, that the gypsy family were just violent thugs and there was no higher power pulling their strings.

Then, one Saturday morning, I was heading across town on the way to the library. I had my Walkman on and I was playing 'Eye Of The Tiger', part walking, part dancing like a boxer tiptoeing round the ring to avoid the blows. I was totally absorbed in the music. I was crossing the road when I saw a car coming towards me with two suited guys in the front seats, one wearing sunglasses. The car was coming straight at me and it didn't seem to be slowing down. It didn't faze me at first; I just took out my earphones and stopped walking, thinking it was just someone going too fast. Then, I realised the car was actually speeding up and heading right at me. I should have run, but I froze. There was nowhere for me to run. There wasn't time. Everything seemed to slow down as I looked right into the eyes of the driver and he looked back into mine. He was smiling. He swerved the car away from me at the very last second and left me standing, shaking, as it disappeared around the corner.

Another calling card. Another message saying: 'We know who you are.'

When I got to the Cave that night I was barely over the shock, still shaking a little, even though I'd downed about five shots of my Dad's whisky.

I didn't tell the guys at first, but they could tell I was wired and maybe it rubbed off on them because they all seemed more hyper than usual. I didn't want to tell them but I knew I had to because if

I didn't I was putting their lives at risk. They needed to know they were in danger.

So I told them. 'We had another calling card today. Some men tried to run me over. Well, they threatened to. They swerved out of the way at the last minute and they were smiling.'

The room fell silent.

'Are you sure it wasn't just some lunatic?' asked the Cat.

'It was a definite, obvious warning,' I said.

Silence again.

Then, suddenly, they were all speaking at once. It was loud and confused, panic-driven babbling mostly but the gist of it was:

'We've got to do something and quick.'

'I don't want to die.'

'Let's blow them up.'

'We've got to get them before they get us.'

I tried to quiet them so I could think.

Then the Spanish said: 'I know where we can get hold of some guns.'

They all started shouting over each other again.

I shouted: 'Guys! Guys! GUYS! We've got this far because we're clever. Guns are the last things we need. We have to use our brains now more than ever. I have a better plan.'

It wasn't true. I had sweet nothing. No plan. Nada. I started to sweat, so I turned away from them.

'OK, Boss,' said Pasquale, looking at his brother. 'We'll put the guns on hold.' The Spanish nodded.

At the door of my office, I turned and looked at them, standing as tall as I could stand, and said 'I'm going to work out the final steps and add them to my written plan tonight. Then we can all meet here tomorrow and I'll reveal everything.'

I spent the next two hours with headphones on listening to the tapes, except I wasn't really listening; my mind was somewhere else. I knew I had less than 24 hours to come up with something that would save our lives and I had nothing.

KING KONG vs GODZILLA

On the way home from the Cave I almost crashed my Vespa because I wasn't concentrating. My brain felt like Joshua, the computer in that movie *War Games*, trying to win a game of Global Thermonuclear War. It was cycling through every possible scenario, rehearsing strike after strike. Every move led to annihilation. I wished I'd given myself more time to come up with a plan. Twenty-four hours! What was I thinking? I knew if I didn't come up with something, the gang would actually resort to getting guns. I'd grown fond of them, but when it came down to it they were idiots. The thought of such misfits tooled up and wired...

I felt desperate. I couldn't eat that night. I couldn't sit down for more than 30 seconds at a time. I sat down to write something and then screwed it up, threw it in the trash and stood up again. I tried to clear my head by watching TV but I couldn't concentrate.

Then something came crashing through the wall of the living room, something big. I found myself lifted up into the air. I didn't know what was happening and I struggled then realised a giant ape had me enclosed in its black, leathery claw. Its fingers squeezed me so I couldn't breathe. The more I struggled, the tighter it gripped. Big, dark, shiny eyes looked at me from a massive face and I stared back up in horror. I screamed, but no sound would come. The ape cocked its head, not aggressively at all. More like a curious dog. I realised it didn't want to hurt me so I started to laugh. I stuck my tongue out at it. It pursed its lips into an 'o' shape and made a gentle 'Oooh' sound. The force of the air from its mouth blew my hair back, its breath stunk of bananas. Feeling like Fay Wray, I blew a raspberry and it cocked its head to the side again.

Then there was more crashing and thudding and everything shook, like another earthquake. Then a loud thud, thud, thud, thud and the most God-awful ear-piercing, high-pitched roar. The giant ape turned its head towards the noise and opened its mouth to reveal a full set of gigantic fangs. It let out a deafening, threatening high-pitched squeal. I wished it hadn't when I saw the huge dinosaur coming towards us through the trees. Without drawing its eyes away from the lizard thing, the ape gently placed me down on a rock. I didn't have time to question why this was happening in my living room and how the rock or the trees got there. All my focus was taken up by terror as a vicious battle raged between the ape and the dinosaur. The noise of roaring and squealing hurt my ears and the ground shook under the colossal monsters. The dinosaur snapped at the air with its croc-like jaws and I knew one bite could end the ape. The ape threw rocks and dodged the snaps and I began to worry about my chances. I knew I might get to live if the ape won, but dinosaur would rip my head off. Then I looked down. I was wearing my designer pyjamas and sitting on the sofa. The TV was on, showing *King Kong Versus Godzilla*. I woke up and laughed out loud. I had a plan.

I grabbed my pen and paper and wrote down:

The Big Boss (King Kong)

The Butcher (Godzilla)

I wrote down everything I'd learned about the Butcher and the Big Boss from the taped phone conversations.

The Big Boss

A cruel gangster, but also an old-fashioned businessman. He doesn't like drugs because he thinks they destroy the fabric of a healthy economy. His businesses, although illegal, still need a healthy economy. He's made so much money trading counterfeit goods without paying duties, he doesn't need the hassle of drug trafficking.

Main income: exporting counterfeit goods/smuggling cigarettes and alcohol.

Sidelines: tax avoidance.

Level of power: superpower. Pioneered counterfeit goods and distribution of them in the 60s. He has goods made in Naples and exports them to Europe and the USA. He controls several ports in Italy and abroad including Greece, Turkey, and Spain. Almost every other gangster in the south of Italy has tried to overthrow him. All have failed. He has held a stranglehold on illegal activity for so long, other criminals have turned to drug trafficking and pornography. These are the only areas left for them to gain power.

The Butcher: the Butcher is the new favourite of many Camorra families. They want to place him as Naples' top dog, replacing the previous top dog, the Bulldog. He's fallen out of favour because he allowed the earthquake funds to be stolen (by us). The Butcher is far more ruthless than his predecessor and more adventurous.

Main income: smuggling, counterfeit goods, drug trafficking.

Sidelines: child pornography and blackmail.

Level of power: owns politicians, judges, the mayor, Naples business owners and law enforcement, including the police commissioners. Some of his business activities appear to be legal and he does business with reputable companies. He has counterfeit goods made in the Far East, where very few venture to do business. He controls criminals in Russia, China, and India where the law might as well be non-existent. Because the Butcher has counterfeit goods made for a fraction of the price, he's the first ever real threat to the Big Boss. His power has grown and he is a serious contender for overthrowing him as the Camorra superpower. It would be only a matter of time before he could displace the Big Boss to take total control of everything.

As I wrote down the bare facts, I felt the gravity of the danger I was in. I realised the earthquake money having rebuilt the city meant a lot of juicy fat construction contracts for the Big Boss's companies. I guessed that the Butcher thought the Big Boss had stolen the earthquake money, which meant he thought I worked for the Big Boss. I couldn't help feeling a bit surprised that I was still alive right now. And I knew that unless I took action, I wouldn't be alive for long.

The corrupt politicians in the pay of the Big Boss thought they 'owned' the 130 million, and so when it went missing they acted like they had been robbed. They assumed it was either the Big Boss or the Butcher (realistically the only two who could have done it). Not knowing which meant they could moan and speculate but could not act for fear of being mistaken. But when the city gets rebuilt they witness all the lucrative reconstruction contracts going to companies that are clearly owned by the Big Boss, they assume it was he who stole the money. Now they are more open to switching sides, handing control of the city to the Butcher (something the Butcher is was already pushing some of them to do with his blackmail).

So the Butcher is profiting from the opportunity that my mastermind plan had created, rather than someone who was aggrieved by that theft.

The Big Boss would know that he was being blamed for the theft, but he would assume it was some sort of false flag ploy by the Butcher. And crucially, he would be expecting an all-out turf war that would inflict huge casualties on both the victor and the vanquished.

These two forces were now locked in a shadow dance, on the verge of a huge battle and I was in the middle. My dream about King Kong and Godzilla made me determined not to get crushed between Godzilla's tummy and King Kong's chest, even by accident. I needed to get myself held in the big protective leathery fist of King Kong. I needed the Big Boss to have no option but to protect me – us – against the Butcher. I had to find a way to make myself indispensable to him. Up until now I had avoided choosing sides in the battle for criminal supremacy in Naples. No longer.

I don't remember getting dressed or riding my Vespa to the Cave because of my preoccupation with the plan. I didn't care that I'd get no more sleep that night. I didn't care it was the middle of the night. I shoved some of my kid brother's toys into a bag and raced to the Cave. I listened to those tapes, the ones I'd marked out as important. And this time I really listened to them. In fact, the plan had made me more focused than ever and my mind felt sharp and clear. I spotted patterns I'd missed and I found new meaning in conversations I'd previously discounted. The grid was filling in.

By morning I had formulated the brilliant plan I'd promised the gang and I was so high I felt on top of the world.

When the guys arrived that morning, instead of the blind panic I'd expected to be in, I was buzzing. I was ready. The guys all sat down, expectant, as I shuffled the bits of paper around on the table and made notes. I was thrilled that I didn't have to pretend to be working on the plan – it was real.

I decided to start at the beginning. I placed two of my brother's toys and a bag of M&Ms under the table in front of me. One toy was my brother's favourite, a large monkey named 'Jacko'. It would have been a soft toy if its face, ears, hands and feet weren't made of rock-hard plastic (hard enough to hurt when he hit me with it). The second was a large green plastic dinosaur, based on a roaring Tyrannosaurus Rex.

I said:

'This is the Big Boss.'

I slid the toy monkey onto the table in front of me.

'And this is the Butcher.' I produced the dinosaur out from under the table.

'These,' I said, scattering the bag of M&Ms onto the table top, 'are us.'

I picked up the dinosaur again and wiggled it around. 'The Butcher,' I said, 'hates the Big Boss.' I pointed to the monkey to indicate that it represented the Big Boss. 'The Butcher is waiting for him to make a mistake so he can pounce.'

To illustrate, I made the dinosaur jump on Jacko the monkey and I wrestled them together awkwardly.

'And the Butcher is also after us.'

I hold the dinosaur so it's looming above an M&M and Gianni's eyes widened – even more than normal – with fear.

'Why?' Gianni asked in a very scared voice.

'I'm getting to that,' I said.

'Anyway, where was I? Oh yes. But he won't kill us – yet,' I moved the dinosaur back to a safe distance. 'Because he wants us to lead him to the Big Boss so he can kill him.' I attacked the monkey with the dinosaur and Gianni looked relieved. 'And then kill all of us.' I smashed the whole pile of M&Ms to bits using the back of the dinosaur's head, with sound effects. Gianni looked like he wanted to scream.

'I still don't get why?' he said.

I had to ignore Gianni's whimpering and get on with my story.

'Now, the Big Boss is one of the richest men in Italy. He's more than a gangster, he's a godfather. He probably thinks he's some sort of benevolent lord, making rules and enforcing them on "his people". I sprinkled some more M&Ms around the monkey to represent his people. 'That no one had ever voted for him doesn't matter to him. Unfortunately for all other gangsters in the south of Italy, the Big Boss has a lock on every lucrative illegal activity, except narcotics and porn. If other crooks want to earn enough money to compete with him, drug trafficking is the only option left. And this is where the Butcher came in.

'The Butcher watched the failures of previous rivals of the Big Boss and knew he couldn't challenge him until he had the right power structure. But the Big Boss owned the politicians and policemen because he paid them off with huge sums of cash, making them rich.

'The Butcher owns Naples' drugs and pornography trade. He's used these to take ownership of Naples' political powers, law enforcement, and legislators. He's lured them away from the Big Boss by giving them drugs and pornography – particularly child pornography, which they all seem to be hungry for. Then he's tightened his grip on them by blackmailing them. So they've granted him more and more freedom of operation. He has judges, police commissioners, the mayor and countless other public figures by the balls. He is becoming unstoppable.

'It's a battle between bribery and blackmail – carrot and stick – and in the end...'

'... the world is only big enough for one of them,' Pasquale finished for me.

I nodded. 'Yes. But, until now, there's been an uneasy truce between them. Neither of them is sure who would win if it came to all-out war, but they know that any war would leave huge casualties on both sides. It would be a pyrrhic victory.'

'A what?' Gianni asked.

I gave him a look.

'All you need to know is that what we did,' I gestured at the M&Ms, 'by getting the earthquake funds back out of their greedy hands and back to where it should be. We have created the spark that will start World War Three.'

'But they was gonna fight anyway,' Pasquale said.

'Take a step back,' I said. 'Who is rebuilding the city?'

Pasquale knew full well because of his job. He listed a bunch of well-to-do government-approved construction companies who were right now digging foundations and pouring concrete.

'Correct. And who owns those companies? Who is making all the profit from the big fat reconstruction projects?'

A light bulb went off in Pasquale's head. 'The Big Boss,' he shot back.

'Right again. And if you know that, then so does the Butcher and all the dodgy politicians. Up until now, they've been loyal to the Big Boss and they don't know for sure who stole the 130 million. For all they know it could be a double bluff by the Butcher. But they're not that clever and they are angry. And, from the sound of things,' I waved some of the tapes from the telephone taps in the air, 'they're ready to betray him. They'll hand the keys to Naples to the Butcher if they get one sniff of evidence that the Big Boss ordered their 130 million euros to go missing. And then, the Butcher will move in for the kill.'

The dinosaur delivered a coup de grâce kick to the monkey's head.

I looked at them one by one. They looked back at me, blinking.

'That's why the Butcher sent the gypsy family to draw you into debt,' said Gianni. 'That's why they did that to your kid brother.'

Something in my gut squeezed as he mentioned my kid brother.

'... to find out who you work for,' added Gianni.

'But we don't work for no one,' Pasquale said.

'Doesn't matter,' I said.

Pasquale reflected and then asked: 'So what you're saying, Boss, is that we're in the middle of a Mafia war. A battle between two all-powerful, evil and lethal enemies, either one of which can snuff us out whenever they want to and they think they know who we are?'

'Yes,' I said.

'It's not looking good so far, Boss,' said the Spanish.

I knew what I'd said had reignited his hunger to get guns and shoot our way out of this. So I swept the crushed M&Ms off the table, reached into my bag and scattered a few healthy and whole ones in their place.

'You haven't heard the plan yet,' I said, looking at them one by one. I summoned up as much of an air of the confident leader as I could, which wasn't hard as I was so sure of my plan. 'This is background and nothing we didn't already know. So give me a chance, OK?'

'OK, go on, Boss,' said Pasquale, shushing the others.

I was a school-kid sitting around my 'den' playing with toys with my mates. As I paused to think about how to go on explaining the plan that would save our lives, it hit me – this was just so surreal. We should have been talking about girls or cars or football but, instead, we were embedded in a war between the most vicious Mafia in the world. I shook the thought off, still not feeling any of the fear I should have been feeling, and continued.

'So they think he did it and they think we work for him,' I said. 'So they're after us and him, but the Big Boss doesn't know the half of it. He knows he's in a battle with the Butcher, yes. He's heard rumours that the Butcher thinks he's responsible for stealing the money because he's the one who benefitted. I mean he knows he didn't steal the money so he reckons he's safe and the discontent will blow over. He doesn't know – he can't know,' I waved the tapes again, 'how immediate the threat is – that they're planning a coup – an epic wholesale betrayal. He thinks it's a rocky patch and still a business-as-usual stalemate situation.'

'So, now for my plan.' I swept the toys and the M&Ms off the table and leaned forward.

I didn't lose any sleep, as it happens. How to get myself face to face with the most feared criminal in Italy became a step in a sequence of events. For an hour or two, I wrestled with elaborate and dramatic ideas. I read history books to find ways lowly people had got meetings with emperors and kings. I imagined myself cramped inside a Trojan horse trundling through the Big Boss's gates. Next was a bomb hidden in my rucksack. I even thought of a giant catapult machine that would throw me straight into his living room. That made me laugh out loud.

In truth, I was daydreaming. I was so used to being the orchestrator of clever plans that gave me an adrenaline rush. I loved to watch my ideas unfold in reality exactly as they had in my mind. Being in control was so addictive, I didn't know how to stop. But now my ideas felt silly, unrealistic, flat and empty. In the end, I knew what I had to do. Knowing I may not see my 18th birthday meant I had no choice. My only option would be to turn up at his house and ring the bell and ask to see him.

Pasquale drove me to the Big Boss's house on his scooter. I clung tightly to the small packet I was carrying. It contained a 'best of' tape of the phone conversations relevant to the Big Boss and a child pornography VHS containing the scenes most incriminating to the Butcher. Creating the VHS had been utterly disturbing. It had nearly broken the gang but it would now, I hoped, be our salvation. It wouldn't be easy. What would he be like? I kept thinking of Marlon Brando in *The Godfather*, but I knew this wasn't right. I understood the difference between Camorra gangsters and Sicilian Mafia. A Sicilian Mafioso would walk the streets and spread good wishes to his beloved neighbourhood, but Neapolitan Camorrists would never be seen in public. They were the invisible brains, the master puppeteers and so much more powerful. Luckily for me, though, the Big Boss was a legend and that meant people loved talking about him. He was portrayed as a kind man with gentle manners and a great love for Naples. But no one had actually seen him and everyone knew he was a cold and ruthless killer. But his address was public information. Everyone knew where his mansion was and stayed well clear of it. It was in the most exclusive neighbourhood of the city, almost 10 miles from my apartment.

Pasquale weaved down the narrow streets, dodging cars, scooters, and people. As we reached the more exclusive side of the city the roads widened and the countryside came into view. I gazed out at the beauty of Naples. All the normal things looked different today and they made me feel different. It was the end of March and spring was full on with all its bright colours. The afternoon sun lit Vesuvius, and it looked like it was glowing from the inside. Even though I'd seen it so many times before, the scenery stunned me every time. Was being born beneath unstable Vesuvius anything to do with this adrenaline addiction? Sometimes the great crater spits and hisses to let us know that it could bury us alive, like Pompeii and Herculaneum.

I made myself a promise that if I got out of this alive, I would never come back to Naples or the shadow of Vesuvius again.

Pasquale dropped me 300 yards from the Big Boss's house. I told him to go and leave me to it, but he didn't move from where we'd parked, watching as I walked towards my fate. To stop my knees trembling, I tried to visualise the Big Boss as a friendly old man. It didn't work and I walked the longest 300 yards of my life.

When I got to the massive grey gates, I found them unguarded and unlocked. This surprised me and I hesitated, thinking I'd got the wrong place. I pushed the giant gate and it swung open a couple of feet and I stepped onto the gravel drive. The instant I put my foot through those gates, two bald-headed, thick-necked heavies stepped from behind the walls. There were five others aiming guns at me. I moved very slowly with a relaxed face and outstretched arms. I was a 17-year-old boy armed with some magnetic tape. I concentrated so much on every aspect of my movement that I actually forgot to be scared.

Stepping further towards me, one of the two no-necks said: 'Are you lost, Kid?'

'I have a meeting with your chief. Tell him the Prince is here and I have what he wants!' I said. It was a speech I'd rehearsed in front of the mirror hundreds of times.

They looked at each other in amazement and didn't know what to do.

I waited for them to make the next move and finally one said: 'Turn around, I need to frisk you.'

He was so rough that I could feel bruises in the making all over my body. Still, I didn't flinch.

They took me to the hallway of the mansion and I passed into the hands of a new attendant, less of a heavy and wearing an impressively expensive suit. I tried to guess from his face how many men he'd killed.

'What have you got for my employer?' he asked.

'It is vital he listens to this,' I said, still relaxed and composed, as I handed him the 'best of' tapes.

The assured manner I had perfected in the mirror was holding up. I had to keep generating curiosity without seeming like any kind of a threat. He stood for a moment and considered me and then the tapes. He didn't know what to do with me. In the end, he took the tapes and walked off.

I stood there without moving under the watch of two more guards, wondering how my legs were holding me up so well.

Thirty minutes later he came back. 'Come!' was all he said.

I could hear my heart pumping as he escorted me through a massive corridor to a huge wooden door. My moment had come and I was trying to pull myself together for the final act of my performance or the final act of my life.

Before he let me in, he searched me again but in a much more gentle fashion. Then he opened the double doors and said: 'Go!'

The Big Boss's office was as huge as a basketball court. I had to walk 40 yards before I got close enough to meet his gaze.

The whole scenario was intimidating and stunning at the same time. The walls were lined with the busts of the Twelve Roman Emperors, each set on a little plinth in its own alcove. Those long-dead emperors watched me walk all the way to the Big Boss as he sat behind his desk. I was happy to know if I died here today, I'd be surrounded by fine paintings and historic books. The floor was immaculate white marble covered with exotic carpets and Roman symbols.

As I approached his enormous polished wooden desk, I thought I was going to faint. I stared ahead but could see in my peripheral vision that either side of him, two men never took their eyes off me.

The Big Boss was nothing like Marlon Brando in *The Godfather* or anything I could have imagined. He did look like a Hollywood actor, but more like George Clooney in a pristine expensive suit. He was so handsome, he looked more like an angel than a gangster. I knew he was in his late fifties but he could have been in his early forties. Slim, not tall, but with an aura and charisma that went far beyond his height. The most powerful man in Italy was before me.

'You must be the Prince. Do I need to bow to you?' he asked with a very clean accent and excellent enunciation.

Lost in his deep-blue eyes, I replied 'That will not be necessary, Sir,' with an impulsive cheeky smile that had not been there in my rehearsal.

Far from laughing he frowned at this frivolity. He leaned back in his massive leather chair.

'You have 30 seconds to save your life.'

If he meant to intimidate me, it had worked.

I was no longer composed but not yet babbling when I said, 'I thought you should hear that tape. It exposes your enemies. I have not come here as your friend, I am not good enough to be that, but I am not your enemy. I am at your disposal if you so wish.'

He relaxed and looked less angry.

He took his glasses off, pushed his papers to one side and asked me to sit down. I was glad because I thought my knees were about to finally give way. With a slight wave of his hand, one of his men gave me a glass of water which I gulped down. As soon as I'd finished it, he waved his hand again and I was given a glass of whisky. He understood I was frightened to death. I didn't drink much alcohol these days but I didn't have the strength to refuse it.

He looked at some written notes on his desk while I drank. Then looked up, put his elbows on the desk and leaned forward.

'As I am sure you can work out,' he said, 'I am impressed and yet puzzled by your visit. You look far too clever to underestimate the consequences of doing this. Which means if you are not mad then you are genuine. And in which case, I admire your courage.'

He paused. I gulped.

'I still have some questions. I strongly advise you not to lie as that will cost you your young life.'

I nodded and gulped again.

He continued 'One: are you really so courageous or very desperate?'

'Desperate, Sir,' I replied quickly.

'So you want something from me in exchange for this information?' he asked.

'Yes, Sir, I want revenge, but my revenge would also advance or at least protect your interests. At this moment, we have something in common.'

I am not sure as his face didn't change one bit but I had the feeling he was starting to like me. He said he was impressed and I felt the hint of it as I was relaxing more and more. It could have been the whisky.

My heart rate was slowly heading back to normal and I stopped looking at his sidekicks as if they were deadly snakes.

He waved the tape. 'Two? Have you got more of these?'

'Yes, Sir. Tell me when and I'll bring them to you.'

Before he opened his mouth again, he took a pause that seemed to last forever. He was not looking at me, he was seeing straight through me.

Then he stopped and turned his attention to the papers on his desk. 'Tomorrow, at four on the dot,' he said. 'And this time I will make sure there are some babàs waiting for you. The best cakes in town.'

He waved his hand again and one of his men got up and walked towards my chair. That was my exit cue.

I stood up. I was so relieved. I could hardly believe I had an appointment with the Big Boss. And the promise of the babàs, the best cakes in Naples, meant he considered it an amicable meeting. I didn't have energy left to breathe and talk – all the air was gone from me. I could only whisper: 'See you tomorrow at four.'

The man walking me out was robotic and distant like the others but much more polite. I had the feeling I was now welcome there. He told me gently: 'Follow me.' He led me outside to one of the many cars parked in the driveway and opened the door for me. He was driving me home. Before shutting the door, he asked: 'Where do you live?'

We did not exchange a single word during the half-hour trip.

I saw Pasquale's scooter buzz past us in some slow traffic. It made me feel more grounded, something and someone familiar to grasp on to.

The car stopped before the gates of the condominium I lived in and the driver said: 'I will pick you up at 3.30 tomorrow. Wait for me here.' I opened the door and got out and he drove off.

When I reached my apartment door, Pasquale was waiting.

I grinned at him as I approached. Then my legs decided they'd had enough and they buckled and I fell on the floor. I was laughing. Pasquale grinned at me, curious. He said: 'What are you doing, Boss?' as he helped me up.

I was laughing too hard and I was too out of breath to answer, but managed to say: 'I'm still alive!'

'Yes, we all are, Boss,' said Pasquale, patting me on the back as he helped his hysterical friend inside the apartment.

The babàs were so good I forgot where I was. They were shockingly and sweetly perfect. The taste had for a moment overridden my fear of where I was, facing the Big Boss for the second time. The syrup hit my senses like a drug and I thought: 'Oh my God!' Then the same thing happened with the coffee. I had never experienced such a depth and complexity of flavour in coffee before. I was, again, startled by the pleasure.

'You like the babàs?' asked the Big Boss.

I had taken another bite of the heavenly cake so I nodded and struggled to swallow it but it had been too big a bite. I felt myself going red.

'Please,' he said, gesturing with his open hand towards the cakes, 'do not rush. Take your time. It would be a sin to hurry such an experience. These are the finest babàs in Naples. We have them delivered every day. I will give you some to take with you.'

As if by magic, a tiny little man rushed in with a cake box. He took four of the babàs from the plate on the Big Boss's desk, placed them into it and handed it to me.

'Thank you,' I said to the small, thin man.

'You're welcome,' The Big Boss said.

I wasn't surprised: the man sitting at the grand oak desk in front of me owned the coffee trade as well as most of the bakeries in the city.

'Who makes these?' I couldn't stop myself from asking. My eyes were wider than I wanted them to be. I was failing at trying to look like an adult.

'They are from a little back-street bakery. But I won't tell you which one just yet,' he said. I didn't know what he meant or why he wouldn't tell me yet, but I accepted it. I wasn't going to argue.

'It's incredible how something as simple as a cake can overwhelm the senses,' he said. 'You are having your own Proustian moment, yes?'

I nodded. I wasn't. I was very much in the here and now. I was flattered, though, that he thought me clever enough to talk about Proust. I felt a little high, like the one I'd had from the cakes but this time it was a hit for my ego, not my physical senses. It didn't last as a realisation reignited my fear. It meant he knew I was unusually well-read for a kid my age. I looked into his eyes and he looked back into mine and I knew he knew everything about me.

'There are,' he said, 'no days of our childhood lived so fully as those we spent with a favourite book.'

I smiled and nodded. We talked for an hour and we moved on from literature to the great leaders of the past, from Caesar to Genghis Khan. I felt exhausted. One moment I was flattered, fascinated and relaxed, the next I was terrorised. Every subject was of particular interest to me and every word had been taken from a blueprint. The whole conversation started and ended with me. He was painting a picture of me in his words, telling me he had me, owned me. At the same time, I could tell that he liked me and he shared some of my passions. I wanted to impress the most feared man in Italy and I felt I had.

Earlier I'd handed over to him a rucksack filled with the tapes and notes. They contained the recorded calls I thought would be most valuable to him. While we talked about books and history, bespectacled suits were poring over the material. The Big Boss got up from his chair and stood facing away from me, looking out of the window. That was when he changed the subject.

'So, tell me something, Prince' he said, his voice softer than before. 'How and why did you get all those tapes and information?'

I knew my reply had to be honest. If I lied to this man he would kill me. I also knew that after my reply he would know everything. I would be in so deep that I might as well not bother to ever try to find my way out. I would no longer be in control of my destiny. He would.

So I crossed the Rubicon. I had no choice.

He sat down, leaned forward and placed his elbows on the desk. He was ready. I started to talk. I told him about the church, the funds in Lugano, the reconstruction orders coming from Rome, the burglaries. The only fact I left out was the hefty 'commission'

I'd taken for myself which I had stashed in a Swiss bank account.

I basically told him it had been me behind all of the mysteries over the last few years in Naples. I couldn't tell if he was surprised or if he already knew, as he didn't move or speak and his eyes never left my face.

We both knew that, by telling him all, I was making a claim. I was establishing myself as a direct cause of events that had been of great benefit to him.

At the end of my 'confession', he kept silent. One of the men who had been examining the tapes came and whispered in his ear and went away again. The Big Boss didn't respond in any way. He asked me: 'So, what do you need me to do for you, Prince?'

'The Royal family,' I said simply.

He nodded. 'They hurt your brother,' he said.

'Yes, Sir,' I said. 'I want them out of Naples.'

'Consider it done,' he said.

I felt a chill snake through me.

'And I want you to do something for me,' he continued.

'Here comes the strings, my shackles,' I thought.

'But first I want you to go back home and finish your year at school. You are far too clever to have such average results. Finish the year and I will send for you to continue this conversation. And when you come back to me bring your school cards. I want to make sure you did what I asked you to do.' For a moment he sounded fatherly. 'And then I will tell you the bakery where the babàs are made.

'Now go,' he said and put his glasses on and started to look over some papers on his desk. I took my box of babàs and left.

***

I had two months of school left and, as I promised, I put everything I had into my school-work. When I did meet the boys at the Cave we watched movies and talked. The Royal family disappeared into thin air. We had no hint of trouble with anyone who could have been connected with them or the Butcher. And all of us noticed we were being treated with more respect in places where previously we'd been invisible. Gianni and I were sitting at a table by the toilets in a restaurant. Then the owner came out to greet us. He treated us like we were celebrities, apologising and ushering us to a bigger table with a view out of the window. It could have been coincidence, but none of us thought so.

In any other circumstances being treated like a prince would have bolstered my ego no end. Now it made me feel like I was being buried alive. Each day that passed was like another spadeful of earth being heaped on top of me.

I analysed every mistake I had made. Particularly the mistakes that led to my breaking my golden rule: anonymity. When all the feelings of revenge for my brother had subsided, I felt only self-anger. So I had told myself the events leading up to my brother being beaten to a pulp had been inevitable, not really my fault. I had told myself lie after lie. Now, for two long months I went to school, I studied, I ate, then I cried myself to sleep at night. Perhaps I was finally becoming an adult.

I finished the year by passing every exam with spectacularly high marks. I took my report cards to the Big Boss, feeling no pride, only a sense of inevitability. I was being swept along by a tide. As I approached the Big Boss's villa for the third time I knew I was someone else's pet, my life no longer my own.

The same 'heavy' picked me up and drove me in a limo to the villa. The driver had previously been threatening but now he treated me with total respect. He opened the limo door for me, offered me cigars, cigarettes and drinks. I wasn't searched when I went through the gates, there were no guns and there was no waiting outside. I was led straight to the Big Boss's grand office and offered every comfort available.

'Congratulations, Prince!' he said as he scanned the results on my school report cards. 'You have excelled as I knew you could. You have lived up to your capabilities.'

I was half-expecting another conversation on art, literature and culture, but not this time. Immediately after I had allowed myself to be complimented and congratulated on my exam grades, it became obvious that my work was about to begin. No longer a social occasion, the visit felt more like the first day of a new job. The Big Boss dismissed me and I was taken to another grand room where I sat at a table with three of his men.

'Is there anything you need?' asked the most intelligent-looking of the three, looking at me over his half-moon spectacles. I shook my head. 'Only to know what I'm expected to do,' I answered.

'We are to explore the material you provided and piece together the actions and intentions of our enemy,' he said.

So we set to work going over the tapes. The men had already connected some of the dots, but they needed me to fill in the gaps. We had to work out exactly what the Butcher and his men had been up to and what they were planning to do. Again I was treated with the utmost respect and I had the feeling that my opinion was highly regarded.

This went on for a week. I was brought every day to the villa to go over the tapes I had listened to so many times already. I began to get to know the Big Boss's men. The way they treated me with such respect made me feel like I was their employer, not that I was actually enslaved to them. After a week, I decided – and it was clear it was to be my decision – we had wrung every clue out of every phone conversation on the tapes. Then I was indoctrinated a little deeper into the Big Boss's world. The Big Boss was aware of my skills and he wasted no time in turning them to his advantage.

For another three weeks he had me improving the logistics and communication of his contraband cigarettes unit. I was introduced to the hierarchy of the organisation and I learned how some of his business operations worked. Each level of the game took me further away from my freedom. The sophistication of the business was impressive. The Big Boss managed it like a Fortune 500 company rather than a criminal operation.

I built them a device that intercepted police calls and low radio frequencies. I also equipped their vehicles with little explosives to be used if the police were chasing them. And I modified their routes from the airports to their distribution centres. I made every stage of their business run more smoothly on a global scale. The Big Boss's USA-based men were grateful for my tips and they implemented some of my ideas in their American operations. This gave the FBI a lot of problems.

The biggest job I'd done for them was to devise a system of radio frequencies connected to a central radio. I created a kind of early GPS system – a centralised way of locating the trucks filled with stolen goods. If they were about to be intercepted by the police, I could use it to alert them to change route. And it was with this system that I caught a rat.

Because I knew the movements of all the trucks and cars in the entire operation. I noticed one of the truck drivers was making off-schedule visits to entities that were not on 'my list'. I started to get suspicious and this was all I needed to begin an investigation into this driver. I put some bugs in his car, his office and house. Three days later I knew he was a mole for the police, but I also found he was one of the Butcher's men. This man was not only a danger to the Big Boss and his operations, he was also potentially lethal to me.

Initially, I'd teamed up with the Big Boss to solve my gypsy problem. But, deep down, I knew, the Butcher would find out for sure that it was me behind the earlier mastermind plan. And he would naturally assume the mastermind plan was the Big Boss's idea.

There was no point being fingered as part of the Big Boss's gang if you don't have his protection. The fact I was just a schoolboy made me a most implausible culprit. So for now, the Butcher's agents are probably not sure about me. Their suspicions (even supported by the Warden's testimony) are just that – suspicions.

If the mole reported my involvement back to the Butcher, it could tip the balance. The Butcher would want to get rid of me. So I had no choice but to lay a trap for the rodent and to catch him.

I don't know what happened to the mole and I don't want to know. It bothered me, though. It added another layer of guilt and shame to the load that was already burdening my subconscious. It was bittersweet because I had caught him and that boosted my status with the Big Boss's men. The Butcher had infiltrated the Big Boss's crew and that highlighted his growing influence.

Other than the drama of catching the mole, the 'work' went on as normal. Being out of control of my life and giving in to the control of others, together with the enforced routine, was hypnotic. I almost forgot they could kill me at any time. The daily visits came to feel familiar to me and I had to remind myself of who I was. I wasn't an ordinary man going to the office, I was a 17-year-old kid working for the Camorra.

I was waiting to be given the main job. I already knew how the Big Boss's mind worked and none of this was going to be enough. He would have a bigger job in mind that would square up the favour he had granted to me. And that coming job was what I was most afraid of.

THE CAPTAIN

I stopped my Vespa at the bakery where they made the babàs and ordered two with a coffee. The place had become my morning habit. The assistant called the bakery owner who, as usual, dropped everything to greet me. He always treated me like a Prince. A sudden burst of happiness broke through the numbness. I don't know if it was the warmth of the morning sun on my face, the caffeine, the sugary sweetness of the cakes or all three.

As I looked out at the people milling about on the narrow street, everything seemed sharper and more 3D. Everyday objects seemed to glow, even the washing hanging high up on lines that criss-crossed the street from one building to another. I was hyper-aware of the noise of the Vespas razzing by and people chatting. Someone was shouting in the distance. For the next few weeks, I was free from working for the Big Boss.

I never wanted to leave this bakery. I wanted to live here in this moment for the rest of my life.

I finished the coffee and babàs. The sense of wonder stayed with me. I smiled and rested my head on the wall, soaking up the sunshine, almost afraid to move in case I broke the spell.

After a quarter of an hour in this state I felt I ought to do something, even though I only wanted to continue sitting there. People would think I'd fallen asleep. So, I picked up *Il Mattino*, the local newspaper. I pretended to read it but I was just reading the same paragraph over and over with nothing registering. Another ten minutes or so went by and I leaned back against the wall again. My head felt empty. Then something from the real world came crashing into my consciousness. Two words: the Captain. I opened my eyes and picked up the newspaper again. The paragraph I'd been 'reading' over and over was part of a report:

'Drugs bust gets police closer to crime family.

'Police arrested 28 Mafia suspects in raids on the outskirts of the southern Italian city of Naples on Wednesday. The suspects are accused of Mafia association aimed at drugs trafficking.

According to investigators, between them the Naples Mafias control cocaine, marijuana, crack, and hashish markets.

'Naples anti-Mafia prosecutors ordered Wednesday's arrests. The suspects are charged with Mafia association, drug trafficking, attempted murder and illegal possession of firearms. A further 14 people are under investigation. Two more suspects are currently on the run.

'Police also uncovered an accounts book. It contained records of profits from criminal activities, monthly payments to affiliates and weapons expenses.

'The investigation also shed light on the ongoing turf war between rival clans within the Camorra and the murders of clan members in January. The Calabrian 'Ndrangheta and the Neapolitan Camorra have posed powerful threats to the legal economy in recent years, outstripping Sicily's Cosa Nostra.

'The volatile situation has claimed at least fifty lives in gang battles this year. The latest came last week when two members of the Camorra hijacked a police vehicle and used it in a drive-by shooting. A few days earlier, the son-in-law of one family boss was executed outside a cafe. An estimated 50,000 people in the city either belong to the Camorra itself, are related to a member, or depend on the syndicate for cash. Many Camorra members are also officers in the Naples police force. The police not involved with the Camorra are hopelessly outnumbered.'

I felt the machine in my brain start to churn and my subconscious again threw out the two words: the Captain. The report was pretty standard for Naples but it was the final paragraph that caught my interest. It ignited a train of thought that led me to start forming a new plan.

The Naples police were in the pockets of the Camorra. But there were a few police officers rumoured to be incorruptible. To uphold the law in Naples is a dangerous game. If you're an honest judge, newspaper reporter or police officer, your life is in jeopardy. In truth, you're not likely to last long. But there was a policeman called the Captain. He had become a sort of underground hero to the anti-Mafia brigade.

I immediately forgot the peace of my moment of bliss, folded the newspaper, stole it, and made my way home. My subconscious started throwing out random ideas I knew I had to pull together. I barely remember getting home.

While working for the Big Boss, I'd listened to hours of taped police phone calls. I'd heard the conversations of a police officer who was trying to dismantle the drug trafficking trade in the south of Italy. He seemed to me to be honest. Since he was no threat to the Big Boss (who did not deal in narcotics), I hadn't taken much notice of him. I'd noted who he was and what he was up to but my only thoughts had been that he was an Eliot Ness type who probably wouldn't last long.

When I got home, I decided to set my subconscious free so I started playing solitaire with a deck of cards. It worked. Patterns seemed to pop into my mind when I wasn't even thinking and I had a much clearer vision of what was going on. One pattern kept coming up over and over again.

Over the months I'd listened to phone tap tapes of the Butcher and his men, I'd heard them talk about an enemy called the Captain. I had ignored it. I skipped over these conversations because the Captain didn't figure in anything I needed and I had no way of finding out who he was.

Now, though, I had the strongest suspicion the Captain was the policeman in the newspaper article. If so, I wondered if I could get him on my side. It was the most unlikely idea – almost a fairytale – but partnering with the Big Boss had seemed even less likely, so nothing seemed impossible anymore.

I needed time to think. If I'd been working for the Big Boss, I'd never have had the time to figure anything out, so the weeks I had ahead of me were essential. Yet my head wasn't clear. I was weighed down with the fear of what my final job would be and my imagination ran wild. Every time I thought I'd found a way to get myself out of the situation I was in, that fear would descend and destroy any confidence in my plans.

I went back to the bakery more than once but I couldn't regain that feeling of peace on the first day of my 'holiday'. The traffic was annoying, the coffee and cakes ruined by exhaust fumes, the laundry blocked out the sun and the bustle was too intrusive.

I decided to go and spend some time with my family. 'A few days away from this shit-hole would do me good,' I thought. I was craving the feeling of closeness and connection with familiar people.

I met up with Pasquale and Gianni in the Cave and gave them all I had on the Captain. I asked them to find out as much as they could about the man and then I left to get the train to Turin. I was looking forward to seeing my family, sharing meals and stories together at the table like we used to. I wanted to play football in the street with my kid brother and help my Mother lug anything that needed lugging. I remembered the time we all lived in the tin shack in the post-earthquake shanty-town. It had been hard but we'd been comrades. It had held everyone together as a family. I laughed out loud at myself, feeling nostalgic about living in a rat-infested hovel.

My family was expecting me, as I'd phoned to tell them I was coming, but there was no warm welcome. My Mother held her cheek out to me as she wiped her hands on her apron and asked me to sit down. There was no kitchen table, just a small breakfast bar with two stools. I wondered where they ate their meals but I didn't ask. I felt responsible for them living here in a strange part of the country. My Father was out at work and my kid brother was asleep in his room. My Mother made me something to eat but it was just fish fingers and bread and butter. She said she was in a rush as she had to go out to her cleaning job. She seemed distant and unhappy.

'Is everything all right here?' I asked her as she grilled the fish fingers.

'We survive,' she said. 'We are outsiders here.' She had her back to me.

I asked how my brother was.

'He is recovering,' she said.

She took off her apron and got her coat out of a cupboard, put it on and checked her hair in the mirror.

'Please watch your brother,' she said, 'your Father will be home soon.'

Then she left to clean someone else's house.

My Father came home half an hour later. He said: 'You're here then, son.' In the fridge there was a meal already prepared on a plate. He placed it in the oven to warm. He sat down in an armchair and started to read the paper. 'Is your brother asleep?' he asked, not taking his eyes off the paper.

'Yes. I think so. I haven't seen him yet,' I said.

He glanced up at me and then back to the paper.

I watched him eat his meal. He had it on a tray in his armchair while he watched the TV.

He was fast asleep in his chair by the time my Mother got back hours later. She washed up his plate and then went to bed, after pulling the sofa bed out for me.

I got into bed and watched some TV but my Father was snoring so loudly that I could barely hear it. I shook him.

'Dad. Wake up,' I said. 'Go to bed.'

He blinked and yawned, bewildered. 'Right,' he said, getting up and staggering towards the bathroom, still drunk from sleep.

'Night, son,' he said as he went into the bedroom.

'Night Dad,' I said.

When I woke at 7 a.m., my Father had already gone out to work. I was staring unhappily at a fly navigating the cracks in the ceiling when an ear-splitting scream made me leap out of bed, my heart pounding. It came from my brother's room. I leaped across the bed and darted straight to his room. I was half-expecting there to be someone in there – one of the Royal gypsy family standing over him, hurting him. My kid brother was sitting up in bed screaming. He'd had a nightmare. I sat on his bed and put my arms around him and tried to comfort him.

'Shh, it's only a dream,' I said, stroking his hair.

My Mother came in and shooed me out. I heard her cooing and soothing him and then they both emerged from the room. He was awake and dressed. I felt something in my insides fall and fall and fall as he limped towards me with his arms out, calling my name.

His left eye looked still and milky, he hobbled rather than walked and when he talked the words weren't formed properly. It was hard to understand him.

I hugged him, although I barely felt it.

After breakfast he left for school, but not before crying and clinging to me because he didn't want to go. I sat in silence as my Mother told me he was being bullied because of his disabilities.

She also said they were all experiencing abuse as southerners did in the north of Italy.

They were living in hell. Even without the bullying, my brother's injuries and the abuse, my Mother and Father lived separate lives. She had to go out to work before my Father got home and he was asleep when she got home. They never got to eat together, to talk or even to sit watching TV. I gave them some money – not enough to be suspicious, but something to help. I said I'd got a weekend job in a bakery and they accepted it without fuss.

I felt responsible for everything that was happening to them. They were being destroyed and I didn't blame them for being cold towards me. I suspected more than once that they knew I was involved in what happened to my kid brother.

I stayed with them for a month. All in all, I didn't find the comfort I'd been looking for but it did help me to stop thinking about myself or worrying about my own safety. The fear and worry, however, were replaced by an engulfing sense of guilt and terrible sadness. A month was all I could bear.

I went to see my other family and joined the gang in Lugano. A great distraction from the crawling despair. Our Swiss business was flying and we still had more than four million euros in our account. I wished I could give more of it to my family, but then they would have to know where it came from. If I turned up with thousands of euros it would be obvious I was to blame for what happened to my brother.

The restaurant was fully booked every night. The car lot was always busy and the boys were planning to open a new restaurant. When we weren't talking about business, the guys' attention went to the Big Boss and what he intended to do with us. They hero-worshipped the Big Boss, like most of the young men in Naples, and they were excited. They didn't share my fear and anxiety.

August came to an end much quicker than I wanted. As September crashed towards me at the speed of a bullet (coming at my own head), it was time to leave for Naples: time to face the music. On the train home I felt like I was rushing towards what I should have been running away from. Still, I wished the train would go faster so I could get it all over and done with, whatever the outcome. Dead or alive, I wanted out of this.

I had three weeks before I'd face the Big Boss again and I knew I had to make the most of it. I had to formulate a real, workable plan to save all of us, one that would mean I wouldn't be forced into doing something horrific. I knew what I'd be made to do would either ruin someone else's life or ruin mine. Everything I'd done so far had been for what I believed to be good. The one thing I'd clung to since I was 12 years old was that I was fighting on the right side, like Luke Skywalker fighting against the dark side. I knew this one final job could pull me over to the dark and I'd never be able to get back again.

Gianni and Pasquale were waiting for me as I got off the train. They greeted me with enthusiasm and made me feel like I was home at last. Their happy faces gave me such a feeling of relief. Two months of misery disappeared as we drove through the city, laughing and joking like normal teenagers. Even the traffic didn't seem as annoying as usual. I felt such affection for these two misfits. As brains tend to do, though, mine searched for its match. It filed through my past and landed on previous similar feelings, throwing up thoughts of my poor kid brother.

'Three weeks,' I thought. 'I have three weeks to make sure no one else has to pay for my mistakes ever again.'

The Captain was my top priority. At the time I thought he could be my saviour. I wanted to connect with this incorruptible police officer and tell him all that had happened, what I'd done and why. If I could work with him under his protection, he would rescue me. I was looking at a future very different to the one I'd imagined myself living. The Captain seemed like the only way I could get that future back. I was gambling. I had put all of my money on one unlikely number: that the Captain would be all I wanted him to be and he'd be on my side. The stakes were higher than I'd ever gambled with before.

My idea was to break into the Captain's home and place bugs everywhere so I could listen to the man, not to the policeman. I had to understand his agenda. I had three weeks. The sense of urgency allowed me to block out worries about my family and Switzerland and, to some extent, even the Big Boss and the impending final job. Focus is a great anaesthetic as it wipes out fear, regret and isolation. If I'm honest, focus was only part of it – what I was doing was dangerous and I was high on risk.

I was so absorbed in my own thoughts, I barely noticed getting to the Cave. I only remembered to check I wasn't being followed at the last minute, so I had to drive past the usual spot where I'd normally drive through the bushes. I did a whole circuit to make it look like I was a kid racing his Vespa on the hillside for fun. By the time I was sure no one was watching me I was late and Gianni and Pasquale were waiting for me, looking worried. I was never late.

'OK guys,' I said. 'I wanted to make extra sure I wasn't being followed.' I went to the fridge and grabbed a soda. I saw them relax. 'So,' I said, 'the Captain?' I looked at Pasquale. Before I left for Turin, I had instructed him to gather information on the policeman.

'Yes, Boss,' he said. 'Well, he's new in town, so that's good.' Pasquale had stolen confidential files from the council where he worked.

'Good,' I said. 'If he's new here, there's less time for him to have been bought like all the other cops.'

'He's come from Milan and he's still unknown on the streets. He's head of the new anti-drug department, as you know. And, from what we've heard on the tapes, he seems ambitious and determined to bring down narcotics trafficking in the whole of the south of Italy. I can find nothing to suggest he's anything other than straight down the line.'

I nodded and looked at Gianni.

'He's married with a young baby,' said Gianni, who had found out as much as he could through his family connections close to the police. 'He lives in the police compound.'

'That's bad news,' said Pasquale. 'Difficult to bug the police compound.'

'Although not impossible,' I countered before he'd finished his sentence.

Pasquale and Gianni looked at me in silence. They knew I was going to get them to bug the police compound.

'Great job, guys,' I said, looking straight at their faces. They'd done a good job researching the Captain but the information we had access to was limited to the basics. I still felt frustrated that we knew so little and his living arrangements complicated things. Still, such limitations had never stopped me before.

'Was there anything on the new anti-drug department itself?' I asked Pasquale.

'Not anything that hasn't already been in the papers,' he said, shaking his head. 'Let's hope it's more effective than previous efforts. I'm sick of finding used needles on my doorstep.'

Even the Government, as corrupt and laid-back as it was, couldn't stand the growing heroin business. It was a cancer, spreading fast throughout Italy. Naples had become an international hub for the drug dealers of Europe. This was how the Butcher was turning into a major superpower. Drugs were coming from South America, processed in Turkey, packaged in Naples and distributed all over Europe. Young guys injecting drugs into their veins was a normal sight in Naples. It had become so commonplace and frequent they'd do it almost anywhere, at any time. After they'd finished with their needles, they'd throw them on the floor and kids would pick them up to play with them. Entire families were torn apart by this horrible disease.

'At least the Big Boss isn't involved with drugs,' said Gianni who, like the other guys, still thought of the Big Boss as a kind of hero. They all thought exactly what the Big Boss wanted people to think – they had fallen for his brand: someone to love and fear.

'No, he's not,' I said, 'but he is a criminal. He is all-powerful, doesn't pay tax and has a massive fleet of ships that operate throughout the world. He has an army of over three thousand devoted followers – also criminals.'

I disregarded the fact that we were technically – or actually – criminals too, but my reasoning told me that didn't count. We'd always broken the law for reasons that were on the side of good.

'Yes, but contraband cigarettes are harmless compared to drugs,' said Pasquale.

I tried to hammer home the situation. 'The Big Boss's business has a turnover of more than five billion euros and he owns everything.' I swept my arms around to illustrate that I meant absolutely everything. Then I added: 'And he owns us.'

'Do you want to be owned?' I asked Pasquale directly. He shook his head.

'Do you?' I asked Gianni. He stared at me, maybe not understanding.

'Aside from the fact that I don't like being owned, the longer we're in the Big Boss's pocket, the deeper we dig ourselves into a pit we won't be able to climb out of. And he will be piling earth on top of us, making sure we stay buried for the rest of our lives.'

I could feel the pitch of my voice rising and the stress showed on their faces. I had wanted this to be like the old days – all for one – but I knew I had to hammer it home to get them to do the job at hand.

'And that might not be very long because we're forgetting one important thing: there are spies, moles, rats, whatever you want to call them. The Butcher's men are all over the Big Boss's operation. We caught one of them already. If we caught one by chance how many do you think there are? And that means the Butcher knows we've been working for the Big Boss. At some point, when he gets the chance, he's going to kill us.'

When I said 'us', I meant 'me', but I wanted them to feel what I was feeling, to motivate them to do what I needed them to do. I didn't tell them I'd been having nightmares of the giant ape vs dinosaur fight, or that every night the dream ended with them both coming after me.

I knew they weren't thinking the way I wanted them to think and I felt explaining it was futile. I lost the little bit of patience I'd been hanging on to and I turned away from them, snapping orders like a Nazi commandant.

'Pasquale, find out how the police compound is run. Who does the cleaning, the plumbing and so on? We need to find a way to get in there.'

'Yes, Boss,' said Pasquale. He didn't question his orders. He handed over a blueprint of the police compound he'd stolen from the council and pointed out where he'd marked the Captain's apartment.

'Good job,' I said, pleased, softening a little.

'Oh, yes,' said Gianni, 'my uncle lives in this apartment here.' He pointed at one of the apartments on the blueprint, on the opposite side of the compound.

'No way!' I said, delighted. What a stroke of luck! Gianni's face lit up. He loved approval. I slapped the table and gave him a big grin and his face lit up even more. He blushed pink, pleased with himself. I felt glad I'd made him happy.

That night, Gianni went home and told his dad he wanted to become a policeman.

It worked like a dream. His dad was delighted. Gianni was showing an interest in something – anything – that might mean a career. The first thing he did was send him along to his uncle's apartment for guidance and advice. Gianni went and had tea and cakes and talked the talk about how he was going to be the 'best' policeman – Italy's answer to Columbo. Then when he got home afterwards, he told his dad he'd enjoyed himself but wanted more information. So he went back the next afternoon. The next day he presented his dad with a police training application form saying he needed help filling it out. That's how we got him invited round to his uncle's for tea every night that week. That was how Gianni became my eyes and ears, reporting to me every detail. Even with his startling lack of social awareness, he'd have made an excellent spy.

A week later, I knew every detail of the police compound, including the companies looking after the plumbing and the electricity. I knew the names of the guards at the reception and the building manager's life story. Gianni blagged his way into full access to every department of the compound except the right part of the living quarters, the area I needed to get into the most.

The only people allowed in, other than police and their family, were the employees of the maintenance company. It was one of the largest organisations in Italy and they had a long-term contract with the police on a national level. They were paid a monthly fee whether they worked or not. This arrangement meant it was in the company's interest to do the best job possible so they'd earn without having to do anything. It also meant they weren't keen on being called on in the first place and there were neither invoices nor records of them turning up. I saw an opportunity to use this to get into the Captain's flat and place the bugs I needed to place.

As soon as I had it all figured out, I called the rest of the gang down from Lugano. I stole a white van like the one used by the maintenance company. I got Gianni to print out some badges that looked like theirs on his computer.

When the guys arrived from Switzerland they brought the most advanced transmitters you could get. I'd ordered them from Germany via our Swiss business at the cost of almost 40 thousand euros. I broke into the police compound's reception telephone system and intercepted their calls, connecting them to the Cave. The Cat's job was to sit and listen to every call in and out of the compound's reception. I was able to see which number they dialled and, if it was necessary, even answer the call myself.

I spent two days training the Spanish and IT Guy on how to place bugs in a way that would give us the best reception. I had no idea of the set-up of the flat but I had to make sure they knew the bugs went inside an electrical device likely to be on when they were home. The bugs had no battery of their own and they would feed from the electricity used by the device in which they were installed. To make sure the transmission would reach as far as the Cave, I had to place a further transmission box in a nearby abandoned farm. That one would collect the frequencies from the bugs and relay them over to the Cave. This device needed electricity too but I got that from the street-lights. I used a transformer to feed the transmitter the correct amount of electricity. It was a lot of work done very quickly and anxiously but, as things were going smoothly, I became confident that I could pull it off. The boys were ecstatic that we were all working together again on something exciting. It felt like the good old days. We were alive again. I was filled with hope and I even slept right through the night.

The Spanish had some basic training in electrical maintenance and that made the whole thing easier. All I had to do was create an upsurge in the electrical supply to the building and blow all the fuses. The police reception would then make a call to the maintenance company, which the Cat would intercept. The Spanish and the IT Guy, dressed like maintenance people, would show up with their fake badges and we'd be in.

The chances of them checking us out were minimal. The company was so large it was unlikely they'd send the same guys for every job, so to see someone new must have been normal for the reception guards. What comforted me more than anything was how you'd have to be crazy to bug a police compound. I'd have been surprised if the reception guards had even dreamt it possible. So I was less worried about them being suspicious of two guys they'd actually called themselves to come and fix the electrics.

I figured the Captain would leave for work at 9 a.m., after which we were set to go into action. I blew up one of the adaptors at the main source of electricity outside the building. As I had the blueprint, I knew which one to do without creating havoc all over the compound. All that interested me was the part where the policemen lived. Everything went to plan and the Cat answered the compound's call to the maintenance company at around 9.40. As planned, the Spanish and IT Guy turned up at the compound in the fake maintenance company van. Gianni was watching from a distance. He kept me updated via a powerful walkie-talkie I'd adapted for long-distance communications.

The compound security let the van in without question. Once in, IT Guy made his way around the flats, pretending to be searching for the source of the electrical failure. Clearly, the only flat we were interested in was Flat 146b, the Captain's residence. Once there, he had to place the bugs and leave as soon as possible. I'd told him to put the bugs in the living areas, including the kitchen where Italians spend most of their time. When he was done, the Spanish would switch back on the fuses in the basement and they would leave.

The whole job shouldn't have taken more than an hour so I was quite relaxed in the Cave for the first hour. I thought everything was going to plan. After an hour I started to feel concerned, calling Gianni almost every two minutes to see if they had come out. To my relief they did come out, but almost three hours later. After the job, they were to drive 35 miles away from Naples. As soon as they found a quiet spot, they would strip the van of all the company logos, get back into their normal clothes and wait for Pasquale to pick them up. They were to be back no later than 12 o'clock. They came back at 4. By which time I was pulling my hair out.

I asked each one of them to go through their version of the operation in minute detail and, to my relief, timing aside, it seemed all had gone to plan. The relayer was connected to the street-lights, so it would only come on when it went dark at 6 o'clock. We waited, mostly in silence. The only thing that unnerved me was the pale face and worried expression of IT Guy.

Six o'clock came and went but we didn't hear a sound. The whole night came and went and we got nothing but dead silence from the bugs. IT Guy admitted he'd had some problems placing the bugs. I asked him to describe the process again but I couldn't find fault in his execution of my instructions. It looked like everything had gone perfectly.

After the most frustrating night of my life, we all went home tired and disappointed. There was a tiny hope that the Captain had taken his wife out for dinner and tomorrow those bugs would start sending the signals.

As I once again lay awake, tossing and turning in my bed, I started to fear the worst. I had to go back to school in less than a week and I knew if the bugs didn't work, my plan would have failed. This time my mind wouldn't allow me the luxury of visualising my escape plan. I was doomed to spend the whole night going over and over the day moment by moment on a loop tape, starting again from the beginning as soon as it reached the end. I had no sleep. When I got up at first light, I couldn't shake off a feeling of dread. I had to bear it for the whole day until 6 o'clock that evening when I would know for sure if the bugs had worked or not.

At the Cave, the atmosphere was tense and the camaraderie had gone. We waited until 10 o'clock, with nothing but silence from each other and from the receiver. We had failed; the bugs were not working. The mission, together with more than 60,000 euros, had gone down the drain.

I turned the loudspeaker off and left the recorder running on pointlessly, like leaving a light switch on when the bulb has blown.

The box in the abandoned farm needed to be removed as soon as possible. If they found it, they'd trace it back to the Cave and send us all to jail. While I was worrying about that, the blame game in my head began. OK, the box would soon be gone, but not just yet.

They all started arguing, pointing the finger at one another. When they'd exhausted all avenues, they started blaming me. I let each of them attack me verbally, one by one, including Pasquale and Gianni. To be fair, I'd never explained why I was so obsessed with bugging the Captain's apartment, so in their eyes they had reason to blame me. After they'd finished their attack, they left. I sat there alone in the dreaded silence that had been the cause of my failure. The silence mocked me and I started to cry.

Much later, I woke with my face pressed against the table. I'd cried myself to sleep. I made myself get up and go home. I rode my Vespa dangerously fast and I couldn't focus on the roads. My mind once again turned towards my escape fantasy: a fantasy that had now become very real. My only choice. My family had gone, my gang had deserted me and I had no friends anymore. Disappearing was the only thing I had left. 'Fuck 'em all!' I said out loud to myself as I sped along Naples' narrow streets to get home and pack my bags.

When I put the phone down after ordering a taxi to the airport, I sat for a moment and finally felt some kind of peace. The morning sun was beaming through the window and it was comforting on my face. I went through everything one more time. My luggage packed, check. Money: my emergency stash of 40,000 euros inside my socks in my case, check. Passport: in my pocket, check. Keys: on the table by the door, check. Taxi to the airport: ordered and coming in 30 mins, check.

The stress seemed to melt away in the warmth of the sun and I recalled the morning I'd felt blissful at the bakery. I tried to pull up some of the feelings from the memory.

I was sitting under an umbrella outside a cafe in London, ordering a beer from a slick-haired waiter. He wrote down my order on a notepad. The street was buzzing. People crowded on the sidewalk behind a thick rope separating the cafe's seating area from the outside. I felt completely free and happy. I smiled at an attractive woman at the next table and she smiled back. I felt excited about my new life. The waiter finished taking my order and, as he turned to go back into the cafe, an ear-piercing alarm bell went off. After a moment's confusion, all the people on the sidewalk started to scream and run. I sat there thinking it was some kind of disaster warning that everyone knew about but me, a foreigner. I grabbed the waiter's arm and begged him for help. 'What is it?' I asked. 'What should I do?'

The waiter wrenched his arm out of my grip, dropped his pad and ran, as the squealing pitch of the alarm got even louder. I got ready to run, only to find myself back in my living room. I was confused and disoriented but then realised I'd fallen asleep. The doorbell was sounding; my taxi was here. I felt dizzy as I stood up and had to grab the edge of the table to steady myself. I remembered that I hadn't eaten for two days because of the stress of bugging the Captain's apartment.

'Never mind,' I thought, still half asleep as I opened the door to the taxi driver, 'I'll have breakfast at the airport. Only another half-hour.' I half-turned around to grab my suitcase but did a double take as the door swung open. It wasn't the taxi driver but the same heavy who had driven me home from my first meetings with the Big Boss. The growling hunger in my stomach turned to lead and I was finally very much awake.

He let himself in.

'Good morning Prince! Heavy night last night?'

'Yeah. Kind of,' I replied, trying to sound casual. He immediately clocked the suitcase.

'Going anywhere nice?' he said. My knees struggled to hold me up.

'What. Ah, that? Uh ... No,' I replied. 'Umm ... I got some stuff for the charity shop. I was planning to drop it off later on.'

'Great,' he replied with sarcasm heavy in his voice. 'We can do that on the way.'

'On the way? Where?'

'You have a meeting with the boss,' he said, picking up my suitcase.

I had no choice but to follow him to the car. He threw the suitcase in the back next to me and we drove away. Instead of going straight to the Big Boss's mansion, we stopped off in the city outside a charity shop. He opened the back door and hauled the suitcase out, smiling at me. I sat frozen and watched him give away the case containing my best, most expensive designer clothes, 40 grand in cash and my dreams of escaping.

All my feeling seemed to ebb away and I found myself grateful for the numbness. Then a gasp of laughter burst out of me. I couldn't believe things could get any worse but my luck seemed to have plummeted far beyond a series of coincidences. I thought something external was controlling the events in my life. I felt I was living in a kind of electronic game, with a dial turning further and further in the direction of chaos and destruction. I imagined an enemy turning the dial while laughing demoniacally at my life falling to pieces. I'd reached a point where nothing could get any worse and something shifted. I felt disassociated enough to be interested in seeing what would happen next, like I was watching a movie. I didn't feel I'd have the strength to open the car door and run, even if the door wasn't locked.

'Very generous, Prince! They loved it! It will go straight to the African kids. Well done!' the driver said as he got back in the car. I said nothing and looked out of the window as we set off in the direction of the Big Boss's mansion.

The door to the Big Boss's office opened and I could see him reading some papers, peering through gold-rimmed spectacles perched on the end of his nose. He appeared so far away it was like I was looking at him through the wrong end of a telescope. The 40-yard shuffle across the great room to his desk seemed like too much effort to bear. I took one step, then another. My only other options would be to collapse onto the floor or run, neither of which would make a difference. It would only delay the inevitable. I finally reached the desk, distracted by the weird time distortion I was experiencing, maybe caused by hunger and exhaustion. Crossing the room had taken hours, not seconds. The Big Boss ordered me to sit by waving his hand towards the chair. He didn't look up. He offered no coffee, nor babàs and he took a full five minutes to finish reading a document before turning his eyes to me. His expression held no warmth, his mouth was set and thin like someone had drawn a dead straight line where his lips used to be. His eyes were hard and icy. He said nothing. I felt the hair stand up on the back of my neck and I didn't know what to do so I looked back at him. I wanted to squirm and shift about in my chair, ask for a glass of water, get up and run away. Most of all I wanted to divert my eyes away from his. I didn't dare.

Then he said: 'You owe me a job.'

I nodded and swallowed.

'Once you have completed the job, you will be free to go any-where you please. Pack a beautiful suitcase with your best gear and find a better place to express your considerable talents.'

I blushed bright red and opened my mouth to babble a yet unborn excuse for my attempted escape. If he'd let me speak, I'd have invented something at the same time as the sounds of my words made their way up my throat and into the world. But he held his hand up to silence me. I closed my mouth again.

'I want you and your boys to bring down the Butcher,' he said.

There it was. The last job in its finality.

I drifted off out of the present as my focus turned in on my thoughts. I found myself watching me, watching him for a moment and then I was back in my own body.

The Big Boss's words were a death sentence.

'I don't care how you do it,' he said. 'Just do it.'

He went back to the pages on his desk. I waited to hear what he was going to say next but he didn't look up again. I gazed around awkwardly for a moment, then got up and made my way back across the polished floor to the exit. The driver was waiting for me outside and he led me back to the car and drove me home. I went straight to bed and slept. For how long, I have no idea. My intention was to sleep to gather enough strength so I could kill myself.

I woke up in my bed, wearing pyjamas I didn't recognise. I thought I was dreaming again but I was definitely awake because I had a headache like someone had hammered a knitting needle into my skull. The door opened and a woman entered with a tray. For a split second, I thought she was my Mother and I felt a sudden wave of relief. I wanted to cling to her and never let go. Then I recognised her. She was a neighbour whose name I could never remember but who the gang had nicknamed Mrs Apron. I felt the sharp loss of the prospect of being a child again and yielding to my Mother's soothing care. Tears welled up in my eyes. With some effort, I refused to let them spill over onto my cheeks.

She smiled and placed the tray on the bedside table.

Not sure what was going on, I said: 'Err ... hello.'

'How are you this morning?' she asked, leaning me forward and plumping up the pillows behind me so I could sit up, then placing the tray in front of me. On the tray were bread rolls, butter, pastries, cereals and a steaming cup of hot chocolate.

'I'm ... err ... I'm fine, thanks,' I said, confused. 'What's going on? These aren't my pyjamas.'

'They're new. I bought them for you as I didn't like to go through your things. Don't you remember, dear?' she asked.

'No, I don't,' I said.

'You collapsed and we got the doctor to you.'

'No, I don't remember. When?' I said. The last thing I remembered was being dropped off by the Big Boss's driver and going home to bed.

'I came home on Monday afternoon to find your door open. When I investigated I found you lying on the floor in the living room, out cold.'

'What? No, I...' I drifted off as I dimly recalled being lifted, undressed and put to bed.

'I tried to find some contact details for your parents but couldn't, so I put you to bed and I've been looking after you ever since.'

'What day is it?' I asked.

'Thursday,' she said. 'You've been out three days and you really need to eat something.' She moved the plate of pastries towards me on the tray. 'I called the doctor straight away. The doctor says you've got exhaustion so we let you sleep but he said you must eat as soon as you wake up. Look, it's hot chocolate.'

I was ravenous so I stopped asking questions and tucked into the delicious breakfast. I scoffed the bread and pastries down almost without chewing and downed the sweet hot chocolate in three gulps.

'What on earth have you been doing to yourself to be getting exhaustion at your age?' she asked, as she fussed and tidied up the bed sheets around me while I ate. 'I suppose it's school – exams and the like – or perhaps a girl?' She stopped and looked at me. 'You're a handsome boy, a heartbreaker. It won't take long for your young heart to mend. You'll have them beating the door down for a date as soon as you're better.'

She continued the tidying, pulling a duster out of her big apron pocket, wiping a mark from the bedroom window-pane and dusting the surround. As she straightened the blinds, she turned and asked me: 'More hot chocolate?'

I held the cup out to her and said: 'Yes, please!' I felt a hope that, even though she wasn't my Mother, I might still feel the relief of relinquishing all responsibility to maternal care. For a while, at least.

I was so exhausted I had to stay in bed for another week. The doctor came again. He said poor diet and lack of sleep had taken a huge toll on my body. He told me I was still a growing boy and, unless I addressed those issues, I'd have long-term damage to my kidneys and liver. He said I had to start eating better and be under less stress.

'You are a teenager, in the best time of your life. What have you got to stress about, son?' he preached.

I let him ramble on, enjoying Mrs Apron's clucking and fussing around my bed.

I felt guilty because I'd totally ignored Mrs Apron up to now. I remembered her smiling at me in the corridor as she bustled by with bags of shopping. I'd ignored all my neighbours in the apartment block, not thinking about their existence at all. The truth is, in the back of my mind, I thought I was too good for them. It was strange that I'd risked my life to get these ordinary people out of squalid, filthy tin shacks and into decent homes, but I didn't even like them much. Mrs Apron knew all our neighbours, of course, and because she'd taken me under her wing, they now considered me one of them.

Everyone in my building came to visit, bringing chocolates, flowers, books and board games and all sorts of fruit and soft drinks and sweets. They clearly thought of me as a child so I let myself be a child. There were more than twenty families living in my condominium and I had lunch and dinner every day with a different family. I played chess each afternoon with the old man from Apartment 2B whose grey beard seemed to grow so fast you could almost see it. I told the middle-aged couple from Apartment 11A about the babàs at my favourite bakery. They were as enthralled as I was at the taste of them but when they brought me some, I couldn't bring myself to eat them. The babàs were too much of a reminder of reality. I wanted to sink, sink, sink into this unreal world where every day was so comforting it felt like Christmas morning when I was a kid.

After all, I really was just a kid. I looked and sounded like a schoolboy and I had only lived 16 years on earth, but I felt a hundred years old.

'Probably too sweet for now,' Mrs Apron had said, looking at her watch as if there was a wrong time to eat sweet things. She carried the babàs away. 'I'll get you some soup.'

I thought I'd offended the couple from 11A but they carried on chatting and smiling while they ate their babàs. I ate Mrs Apron's delicious home-made soup.

In the afternoons, before tea time, Mrs Apron would allow neighbours young and old to crowd into my room at once. They'd laugh and joke like it was a party. They sat on and around my bed, the men patting my head, the women giving me kisses and hugs. The kids played sword fighting or pretended my bed was a racing car. Mrs Apron clucked about like a mother hen looking after her brood. I lay in bed, still weak, pale and thin, but smiling and grateful for their gifts and their love. I felt touched and humbled by it. I'd spent so much time with ugly and evil people I'd forgotten good people existed. They didn't know me but they cared for me simply because I was a kid who was sick with no one else to look after me. I fell in love with every one of them.

When they'd gone, I'd lie there smiling. Mrs Apron was always in my apartment, cleaning, cooking, folding my things, checking my temperature and fluffing my pillows. She left my bedroom door open and I could hear her singing while she did the dishes. I knew I only had to call and she would be right with me.

When I was well enough to get out of bed, I felt scared because I didn't want my temporary childhood to end. I didn't need to worry as, even when I was up and about, everyone still came to see me, bringing food. And Mrs Apron continued to mother me. When I went back to school, I came home to find her in my apartment having cleaned the whole place. She cooked my dinner and she would shower me with hugs and kisses. Each evening a different group of the neighbours would come by to check on my health or bring me something nice. I still played chess with the old man from Apartment 2B.

Filled with good food, warmth and a sense of community, I felt happy and healthy, more so than I had in ages. At school I went through a routine, not speaking to anyone at all, not even Gianni. He kept his distance from me but I wasn't bothered. I had all the love and friendship I needed at home.

Then one day in October the Big Boss's driver was waiting for me outside the school. He took me by the arm and ordered me into the car. I had no choice but to get in the back seat and I saw Gianni standing on the sidewalk watching me as we drove off. Our eyes met but his expression didn't change and I thought: 'Good for you, staying out of it. Why should you destroy your life because of me?'

The driver didn't take me to the Big Boss, as I'd expected. He drove around the city asking me questions. He said he was watching me. Then he asked: 'When are you going to do the job?'

He said the Boss was waiting for news. I somehow managed to convince him I had a plan and was following it. He seemed satisfied and he dropped me off at home.

In my apartment, Mrs Apron said I looked pale and she sent me to bed, worried I was having a relapse.

My trip back to childhood was over and I knew it. The next morning I plucked up the courage to go to the Cave and see if I could come up with anything.

No one had been there for almost a month and dust was settling. Everything was in its place, from the *Rocky* posters to the documents we'd stolen and most of the tapes I'd kept. I opened the safe and I was glad to find three grand. I hadn't paid the bills at home for a while and the electricity company had started sending termination letters. I also found two loaded guns in the safe: weapons bought by the Spanish in case of an emergency.

I sat on the floor in the middle of the basement and burst into tears. In the place where it had all began, just a few years before. I felt it was the end.

I turned over all that had happened in my mind: our victories, our defeats and those long nights spent fighting a system that had now beaten me. I missed the guys and I felt overwhelmed. The loss of my family and my close friends weighed heavily enough at that moment but I was also scared. I knew a war had broken out between the Big Boss and the Butcher. Whoever won would get full control over the city and all illegal activity in the south of Italy. And now I was contracted to kill the Butcher. I couldn't quite believe the enormity of it all.

The Butcher had an army of mercenaries working for him and they were as brutal, if not more brutal, than him. They were loyal to the massive wages he paid.

The Big Boss paid his people well but never well enough to get away from him. He used to say: 'You have to keep people like you keep a bird in your hand. If you squeeze too tight, it will die. If you keep it too loose, it would fly away.' That was the way he had built his 'family' and his empire. The Butcher paid four times what the Big Boss did but disloyalty or even a simple mistake led to unthinkable punishment. The Camorra had a kind of code of conduct: never hurt wives or children. The Butcher not only violated that rule but he took it to another level. The street legends said he had a kid of only five years old dipped alive in sulphuric acid to punish a disloyal father. It took the police four months to work out the identity of the 'body' as there was very little left: a few bones and a couple of teeth.

It made sense for the Big Boss to unleash me on his now sworn enemy. If I succeeded, great. If I failed, he could claim he had nothing to do with it and let me be the next kid to be dipped alive in sulphuric acid. I was a little pawn in his chess game against the Butcher.

I felt daunted by the task ahead and as lonely as I'd ever been. I picked up one of the guns and went outside.

I started to cry again. Not because of the Big Boss or because I had to kill the Butcher but because I missed my Granddad.

I stopped crying after a while and wiped the tears and snot off my face with my sleeve. Then I sat outside of the Cave on a stone and looked at the sunset. The sky was beautiful.

I checked the bullets and the gun and I felt peaceful. I kept looking at the dying sun, waiting for my cue to go.

Despite being a full-time 'criminal' for the last five years, I had never held a real gun before. This wonderful piece of engineering capable of such force was astonishing.

'How can such a small thing cause so much fear and death?' I asked myself.

Holding a gun in your hand gives a great sense of power. You're aware you can end someone's life in a second. Puzzled by it, I fired a shot to see if it was working. I tried to hit a small tree not further than ten yards away but the kickback was so violent I completely missed.

'American movies,' I muttered to myself, 'they make it look so easy!'

I tried again and again, but I missed every time. My near misses only reminded me of what my life had been about. 'I can't even hit a tree a few feet away!' I thought. Deep in contemplation of my persistent failures, I heard a shout coming from behind me. It was Gianni's squeaky voice shouting: 'Prince!'

I turned and saw Gianni and Pasquale, pacing towards me.

'Put. The. Gun. Down!' said Pasquale.

The sight of them made me angry. 'Keep a safe distance. The kickback on this thing is vile,' I said as I waved the gun around dangerously.

They were scared but I didn't care. I hated them in that moment. Pasquale, with his arms held wide open, was now talking very quietly: 'What are you doing? You aren't 18 and you ain't got no licence. You really wanna go down for that after all you've done?' I looked at him without moving and he ordered: 'Put it fucking down!'

They knew nothing of the arrangement I had with the Big Boss and now was not the time to discuss it. I had no intention of carrying on with the plan or my life. I had my gun pointed at Pasquale and Gianni.

'Who are you to give me orders? I call the shots around here. Literally, as you can see, I am the one holding the gun,' I said. I sounded evil. 'You show up, finally.' I carried on. 'Long time no see, my dear friends.

'Nice little stunt you pulled in there a month ago. Well done! You left me high and dry, alone to deal with everything. Is that what you call friendship, is it? You would be nothing without me.'

I pointed the gun at Gianni. His eyes widened in fear.

'You,' I shouted, 'would still be a sissy with the assertiveness of a mouse and bad results at school if it wasn't for me.'

I turned and pointed the gun at Pasquale who held his hands up as if they would protect him. 'You,' I said, 'would still be a two-penny street hustler making a hundred euros a week. Maybe you'd be dealing in drugs by now and waiting to get shot at any time.

'As for the other three pieces of shit, well, they would keep you company in the gutter, where you all belong! I gave you an iden-tity, a job, a career, a business, a house, money! What did you do? When push came to shove, you fed me to the wolves and walked away. Miserable bastards.'

They were shaking with fear. I had no intention of killing them – I wasn't a killer. They were an easy target and, to be fair, they would have had a hard time arguing with what I'd said. At the end of the day, though, I was the one who went to them. I engineered the gang, the Cave and my revenge against the world. I only used them. Looking back, I did to them what the Big Boss was now doing to me. They were not to blame for anything. It was me all along and it was me that had to pay. I put the gun to my head. Gianni started screaming and Pasquale ran towards me. I closed my eyes and fired. Everything went dark.

I woke up sitting in the Cave with my back against the wall. The whole gang was staring down at me. I had my arms stretched out on either side of me and they'd tied my hands to the pipes. I felt like Jesus on the cross. For a minute I thought I was dead; then I figured I must be alive because I was trying to work out why I wasn't dead.

'You used all the bullets shooting the tree,' Pasquale said, as if he'd read my mind.

'Fuck!' I said. I couldn't even kill myself. I struggled to get free from the nylon ropes but they were too tight. I stopped struggling and faced the gang. I stared them out one by one as they sat there in silence looking back at me. I was still angry at them, but more at myself for yet another failure.

The IT Guy was first to speak. 'We owe you an apology, Prince. We want to make it right.'

'It's too late!' I spat out.

'We hope...' Pasquale interrupted with so much confident command in his voice that it startled me into silence. 'We hope you'll accept our apologies.'

'And what if I don't?' I replied.

'If you don't,' said Gianni, taking over as speaker, 'then you're going to stay tied up until you do.'

All eyes were off me and onto Gianni. They were as shocked as I was that he'd spoken with authority. So out of character for him. He'd wagged his finger at me, rolled his eyes and pursed his lips. He might as well have added 'girl' onto the end of his scolding. The whole gang burst into laughter, even Gianni himself was giggling. I looked away from them as I felt laughter making its way up from my stomach and I didn't want to laugh; I wanted to be aloof and indignant. Avoiding eye contact worked for a few seconds and I tried to focus on how I was going to escape. But they were out of control and shrieking with laughter. Even though I was so angry at them, I couldn't help feeling glad to see them. I'd missed my gang after all these weeks of abandonment. To see them clutching their sides and choking with laughter was like coming home.

Gianni's effeminate reprimand played through my mind again. It caused a crack in the dam I'd built to stifle the laughter. I had a split second's real awareness that I'd shot myself with an empty gun because I was worried about being killed! I had no choice but to give in to it. I let the laughter jet out of me in snorting torrents. The laughter subsided, as I needed to take in air, and then rose again as the whole farcical situation forced its way again and again into my mind. It was as if laughter were punching me in the gut repeatedly. In the end I was gasping, my stomach aching painfully because I was unable to bend or clutch it as my hands were tied. The ridiculousness of that only made me laugh even more.

'So,' said Pasquale, who had fully composed himself, 'will you accept our apologies, Prince?'

That they'd tied me up and refused to let me go until I accepted their apology almost started me off laughing again, but I managed to contain it. I tried to think of what to say to them. I was all mixed up. I still blamed them for abandoning me while also being glad that the less involved they were, the safer they were. I toyed with the idea of telling them about the final job but decided it would be selfish to offload my problems. The less they knew, the less danger they were in. I couldn't see a way forward with them involved and to see more people suffer as a consequence of my actions was something I could no longer bear. I'd survived my suicide attempt but I was still finished inside. I had nothing to give anymore and I still wanted out. It was over, as simple as that.

I sighed. 'There's no need to apologise,' I said. 'No need for you to be here. I should be the one to apologise to you for putting you in danger and getting you involved with the Big Boss. I want you to go home and I will take care of the rest. This is my gig, my risk and not yours. You should all go and get on with your lives.'

The gang looked at me with what was probably sympathy but I saw it as pity. They used to look at me with awe and respect and now they felt sorry for me. Something in my chest fell and I thought I was going to cry again for a moment.

The Spanish then spoke up for the first time. 'We are where we are thanks to you,' he said. 'I'm sorry for leaving you alone. I can't speak for everyone but as far as I'm concerned, I'm here for you, Prince, to the death if necessary.'

I'd never heard this Neanderthal hulk speak so softly and sincerely. His rough dialect had softened and improved thanks to his life in Lugano. I saw a depth in him I hadn't noticed before. I wondered if it had developed because of his rich life or if it had always been there and I'd been blinded to it by my own arrogant assumptions. Probably the latter.

The IT Guy then said: 'I'm at your service, Prince. Say the word and I will kill for you.'

The Cat, who never spoke much during our meetings (or at any time really), added: 'I'm grateful to you in a way that you could never imagine. You know I'm no good with words because I never went to school, but I now have a business and a future I never would have had. Without you I'd be in jail or even dead. I owe you my life. I am your friend and you are like a brother to me.'

I was distraught by whole thing and touched by their sense of solidarity but I had genuinely run out of energy and ideas.

I looked up at the IT Guy and he said softly: 'We've had some rough times, Prince, but no one will ever forget what you've done for us. Especially me.' His eyes were full of sincerity. 'We started together, as a gang, and we'll finish together.'

Gianni stood up and stretched out an awkward right arm in front of him.

'What are you doing?' I asked after I'd let him stand there for a few seconds with everyone staring at him.

'All for one!' he shouted. 'Come on!' He waggled his arm about and gestured towards it with his head. 'All for one!'

The IT Guy grinned at me, got up and placed his arm out with his hand on top of Gianni's. They all followed and when Pasquale's hand, which was last to join the pile, landed, Gianni said again: 'All for one!'

'And one for all!' they shouted together.

It was stupid but I felt left out, tied to the pipes with my arse stuck on the floor. The Spanish untied my right arm, evidently not comfortable with letting me go completely. The pile of hands came close enough to me so I could reach and I placed my hand on top. Then we all said together: 'All for one! And one for all!' and cheered.

The atmosphere had changed and, after they'd untied me, we all stayed together in the Cave for the rest of the day. Pasquale went out to get beer and pizza and we ate it while chatting, joking, making fun of each other and pretending to fight. We watched movies, including *Rocky*, of course.

After enjoying one of the best nights of my life with the boys, I threw myself into my school-work, hoping my big problem would go away by itself. I was hoping for a miracle. I studied hard all day at school and then went home and studied some more while Mrs Apron looked after me. It wasn't necessary for me to study so much. I was way ahead of the school-work game, always had been. I challenged myself to learn more and more as a method of avoidance. My exams would be child's play but, as long as I kept my brain busy, I didn't think about the Big Boss. I was strangely happy. Happiness worried me. As long as I was miserable and suicidal I didn't feel the terror of losing my life. I knew whatever was likely to happen to me at the hands of the Butcher would be prolonged and painful but, when it was over, that would be that. I'd have lost nothing but a miserable existence. But when I felt happy, I had something to lose and I was afraid.

On the Saturday, a week after my suicide attempt, things changed abruptly for me, for all of us. I went to the Cave and found everyone else already there. They were sitting in a circle in the middle of the room, drinking sodas. As soon as I walked in I could sense something in the atmosphere and I knew right away it was fear. They turned their heads to look at me with serious faces and wide eyes. I didn't even greet them. I just sat down and joined the circle, not wanting to hear what they had to tell me.

'Prince, we have a problem,' said Pasquale.

I said: 'What is it?' but I thought: 'Yeah, tell me something I don't know.'

The IT Guy spoke. 'All of us except Gianni have had a visit from the Big Boss's men.'

I took an involuntary deep breath and stared at the floor. The heavy weight of guilt pushed down on something in my chest.

'They told us,' he continued, 'if we don't do what we promised we'll all be dead. And so will our families, friends and anyone else who has been seen interacting with us, even if it was just a handshake.'

'What have we promised?' asked Pasquale, sitting next to me, his head twisted towards me.

I was unable to look at him and my eyes remained staring at the floor. 'OK,' I said. 'I suppose it's time to tell you.'

'Tell us what?' said the Spanish.

'Try to stay calm,' I said. 'Getting wound up won't get us anywhere.' I tried to pluck up some courage from somewhere deep. I took another long breath inwards before starting to tell them the burden I'd carried all by myself for two whole months. I'd been so desperate to keep them out of this and I thought I'd never have to tell them. I could see now that my silence had been making them more anxious.

'I wanted to protect you from this and I didn't know the Big Boss knew your identities. He knows you exist but not who you are. It can't have been hard for him to find out, I suppose. I know he's aware of some of what we've done in his territory but I'm sure he still doesn't know the extent of our success. He can't know about the money and the business in Lugano. At least that's some good news.'

I was stalling and they looked impatient.

'But what is the promise?' said Pasquale, irritated.

Finally I managed to blurt out, 'We owe him a fee and he wants us to pay it. He wants us to do one last job for him before he'll set us free.'

They were silent and then the IT Guy said: 'Well let's do it then. Get it over and done with and then we'll all move to Lugano and forget all about this shit-hole.'

The guys all nodded and agreed.

My hesitation had backfired because I'd given them hope where there wasn't any, which made my next sentence even harder to say. I clammed up and I had to fight back tears. I felt so angry at myself for that. They saw it and I felt the hope drain out of them.

'Prince! Just say it already. What the fuck does he want?' The Spanish had desperation in his voice.

'He wants us to bring down the Butcher, dead or alive.' My voice sounded flat and monotone but the words filled me with fear. It was as if I were hearing them from someone else's lips for the first time.

'What?'

'The Butcher!'

'How?'

'And why us?'

'Is he mad?'

'You are kidding ... Are you?'

They all spoke at once.

'I will say this again: if we do not get rid of the Butcher, he will get rid of us.' I put my head in my hands to hide the fact I hadn't managed to overcome the urge to cry. The gesture gave away all the desperation I had been hiding for the last two months.

After a short silence, I finally had the courage to raise my head and look at them in their faces. I'd never seen them like that. The Spanish, never afraid of anything, had gone white. His brother hid his face in his hands. The Cat, the most stoic of us all, started to sob. The IT Guy had gone outside and was throwing up. The calmest was Gianni. He didn't know much about the Butcher nor was he familiar with the kind of punishment he inflicted on his enemies. He was trying to cheer the other guys up, which only angered Pasquale.

'It will be *all right*?' he repeated back at Gianni. 'Do you know who this guy is? Do you know what he did to a mate of mine two years ago? He's got an army of over five thousand people. They kill, you know, and they enjoy it! And the worst thing is, they're good at it! How are we going to take him on? With water pistols? What are we going to do to him, kick him in the shins and run away?' Gianni was now more intimidated by Pasquale than by the situation we were in.

When the IT Guy came back, he looked half the man he was when he went outside.

The second I looked at the IT Guy's pale face, the sickness I'd felt inside for so long subsided. The all-consuming fear seemed to shrink like it was collapsing in on itself, condensing into a point in my solar plexus. I was accustomed to the out-of-body experiences I'd been having lately and now it was happening again. I felt like I was standing next to myself and I was more aware and more awake than normal. I don't know what kind of alchemy went on inside me right then. But seeing the gang displaying the fear that had been, up to now, only my own seemed to lessen my own burden. I wondered if fear was a finite weight that became lighter when carried between people. My fear continued to get smaller so rapidly that I thought it had disappeared. Then I knew it had simply changed to something else. I didn't have any more time to ponder the nature of fear because I popped right back into my body. That 'something else' expanded as rapidly as the fear had collapsed. It filled my heart, my brain, my eyes and it took over my whole body; I knew it like an old friend. It was rage.

I shouted: 'OK, guys, sit the fuck down! If we start screaming like little girls, we are as good as dead.'

The Spanish looked up and whispered: 'Have you got a plan, Prince?'

'Of course I do!' I replied confidently. 'We are going to show these fuckers that we are not people to mess with! We have done it once and we are going to do it again! All right?'

Just to have a break from the fear made me feel so full of relief. I must have appeared like my old self. I knew the guys had memories of me as a strong leader who had taken them into battle before. And we had won. The fact that we'd been anonymous and now we were exposed, and that this time our situation was all but hopeless didn't matter. All they saw was the Prince with a plan; to them that was hope and hope was all they needed now. They sat down again and began to look more composed.

I sounded, or tried to sound, like Winston Churchill or Mussolini. 'We are going to do this. Before we start working on my plan, I'm going to see the Boss. I'm going to tell him that he does not scare anybody: certainly not me. If we stay focused and find our strength again, we have a chance.'

I looked at each of them. 'Do not be afraid,' I said. 'Do not show fear or behave any differently. And do not do anything until we meet here again next week when I will tell each of you your part in the plan. OK?'

They nodded one by one. It had worked. They were calm. I felt like a giant bird protecting its chicks. Even though I was only 17, I was wise enough to know that protecting these men was the single cause of the planet-sized anger slowly turning inside me. Normally I'd have felt proud of myself for a realisation like that and might even have taken a moment for self-congratulation. But the rage was so massive that there was no room for pride. There wasn't even space for the worry I should have been feeling about lying to the gang again. I'd told them I had a plan when actually I didn't have a clue.

I woke up the next morning – a Sunday – without my usual feeling of dread; I hadn't had any nightmares, which was rare. Mrs Apron must have been having a lie-in because there was no smell of hot chocolate drifting into the room. I got up and dressed in the best clothes I had, after my involuntary donation to the charity shop. I got on my Vespa and rode straight to the Big Boss's house unannounced. I beeped my horn over and over outside the closed gates until two guards came out to see who was making a noise. They knew me.

'Have you got an appointment?' the burlier of the two asked.

I said: 'Yes, he's waiting for me.'

I no longer cared about my own life and so I felt I could be cocky and insolent. The tables had somehow turned in my favour and I wasn't afraid at all. The gates opened and I wheeled my Vespa inside.

I followed the usual procedure. I thought the guards must have believed I had an appointment because they took me straight to the Big Boss's office. Nevertheless, I wasn't stupid and I knew they'd be communicating everything with the man himself. If he hadn't wanted to see me, hadn't been curious why I'd turn up out of the blue on a Sunday morning, there was no way I'd have got past the front gates. In his office I made the usual 40 yards and sat down without waiting to be asked.

He sat at his desk as still as ever, looking over his gold-rimmed spectacles at me with his cold, expressionless eyes.

'I will do this Butcher business,' I said without emotion. My lack of regard for my own safety had given me what felt like equal power to him. 'Then, after the job, you will let me and my boys walk away from here forever. In the meantime, you will never get your men to approach or threaten my boys again. Do you understand?'

I thought he'd order those two lumps standing either side of his desk to put a bullet in my head or to beat me senseless, but he didn't flinch. He leaned back into his massive leather chair and placed his hands together in front of him like he was praying. But he wasn't praying, he was thinking. Then he surprised me by saying:

'I am sorry to have scared your boys.'

I lost my composure for a second from the shock of him apologising to me instead of killing me.

He went on: 'Maybe my men got a bit rough on them but this was not intended. I wanted to remind you of our arrangement as I had the impression you were not taking the affair seriously. I can see now that you are so accept my apologies and let us move on to the next item on the agenda.'

I pulled myself together, nodded and said: 'I'm sure you have a file on the Butcher. I would like to have a look at it. If I need anything, I would appreciate your unwavering support. I'm sure that you realise I'm not trying to rob a candy store here. What you are asking me to do is almost ... well, unprecedented.'

He replied: 'Of course. I will help you. I have to keep my distance from this thing for reasons you might well understand but if I can give you a leg up, why not? You are far too clever to die young. I want to get this business over and done with and then you can give your talents to medicine or law or whatever brilliant future awaits you. One day you might find a cure for cancer. Who knows?'

As soon as he finished his sentence, as if he'd communicated with his men telepathically, one of them handed a file to me. It was all the information he had on the Butcher. I opened it and saw the picture of a young man in his twenties and a dossier of about 25 pages.

'Look it up in your own time, son. I need to go for lunch as my family is waiting. If you had told me you were coming, I would have had a seat ready for you. In the meantime, I wish you a good day and I will be looking forward to some news. I am sure you will do this job well.' One of the men came to my chair as if to invite me to get up so I took the file and left.

On my way back home, I had an incredible sense of satisfaction. I had gone to that gangster's house and I had put him in his place. 'Fuck him,' I thought, enjoying the feeling of anger that made me powerful and invincible again.

At home I pored over the file, memorising all the information it held about the Butcher. Then, having thrown the file on the floor, I sat on my bed and tried to take stock of what weapons I had at my disposal: a traumatised gang with a suicidal leader; an employer who might kill me at any time; two years of failure behind me and not a stitch of a plan. With this, I had to bring down one of the most powerful gangsters in the world. He and his army of five thousand assassins were ready to slaughter me, my family and my friends.

As my head fell into the pillow, I wished I'd killed myself when I had the chance.

ONE FOR ALL

When I woke on Monday morning I felt better than I had in months. I was hungry and my mouth watered as I thought about Mrs Apron's breakfasts. I got up and went to greet her, but she wasn't there. Yesterday, for the first time since she had found me collapsed on the floor from exhaustion, she had been absent. Now it was two days on the run. I missed her but I felt like I had no right to feel that way; I knew I could never make demands on her or expect her to take care of me. She had done enough and had been so kind. She was probably too busy with her own life to care about me now I was better. Still, the thought of that thick hot chocolate and pastries made my stomach hurt. And there was another type of hollow inside me that expanded when I walked through my empty apartment.

I checked the fridge and the kitchen cupboards for something to eat and found a loaf in the bread bin. I made hot chocolate and cut myself a slice of bread but the butter dish was empty. I'd have to make do with the hot chocolate but it didn't taste the same as when Mrs Apron made it. I left half of it and decided to bunk off school and do something productive instead. I wandered around my apartment looking at the mess I'd made in the short time I'd been left alone. I tidied up, washed the dishes and then stood for a while staring at the pile of unpaid bills that Mrs Apron had neatly stacked on the counter. Another final demand dropped through the letter box. I knew if I didn't pay them soon I'd have to spend the winter with no heating, no water and no electricity. The thought cheered me as up. I hadn't thought I'd still be alive for another winter. Worrying about my utility bills meant I had some hope of being here long enough to suffer from the inconvenience.

The belief that I'd soon be dead had been the real reason I'd neglected to pay the bills. I could afford to pay them. I had the three grand I'd found in the safe. After I'd lost the 40 grand in the charity shop débâcle, I'd withdrawn my 10,000 euros share of the profits of the Lugano business. So, with a small hope of a future, but still a niggling doubt I'd live long enough to reap the benefits of paying the bills, I decided to clear up my life. I didn't want to leave any debts behind that my family would have to deal with after I was gone. I ripped the envelopes open, added up how much I owed, grabbed a giant wedge of bank-notes from the much larger bundle and hurried out.

After I'd taken care of the bills I found myself in the city with a good deal of cash in my pocket. I decided to go shopping. Impending death playing on my mind meant I was reluctant to spend money on things I probably wouldn't be using. I saw a magnificent white suit in a tailor's window and wondered if I should buy it to wear at my funeral. I was half-hearted even about that – a bit of hope still clinging on. Besides, I thought, there won't be much left of my body to put in the suit if the Butcher has anything to do with it. I looked in the window at the suit and imagined it filled with dismembered body parts, stained with blood. Then I thought of myself lying in an open coffin in that pristine white suit but with my features dissolved away by an acid bath. I laughed out loud. I looked around in case someone had heard me and walked on.

I went to the market and ordered a hot chocolate from a cart cafe. I sat at one of the small tables and watched people milling about buying fruit, vegetables and fresh fish. The hot chocolate was not as good as Mrs Apron's. Still, it was sweet and hot and I let the foam collect on my top lip. The people around me, I knew, were worse off than I was. They were my people. Neapolitans. Good people who work hard all day long and still struggle to make ends meet. Their only joy is their families and gathering around the table for a Sunday roast. Still, here they were with beaming smiles and twinkling eyes. The women stopped to chat every few yards as they bumped into yet another familiar face. The men laughed and shouted insults at each other in good humour. The market traders called out the prices of their goods with such energy. I wondered why people, who had it so much worse than I did, were so happy and without complaint when I had been so filled with anger and revenge that it robbed me of any peace. There I sat, a millionaire at the age of 17. I was healthy (if I looked after myself), good-looking, with my own apartment. I had my trusty Vespa to take me wherever I wanted to go. I regularly threw away money like it was confetti.

I remembered why I had started all of this in the first place: what I had been fighting for since I was 12. The people around me were the real victims of the criminal activity in which I had become so entrenched. I couldn't let myself be killed. Without me, who would help my family to a better life? This city refuses to lie down in spite of such hardship. I thought: 'If they can do it, so can I.'

I had an idea for the best way to deal with the cash that was burning holes in my pocket. I wanted to square my debt to Mrs Apron and the families in my building. I found a florist and ordered every family a huge bouquet of flowers. I asked them to deliver them that afternoon. Then I bought more than 20 boxes of the finest chocolates I could find. I felt stronger with each passing hour. As if I wasn't weighed down enough with bags filled with chocolate and presents for the kids, I then went on to spend a few thousand euros on clothes – including the white suit which I was fully determined to wear on a whole living body unscarred by acid. I had most of the clothes delivered to my house because I was unable to carry them all.

The flower delivery van arrived as I got back to my apartment and I watched for a while as the sole driver struggled with so many orders of huge bunches of flowers at once. He took them out of the van two at a time and placed them in the stairwell ready to take up the stairs. I put my shopping bags down and stopped him as he started up the stairs with the first bouquet.

'It's OK mister, I will deliver them,' I said.

He looked at me with suspicion. I didn't blame him. I must have looked like a kid about to steal his flowers to sell on somewhere else. I smiled my best, most honest smile and told him to wait. I left my bags where they were, took my new clothes into my apartment and grabbed one of my kitchen chairs. I put it by the main door and made him sit in it. I grabbed a bunch of flowers, a box of chocolates and a bag of toys and I ran up the stairs. I started from the top down and delivered to every family in that block, giving toys to those with kids. My neighbours were delighted to see me and they were so humble and grateful that I almost cried more than once. People came out into the corridors to help deliver the gifts so that in the end, everyone was milling about the block and it felt like a party. Smiling, friendly people surrounded the delivery man. They brought him coffee and cakes and he looked very happy about his unexpected break. I felt like Santa Claus.

I had only one delivery left: the most important one. I was so tired from being squeezed in bear hugs and kissed all over my face that I wanted to shove the delivery man off his chair and sit down on it myself. The party was winding down and everyone had started to go back inside when I knocked on Mrs Apron's door. I was half-wondering why she hadn't come out before now because of the racket. I thought she might not be in and I was right as there was no answer. I decided I'd have to wait until she came back so I gave the delivery man a handful of euros as a tip. He was so shocked at the size of the bundle of notes, he stood there with his mouth open looking at me and then looking at the money.

'Are you sure?' he asked.

I nodded and grinned at him, thanking him again for delivering the flowers. He said: 'No. Thank you, Sir!' Then he left, folding his hands around the money like he was holding a live bird. He was still smiling even as he drove away. I took Mrs Apron's gifts and flowers into my apartment and tried on my new clothes while I waited for her to return.

A few hours later I went down and knocked on Mrs Apron's door for the fifth time. I was about to walk away once more when a second person turned up and knocked on the door. It was a woman wearing a similar apron to Mrs Apron's. She smiled at me and we stood there waiting awkwardly.

'Do you think she's out?' the woman asked.

'She's been out all day. This is about the tenth time I've tried. Do you think she's ill or something?'

'She'll be working at the factory,' she said. 'She does shifts there when they've got work for her.'

'At the textiles factory?' I asked, wondering why she wouldn't have told me that. 'That's a total sweatshop.'

The woman bit her bottom lip and stared at me in a way that said she was thinking she should keep her mouth shut.

'It's OK,' I said. 'I'm her friend. I live upstairs.'

'Well, I wouldn't want her to think I was gossiping about her behind her back,' she said, checking the corridors for eavesdroppers. I could sense the urge to talk about Mrs Apron behind her back was much stronger in this woman than any sense of loyalty. I smiled my best smile and said: 'Of course, not! You can trust me. Hand on heart,' I put my hand on my heart. 'I am very discreet,' I added in what I hoped was a conspiratorial manner, putting my hand on her arm. It might have come out as more flirtatious than I intended, going by the woman's reaction. She blushed, pulled a handkerchief out of her apron pocket and wiped her forehead. She wafted the handkerchief at me, giggling. 'Go on with you!'

I laughed with her, flirted with her and grinned as she spilled all she had always fully intended to tell me about Mrs Apron.

'Well, she works at the textile factory, as I said,' she said. 'But she doesn't like people knowing because, you know ... what they do there.'

'Knock off designer clothes?' I asked, but I already knew the answer.

'Yes. She's a very upright woman and she's never broken the law in her life, but circumstances mean she has to do what she has to do.'

'Circumstances?' I asked.

'Yes, she's fallen on hard times and she's got that...' she looked around to check no one was listening again and dropped her voice to a whisper. 'She's got that retarded son to look after.' When she said 'retarded' she mouthed the word without any sound. 'He's a handful and he's not going to be bringing in any income any time soon.' She pursed her lips as if in disapproval.

'Right,' I nodded, pretending I already knew.

'I think she's ashamed, between you and me.'

'Ashamed?' I said enthusiastically, as if fascinated.

'Yes, I expect so. After all, the father left soon after they found

317

out the boy was, you know ... slow. And it's bothered her, being a single mother. Her family shuns her because of it. I'm her only friend. And now she has to work for a company that's involved in criminal activity. I don't blame her either. She's always been a proud woman and I think this time, pride did come before a fall.'

'Right,' I said. 'I'd better get back. If she comes back, I'll tell her you called, Mrs...?' I took her hand and kissed the back of it.

She giggled. 'Call me Matilde.'

I half-bowed in an old-fashioned way – I almost clicked my heels together but managed to suppress the urge. I turned and left, wiping my mouth with my sleeve, feeling like her hand had contaminated me. I looked back before I turned the corner to the stairs and she was still leaning against Mrs Apron's doorway waving the handkerchief at me. I bounded up the stairs two at a time, wondering how I hadn't known all this. I was working out in my head how I was going to rescue Mrs Apron from her 'circumstances'. Matilde was not her only friend. She had me.

I knocked at Mrs Apron's door once more that night before falling asleep on the sofa, only to wake up at 6 a.m. the next morning. I didn't want to disturb her at such an early time, so instead of knocking I put my ear to her door before I left for the Cave. I could hear a radio playing very quietly. So she had come home. I felt relieved.

On my Vespa, driving towards the Cave, I looked up at Vesuvius, lit in sharp relief against the sky by the early morning sun. I knew that inside its unchanging and peaceful exterior, there was a hell of boiling rock waiting to burst out and destroy all that surrounds it. It made me think of myself. This shook me as I didn't know why I was such a destructive force. I was so determined to work hard to make everyone's life better. I brushed off the feeling and focused on the hope I'd had a few moments ago – that anything was possible.

Inside the Cave I made a list of all my options. I wanted some sort of plan. I wrote several possible courses of action, including 'run away to another country' and 'kill the Butcher'. I underlined the latter, thinking it was probably my only option. Kill or be killed. Then I got up and started cleaning up the mess the guys had left from one of what they called their 'snackathons'.

I stopped what I was doing and took a moment to laugh at myself, realising the last time I was here I'd intended to kill myself. Now here I was making a plan to kill someone else. Planning a murder while clearing up pizza crusts, popcorn and candy wrappers, and feeling annoyed at the mess, was surreal and ludicrous. Still, I continued. I noticed that in my office someone (probably Gianni), had left a packet of biscuits that had crumbled out all over the table. I swore under my breath at Gianni's messiness. In my office! I scraped the crumbs into the bin with my hand. I picked up the packet to fling it away then found there was one biscuit left. As I ripped open the packet, retrieved the biscuit and pushed it whole into my mouth, I noticed something flashing out of the corner of my eye.

I stopped chewing and slowly turned my head towards the flashing red light, my heart pounding. Bugging the Captain's apartment had failed and so I'd given up on seeing the light that indicated the bugs had actually recorded something. Hoping and doubting at the same time, still struggling with swallowing the huge mouthful of now too-dry biscuit, I pressed the play button. The sweet sound of the Captain's voice filled my office. He was talking to his wife about groceries. Destiny might be on my side after all.

THE CAPTAIN'S VOICE

At school I felt so excited about listening to the Captain's conversations that nothing bothered me, not even the teacher's sarcastic tone when he called me 'Prince'. I almost floated home. The future seemed brighter than it had in a long time, not least because there might be a future. I had the barest seed of a plan, but it was enough. I had nothing to guarantee my success, or even my survival, but I had tangible hope and that was something new in the game.

I picked up Mrs Apron's flowers and chocolates from my apartment and knocked on her door. She opened it this time, just a crack, and peeped through. I held out her gifts with a big grin on my face. She opened the door and stepped through, pulling it almost closed behind her. She wiped her hands on her apron, glancing back into her apartment as if she didn't want me to see what was in there. She smiled, glad to see me.

'Are those for me?' she said. 'You shouldn't have bought me anything. Oh, my! Aren't they beautiful? And chocolates, too. You really shouldn't have. How lovely.'

I handed her the bouquet and the chocolates. 'After all you've done for me. Yes, I should have,' I said. 'It's the least I could do.'

We stood awkwardly for a moment and I felt her hesitation. She knew she had to take the flowers and chocolates in, but I noticed she didn't want me to go in. My curiosity overpowered my manners. I waited with obvious expectation, ignoring her efforts to stall me. In the end, her desire to hide something was overtaken by her need to be polite and she backed in through the door and said: 'Come in, of course.'

Ever since she had been caring for me, I'd never seen the inside of her home. I was expecting a spotless, warm, homely place full of trinkets and the smells of cooking. That was not what I found. The apartment was a tiny, two-room bedsit. There were two single beds with a curtain to separate them and two uncomfortable-looking wooden chairs at a small table in front of a hearth.

A fridge rattled and buzzed, almost drowning out the chatter from the tiny portable television on top of the 'kitchen' counter. Next to it, a pot boiled on a tiny two-ring stove. It was spotless, as I expected, and the curtains were bright and cheerful but the wallpaper was peeling off and one wall was bare plaster. A closed door, also with peeling paint, led off to what I presumed must have been a bathroom. Mrs Apron's face blushed red as she looked around and then at me. Then her chin lifted and I saw a sense of pride return to her face as she nodded for me to sit in one of the chairs at the table.

'Take a seat and I'll find a vase to put these in,' she said, gesturing to a chair. She opened a rickety cupboard and pulled out a large chipped vase. She filled the vase with water, unwrapped the flowers and began to arrange them. I watched her for a moment, saying: 'I'm glad you like them. I wanted to give you something to say thank you.'

She nodded. 'It's very kind of you. I'll make you a hot chocolate when I've done these.'

I felt sorry that I'd barged my way in. The last thing I wanted was to embarrass or hurt her and I felt my face flush as red as hers.

We were being unnaturally polite. She tried to fight her embarrassment with her usual elegance and pride. I was ashamed and tried to fight that, reminding myself my motivation had been to help her. I was determined now, more than ever, to do so.

When she finished arranging the flowers they looked even more beautiful than when a professional florist had arranged them. The ugly vase became insignificant in their shadow. I marvelled at them and smiled as she placed them on the windowsill. 'Wow! That's amazing,' I said. 'You've got skills there.'

'Thank you,' she said, blushing again. 'I enjoy flower arranging and it's been a long time since I've had any.'

She made hot chocolate in a pan on the tiny stove. I thought about asking her if she wanted to come over to my apartment but I realised that would seem like I thought it was better than hers. Maybe she'd think I wanted to get out of there. I did, but I didn't want her to know that. I wanted to get her out of there, too! I felt exactly like I would have had she been my real mother and there's no way I'd have left my Mother to rot in a hole like this.

'Is that your son's bed?' I asked, pointing to the rickety bed in the corner with threadbare blankets and a pillow greying with age. I knew it was because there was a poster of Giuseppe Bruscolotti, a.k.a. 'Pal e fierr' (iron pole), the heroic Captain of Napoli, on the wall above the headboard.

'Yes. He's out at the moment trying to find work,' she said. 'He's struggling. He's upset that no one will take him on because he has a condition.'

'A condition?' I asked cautiously, remembering the way Matilde had said 'retarded' under her breath.

'Yes, he's got autism. He has trouble making friends and people think he's a bit strange. He has difficulty judging what people expect of him so he can get himself into trouble by saying and doing the wrong thing. He's not good at job interviews. But he's very clever in lots of ways. He has a wonderful memory and his drawings are indistinguishable from what's real.' She went over to his bed and pulled out a large sketchbook from under the mattress.

'Look,' she said, peeling back the sketchbook cover.

The picture was of Mrs Apron herself. It was so realistic that for a moment I thought it was a photo. When I looked closer I could see the entire image was made up of tiny dots. Just pen dots applied with varied spacing to give the illusion of light and shadow. It looked like a finer and more detailed version of a newspaper printed photograph. But it was better than a photograph because he seemed to have captured more of Mrs Apron's character than a camera ever could. It was like he had captured her soul. I took the sketchbook and turned the pages, marvelling at the drawings. Each one was executed at a level of artistic genius I had never seen. 'These belong in a gallery, not under a mattress!' I said.

'That's what I say to him,' Mrs Apron agreed. 'But he won't let anyone see them. He even hides them from me.' She took the sketchbook gently out of my hands and returned it to its hiding place under the mattress.

'Would you like a chocolate with your hot chocolate?' she asked. She handed me a cup of the hot chocolate I'd been craving over the days she'd been absent.

'No thank you. This is all I need,' I said, taking a gulp.

'Another reason I called,' I said, the words coming out of my mouth at the same time as I thought of them, 'is because I was going to put an advert in the paper as I'm looking for a house-keeper and cook. I wanted to ask you what I should write in the advert. You did such a good job of taking care of my apartment when I was ill. I know you will know the right way to word the ad, what the job entails, what skills to ask for etcetera.'

'Of course,' she said. 'I'd be glad to help.'

She looked at me doubtfully for a moment, as if she were think-ing I'd lost my mind.

'What's wrong?' I asked.

'Well, it isn't my place,' she said carefully.

'No, please ... go on,' I encouraged, curious.

'How are you going to pay a housekeeper? It's none of my busi-ness, but I wouldn't like to see you get into a situation where you're obliged to pay someone and find yourself without the means. I mean, I did notice that you seem to be, well, short of money. Understandable at your age, with you still being at school.' She smiled at me sympathetically. 'I'm presuming your parents are paying for your place but if you can't keep up with your bills, do you think a housekeeper is a good idea?'

'Ah, the bills,' I smiled, realising that my leaving the bills unpaid had given her the impression I was poverty-stricken.

'I'm not short of money. I'm lazy,' I grinned. 'I have enough money to pay the bills and employ several housekeepers, if I want them. But I only want one. Ideally, that would be you, Mrs Apron, but you may not have the time or the desire to spend your days cater-ing to the likes of me. So, on the basis that you've got better things to do, I'm putting an ad in the paper. I hope to find someone with the experience and ability to do everything as well as you have done it. I will accept nothing less – and I will pay them well for their trouble.'

I watched her face to see if my plan was working. I didn't want to risk hurting her pride. This woman had dignity and she wouldn't have responded well to any offer of charity.

'Say that again,' she said frowning. 'You'll pay them how much?'

'100 a week,' I said knowing this was three times the amount she would be earning at the factory.

'And you can afford that?' she asked, her eyes wide. I knew this was more than she would ever have earned and more than enough to keep her and her son in food and clothes and more.

'Yes, of course. I'll pay in advance, too.'

Mrs Apron stood silent for a moment. Then she sat down on one of the chairs opposite me and all of the tension seemed to go out of her. 'And you say ideally you'd want me to do the job?'

'Yes, of course!' I said, with genuine hope in my voice. 'That would make me very happy because my apartment only feels like a home when you're there.'

I looked up at her and the realisation that there were tears welling up in my eyes startled me. I had to fight the cold mass of loneliness that threatened to escape from its hidden compartment where I kept it sealed away by sheer force of will. I had hidden it even from myself and I felt shocked by it. I realised it was an effort that was always present and I felt suddenly tired.

I thought about my gallant plan to rescue this woman. I had to cough to hide the burst of snorting laughter that I couldn't control.

'Who is rescuing who?' I thought.

'Well, I'd be glad to take the job,' she said, smiling.

'Really?' I said, feeling excited.

'Yes, but the pay you're offering is a little too much.'

'No,' I said. 'No, it's not. This is something I won't budge on. I have the funds and I've worked out how much I want to pay and I insist, particularly because it's you and you've proved yourself more than worthy. I actually think it's not enough, considering how valuable you are ... err, your work is to me.' I corrected myself but she smiled, knowing what I meant.

'Very well, then,' she said, holding out her hand for me to shake. 'You have a deal.'

The day was getting better and better.

I left Mrs Apron in my apartment cooking one of her dinners and I sped off to the Cave on my Vespa, feeling all the security of home I'd felt as a little kid. On top of that, I was on an unstoppable roll of good luck. How could I have thought I was going to die when there was so much hope?!

We had recorded 18 hours of tapes from the Captain's flat. I worked out why it had looked like the bugs hadn't worked and I slapped myself on the forehead at my stupidity. I'd designed the bugs to be triggered by sound so we wouldn't have to trawl through hours of blank tape. This meant there was no recording when the Captain was sleeping or out at work. I hadn't figured out that the bugs were working fine and the Captain might simply not have been home. I felt foolish: a feeling I figured was good for me as I often assumed I was a genius and much cleverer than my enemy. A bit of self-abasement and seeing my plans fail meant I was far more careful than usual.

With these hours of the Captain's conversations I could revisit the plan I'd shelved but, before I started any real thinking and figuring out details, I had 18 hours of tapes to listen to. It was a boring job but I could do it an hour at a time over the coming days. I decided to start right away. I felt grateful now that I didn't have to listen to long stretches of silence. The first conversation I heard was the Captain's wife asking him if he'd enjoyed his trip and all became clear. I wondered where she'd been if he'd been away and why she hadn't triggered the device. I decided to take notes.

I spent an hour listening to the Captain and his wife. Mundane discussions about what was in the newspaper, what to get from the shops, comments about family and some memories of years ago. I figured they'd been childhood sweethearts because they talked about things that happened when they were very young. Then, as they were remembering when the Captain's father had let them drive the car on the beach when they were toddlers, she referred to him as 'dad', too. It dawned on me that this wasn't his wife but his sister.

'The Captain is unmarried and he lives with his sister,' I wrote in my notebook with several exclamation marks. Then, as I wound the tape forward, I heard his sister say: 'I'm off home, now. See you tomorrow, love' and I scratched out the last part of the sentence and wrote: 'He lives alone.'

I thought of Mrs Apron at home and the delicious meal we were going to share and I felt sorry for the Captain. I knew what it was like to be alone.

When you're a kid, time goes by slowly, but I still felt alarmed at how quickly December and Christmas came around. I'd been basking in Mrs Apron's loving care, seeing the guys at the Cave and enjoying myself, all the time pretending I was perfecting a plan I didn't have. I had yet to work out some way to give the Big Boss what he wanted: the Butcher's head on a plate. That or die.

I was feeling so full of life at the thought of Christmas, I had let go of the latter option. The determination to live was strong in me. The worry that a violent death awaited still lingered like a shadow though and I was living in a kind of corridor, squeezed from both sides. Death could come from either direction. The Big Boss could kill me because I hadn't done what he asked, or the Butcher could find out I was plotting his downfall under the direction of the Big Boss.

The former was the most urgent. The nagging voice in the back of my mind ruined my new optimistic mood so I decided to pay the Big Boss a visit to buy more time. I wanted to have a Christmas without the looming threat hanging over me. In that one respect, I was like any other kid my age. I wanted to sit around watching TV, eating chocolates and opening presents.

My meeting with the Big Boss went the same as the other meetings. I turned up at the gates, waited until they opened them, took a long escorted walk across the huge office. He didn't look up from the papers on his desk until I was seated in the chair opposite. We talked as usual, with him leading the conversation and me deferring to him and mustering up as much respect as I could for someone I loathed. This was made a little easier by the fact that I admired him at the same time. Even though all of this was so familiar to me, the hair was standing up on the back of my neck. Something about it was different. I couldn't quite grasp what it was.

I told him the reason for my visit – an update on my progress. I said I wanted to reassure him that while it was taking time to execute, I had a plan that was being followed. He didn't ask what the plan was, thank God, because it was a lie.

'Time is ticking by, Prince,' he said. 'But I am a patient man.'

I felt my Adam's apple bob up and down as I swallowed but my eyes didn't leave his face.

'I know this is a slow process, but I want to be thorough and I need time to make sure there are no mistakes. One wrong step and the outcome may be very different to the one required,' I said.

He paused. He was like a frozen statue for what seemed like a long time. He looked me directly in the eye like he was reading something there. Then he nodded, as if satisfied with what he'd read, and re-animated, reaching for a pen and going back to the paper on his desk. This usually signalled that he'd finished with me and I put my hands on the arms of the chair and pushed myself up out of the seat.

Then he said, without looking up: 'It is unfortunate that in each day that passes while you are executing your "plan"...' His emphasis on the word 'plan' sent a shiver up my spine. I sat down again. '... The Butcher grows stronger. The continuing successes of his operations mean he is quickly becoming a superpower in every sense. He is making considerable amounts of money and his reputation is expanding. He is feared. Money and reputation are and always have been the source of ultimate power for all men. Men like us use money and fear to surround ourselves with protection and to get others to do our bidding.'

He gestured towards the various suited heavies in the room. I looked around at the one that had escorted me to him, the one standing to attention behind him, staring into the middle distance, and the one by the door.

'We are direct rivals, the Butcher and I. The more power he has, the less I have. And, while I have every confidence in the people I am surrounded by, there are many under my employ. As you know from your own work with me, I am not able to keep all of my men from going over to the other side. The bigger an empire he has, the more unstable mine becomes.'

I looked again at the heavy behind him and the one standing

by me but their expressions didn't falter or change. I understood what he was saying and I knew he was right. The Big Boss's people feared him enough but there was a growing risk that some of them could be compelled to desert him. They'd betray him for a man they feared more and for a bigger pay packet.

'I understand,' I said. 'I will do my best to get the job done as quickly as possible.' I hoped I sounded confident and efficient and I think I pulled it off.

All the time I was thinking that while the rise of the Butcher was making the Big Boss feel unstable, it was actually the best thing for me. The bigger he was, the more activity there would be surrounding him, meaning more opportunities for me to find his weak links. The downside was pretty considerable though. If the Big Boss's men were betraying him to the Butcher, they would also be likely to pass on information about his operations. He could find out who was working for him – including my work and my identity.

As if he'd read my mind, or seen the flash of fear on my face at the thought of the Butcher finding out I'd been hired to bring him down, he said: 'I don't want you to come here again.'

I couldn't help my muscles relaxing with the feeling of relief at the prospect of never again sitting in this chair. I almost let out a small gasp of breath held in by the tension I felt, but I managed to stop it.

The Big Boss gave me his direct phone line and a password. I was to use it should I need to speak to him in future. 'Call this,' he said, 'and we can arrange to meet somewhere more convenient and private.'

That he still meant us to meet and not just communicate by phone was a blow. The tension I'd let go rebuilt itself, like a self-assembling string of cells under a microscope.

That he wanted to meet anywhere but his own home showed how much trust he was losing in his men and the magnitude of the power ebbing away from him.

I'd been watching the Butcher's house for months to find out more about his day-to-day activities, who came to see him, when and if he left and where he was going. We had set ourselves up in a good position. Across the wide road from his villa was a block of luxury apartments. Built into the ground floor was a pizza restaurant with chairs and tables outside. It was a quiet part of the city so the restaurant was exclusive and frequented mainly by rich residents from nearby. The apartment above was rented by what appeared to be a normal Neapolitan family but, in fact, it was us. Dad was the IT Guy wearing a thick black beard, Gianni was his 'lovely' wife (he got into character very comfortably) and the Cat and Pasquale were their two sons. I dressed as a girl when I visited the apartment and I couldn't believe how convincing I looked. I was a bit broad and tall but my face was remarkably pretty; it was unnerving. I was barely a man. The changes I'd been through and the increasing masculinity that I'd grown used to felt under threat. I didn't like the laughter and constant mocking from the guys that now came whether I was dressed up or not. The decision to wear disguises might seem over-dramatic but it wasn't taken lightly. We didn't dress up for fun. The Butcher was likely to have men living in the building and they would be paid a lot of money to keep watch over his house and the surrounding area. If we were found out, we would die. So, our 'costumes' were carefully devised to look as real as possible and we were pretty convincing. But I didn't enjoy it at all!

We took reams of photographs of the entrance to the Butcher's house every day. We couldn't use a flash, so we were restricted to taking pictures in daylight hours. When it was dark, we took it in turns to watch and take notes. Every time anyone paid the house a visit during the day, we took as many shots as we could. We hoped to capture their faces, their number plates or whatever information we could use to identify them. Then, back at the Cave, we would develop them and I would pore over them to find I didn't know what until I'd found it.

We rarely saw the Butcher.

Three months in and coming up to Christmas, we had more than 20,000 photographs with nothing of any use in them. The boys were bored and tired. It felt like a dead-end mission. I spent any spare time, when not watching the gates or listening to the tapes from the Captain's apartment, examining the pictures. I filed them into order based on the time and date they were taken. 'At least I know what time the bread is delivered,' I thought as I slotted the latest photo into its correct place in the file.

The Captain's tapes seemed to be just as fruitless. His sister had gone up north and the only thing I would hear was him cooking, or the music he played and the movies he watched, and every time he farted. After a while, even that stopped being funny. If it hadn't been for the company of Mrs Apron at home, and her cooking of course, I would have died of frustration and boredom.

Morale was at rock bottom yet again, and not just for me. We all felt we were going nowhere. The prospect of a Christmas spent away from this mind-numbing task, being with our families, seemed like the most exciting thing in the world.

Before I left Naples for the holidays, I took a look at the finances I'd been ignoring. I immediately wished I hadn't. I'd spent almost 900 grand: the printing shop; the flat; the electronics for bugging and listening; photographic equipment; transport and more. It all amounted to a fortune and I had nothing to show for it apart from tons of badly taken, useless photographs. My share of the eight million euros we had kept for ourselves had gone. I was now tapping into money that belonged to the rest of the gang. Some of the stuff we'd bought could have been seen as 'assets' that might increase in value, such as the shop and the apartment. This was a comfort. But, in our rush to get everything set up, we'd paid a much higher price for these than we should have.

A recession in Europe also meant the shop in Lugano wasn't doing well any more. We still had more than two million euros in our Swiss account but we were spending it so fast, I couldn't see it lasting more than a few months. No wonder the IT Guy wasn't pleased. No wonder he'd stopped telling the rest of the gang about our collapsing financial situation. We had no money coming in, but it was flowing out like our bank account was a burst pipe.

I felt depressed and worried as I left Mrs Apron and her son. I'd suggested both stay in my apartment over Christmas to 'keep the place secure'. I was off to my Grandmother's house to be with my family. I'd arranged for one of the neighbours to dress as Santa and deliver presents to Mrs Apron and her boy on Christmas morning. Thinking of this made me smile despite my financial worries.

I had a warm and comfortable Christmas at my Grandmother's. My family were almost back to normal. My kid brother was much better, apart from his left eye and his leg. Emotionally, he was much improved. My parents were full of Christmas cheer and they were more affectionate towards me – and each other – than the last time I saw them. Being with them made me realise how lonely I'd been. We ate and drank and chatted and laughed. I forgot about everything when I was with them. I didn't have to do anything but sit around and eat, open presents and watch TV. Most of the time it was like being five again.

I took lots of walks through the village and the forests. These were the times I tried to drag my mind away from being a five-year-old with no responsibilities, to working out what to do. I sometimes sat in my Granddad's garage, where he'd taught me to open locks and get into safes. I hadn't had time to think about him in a long time but now I missed him so much it hurt.

My Granddad would have known what to do. Not that I'd have told him about any of this. He was an honest man and I doubt he'd have approved of how I'd used the things he taught me. Now, in his garage, I could feel him all around me and I felt like I was asking him for help. I remembered him teaching me how to unlock my first safe right here in this room.

'I've finally found a safe I can't open,' I said out loud.

How can the Butcher run such an empire without ever leaving his house or making a phone call? I knew he must interact with people. He must do both of these things but I couldn't figure out why I'd never seen him or been able to intercept a call from his villa. I felt like giving up. But the image of a safe kept coming back into my mind.

It really was like an impenetrable safe and thinking of it like this helped. If it were a safe, I would have the patience and the confidence to eventually break it. With a safe, I'd never give up and, no matter how many times I failed, I would just keep going until I'd opened it.

While I was sitting in there, looking around at my Granddad's kit, torturing myself with my un-openable safe, there was a gentle knock at the door.

'Come in, Grandma,' I shouted.

The door opened and my Grandma came inside. 'I've brought you some hot chocolate,' she said, handing me a cup. 'How did you know it was me?'

I laughed. 'I could tell by the way you knock,' I said. 'And that you did knock.'

Mum or Dad would have barged in but my respectful Grandma would always knock, even when Granddad was in here. She'd have known he might be concentrating on something or in the middle of doing something that he might drop or make a mistake with if she startled him.

I grinned at her as I sipped the delicious hot drink.

'Your grandfather was always in here,' she said.

She looked sad as she looked around.

'I know. I was just thinking about him,' I said. 'I'll be in in a minute,' I added.

She nodded and left, softly closing the door behind her. I smiled to myself about recognising her knock; I would even have known it was her closing the door if I hadn't been looking, she was so gentle. If my Dad had brought me the drink, he would have swung the door wide before striding in. Just then, the nature of the lock on my metaphorical safe fell into place in my mind and I suddenly knew how to open it.

I laughed out loud, looked up and said: 'Thanks Granddad.'

I went back to the Cave to meet the gang as soon as Christmas was over. I had a plan, thanks to my Grandmother, and I was burning with excitement. The guys were the opposite. They lolled about, legs sprawled across chair arms or out in front of them and heads against the walls. They all looked desperate for sleep. Dull eyes stared out listlessly from pasty faces, puffy from Christmas overindulgence. I stared at them one at a time. I thought about how to explain the plan, then decided waking them up was a better idea. I slammed my hand hard on the table, startling them so much they almost fell out of their seats. The Spanish jumped up ready to defend himself against the 'attack' and Gianni screamed. Their reaction made me laugh so much they couldn't help laughing, too.

'So, are you ready for the next stage in our plan?' I said. I was serious now and I had their attention. 'We haven't been able to discover the identities of the Butcher's visitors, right?'

'Right,' they said in unison. It was a dull and lethargic agreement, but it was an agreement.

'Now we have a way to find out who they are.'

I waited for them to ask how, but no one spoke. I continued: 'I was in my Grandfather's garage over Christmas and my Grandmother knocked at the door. I knew it was her by the way she knocked. Only she was polite enough to knock and then wait for a reply before opening the door and coming into her own garage! My Dad wouldn't have even bothered to knock. My Mum might have knocked but she'd have rapped twice and then entered without waiting for me to answer. And my kid brother would have shouted at me and bounded in.'

I looked around at them one by one, but still no real response. They were actually looking at me though, so I was thankful for that at least.

'So knocking is as individual as the personality of the knocker,' I added. 'This individual knocking pattern triggered an idea. Each of the visitors to the Butcher's house would have their own pattern. They won't be knocking, obviously. Theirs will be a pattern of behaviour. We could watch and learn the Butcher's visitors' patterns and build up a profile for each of them. Yes, they take the precaution of driving different cars every time they visit and they arrive and leave at different times. But, if we followed them and tracked everything they do, we would come to recognise a pattern of movements unique to each visitor. We could then define them as "visitor a" or "visitor b", or give them code names. We could build up a profile and then, eventually, when we found a way to take their picture or work out who they are, we would be able to match them to these profiles.'

I wanted to infect them with my enthusiasm. Their failure to react showed me what was going on inside their heads. They'd given up. Their minds were full of negativity and resistance, both of which I'd have to destroy.

'So we can't identify them, but we can identify what they do,' said the IT Guy. 'We can spot similarities and repeated behaviours and give them a name. But we don't have a plan for finding out who they are after we've done that?'

'Yes,' I said. 'So it's not a full plan and I know you can't see its brilliance yet, but you will. Trust me, this will work.'

'So how are we then going to put real identities to the identities we've made up from these patterns?' asked Pasquale.

'Good question, Pasquale,' I lied, hoping to flatter him into some type of enthusiasm or at least support. It was a very poor question indeed because I didn't yet have an answer. 'But we should take this one step at a time. I have a full plan. You'll have to trust me. I know how we will identify the people from the patterns,' I lied again. 'If I tell you now, though, it will distract us from the work we need to do to get this idea underway and working.'

'We're going to need every piece of equipment and all the knowledge we've acquired over the last five years as a gang. We have to be at our peak, working as a team. We have to time everything to perfection. We'll have to fix up radio transmission equipment and work out the best way to follow our targets without them seeing us. We'll have to develop and learn a code so we can communicate safely.

'We all have to be in this,' I looked around the room. 'We're a great team, genius even, when we work together on a plan.'

I wanted them to feel flattered and to manipulate them into accepting the plan but I also meant it. I thought: 'We are a genius team.' Something in my eyes must have changed when I thought that. They started to shuffle about and Gianni said: 'We could fix up some of the helmets with transmission.'

I knew I had them after that. I unfolded the map I'd drawn on a sheet of A1 paper, showing the roads outside the Butcher's home. I used my pencil as a pointer to illustrate how we would work.

'So, from now on, as soon as a chosen target leaves the mansion, he or she can only turn right or left. At the bottom of each road, there will be one of us on a moped, ready to follow him. That moped – Moped One – will then inform the second moped driver of the target's movements and where he's heading. Once Moped Two has caught up with them, Moped One will go its own way. Moped Three will be following Moped Two at a distance, being informed via radio and secret codes of the direction taken by the target. Once the target stops at his destination, Moped Three will catch up with them and Moped Two will ride off.

'Whichever of us is on Moped Three will take pictures using a small camera tucked in under his jacket and inform Moped One where he is. When One has caught up with Three, he will stop to wait for the target to leave his destination. He will then follow him to his other destination, alerting the others and so on and so forth. In simple terms, the same moped will never stay behind the same target for longer than a certain period of time so as not to raise suspicion from the target.'

The gang were concentrating and I felt pleased. I knew things would run smoothly from now on.

The heavy traffic of the city was a big advantage to us, as mopeds move a lot quicker than cars. We didn't follow the same target all day. Sometimes we stopped at just two destinations a day and we moved on to the other ones. We rehearsed the code language and the procedure to death before we actually got into action. We documented their every move in every possible detail. We kept a record of the disguise we wore while following our targets, so we could change it the next time.

As Gianni and I were busy during the day with school and Pasquale was at work, the day shift was up to the IT Guy, the Cat and the Spanish. I'd have given anything to do the work myself but I couldn't afford to risk the school calling the authorities. I had no choice but to go to school as usual. It was a very busy time for us and we struggled to keep up with the massive amounts of information. Nevertheless, apart from minor set-backs, after a month I knew every movement of my chosen targets. We built up a picture and, as luck would have it, the intense focus on each of them turned up several opportunities to photograph them. So, we managed to overcome the second hurdle I hadn't worked out yet. We got pictures of their faces as well as their addresses.

Two of them had legitimate jobs. One was a lawyer and the other a very famous accountant in Salerno. I didn't need to use my imagination to work out which roles they covered in the Butcher's organisation. Of course, I had to bug their phones and offices.

Whenever we disguised ourselves, I had the feeling we were playing or getting ready to be in a school play. It felt theatrical and non-serious. It made me feel as if I were in a child's fantasy which diluted the sense of danger. It also meant we would always crease up laughing when deciding on what role to play, especially buying our outfits and trying them on. I was never quite sure whether this distraction was a good thing or not. On the one hand, it was a relief from feeling nervous and scared and so gave us all more confidence in what we were doing. On the other hand, it made us a little cocky and less vigilant. It was hard to see that we were walking into something that could kill us all while lying on the floor, helpless with uncontrollable laughter.

Our disguises were brilliantly realistic. The IT Guy dressed as a businessman for one mission and I could have walked past him in the street and not recognised him. My own reflection showed an older man with all the worries of running a business mirrored in weary eyes behind gold-rimmed spectacles.

I combed my hair to the side with a straight, neat parting, adjusted the knot on my silk tie and I was done.

Dressed as businessmen, the IT Guy and I paid two targets a visit. We went to see the lawyer and the accountant to hire their services for our 'new business venture'. I'd spent three full days creating a fake but viable business plan and cash flow forecast. I impressed myself. I already thought I was a genius but my finished business plan was so brilliant that I surprised even myself and surpassed my own vanity. It crossed my mind that, had I focused my talents exclusively on building such a business, I'd have been even richer and more successful. It would also have been legal and without all the stress and risk!

So, we pretended to hire the lawyer and the accountant to work on our fake business. Our real motivation was so I could have a look at their security systems. When we were in discussion, though, I felt myself getting carried away with the role and part of me believed we were there to hire them!

Our convincing disguises, my brilliant business plan and their arrogance (they thought they were untouchable) came together to make our mission an easy one. They left us alone more than once in the 90-minute meetings and their security systems were basic. The fear they instilled in people meant they didn't ever imagine they could be targets. Bugging their phones was easy. I worked out how to exit and enter, meaning I could break in to both offices over the same weekend, without leaving a single fingerprint. I'd bought a state-of-the-art metal detector that found their safes immediately and I photocopied every document they had under lock and key. I was surprised by how little attention they paid to such important (and incriminating) records.

We all had to fight the temptation to steal the immense amount of cash and jewellery we came across. We managed to win that fight so everything went without a hitch.

It took many hours of work to unravel the complex web of business, bank accounts, partners and so on. I worked out who was doing what and how, and we ended up with the full picture of an entire network of efficient criminal activity. They were like ants, all carrying out their role and keeping the nest working to support the bloated and immobile queen: the Butcher.

This picture of their network led me to spend weeks bugging the personal telephones of as many of the main figures of the organisation as we had time for. We were listening to and recording every word they said. We had so much equipment by now that the Cave looked more like a NASA headquarters than a derelict building. We had to get more generators to run it all. The guys had to keep buying petrol from different petrol stations to keep the generators running day and night.

I was so tired that sometimes I fell asleep at school during lessons.

The more I found out about the Butcher's enterprise, the more impressed I was. It ran like a Swiss clock. The Butcher didn't communicate with the outside world because he didn't have to. He had six 'managers' that he was in touch with. Apart from his security – his army of heavies that weren't involved in the business – he didn't speak to anyone else. His orders filtered through a machine designed with such precision and timing, even I was in awe of it. They worked everything out in detail in advance before even the smallest step could go ahead. Every possible eventuality was foreseen and a procedure put in place to counteract any problems.

The Butcher had made himself into the Invisible Man. He had taken the concept of divide and rule to a new level. All transactions were controlled by him, but not connected to him. Different bosses looked after different sides of the business. They didn't know each other or, if they did, they didn't know they were working for the same person. Each 'underboss' controlled his own small operation and was never given a chance to grow too big for his own boots and put the whole organisation at risk. If the Butcher had a problem with one of them, he would replace him and carry on without compromising other parts of the enterprise. He even pitted his own underbosses against each other, creating tension between them. This made them need him and so increased his power.

He imported drugs and fake designer goods of all sorts from the Far East, Russia and South America. He then sold them in Italy, Europe and the USA without paying duties or copyright fees to anyone. The Butcher pioneered the illegal trade with the Chinese. They were hungry for exports and had non-existent local regulations. They'd manufacture anything the Butcher wanted and export it for a fraction of the usual price. Once the goods reached the ports controlled by him, they disappeared into shops all over Europe as if they were originals. On top of all this, he was a giant money lender at extortionate rates (as my own grandfather found out to his cost). If you'd arrested any of his global trading partners, you'd find that none of them knew they were doing business with him. They were trading with his underbosses. Arrest every single person involved and he would have replaced the whole machine in the space of a couple of months. He always had ambitious young people waiting for their big chance. Even though I had all this evidence against him, if I handed it to the police, they'd arrest the small guys. The Butcher would remain untouchable. After a couple of weeks it would be business as usual.

He handled such a complex machine with relative ease and little risk to himself. I hated the man with all my heart but I had to acknowledge his incredible genius.

THE TIP-OFF

As I learned about and followed the web of connections through the structure of the Butcher's organisation, I built it into a 3D memory palace in my head. I saw each player in the game as a chess piece according to their importance. The image was quite beautiful; the pieces shone like stars of varying intensity. Each linked to another by golden threads on a vast board of dark and light squares.

I knew the politicians – the knights on my chess board – were involved with the Camorra, but I'd never had such clear proof. And now I knew which ones they were. The Christian Democratic Party was trading favours with the Butcher in exchange for votes. The CDP contained members from right across the political spectrum, from the far left to the far right. They were divided up into factions that maintained individual power over whichever area they presided over. By design, they were much like the Camorra itself. The Butcher had so many pawns in his game that it was easy for him to make sure they voted for whomever he told them to vote for. And he was in control of the selection and election of local politicians, so he owned them.

While it was beautiful in my mind, it was also evil: an evil that was tearing the heart out of my beloved city, my home. The people in Naples were not free. They knew that. They knew they lived under a net of corruption.

Now I could see all of it, my arrogant ego was whispering: 'Go on, you can do it!' But I knew it was much, much bigger than I could handle by myself.

The Butcher had got his claws in deep. He owned the Government itself. In the face of his power, I knew either the Butcher would get me or the Big Boss would for not having got the Butcher.

The Butcher's cold and evil hand reached so far into the establishment, I couldn't ask for help from the police or any of the usual sources of justice. There was only one man I could reach out to. I only knew one uncorrupted person who was good. The Captain.

I'd been listening for ages, and all I really knew were his tastes in pop music and soaps. I felt sure that he was as pure as snow.

I had to get his trust.

My opportunity came through two useful events.

The wiretaps were alive with talk of a big shipment. It was coming from Spain but had originated in South America. They spoke in code about the cargo, so I didn't know what was in it. Most shipments were ordinary goods: part of the underbosses' regular business deliveries. It could have been tea and coffee and totally legitimate for all I knew. I'd have to take a gamble that it would be something much more incriminating to the Butcher. Counterfeit goods would be good but drugs would be even better.

I listened to the underbosses' conversations and I picked the one shipment that was generating the most attention.

I knew when and where it would arrive. This intel was gold dust if I could use it. The gang, including myself, looked like a bunch of freaks. The Captain would think we were insane if we approached him saying: 'Hey, there's an illegal shipment coming in organised by the top criminals in Italy.' We had to find a way to make ourselves known to him and get him to trust us. We'd need him to check out the information we were offering. To do that he'd have to arrange a massive operation involving the corrupt police force and authorities, at a great cost to the city. We had quite a task on our hands.

It started off in a mundane way, involving more eavesdropping on the Captain. We had to get an idea where he'd be going so we could work out a way to approach him and make contact. I was lucky (if you count more than 30 hours of listening to the Captain farting as lucky). A week before the shipment I heard the Captain confirm an appointment with his doctor. Now I knew where he would be in advance. The gang and I had no time for a waiting game. Instead, we'd have to play the waiting-room game.

The doctor was expensive and private. A visit established he was not taking on new patients so we ruled out booking an adjacent appointment and approaching him in the waiting room.

I breezed by the security guard at the main entrance to the

building but the receptionist was not so easy. She was so efficient and organised with eyes like a hawk. Her management style was almost military. I found myself following her home from work.

Three days later, on the night before the Captain's appointment, I revisited her house with a small bag of my favourite chemicals.

One hour before the Captain's appointment, her neighbours heard a small bang and then water came pouring through the ceiling. Her downstairs neighbour was soon on the phone to her.

'Oh my god! Come quickly. Your water main has burst; you must come and turn it off.'

I watched from my vantage point opposite the doctor's building. She left 30 minutes before the Captain was due. Right on cue.

As soon as she'd gone, the IT Guy made his way up to the doctor's office claiming to have an appointment. Without his secretary, the doctor was in chaos. He couldn't find the IT Guy's appointment in the book. The secretary would have sent IT Guy packing in an instant but the doctor charged 450 euros an hour. He wouldn't turn anyone away.

The IT Guy was ready, alone in the waiting room when the Captain arrived. A female patient had gone in to see the doctor. It was now or never.

The IT Guy started his well-rehearsed script.

I had gone over this scene with the IT Guy almost fifty times and by the end he did a great job.

The IT Guy was waiting by the doctor's office door. When the lift stopped and the doors opened, he nodded hello. The Captain nodded back and made his way into the nicely decorated hall and took a seat in one of the three posh chairs next to a glass table. The IT Guy sat in the third chair, one seat away from the Captain. After a minute of 'waiting' he pulled a handkerchief out of his pocket and dropped a picture of a teenage girl on to the floor. The Captain picked it up and passed it back to the IT Guy, who thanked him and started to cry. The IT Guy had lost his wife and child in the worst possible way, so it was not difficult for him to act this scene. His stutter made things seem even more tragic.

The Captain, robbed of his own sweetheart by a gang of drug

dealers, asked: 'Are you OK? Can I get you some water?'

'They killed my baby girl. I cannot cope with it anymore,' sobbed and stammered the IT Guy. 'I want revenge. I want those drug dealers to die like she did! She was found in a ditch with a massive overdose. My wife is no longer herself and I do not know what to do.'

This was the point when the Captain was supposed to connect with the story. But he stared at the IT Guy with suspicious eyes. He may have been receptive in principle but in practice he was a cynical, hard-boiled cop who would never fall for a story without evidence. Or maybe it was too convenient for a guy to be saying all this to a policeman whose job it is to catch the criminals he's talking about.

The IT Guy realised he was failing to connect. He knew he was on the verge of an epic fail. So he abandoned the script. 'Okay, I can see you're not buying it,' he confessed. 'Sorry I insulted your intelligence. I know who you are. I'm here because I wanted to meet you to give you some crucial information. Information that cost lives to get and will cost more lives if you don't act on it.'

The IT Guy handed over a letter containing the full details of the shipment that was due to arrive.

'Who are you? And what is this?' the Captain asked.

'Just read it and I will do my best to answer questions, but quickly while we are still alone and unsuspected.'

The Captain read it. The letter was simple: a tip-off. It had the name of the vessel and the time of arrival. It described the merchandise as illegal drugs. At the end was the time and place where he could meet us if he needed to. I wasn't sure if the vessel definitely carried drugs. I knew it would be illegal, but I only hoped that the content were heroin or cocaine.

'How do I know this is true?' demanded the Captain.

'It's true,' said the IT Guy. 'You must act on this or more people will die. You're the Captain of Police. I've done my job, you do yours!'

'What if this turns out to be a shipment of coffee from Columbia? I would lose my job.'

'This is either the biggest bust you'll ever have or the most elaborate hoax. I wish you luck making the right call. Nothing I can say now will help you to decide, will it?'

'Why did you come to me?'

'That's easy. You're the only uncorrupted cop in the city.'

'And I could be last one if I lose my credibility over this.'

'How have you been doing so far? A few small busts? A drop in the Bay of Naples, let alone the ocean, compared to this,' said the IT Guy, pointing at the paper in the Captain's hand. 'Ask yourself this – is it time to think big or same old same old? Stick or Twist?'

'Suppose I believe you,' said the Captain. 'A bust on this scale will take some organising. I'll need a warrant from Rome and the SWAT team and I know for sure they are compromised.'

The IT Guy looked blank. 'Compromised?'

'I mean corrupted' added the Captain.

'Don't tell the SWAT team the date of the shipment until the day before. Don't tell them where until you've seen it dock with your own eyes. A boat with a cargo like this can't run away.'

The Captain fell silent.

The doctor's office door opened.

The doctor said to the Captain: 'I will see you now.'

The Captain folded the letter, and stepped into the doctor's office.

He turned once more to look at the IT Guy.

'Good luck,' said the IT Guy.

'No one needs luck when they are in my care,' said the doctor as he shut the door behind them.

The next four days were excruciating. Had he taken the bait? We monitored his wiretap 24/7 but the Captain was on communications lockdown. No phone calls. Whatever business he was doing it was all under our radar.

I was so fretful but I tried not to show it to the gang. The vessel had all the paperwork in order and the illegal merchandise would be cleverly hidden. If he didn't find what he was looking for, he'd be relocated or even dismissed. Pissing off the highest authority was not a welcome exercise in Italy, especially if you pissed them off for no reason. In other words, the Captain was not only risking his career but also risking my only hope. We still had nothing on the Butcher. We needed a victory for our sagging morale but all I could say to the boys was 'Let's keep our fingers crossed.' It was February 11th and, as much as we needed a victory, so did the Captain. I clung to that for hope.

ST VALENTINE'S DAY MASSACRE

The day of the shipment came and I woke up covered in sweat. This was it. All morning my veins were pumping mercury. My body felt like it was wired to the mains and I couldn't shut it down. I had to stay home. In the late afternoon I switched on the TV dreading and hoping to see some news relating to the shipment. I flicked through the channels but there were American sitcoms, and an old movie – no news.

I left the TV on and tried to distract myself by getting drawn into the movie. It was black and white and in English with Italian subtitles. The story was about a guy whose kid had been abducted and he was fighting back against the kidnappers who were demanding millions of dollars. It was a good distraction for a while and I began to feel calmer. The guy in the film had won against the kidnappers, killed most of them and got his son back without giving up any of the ransom money they'd demanded. The kidnappers had picked the wrong man to mess with. It fired me up and I started to feel like I could do the same.

When the movie finished I looked at the other channels again and the news was just starting. My veins burned again and my heart thumped against my ribs once more. I half-expected to hear nothing, though, which would be really bad news. But then, in that first part of the news where they highlight the coming lead stories, before the theme music kicks in, the newsreader's voiceover announced a colossal, unprecedented bust – what they described as the biggest illegal drug shipment ever known to have docked on Italian shores, with an astronomical street value.

'Yes! Yes! Yes!' I shouted, jumping up and punching the air.

I ran out of my apartment, leaving the TV on, and rode my Vespa like a drunk to the Cave, speeding and taking risks I wouldn't normally take. It was impossible to focus. The guys were already there and when I ran in, I was already shouting. The guys couldn't contain their excitement.

The news spread through the city like wildfire. Every TV channel that day, local and national, was devoted to this bust.

'The biggest drug shipment ever confiscated by Italian police. That's gotta hurt,' I said when everyone had calmed down a bit. My throat was raw from the shouting and cheering. I swigged from a bottle of beer to soothe it. I didn't usually drink but I needed to do something to celebrate and to kill the wired feeling, now growing more and more intense. The wooziness and the warmth of the alcohol were the perfect antidote. When the anxiety was medicated, I was on top of the world.

I had both dreaded and hoped that the Captain would take the bait. In that conflicted state I hadn't thought about the next step. This underlying terror of what was coming after this was the cause of the anxiety.

The Butcher would retaliate. I was pretty sure it wouldn't be directly against us, but I sensed a coming full-scale war between the Butcher and the Big Boss. I had no idea how this was going to manifest but I knew it would be violent and that made me nervous.

Policemen and politicians, whose voices I recognised from the wiretap tapes, were taking credit for this 'victory for the State in the long war against organised crime'. I wasn't surprised by this as it always happened, but they disgusted me. My hatred of these criminals never wavered.

At least I was now sure that I could trust the Captain. He and I would be a match made in heaven, like Batman and Robin. The fact that he never gave an interview and wasn't ever mentioned in the media, despite being the hero of the operation, concreted my trust in him. He wasn't after glory or fame, he just wanted to make the city safe.

The day after the shipment, I felt so worried about possible retaliation by the Butcher that I called the Big Boss to warn him. I used our recently arranged secret code to protect my identity from the traitors within his ranks.

'Yes, Prince. What can I do for you,' he said. He sounded depressed. And for the first time, he spoke to me with a great deal of consideration. He'd set me the task of hitting the Butcher but I could tell from the difference in the way he addressed me he was surprised I'd actually done it.

'I'm very sure the Butcher is going to want to do something extreme in retaliation for this,' I said. 'He will not let this go without a violent response.'

'No, he will not,' he replied. 'He is a powerful man. More powerful than we thought.'

'Yes,' I said. 'I know.'

I sensed the Big Boss's embarrassment and was wary of highlighting it so I decided to say very little on this subject. The Butcher had defied the Big Boss openly by bringing in illegal drugs to the Port of Naples. Naples and its port belonged to the Big Boss. The Butcher had not asked permission and he had not paid the usual commission. This was a blatant act of defiance, a show of power and a declaration of war.

'It is not my place to ask you,' I dared, nervousness rising up like hands around my throat. 'But please don't try to provoke the Butcher. I still have plans to further bring him down and any strike from you now would ruin what I have in store,' I lied.

'I will think about it,' he said. 'But no guarantees.'

I put the phone down feeling little of the relief I'd hoped for.

I rode my Vespa through the streets and the tension in the city was tangible. The atmosphere was thick with fear and suspicion. I asked the IT Guy to meet me at Gianni's house and, for a while, not to be seen with me in public. That afternoon the gang transferred all the evidence, the documents and tapes, from the Cave to Gianni's grandmother's big house. She was kind and gullible, unsuspicious of us borrowing her huge cellar.

Back at the Cave, I told the Cat to keep the tape recorders running day and night. Now, more than ever, I needed to know everything that was happening around the Butcher and his people.

Three days after the drug shipment, on February 14th, St Valentine's Day, mass devastation descended upon my city.

The Port of Naples was bustling with people as usual. One of the port bars was filled to capacity with people smoking, drinking beer and coffee. Forklift trucks, cranes and containers were all being moved and operated by dock workers, and tradesmen were milling about doing their business. No one would have thought anything of it when several cars pulled up on the main street running through the port, so no one was expecting gunmen to open fire on the bar and the surrounding area.

Sixty-seven people were shot to pieces that day as they sat sipping their drinks. Another 36 tradesmen were killed going about their business nearby. Most of the dead were in the wrong place at the wrong time and not connected to any shipment or criminal activity, but the message came loud and clear.

People who had been alive in Naples as that day dawned now lay dead. And it didn't just happen in Naples. Massacres were being carried out all over the world: Bogota, New York, Miami, Valencia, Istanbul and Rio de Janeiro. Everyone, no matter how remotely connected to the shipment, was assassinated to protect the Butcher's operation and to send a message. Brutal but effective.

I felt responsible, of course. I was aware that without me, these people would still be alive. I imagined the pain their families were feeling and I kept making up a little story in my head where I could turn back time. I saw the people leaving the bar in the Port of Naples that day, alive and well, a little bit tipsy maybe and going home to their loved ones, perhaps with flowers. I tried to rationalise the self-disgust away by looking at the facts. A war between the Butcher and the Big Boss had been on the cards long before we'd come on the scene and we had, in fact, tried to prevent this from happening by using the legal system to bring down the Butcher.

Clearly the retaliation wasn't aimed at me directly or even the Big Boss, he was really just wiping out anyone who knew about the shipment and thus could be a traitor. But I was the Prince of Naples, and I loved my people, and so I took it personally. Plus by this point I was more than a little paranoid, so I took literally everything personally.

Either way, the massacre meant I had more to do, much more. I had to take this to the end now and I had to do it well because if I didn't, all those deaths would be in vain.

Mrs Apron was my comfort, my Mother, my home. I couldn't live without her. She kept me going while I was in this heightened state of fear, and when I wasn't. She was there when I got home from school every day. On the rare times she was absent, the place would be spotless and there was always a meal ready to eat or warm up.

The day after the massacre I got home to find my apartment empty and there was no meal waiting. I had spent two whole nights tossing and turning, worried about meeting the Captain, so I had lost track of her schedule. I thought it was her day off but I felt a sick feeling. I wasn't worried about her: I felt abandoned.

The next day the abandonment turned to frustration when she didn't turn up again. I was so distracted and stressed that I just grumbled to myself as I got my own breakfast, thinking she should have the decency to call me if she's going to take time off. Then I remembered she had no phone in her apartment and so it would mean she'd have to go out and she may be feeling unwell. There was a flu bug going about and I thought to myself she might have that. I planned to take flowers down if she wasn't back the next day. Then I changed my mind and decided to send them instead because to catch flu now could be too dangerous.

I sent the flowers but two days later when there was still no word from her I went to see her.

I tried ringing her doorbell – several times. There was no answer. My chest tightened and I couldn't explain why. I was about to walk away when a door opened across the hall and an angry head poked out. Someone I'd never seen before.

'Leave her alone!' shouted the head. 'She doesn't want to be disturbed. By anyone.'

'Why?' I asked.

'Just go away!'

I didn't. I should have. I had done what I came for. I'd established she was alive. Anything beyond that was none of my business.

Mrs Apron would surely come back to work when she was ready. My flat would be dirtier than usual. So what? Get over it.

I decided to stare at the woman until she told me what was going on. She fixed me with a gimlet gaze as if to say *don't ask*. Still, I stared silently back.

'Her son was shot in the massacre,' she finally blurted out. 'And before you say anything, the boy was just working in that bar not drinking.'

She slammed the door shut. My knees went. I needed to sit down. The moment I slid to the floor, she opened the door again. When she saw me on the floor she softened.

'Do you want to come in for some water?'

I nodded. Once inside, the interrogation started. She asked me who I was and what I was doing there. Simple questions. The answers were simple, too. Or they would have been if I hadn't been totally numb. I was already feeling guilty about being the catalyst for the massacre but now the tide of death had flowed right into my own life.

'She cleans for me and I missed her these past two days,' I said.

She nodded, as if satisfied and said: 'The poor lady, she's devastated. Her boy was a bit slow, you know, retarded or something. Now, they've got no friends around here and suddenly no one wants to know. She is too ashamed of her son and of the fact that she is, err, was a single mother, you know. I don't think anyone will go to the funeral. Poor kid.'

My despair turned to anger.

'The boy wasn't retarded, but severely autistic,' I said. Autism wasn't well known then, like it is now. Although I knew about it as I was interested.

'The father disappeared after he was born,' I continued.

It occurred to me as I spoke that, as she'd never married, she was technically Miss not Mrs Apron.

'Her family abandoned her, too,' I almost shouted, as if it was all this woman's fault.

'Who the hell are you, anyway? I live here and I've never seen you before!'

The woman explained that she was the mother of Franco Martinelli, the man who owned the apartment and that they'd gone on holiday.

I wasn't really listening. I was thinking about Mrs Apron and how she had carried the shame of single motherhood and how hard that must have been. I felt ashamed of my people and their ignorance. The 'good' people of Naples were no more than cowards, hiding behind the image of respect for the sanctity of family, but when push came to shove the respect was empty and their behaviour was the exact opposite.

Mrs Apron's eyes never betrayed anger: she worked hard to give her son whatever he needed, without complaining or criticising. She was an angel and we were the unfortunate souls. None of the rest of us could dream of carrying ourselves with such dignity. And look what we had done.

Mrs Apron was frail and fragile but she would still get up in the morning and do manual labour, without accepting handouts or charity. I loved her. She was a mother to me. She had, in fact, replaced the Mother I felt I had lost. Despite my independence and belief that I was a grown man, I was really still a child and my child's heart had clung on to Mrs Apron. I needed her. She was a good woman.

I felt responsible for the death of Mrs Apron's son and I blamed myself, but I also blamed the men I had been working for, and against, and all of their associates. The sense of injustice went far beyond the killing itself. The majority of the people assassinated deserved to go: they were gangsters selling death and destroying families and young lives to enrich themselves.

Later that day, I went to see the IT Guy to discuss the meeting with the Captain but I couldn't focus.

I could think of nothing but Mrs Apron and her poor boy. I decided to change the subject of the meeting and I told the IT Guy what had happened. He took off his glasses and cleaned them with a handkerchief. He wasn't looking at me and I could tell he didn't want me to see that he had tears in his eyes. I looked away and pretended to be going over some notes.

'We must take care of the funeral,' he said. 'I doubt she'll be able to afford it.'

I knew he was right. And so that was what we spent the meeting discussing. We drew up a full plan to organise and pay for Mrs Apron's boy's send off from the world.

When the Spanish arrived, I told him to use whatever means necessary to ensure as many people as possible would turn up at the funeral. Despite all my talents and resourcefulness, I could not bring the boy back to life, and I felt powerless. So I put all of my energy into the one thing I did have power over: the funeral. It was all I could think about.

The meeting with the Captain, supposed to happen the day after the funeral, would have to be improvised instead of planned and rehearsed meticulously. Suddenly it didn't seem to matter as much.

I didn't see Mrs Apron. I posted notes under her door, first telling her I would take care of the funeral and asking if she had any requests. If she did, she was to leave them on a note under my door if she wanted to be left alone. Then I would slide notes under the door regularly throughout the day, telling her of the funeral's progress and giving her any details. I wanted her mind to be totally at rest and for her to use the time to grieve, rather than have the stress of organising this terrible event.

The IT Guy and I had chosen the coffin – the best we could find – but when it came to the lining, we were about to purchase the finest white satin when we found out from the morgue that the coffin would have to be closed because the boy's face and body had been mutilated in the shooting. We paid the undertaker 5,000 euros to reconstruct him and make it so that he would look complete so Mrs Apron could see her boy and say her goodbyes. Needless to say, I neglected to mention this detail in the next note that I slipped under her door.

When the funeral day came around, I'd had only one note from Mrs Apron. It just said: 'Thank you.'

The Spanish and Pasquale did well. The church was packed to

the rafters with guys from the boy's neighbourhood. The attendees, despite most of them not even knowing the dead boy, behaved as if one of their own family had died. No one was prepared to step up and address the mourners, though, so we paid someone to give the eulogy. I'd never felt so sad or angry in my life.

I felt the funeral was not just the funeral of a wonderful boy, but also the funeral of our conscience. Mine and all of my people. That we had had to threaten and blackmail people to attend the funeral of one of their neighbours, a member of our community who stayed away from trouble and lived his life lawfully, it disgusted me. The status quo of Naples hit me very hard. If you weren't involved with the Camorra, people didn't want to know you, you weren't respected, you were ignored by everyone, including your friends and neighbours. Being a criminal was not only the best way to get rich but also very fashionable.

The actor we paid to delivery the eulogy really nailed it, learning enough about the boy to appear genuine, I rested my eyes on the only holy person present in that shit-hole: my beautiful cleaning lady. She sat there, upright and decently dressed, tears on her cheeks but quiet and composed. She didn't scream in anger, even though she was entitled to. She had the elegance of a real queen. She was a class above everyone else. She had a soul, a real one. She was incorruptible, clean and worth all of us put together.

I cried and couldn't stop crying. So did every other member of the gang, even though they didn't know her as well as I did. I was glad of one thing at least, her boy's final goodbye was taking place in a beautifully decorated church, plenty of people in attendance and with all the costumes and artefacts usually reserved for the rich of the city.

The city went back to normal after a few days. Curfew was lifted. Martial law lockdown dissolved and the soldiers left. The media spotlight shone elsewhere and the battered and bruised people of Naples got up from that knockdown to fight another round. The only memorial was the bar by the port, which had become an empty and depressing shrine. I felt drawn to it, knowing only too well my part in how it came to be. I stood looking at it for over an hour with dread in my heart. It had been a buzzing hub of social interaction and a place where Neapolitans went as part of their daily routine. And now it was dead. The shooters had killed the place as surely as they'd killed the people in there that day. It was quiet and still with boarded-up windows and patterned with craters where the bullets had smashed into the brick.

I dropped in on Mrs Apron as often as I could, but she was quiet and still, too. I couldn't stand to see the pain in her eyes. I brought her food and made sure she was comfortable but I couldn't do anything about her loss and I felt helpless. The meeting with the Captain was so close now but it was hard to focus when I felt responsible for this woman's grief. Finally, when I woke up in the night screaming after a terrifying nightmare, I knew I had to let go of my guilt over the death of Mrs Apron's son and concentrate on the job in hand. If I let guilt consume me, I would become ill again and be unable to finish what I'd started. That would be of no help to anyone, not least Mrs Apron.

I'd never have dreamt in my life that I would use something as big as meeting with the Captain – the event I hoped would keep me alive – as a way to avoid feeling my own shame. But that's what I did. I focused on that instead and it worked. I wrapped the guilt up in layers and layers of excuses, such as 'I did what I had to do,' and stored it away in the furthest room in the memory palace in my mind, the room I never went into: the room that held all the pain I couldn't face. And I turned my mind towards the Captain; the man I hoped would save us all.

I sent the gang away to Lugano on holiday. They had all looked so sick and tired, I felt I owed them and I wanted them out of the way so I'd have no distractions. I went to school the morning of the meeting with the Captain. I decided it was safer to wear my school uniform to meet him. I weighed up the disadvantage of him not taking me seriously with the advantage of the disguise it afforded me. No one would suspect anything shady of a schoolboy. I chose the latter as I felt safer 'dressed as a kid'. It genuinely didn't occur to me that I actually was a kid, so I naturally assumed he would see through my 'disguise'.

I'd arranged to meet him at a bar in Sorrento at 4 o'clock. I was quite often a reckless driver, but this time I left early and took it easy on the roads on my Vespa because I knew my mind was occupied. If I got killed or injured on the way it wasn't just my life I'd be messing with. Besides, I wanted to get there before the Captain so I could watch him arrive.

I arrived more than an hour early and sat at a table opposite the entrance. I ordered a coffee – not as tasty as I was used to, but I sipped it anyway. I felt anxious and exposed and I was half-convinced every person in there could be police – even old ladies and kids. My heart was beating far too fast and I decided coffee was probably not going to help with the paranoia, so I pushed it away across the table. I looked at my watch a thousand times a minute but time seemed to have stopped. Even though I could clearly see all the people approaching through the bar window, my stomach lurched every time someone walked through the door.

The Captain turned up 20 minutes early, probably hoping to get there before me. He was in jeans and a denim shirt and under his arm I could see the bright pink paper of the *Gazetta dello Sport*. He had his jacket over the other arm. 'He has a gun,' I thought. He walked slowly and I could see he was scanning the bar, looking for me. He came into the bar and looked like he was choosing somewhere to sit but his eyes discreetly took in each person one by one. I looked away to the side of him and tried to look like I was staring into the middle distance as his eyes crossed over me, then

I looked back to see him take the table over in the far corner of the bar, so he could see everyone coming in and going out. He opened his paper and looked like he was reading, but his eyes remained fixed. He looked relaxed. I felt envious of this.

There was something solid about him, something that said: 'I'm the good guy.'

The waitress came over and took his order. I heard him say: 'Chocolate ice cream,' which surprised me. That made me like him even more. I wished I'd ordered ice cream instead of coffee. The waitress said something I didn't quite hear and he laughed. He was at ease with himself. He was polite and handsome and when the waitress turned and left his table she was blushing and smiling to herself.

The thought that I should be more like him flashed across my mind. I decided, if I survived, I was going to work on being more relaxed, giving off more of an air of self-possession. I'd never lacked confidence. It wasn't that. But I had the tendency to be arrogant to cover up my age and I wasn't without fear. This man was. He was genuinely charismatic. I wanted what he had.

All I had to do now was get him to like me! The waitress brought his ice cream and left. I let him eat a few spoonfuls and then decided it was time. I took a deep breath, stood up and walked over. I tried to keep my breathing measured, to draw on every ounce of confidence I had. This was live TV, no retakes. He looked up from his paper, took in my school uniform and, unimpressed, raised his eyebrows in a silent question. I responded with a smile that I hoped said: 'It's me, the person you're waiting for.' I failed to convey this. Impatient, he said: 'What do you want, Kid?'

'Good afternoon,' I said. 'Thank you for coming to meet me.' I held his eye in as confident a way as I could.

He looked back at me with no expression. It took him a long time to respond.

'I'm not sure what you mean,' he said. 'I'm not meeting anyone. I'm just having an ice cream.' He gestured towards his chocolate ice cream with his spoon.

He took me completely by surprise and, for a moment, even I

thought I had the wrong man. I was dizzy with confusion and my mind raced for a response. I stuttered, then managed to pull myself together.

'Relax, Captain,' were the words I managed to form in a voice with a confidence that surprised me. 'The man you met in the doctor's surgery works for me. Don't let my appearance cloud your judgement.'

He looked again at my school uniform.

'I am young, yes,' I continued. 'But give me a chance. I have chosen to trust you and I don't trust any other members of your profession. Lives are at risk. We are the resistance. We need you but you need us more. Give me a chance and you will see that. What have you got to lose? I am a kid. What can I do to hurt you?'

'How do you know who I am? What is it that you want from me? Who are you?' He fired the questions back at me in a flat and quiet voice that was laced with a deadly threat.

'I'm a boy in trouble,' I said. 'I need your help.'

This appealed to his noble nature.

He said: 'Go on.'

I handed him a letter.

'Go home and read this letter. You will find three bugs in your apartment. Don't be angry. They were totally necessary. Without them, I never would have known I could trust you. Meet me again tomorrow at my apartment, you'll find the address in the letter. Please come alone, as I'm worried about your people. If they find out who I am, I'm dead, along with my family. We've had enough death in this city.'

He looked shocked. I presumed he had expected less of me. I walked out before he had a chance to object.

The whole meeting had lasted only minutes but I left the bar feeling exhausted, as if I hadn't slept for a week. I barely remember driving home. I was in a dream.

I decided to go straight to bed, even though it was still light outside. I ate leftover pizza in bed and just before I fell into a long and deep sleep, I remembered it had been my 18th birthday.

The next morning I forced myself to go to school again. I had to pass my final exams. This was just as important to me as taking down the Butcher. I didn't want my life, if I was going to stay alive, to spiral out of control. Plus the school routine gave me a sense of normality that I craved. I did go home and change out of my uniform before the Captain was due to turn up, though. I wanted him to see I wasn't just a kid.

I watched him approach the apartment block from my balcony. He strolled up the road without a care and with no visible escort. Dead on time. Well done Captain. That he had followed my instructions in the letter gave me confidence. I went to the block entrance, and opened the door to him. Wearing just jeans and a T-shirt, I held my arms wide open so he could see I was unarmed, but I still had to turn around so he could search me.

'Good afternoon, Captain,' I said. 'It's good to see you again.'

'OK, I'm here,' he replied. 'What next?'

He had a pistol in a shoulder holster and I was sure he was ready to use it if he had to. I was equally sure I wasn't going to give him a reason to.

'If it makes you feel more comfortable, feel free to point your gun in my back, but please follow me.'

I felt the barrel of his gun in my back and he followed me up the stairs to my flat. When we got to the open door, he half-guided me, half-pulled me around the place to make sure we were alone. Then he checked all the windows were shut and the door closed and locked. I think he was expecting some sort of ambush.

Once he was sure that wasn't going to happen, I gestured towards the kitchen and asked him to sit down while I made him a coffee. He sat at the far end of the kitchen table with the gun laid on the table in front of him.

I handed him the coffee and he looked at it, then at me. 'I must have been crazy to come here,' he said, shaking his head. I sat down opposite him with my own coffee and I was careful to keep my hands clearly visible.

'No, you're not crazy,' I said. 'You're as desperate as I am. You need my help and I need yours.'

'Who are you?' he asked, sternly.

'I'm not your enemy,' I said.

He put his hand in his pocket, his eyes never leaving my face, and pulled out a few of the bugs we'd placed in his apartment and slammed them on the table in front of us.

'Unless you want to spend five years in jail, you will tell me everything,' he said.

'Yes, I will,' I agreed. 'That's why you're here.'

It took me an hour or more to tell him the whole story. I omitted some things, such as the stolen cars, the Royal family, the business and the millions in Lugano. But I told him everything else, right from the beginning to the end. I wanted him to understand what I was capable of and that I was in a mess and we needed to work together to bring down the Butcher.

I hadn't realised the effect telling the story would have on me. I had been holding so much inside for so long that I found myself crying and then sobbing. I couldn't hold back the tears. I still went on.

When I had finished he said: 'So you want to bring down the Butcher?'

'Yes.'

'Police from all corners of the world are after him and you think you can bring him down?'

'Yes.'

He laughed.

'Remember this,' I continued, feeling annoyed. 'I have achieved more in that regard in four months than you and the police have done in four years.'

'And look at the consequences,' he said. I thought of Mrs Apron's son and felt the familiar burning shame.

I also felt myself getting angry but I tried to push it down. I got up and made him another coffee while I dealt with my anger. Then I said: 'It was my tip-off. You did the bust. You got the promotion.'

'And you are screwed,' he said half smiling.

'Then so are you,' I said, looking him in the eye. 'I've collected more than forty hours of tapes with conversations between many of his underbosses. I've taken several thousand photographs of their movements. I know how they launder their money and I have bugged many of their houses. How does that sound to you? Does any of that give me the qualifications to work with you?'

As I looked at him and then down at the bugs on the table, I noticed one was missing. There were two here, and not the three I'd tipped him off about.

'Only two?' I asked.

'I left one there – for now,' he replied. 'If we are to work together, we might need to communicate.'

There it was. He had basically said we would be working together and he'd known this before he came here. I began to relax. So did he. He put his gun back in its holster and leaned back in his chair, sipping his coffee.

We fell into silence. I wanted to let him think about everything I'd told him.

'Can you prove all this? The documents, the pictures and the rest?' he asked.

'Of course,' I replied. 'When I do prove it, when I show you the proof, will you be with me on this?'

'You have to appreciate my amazement,' he said. 'No disrespect, but you are a kid. Yet here you are seriously discussing how to destroy a criminal empire worth billions. You must admit, it's far-fetched. If it wasn't for the tip-off turning out to be correct, I wouldn't even be here.

'And your safety concerns me, also. My job is to protect people like you – kids – not to get them involved. I hope you aren't think-ing of this as some video game. The risks you are taking...' He shook his head. 'I don't know what to make of all this.'

I decided that sounding defeated would be my best bet. I wanted to appeal to the empathic side I knew he had. 'I have no choice here,' I said. 'I tried to get out of all this but there is no way out. You couldn't involve me any more than I am already involved. I am in deep. All the way up to my neck. I have to bring that piece of shit down and then I will disappear and live my life again like a normal human being.'

I felt tears well up in my eyes again. I'd wanted to sound defeated and it wasn't difficult because I was close to being defeated. I was clinging on to one hope – the Captain.

After what seemed like a long time, he stood up and offered me his hand to shake.

He said: 'OK. I'll do what I can to help you, if you will help me.'

I shook his hand and he added: 'Hell, maybe you are just the secret weapon I was looking for.'

I grinned and shook his hand more enthusiastically.

'What's your name?' he asked. 'Can I know your name, at least?'

'Just call me Prince,' I said. 'Everyone else does.'

It was time to take him to the Cave. 'I need to take you somewhere, to my headquarters. Will you come?'

'Now?' he asked.

'Yes, now,' I said.

'OK.'

We managed to get to the Cave safely without being followed. He looked a little apprehensive about going through the bushes, but I asked him to trust me. When we reached the place, he looked it over. He didn't look impressed. I opened the door and gestured for him to enter. He hesitated and I saw his hand momentarily hover over his gun, but he made a decision and walked through the door in front of me. As he looked around, his mouth fell open and he couldn't hide his surprise. He took in my sophisticated recording equipment, the lab where I made explosives, the machine that made keys and the lock-breaking equipment, the tape recorders, which were running, the furniture, the car seats and the *Rocky* posters and boxing memorabilia.

He stood in the middle of the room and gestured widely with his arms as if to say 'I give up! Look at this place!' Then he looked around again slowly and finally looked at me, shaking his head. I saw that he now understood for the first time that I was no ordinary teenager. I saw the place through his eyes and I felt proud. It was like a sort of Batman Cave. It was my place. I felt like a hero.

'What are you?' he asked.

'Would you like to see my office?' I grinned at him.

'You have an office?' he said, then shook his head again. 'Of course you do.'

We went to my office and I got him a beer from the fridge.

'I haven't got an office you know,' he said as he took the beer.

We looked at some of the photos I'd taken of the Butcher's visitors and house. I'd kept most of it back and had removed it from the Cave as I hadn't known what would happen today. I told him I'd stored most of it in a secret location and I would give it to him when the time was right. I no longer worried about this because I now knew we would be working together.

We talked for a long time and he agreed with me that the Naples police were corrupt and that neither of us could trust them. He gave me some names of the officers he'd brought with him from Milan and told me they were the ones to contact if anything happened to him. We were bonding. I knew he felt relaxed and I was relieved. He seemed a little in awe of me and I felt in awe of him. I was excited that I could count on a man of his calibre. I loved my gang, and no disrespect to the boys, but they weren't exactly A-team material. This guy was like the star of an action movie – but this wasn't a movie. This was real.

Once the emotional moment passed, we got down to work and I asked him about the people I had photographed. He knew some of them but not all; the ones missing were the ones I had put on top of the tree of the Butcher's organisation. I made him listen to some of the tapes as well but, as they talked in a kind of code, I had to help him understand them. More importantly, we agreed on how to speak to each other and how to meet up without anyone knowing. He could leave a message just by speaking into the bug; when the guys got back from their break I would be informed of the message within twenty-four hours. He was amazed by how methodical and risk-averse I was and, by the time he left, I had the same rapport with him that I had with the other members of the gang.

Victory; I was on a roll.

'I have some American colleagues I want you to meet,' the Captain said. 'They work for the FBI.

'You shine too brightly to be hidden. The wider world could use your talent,' he added. 'I will do what I can to keep you alive and so will they.'

I had a strong feeling that my life had suddenly gone in a different direction.

The FBI guys were seven Italians-Americans from New York. I loved the way they talked. The ebb and flow of their language was poetic and I decided I was going to become fluent and one day speak English even better than they did. Most of them understood Italian, which made communication with them easy, as long as I spoke slowly.

We met in their headquarters. We had to walk through a long building full of desks and office workers and I trailed behind the Captain, dragging my bag along like I was a school-kid coming to see where the police did their work. The Captain played his part by rolling his eyes and saying 'Don't drag your bag, Kid,' with impatience in his voice. He snatched the bag off me and we continued on with him carrying it for me. I almost laughed when I caught his eye but I managed to stifle it.

In the HQ, the FBI guys were all sitting around drinking coffee and smoking. When the Captain introduced me, I could tell he hadn't warned them I was a kid. They were under the impression I must be someone's son or nephew and even when he did introduce me, they thought he was joking.

'This is the guy!' the Captain said. 'Yes, he's a kid, but he's our guy. The one I told you about.' They all laughed.

I was getting tired of being underestimated. These guys had failed again and again at bringing down the Camorra. Not only that but their actions – the way they'd jump in and act as soon as they had the tiniest bit of evidence – had made the mob stronger and better. I knew if I let them have any of the stuff I had on the

Butcher and his people, it would only lead to another massacre. I had to take control of this situation.

One burly guy, who looked more like he belonged in the Mob in 1930s Chicago than the FBI, reached his hand out and I knew he was going to ruffle my hair. With a lightning reflex, I grabbed his wrist and bent it away from him while looking straight in his face using my most threatening expression.

I later found out he was called Arnold, but I never knew if that was his last name or his first.

'Hey kid! Go easy,' he said. He wasn't laughing any more. He was rubbing his wrist.

This made the others laugh even more.

'Well I'm not going to hit a kid,' he said to them, sulkily.

'Settle down now,' said the Captain. 'This is no ordinary kid. This young man has impressive surveillance skills and has found more information on our targets than we have in the past decade. So please, no laughing. Have a little respect.'

One by one, they stopped laughing and their grins subsided to disbelief as they realised he was serious.

I looked at the Captain and he nodded once to signal that I should speak. I stepped forward and faced them.

'I know the Captain has told you about the evidence I've collected on the Butcher, but I'm not giving you anything until the time is right.'

I paused and there was a silence. They just stared at me. Then one of them said: 'So you're saying you've got some stuff on the Butcher?'

'Yes, I have,' I said. 'A great deal of "stuff".'

Another one piped up: 'If you have got something, you have to tell us.'

I shook my head. 'I will work with you,' I said, 'but I will not give you anything I've found. I will continue my own operation and I'm not going to give you any updates on my ongoing progress. Right now I don't have enough evidence to bring him down.'

'So you're saying you have enough to bring someone down?' said Arnold, still rubbing his wrist.

'Yes, we could use what I have to bring some of his organisation down, but we're not going to.' I was getting tired of repeating myself. 'If we do that we'll just be giving him the help he needs to weed out his weakest links and he will only become stronger. We need to bring the whole thing to an end, including him. It needs to be coordinated perfectly, like a series of simultaneous explosions that will cause his world to fall all at once without giving him a chance to regroup.'

'Then what are you doing here?' asked a ginger-haired weedy guy called Doran who lit one cigarette with the butt of the other.

'I'm here to teach you your job,' I said. I was frustrated and I wanted to get out of there.

The Captain stepped in. He'd told me to be polite and I could tell he was now both annoyed with me and trying to protect me. 'The kid is here to teach us his surveillance techniques,' he said as he dumped my bag on the table.

They all started laughing again. So I just waited for them to stop, then I stepped forward and unzipped my bag. As I unpacked the bag of tricks – tricks they'd never seen before or even had the brain capacity to think of – their disbelief dissolved and was replaced at first by shock and then by awe. I'd brought along bugging systems, phone taps and keys, lock-picking devices and all sorts of prototypes for surveillance and burglary. I enjoyed showing off my skills and the equipment I'd invented.

Over the next few weeks I met with them regularly and I gave them everything I'd learned about how to spy on people without them knowing, how to break into houses and set up bugs and tap phone lines. I gave them details of the equipment and electronics I'd invented to gather information on our enemies.

I got very little from them. In fact, the only thing I did get was a feeling of pride in myself. Looking through their eyes at how far I'd come and the things I'd done gave me a fresh perspective and even I was impressed with myself. I realised I had a special talent. I'd underestimated my skills so I decided to stop that. I was also no longer underestimated by the FBI. I did, however, find that I had overestimated them.

The hope of a bright future – or any future at all – that had arisen when I met the Captain started to fade. I slowly realised that my life wasn't going to be changed by these guys. They wouldn't or couldn't change their ways and they continually pestered me to give up the evidence I had so they could make arrests. The Captain kept the Cave a secret; I don't know why he stayed loyal to me but I was grateful. I began to feel like he was my true friend. But the others weren't going to be any use to me so I needed to get my guys back on track and get the evidence we needed to bring down the Butcher ourselves.

By the time I got the gang back together, I was feeling weary and let down. I was on the edge of defeat yet again. To make it worse, the recent busted drugs shipment had warned the Butcher and his men and they were being especially careful. They stopped talking on the phone and my tapes went silent. We carried on watching and listening, though, taking pictures of visitors to the Butcher's mansion, but the same people we already knew kept on coming. We could find nothing new. We needed more to complete the diagram of the hierarchy.

We started watching the house at night, hoping the Butcher's late guests would turn up something new. It was a lot more risky than working the day shift. In the daylight, the streets were busy and no one would take any notice of a young guy on a Vespa. There were hundreds of them. As long as we did the changeover and it wasn't the same moped behind a car for too long, there was little chance of getting caught. And we could use natural light to take photographs. At night, it was a whole different scenario.

Following the cars at night was no problem in the busy cities, but we had to end the tail on the quiet streets or we would have been seen. We couldn't take any pictures because the heavies would definitely notice a camera flash. It would have been certain death if we were caught.

The task ahead was enormous. Too big. I knew it was going to take incredible skill to bring this monster down. I was weary and I felt 100 years old but I couldn't stop.

While I was trying to work out a plan, I was collected and taken to meet with the Big Boss. I knew it was something bad because we had only been communicating by phone and this was confirmed by the sight of his stony face as I trod the familiar path across the massive room to his desk.

'You are out of time, Kid,' he said. 'You haven't done what I asked you to do. The Butcher is still alive and operating and taking money from me, not to mention my men. I gave you a job and you have failed.'

'I just need a little bit more time,' I said. 'I'm nearly there.' I tried to sound confident, but I think there was a slight tremor in my voice.

'I'm sorry, Kid. Time's up.'

'What are you going to do?' I asked, meaning what was he going to do to me. He misunderstood.

'I'm going to get the job done myself. I'm going to launch an attack on him and his men on an unprecedented scale,' he said. I stared into his eyes and saw nothing but coldness and hardness.

'But thousands of people will die and the aftermath will be even worse,' I said.

'Yes. If it has to be, it has to be,' he said casually.

'Give me one month more. Then if I haven't done the job, you can do what you have to do ... with me and the Butcher.'

He was quiet for a moment and his eyes never left my face. I stared back at him, wanting to look away but not daring to. I felt scared but I also understood him. He was being forced into a war that he knew he could never win.

After a long time he said: 'Very well. Four weeks.'

Then he turned his back.

As I retreated, I wondered if I would be using the month I had to destroy the Butcher or run away. But I knew that no matter how far I ran, he would find me. Or, more specifically, the Butcher would. The Big Boss would simply 'throw me under the bus'. I'd become the scapegoat, used to build bridges between the two men.

I spent the first week thinking about the ways I might die and going over and over the material we'd photocopied from the various burglaries of the previous years. It was a monumental task and I felt so tired and ill that I just wanted to stop. I don't know how I got through it. I counted more than 300 companies involved in what appeared to be legal business that traded seemingly legal goods. Some of the names on the documents were people we'd identified when watching the Butcher's house but there was absolutely nothing to connect those businesses to him. These companies were spread throughout Europe, North America and South America. Their trading accounts were held in reputable banks. I could find nothing.

When we began night-time surveillance I didn't hold out much hope since we were so vulnerable to discovery. The Big Boss's deadline pushed me to the limit, though, and I was desperate. The guys kept asking me if I was all right. I must have looked like a ghost.

I had to take a risk. I devised a really complicated and time-consuming way to follow the Butcher's visitors. It was so dangerous and a hell of a task for the boys but they accomplished it with great success. After two weeks of very hard work, we finally got somewhere.

We discovered the identities of some new visitors, men we'd never seen before, and after investigating them, we found out they were the Butcher's 'prestanomi': the men of straw or figureheads of his businesses. They were a respectable and legitimate front used by the Butcher as a cover for his illegal activities. The businesses and all the money from those operations theoretically belonged to the prestanomi so if any business were raided or investigated by the police they would be the ones responsible for any crime. The Butcher would have been paying them handsomely for their risk as it wasn't unknown for these front men to go to prison for years. They were paid to take the risk and do the time.

So, after spending 1.6 million euros, conducting five months of intense stakeouts and taking more than 9,000 photographs, we had finally found the 12 prestanomi used by the Butcher to run his organisation. I knew the turnover of his businesses, what their merchandise was, how they bought it and where they bought it from. I knew who authorised the shipments to come into Italy unchecked, where the money went and how it was spent. I knew who cleaned the funds, how they were laundered and who was in charge of what.

I still had nothing on the Butcher.

I had to admire him. I mean, the sheer brilliance of the man! The empire he'd built – such an empire – and he was all but invisible. I knew more about him than anyone, certainly more than the FBI, but I still had nothing that I could use to bring him down. The drug bust that led to what I called the St Valentine's Day massacre had hit him hard in the wallet but he'd come back stronger than ever. He'd expanded to Russia at a time when no one did business with the Russians because they were seen as dangerous and unreliable. The Butcher didn't care. He was trading gas and oil with them through petrol stations in Europe without paying duties to anyone.

The man was a pioneer, no doubt about it.

His men, not so: particularly the prestanomi. They were reckless with their movements and security. They probably felt protected.

I still refused to give anything of what we had learned about the prestanomi to the Captain and he engineered it so our meetings dwindled to brief conversations. I think he was frustrated with me and had started to think of me as unhelpful. I felt let down and hurt; it had felt like such a relief to have someone to trust and I genuinely liked him. I had not felt so alone when I was working with him. He had become obsessed with swift victories, no matter how small and no matter the cost. I knew I would be killing many people, including me, if I gave in to his demands for more information. What hurt the most was that I lost his support at the time I needed it most. Still, that didn't stop me from harbouring thoughts of redeeming our friendship in the end. Again and again I imagined various scenarios where he apologised for doubting me and congratulated me on destroying the Butcher and his empire. I couldn't help myself, even though I knew it unlikely. In fact, all hope that I would ever destroy the Butcher was rapidly dwindling.

The news of violent murders throughout Naples had become so

regular that it was no longer news. Hundreds were being killed all over Italy. The Butcher was decimating his enemies, destroying anyone who was not with him. Most of the people killed were associates of the Big Boss. The Butcher was systematically weakening the Big Boss's position by dismembering his organisation. It wouldn't be long before this process of elimination reached me. And I'd be targeted by both parties.

Even the Lugano businesses looked bleak, with massive financial losses. Our Swiss bank account had reduced from over eight million euros to under 147,000.

I had failed at everything. I couldn't even make sure my friends had a future.

All of this failure suddenly fell in on top of me one day when I was at the Cave looking over the books for the Swiss businesses. I dropped to my knees and cried. I cried for my little brother, for my friends, the members of my gang, for all of the families torn apart by the Butcher, for Naples and for myself.

The only thing left to do now was to make sure the boys would escape unhurt. I hoped, with me out of the way, my family would lead a long and happy life without those bastards ever bothering them again. When the boys turned up at the Cave, I was sitting there in the middle of the floor, surrounded by the havoc I'd created, in more ways than one. There was no *Rocky*, not even pizzas or beers. There was only me, without even the strength left to cry.

The guys joined me on the floor one by one, sitting in a circle around me. I like to think they were showing solidarity but it was more likely because the chairs had all been flung about the place.

I looked at their faces. They were expecting some flash of inspiration like there usually was, I could see it in their eyes. I couldn't live up to their expectations. Instead, I said: 'I'm so proud of all of you. You have been brave, audacious and loyal to me and to our cause.'

I paused, not for effect, but to swallow a lump in my throat.

'I feel no shame in admitting now that we have failed. We have lost this war. I take full responsibility and I will do my best to take all the blame and protect all of you. I want you to go back to Lugano and rescue the only good thing to come out of all of this mess – the businesses – in my memory.'

My voice broke as I thought of them all living to be old men. Something I couldn't have.

'I'm going to give myself up. The Butcher is still killing people, looking for the culprit of the confiscated shipment. All this bloodshed has to come to an end.

'Goodbye my friends. I wish you all possible happiness from the bottom of my heart.'

They were stunned. Not one of them moved as I walked out, as quickly as I could, struggling to hold back my tears. I rode my Vespa through the city as fast as it would go, determined to spend my last few days alive in the best way I possibly could.

I rode my Vespa as if on autopilot, thinking about what my life would have been if I had not got involved in all that mess. My journey to my Nan took twice as long as usual. I could not help wondering if I had not known Cocco, if the earthquake had not happened, if the restaurant owner had paid the wages he owed to Pasquale ... then I would not have entered the criminal world. Then I got tired of wondering, it was utterly pointless.

Then I wondered if I would have got married, had kids of my own and had a family that cared about me, as my own hardly even spoke to me anymore.

Next, I got distracted by the beautiful smell of the lemon groves.

Soon, I would have to face my destiny and it would be better for me that I came to terms with it as quickly as possible. Running away was no longer an option as not only would my enemies have hunted me down to the end of my days but the very first people to pay would have been every member of my family. The plan was simple: pay my Nan a visit, leave some flowers on my Grandfather's grave for the first time then go straight to the 'Big Boss'. I would offer myself to him as the olive branch for the Butcher; the Butcher would find the cause of the loss of his drug shipment; the 'Big Boss' would go in the good books of the Butcher; the whole thing would go away without any further loss of life, especially my family's and my boys'. It was the only way to minimise the bloodshed.

When I barged into her home, my Grandmother was reading the local newspaper, lying down on my favourite sofa. She was surprised and delighted in equal measure. She hugged me so hard she almost crushed me but I really enjoyed her love and affection. After the customary shower of kisses, she rushed to the kitchen to prepare my usual cappuccino along with my favourite cakes.

As she enthusiastically jumped off her sofa to go to the kitchen, she dumped her newspaper on the table. I picked it up to keep myself busy. Two pictures immediately attracted my attention: mug shots of two of the Butcher's prestanomi.

The headline read: 'Two businessmen killed by the Camorra for refusing to pay the racket'; the article made them look almost like martyrs. 'What a load of rubbish!' I thought – they were the ones collecting the racket and obviously keeping too much for themselves. They were found with their own genitals in their mouths, a graphic message from the Butcher to other members of his organisation. Over the coming days five more such deaths hit the news.

Consciously, I paid little attention to the article as the matter, as far as I was concerned, was decided – ancient history in effect. Subconsciously, some parts of my brain picked up on it and started to work on it on their own. All the while I was enjoying my cakes and chitchatting with my Grandma.

'So, what a pleasant surprise, my beautiful boy. What made you come here?'

'I just wanted to see you before I get down with my final exams. I would like to put some flowers on Granddad's grave too, so he can wish me luck.'

'Wonderful,' she exclaimed with glee before continuing more calmly. 'You've never seen the chapel that I have built for him, have you? I took some of the money that I got from Cocco's son for the vineyard and I built a beautiful chapel for him and for me when I am gone. Do not worry, though. You won't get rid of me for another 20 years, at least. I want to see you married first!'

Now, I had real difficulty holding back the tears. If she could have imagined what was about to happen, she would have died on the spot. I had to take several deep breaths to prevent myself bursting into tears. I told her to get ready to go out as I would have to go soon.

I admired her as well as loved her. She was nearly 70 but she still took a lot of pride in the way she looked. We were only going to a cemetery but she was getting ready with the same enthusiasm as if she were going to a wedding. She looked amazing for her age too, at least 20 years younger and not a hair out of place; she was articulate, intelligent, funny and completely devoted to her family. I missed her already.

As she took forever to get ready, I was looking around the kitchen for old memorabilia until I stumbled upon a thick black magic marker pen. I went downstairs and, at the back of my Vespa, I wrote: 'Live fast, die young, leave a good-looking corpse,' supposedly James Dean's motto. I just hoped that my killer would not shoot me in the face.

Even though death had been a regular visitor in my life, this was the first time I had actually visited a cemetery. I didn't believe in putting a bunch of flowers on a stone to rot while pretending your loved one was there to see it. I carried my Granddad in my heart, all day and every day, so I never felt the need for what I believed to be an old-fashioned superstition for over-zealous Catholics of poor education. Still, that day, I felt different about it all. Moreover, it made my Grandmother happy and that was what mattered.

What my Grandmother never knew was that the chapel and little mausoleum had been built with my money all along. Well, with the money I had stolen and given to Cocco's son. I was the one that bought the vineyard and the one that paid 50 grand for my Grandfather' share so she could inherit it. It was way too much for such a barren piece of land but, when I finally saw his last resting place, I certainly couldn't think of a better way to spend it. I was glad and proud that my Granddad had such a royal tomb, one worthy of a king, never mind a prince.

When I entered the gates, I was flabbergasted by how clean my Grandmother kept the place: fresh flowers in every corner, candles and crucifixes and saints' pictures hanging on the wall. 'Real live human beings live in worse conditions,' I thought cynically.

However, when I saw the large picture of my Granddad, I did feel something extraordinary. His beautiful eyes and his curly black hair had almost come alive. I felt the warmth of his hand going down my cheeks like he used to do when I was a kid. I did not hear a sound, just felt a great sense of peace. Everything had magically disappeared and I was now in a better place, all white and just love around me. I dropped to my knees and I cried gently, with my head leaning against the marble covering the grave. For the very first time in a long time, those were tears of happiness.

My Grandmother brought me back to life with a warm hug and some mumbled nonsense. I turned around to hug her too but I got annoyed because I realised she was not talking to me, but to her dead husband! I was upset by the fact she had disturbed me during such an intense and enjoyable experience, so I went outside to sit on the stairs of the chapel, hoping that I would be able to go back to the place I had just been to. Unfortunately, my Grandmother did not let me go anywhere as she stopped mumbling to her dead husband and started chanting at him.

'What the hell is she doing?' I thought, now completely irritated.

'Who is she talking to? An expensive piece of marble? Why is she shouting? Why is she telling him all that? He can't hear you, you dumb cow!' I complained silently to myself.

She was talking, very loudly, to my Granddad just as if he had been alive. She was recounting the local news: things going on with the neighbours, with the post office and almost everything that had happened to her since her last visit to his grave.

In the south of Italy, apparently, that was quite a common thing to do as they take death very seriously indeed down there.

'The power of religion!' I said under my breath as I marvelled at her crazy faith.

Nevertheless, she carried on talking to him like he had been there, even begging his spirit to come down and supervise me during my exams.

'Incredible,' I thought. 'Such an intelligent woman ... doing such a thing.'

She went on like this for a while. I had plenty of time to think on my own, but I couldn't because she was so loud. So all I could do was think about what she was doing. And then...

All of a sudden, something happened to me. My tears stopped, my heart started pumping faster and my muscles tensed. I could hear the Bill Conti track 'Going The Distance' from *Rocky* as if it was playing in my ear.

I stood up and I felt a new lease of life embracing me. Ironically, it had come from a dead man. My nonno (Grandfather) had come back to save me. It was *my revelation*.

THE END

I had no time to waste, so I hugged my Grandmother, and jumped on my Vespa to race back to Naples. I left her bemused at the cemetery.

Gone in seconds. If I had known I would never see her again, I would have made more of an effort to say goodbye.

Having contemplated an act of personal sacrifice which amounted, no more or less, to suicide, I felt like I was born again.

I travelled back as fast as I could without actually killing myself. The way I cut through the heavy traffic it was lucky I didn't. Instead, I left a trail of fuming car drivers in my wake.

If I could get off the ropes and land one knockout blow I could yet emerge victorious, from a fight that hitherto had looked like having only one winner. 'Going The Distance' kept playing in my head.

I managed to catch up with Gianni on his way back home from school. When he saw me, he shouted: 'Prinze! Good to see you. We were all worried about you!'

He literally jumped on me; hugging me. Actually, I knew his affections weren't sexual but it still made me uneasy, so I pushed him away.

'I need everyone at the Cave as soon as possible. Please get them all back from Lugano. I'll wait at the Cave, OK?' I ordered.

I then disappeared, taking for granted he was off to do exactly as I had asked.

When I walked back into the Cave, I got down to work.

I made a list of all the bugging and electronic equipment available to me as I had no time to buy any more material. As I was recalibrating some of the transmitters, the guys made their way in, all five of them; they paraded silently in line like a squad of soldiers. They were looking at me with a clear sense of anxiety, my moment of suicidal madness, evidently, still fresh in their minds.

I paused for the emotions to settle then I gave them their work to do. Gianni would be the busiest. He had to apply a heavy disguise for Pasquale, the IT Guy and the Spanish.

The Cat's job was to find out where and when the funeral of the two 'Names' killed this week was to take place.

No more time for talking, we all had work to do. The task was easier than others we had done recently but time was of the essence and mistakes could not be tolerated. I worked through the night to readjust and calibrate the sensitivity on the bugs and the transmitters for their new jobs.

The Cat had no problem finding out where the 'magnificent seven' were to be buried. We couldn't be in two places at once. Ideally, all the funerals would take place at different times so the gang could attend them all. Luckily they were.

Everything was in place. After that, it was my turn to pay a visit to the dead, and climb into four different cemeteries. During two long nights, I had to visit each grave twice: once to measure up where I would put the bugs and the second time to place them effectively. On the day in between the two visits, armed with the distances from bug hiding spot to headstone, I finalised the sensitivity settings on the bugs and tested them outside the Cave.

Apart from the fact that the cemetery is not a merry place to be in the middle of the night, that was not the most difficult job I had accomplished in my 'criminal career'. All the bugs were well hidden. The chances of anyone finding them were negligible. Within four days of the burials, each of the seven graves was now under surveillance. I could hear a pin drop at a graveside while sitting in my office at the Cave. I prayed that some of their friends and families would be crazy talkers like my Grandmother – crazy enough to try to talk to the dead. Thank God for the Catholic Church!

The first few days we got complete silence, I was initially a little shocked but before I had time to dream up any kind of 'Plan B', some guests finally paid a visit to my circus. Many of the 'colleagues' of the deceased did not attend the funerals, as they could not be seen to be connected to them in any way. They paid their respects individually, later on, at different times over the course of the evening, when it was quieter.

Their relatives, brothers, sisters, cousins, and parents, came during the day. The bugs were sound activated (and if the bug did not hear any sound, it would switch itself off). I relied on the cemetery being fundamentally quiet in between times or the battery would have died too soon.

The batteries did die. But they were not wasted. I had to pay those graves several more visits in the middle of the night to replace them to keep my show on the road. And it kept getting more interesting.

In all the weeks, I accumulated over 36 hours of 'Confessions from the grave'.

The mourners were kind enough not only to mention the name and surname of the Butcher during their conversations but also tons of other incriminating evidence. It went far beyond even my wildest imagination. The other members of the gang, sometimes present with me while listening to the tapes, were amazed by how much detail the events were described in. These guys obviously had a lot on their minds and needed to unburden themselves. Tony Soprano from the famous TV series had a shrink. Well, these guys didn't, but they surely needed one all the same. These graveside outpourings were clearly the next best thing.

Now I had what the Captain and his FBI mates really wanted and had been waiting so long for me to deliver.

I imagined the Butcher as if he were a city protected by powerful walls. Until now, I had laid siege to that city, thrown every piece of artillery at it that I had and I'd not made a single scratch. The walls were impenetrable and all I was doing was wasting time and energy. All it had done was demoralised my team. The police had made the same mistake.

The 'Confessions from the grave' made me look at those walls differently as I now had an insight into what was behind the fortress and how those walls were built. The empire that the Butcher had built was not protected by stones but by a precise combination of FEAR–TRUST–GREED. The Butcher controlled his closest allies thorough fear. As a consequence, he could trust them and, in exchange for large amounts of money, they worked for him and did almost anything he wanted. If I were to bring down those walls, I had to undermine the Butcher's ability to control this equation. I knew that, if I took away one stone at a time from his city walls, the Butcher would rebuild before it collapsed. If I took away a majority of the cardinal stones all at the same time, the fortress would collapse in a second.

I needed inspiration from history. Who doesn't in times of trouble? This time it was the battle of Alesia. In 52 BC Julius Caesar laid siege to the city of Alesia, home to a rebellious Gallic tribe. The city's walls were impregnable so the Roman general did not attack them. Instead, he built a new set of walls around the city and starved Vercingetorix, Asterisk, Obelisk and the rest of his people into submission without throwing a single stone. All he did, after he had cut off their food supply, was to wait until they came out to beg for their lives.

The recordings had no legal value whatsoever; they would have been thrown out of court. Moreover, if the Butcher's lawyer could not silence the witnesses then all the 'accidental confessors' would simply have been killed themselves in turn and replaced in the space of a month. Like Caesar, I had to go against convention. The taped confessors talked about future killings, promotions, demotions, who was doing what and, in some cases, how much money they were being paid to do it. In front of others, the confessors were very good at hiding their discontent, especially from senior members of the Butcher's Family. Most of the discontent stemmed from losing close family members during one of the Butcher's frequent purges of his 'org chart'. As the Butcher kept all his prestanomi and underbosses at a safe distance from each other, they were also in competition with one another to make more money and to get up the criminal ladder faster than anyone else.

In Italy, the law of silence, known as the Omertà, was the first commandment of the underworld. Anyone involved would always refuse to talk to the police. And so prosecuting the Mafia was very difficult. My tapes started a wave of 'pentiti'. Pentiti is the plural Italian noun for those people who cooperated with the police.

They did so in waves. Waves that led all the way to the USA where the same tactics led to the arrest of hundreds of senior members of the Cosa Nostra (the Sicilian equivalent of Naples' Camorra).

It was time to make another 'best of' tape and then get into disguise.

As Gianni was dolling me up with a wig and make-up, he said: 'You look hot.'

I hated dressing up like a woman. I lost count of how many whistles I heard on my way to the police compound but that did not bother me as much as the fact that I enjoyed it! What an ego.

Even the police at the reception of the compound gave me larger smiles than usual. I gave my name as that of the Captain's other sister, knowing this was our ancient pre-arranged code, and somewhat confident that he would remember and comply.

When he came down to pick me up, he looked so empty and distant that he would not have recognised me if I had turned up as myself!

In my best female voice, I told him that I had some personal and important issues to discuss with him and asked if we could go somewhere private. He did not hesitate. When we finally walked into a meeting room, I took my blonde wig off.

'Listen to this,' I replied confidently while I got the tape out of my bra.

Before we were halfway through the tape, he asked: 'Have you got more of this?'

'You betcha!' I replied, fending him off as he tried to hug me.

'I've got some other news for you' I added as I pushed him away as hard as I could.

'What kind of news?' he replied, his epic euphoria quickly subsiding.

'I am working for the Big Boss' I said. I'd shared most of my crimes with him before but this was next-level bad, so I expected him to take it badly, too. But he took it well. Too well.

'Fine. As long as these tapes are genuine and there's more of them, I don't care,' he replied matter-of-factly. 'Go away, keep a low profile, get me the rest of the tapes and come back in 24 hours.'

'And the magic word is...' I said.

'Please!' he added cheerfully. I could be as cheeky as I wanted now, it seemed.

'Good, will you see me out, and don't stare at my arse,' I said as I put the wig back on.

The rest of the gang had to work very long hours to cross-reference and identify the voices on the tapes with the names and addresses of our surveillance targets.

Because the tapes were useless in court, what the police and the FBI had to do was simple: get the subjects of the tapes to listen to what was being said about them behind their backs and overturn the 'FEAR–TRUST–GREED' equation. If one of the underbosses, after listening to the tapes, knew that he, or his loved ones, was slated to be 'whacked', then he would no longer be scared of getting on the wrong side of the Butcher. A dead man walking has nothing to lose and can no longer be manipulated with threats. If the FBI and the police granted him protection, he might cooperate and break Omerta since he would be killed anyway. Greed was satisfied in a sense that his reward was not only the possibility of his survival but also the chance of starting a better life from scratch. Like cancer or a virus, we had to reprogram the cleverly structured cells of the criminal organisation to do our work for us.

To complete the last part of the puzzle, we carried on taping the 'Confessions from the grave' from mourners of other killed members of the Butcher's crime family, and we made copies: one for law enforcement and one for us. Despite everything, I still could not fully trust the police. There were so many of them on the Butcher's payroll.

It was going to be hectic: we all smelled blood and we had to go in for the kill.

When I turned up at the scheduled meeting a few days later, I was taught another lesson.

Dressed as a drug-squad cop, I waited while the Captain carefully tapped in a code to open a door into a secure meeting room. As the door opened, I nearly fainted on the spot.

The Big Boss, one of the most feared criminals in Italy, sat comfortably at the table, in a room inside a special police compound designed solely to destroy people like him. My reaction was in turns amazement, indignation, disgust. The grand betrayal that this signified made me sick.

The Captain and the Big Boss were in this together.

Surprising? In hindsight, not at all. The Big Boss professed a different kind of criminality that worked very well with the existing powers. He kept control of the city. Although his control was waning, he kept hard drugs off the streets wherever he could. He was business-friendly, so to speak. This meant he preferred to keep business flowing rather than engage in bloodshed and turf wars because of some slight. By managing the micro criminality himself, he had reduced the workload on the police force and made the city a better place to live.

The police, on the other hand, were rather complacent. They had by and large accepted his activities as they did relatively little harm to society (in their view) and, for a lack of a better way of doing things, they preferred to allow him to remain in charge than allow someone like the Butcher to take over.

It was the classic compromise, a concept too difficult for a young idealist like me to understand. No matter how clever I was I couldn't get my head round it. With experience comes maturity and perspective. Looking back, during the reign of the Big Boss, Naples had become a prosperous place and, by Italian standards, efficient and dynamic. The city was kept clean, the streets with little or no crime, with a thriving economy and a stable international trade. The Butcher, on the other hand, brought with him death and destruction as drugs ravaged families, destroyed young lives and increased street violence. If the police couldn't defeat both of them then they chose to protect the lesser of the two in order to empower him against the greater evil.

I understood, for the first time, that democracy does not work. People, especially Neapolitans, do not respect the rules unless they fear the ruler. The Big Boss acted as de facto ruler and the system around him was no more than an illusion. I felt naive and childish, that I hadn't foreseen this.

384

Despite my deep affection for Naples and Italy, my country and my people, I promised myself that I would leave and never come back.

The 'Big Boss' spoke first.

'You look surprised. Sorry but this is one secret that had to be kept. Until today.'

I was still shocked and disgusted. And angry, because I did not like being played.

'Let me continue by expressing my admiration and gratitude for all your hard work and ingenuity without which we wouldn't be here today.'

I still couldn't say anything. I couldn't even mutter a basic thank-you.

'Rest assured I will offer you our full protection going forwards.'

I think he must've thought I would relax at this point. But I didn't. I was still like some rabbit in the headlights.

'Your obligation is complete.'

It finally dawned on me. I was free. The mission was over. The Prince had led his team to a glorious victory. By team, I meant not just my gang, but the Big Boss and the Captain – all those sorry people who without me would not be here today celebrating. Now I started to relax.

'Now, let's talk about your "Relocation Package". I and the Captain have powerful friends in the USA. I think this might be a good place to go and live to get your life back on track. You are still young.'

He was pushing on an open door here. I had vowed to leave Italy so the USA would fit the bill nicely – to start with anyway – the world was my oyster, so they say.

I nodded but I still did not reply, not a single word. I did not ask if the Captain knew all along about me, if it had been a massive set-up for them to exploit me or any of the many other questions that were raging within me.

'Finish the job, take your final exams, sort the guys out and go away,' I said to myself. My obligation to the Big Boss was complete but my obligation to me and my people was not.

I would have to leave the gang and my family behind. My family didn't know then what I had done and, over 40 years later, they still don't. It's one of the reasons I waited so long to write this book.

I was anxious to finish the job. That feeling trumped the feelings of disgust about the corruption, and the compromises that accompanied it. Actually, I was disgusted about everything that had led me here too.

I spent 12 hours a day, 12 days straight in a room with 15 people (6 FBI agents, 3 from Interpol, an Italian magistrate, and the Captain and his close team). The Magistrate was from Milan, far from the corruption of Naples. He was young and like the Captain hungry to succeed where so many had failed. Imagine how funny it must have looked: a teenager teaching these big men how to do their jobs.

I handed over every document and, the more I gave away, the more I felt like a mule finally being unburdened.

As the operation continued apace, other members of the clan were killed. We kept on bugging their graves, houses and office phones. Apparently, by the time they went to trial, the agents had accumulated over 5,000 hours of relevant conversations. I think I had 350 hours taken over the period of three and half years. So you can see they took my idea and ran with it, many times over.

On the last day, when I had told them everything I knew, explained everything I had understood over the previous four years and finally given every piece of evidence I had in my possession, I brought down the final curtains on my show.

When I gave my final speech, one person, among others, left me with something I still treasure. He was a very senior member of the FBI, the man who, although not Italian himself, led the largely Italian team to victory. He was accompanied everywhere by a translator, an FBI agent of Italian descent. At the end of my final session of exposition, he invited me to a private room where I had been working. He looked at me in a way that no one else did: with genuine gratitude. Everyone else resented a kid telling them what to do and never missed an opportunity to ridicule me. I'm sure they were competent enough at their jobs in a narrow sense but like lots of Italians they had big 'Mummy's boy' egos and very little emotional intelligence.

Anyway, on my last day, that senior FBI guy shook my hand gently with respect, without trying to crush it to prove he was a man and I a boy. He spoke slowly to give the interpreter a chance to translate.

'Son, it has been a privilege to have worked with you. You have done a great thing. Mankind will be eternally grateful to you. Your flash of genius has changed the way we fight the underworld forever. Unfortunately, you will be forgotten. History cannot record you and your heroic deeds but I will not forget. If you ever need anything, just give me a call. My country will be honoured to welcome you.'

He then gave me his business card, which, together with the memory of those beautiful words, I have kept to this day and will continue to keep until I die.

'Thanks but you do not get rid of evil that easily, chief!' I thought but didn't say.

I never saw him or any of those FBI agents again. I didn't properly reply to those kind words at the time but, if you are reading this, I have meant to thank you for the past 40 years.

As soon as I left the police compound, I went home to get changed and to focus on my last two jobs:

Firstly to pass my final high school exams (the ones I had had simply no chance to study for) and, secondly, to leave my country once and for all – probably to the USA – although I hadn't decided for sure yet.

My exams started in three days, so I booked an international flight for four days later, and paid for three months' accommodation in advance through a travel agency in Rome.

On the train back from Rome, I kept myself busy analysing my chances of passing the exams without having done a shred of studying. Despite my high IQ, my chances were not good. With my general knowledge, my powerful memory and a dose of good luck, I could just scrape through. As Lady Luck had been far too kind to me recently, I decided not to rely on her for the time being.

Instead I would do what I was best at: cheat.

I made all the plans. I would pretend I had a car accident. Then Gianni could bandage me up to conceal a microphone, earpiece and two-way radio. On top of that, I'd hire a van full of top-notch undergraduates to park outside and act like it was 'phone a friend' on *Who Wants to be a Millionaire?*

It was all lined up, the bribes for the students were arranged, and then I thought to myself...

'What's the point? Who am I trying to prove it to? I am the Prince and I can do this, and if I can't then I have a good excuse even if it is one I can never tell anyone about.'

With all the hassle of trying to get complicated questions and answers in and out over a radio, maybe I would do better on my own than by spending 10 grand on cheating and at least I could avoid the agony of fake bandages and wires.

These exams were meant to be the start of my new life as a child once more. In my heart this had to start now, not when I boarded the plane.

Did I cheat? It doesn't matter how I did it, because all I did was scrape through – I got the minimum grades to pass and we all know I'm better than that. In the end, though, I was just happy to be alive and to have another crack at living a normal and happy life.

After the exams, I had just a day to pack my bags, cut my ties with my place of birth and, more importantly, to say goodbye to my friends, those five fine soldiers who fought many battles with me. I hate goodbyes and this time was no different. I spent the penultimate day of my Italian life by myself, going round the flat collecting various important documents to send to my family. I basically had to prepare the flat to be safely left empty, and I forwarded them the paperwork, in case they wanted to sell it.

Then I called my Mum. As usual, I did not tell her the whole story. I said I had been accepted by a foreign university. This was half-true as I was sure I would end up going to university after I left. And I did, but with my grades it certainly wasn't easy to get in!

I told her they would pay for everything – not true – my Swiss bank account would supplement that hugely. She believed everything. For a long time, I spoke to her only by phone. I didn't see her again in person for another 12 years.

I thought very hard about how to say goodbye to my other family, my gang. This would be the third and last goodbye, the first being when I tried to commit suicide by my own hand, and the second when I planned to give myself up and commit suicide at the Butcher's hands. I was pretty confident that it would be 'third time lucky'.

I called Gianni to tell him to gather the gang at Naples' airport departure terminal at noon the following day. I hoped they would get the hint about what I was about to do. My check-in was at 2 p.m., so enough time for my last speech but not enough time for the long goodbyes to drag on and get too emotional. I packed all my best clothes like the last time I had tried to leave. This time I hoped to be more successful.

I went to the airport early that morning by train and, because I had never really travelled internationally before (Switzerland aside), I wanted to do some homework before I flew out of the country. I had just 900 euros in cash, although my accommodation at the destination was paid up for the next three months.

At 11 a.m., one hour before the guys were supposed to turn up, I went to the airport cafe for one last Neapolitan cappuccino. I swore that I would never go back to Naples. For 15 years I kept my promise. I sat there, in this faux coffee bar bustling with people. I was flooded with memories. Everything around me reminded me of something that had happened in the last five years. It was difficult not to cry. I was leaving my home and my friends. The only thing that made it easier was that my family had already left.

The guys turned up half an hour before scheduled, looking sad and resigned. I had not told them my plans but I soon saw that they knew this was the big goodbye. I had not taken them by surprise this time. They walked single file towards me, like the five soldiers that they were. They were all dressed up for the occasion and even the Cat had made an effort to look like a human rather than a feral beast. Without saying a word, they all sat around me, like we used to do during the good (and bad) times in the Cave.

Inevitably, it was up to me to open the dance. Struggling to hold back my tears, I started:

'I can see you have already understood what I am doing here, so I am not going into that. Before I say what I have to say, you have to do one little thing for me, this will the last thing I ask of you, call it my parting gift.' I chuckled then paused before resuming...

'Please, get rid of everything in the Cave. Do what you want with it, but empty that wretched place. Keep anything you want as a memento. Now, my real parting gift... As I have taken so much from you, I hereby, officially, give up my share of the business in Lugano. Share it equally between yourselves, and make sure that you carry on making a success of the business, and of your lives.'

Then the wave of protests started.

'We did it together, it belongs to you too!' the IT Guy shouted.

We all knew that it was always supposed to be shared six ways. I was moved by their generosity and honesty. The business in Lugano, even though it was not doing as well as before, had stabilised and my share was a nest egg to start again in the USA. They tried to refuse my gift but I was in no mood to negotiate, and anyway I wanted to be forced to get a job in my new country.

'Listen, will you! We had fantastic five years together. We fought many battles and we went to hell and back many times together. You are not just my friends ... you are like brothers to me. In fact, you are part of me and I will never, ever, forget you. Unfortunately, the combination that we create when we are together is not conducive to peace and quiet, if you know what I mean. Therefore, I have decided to have a clean start and to give you guys a clean start of your own. I think it will be best if we never see each other again, as our enemies might find out who I am and harm you as well as me. We have to delete the record of the time spent together and hope it will never come back to haunt us. This is it. It is over and it has to stay over. Please, do not make this any harder than it is.'

My neck was now struggling to hold my head and I just could

not look up anymore. Pasquale grabbed my hand and shook it so vigorously he almost broke it.

While the rest of them came over to hug me, we received some unexpected visitors.

I don't know how they found out that I was leaving the country, that I was at the airport or that I would be at the coffee bar at that particular moment. Then again, I was tired of asking questions, of trying to understand and, most of all, of being suspicious and angry. Whatever the truth was, the Captain and his team showed up in high uniform. They might have been the finest officers Italy had to offer but I would not have swapped them with my boys, my five heroes. It is fair to say that I was not happy that our private goodbye was being hijacked by the boys in blue.

The Captain sensed my displeasure immediately and did not look surprised by it. He merely took a step back. My boys rallied to form a wall in front of me, as if to protect me.

'What were they going to do now? Arrest me?' I thought, suddenly worried I would miss my plane while I dealt with bureaucracy gone mad down at the police station.

Instead, the Captain cautiously said to me in a low tone: 'I think you should know that the judge has signed all the warrants and the Special Forces have taken the Butcher into custody. We have arrested 67 of them. We are sure they will be going down for multiple life sentences.'

The Captain went and stood in a line-up with his team and then, in a solemn but much louder tone said: 'Prince, in name of the Italian Republic and its People, we salute you and your team' and, as soon as he finished, they all performed a military-style salute and clicked their boot heels together so loudly that you could have heard them in Rome. I wanted them gone. They were stealing my last precious seconds with my boys away from me. In his own way, he was trying to thank me but I did not respond. They took the hint and they all left, walking back through the coffee bar while the other customers stared in shocked silence.

When they finally disappeared, the guys and I hugged, cried and hugged again as violently as we ever had. We did not say a word more. We did not need to.

Whenever I go back to that moment of my life, those scenes are fittingly accompanied by the last song of the *Rocky* movie, 'The Final Bell'.

My time had come and I had to go. They walked me silently to passport control. When they hugged me for the last time, I felt the warmth of their tears on my face. I still remember the emotions I felt that day. I cannot find the words to describe the love that existed between us but I had the impression that I could touch the energy that, together, we were generating. I felt the same energy when I saw my Granddad dying.

I could not take it anymore, so I turned around and left. As I was showing my passport to the airport guy, I glanced behind me for one last look. I took a mental picture of all five of them, lined up next to each other, staring at me in the forlorn hope I would change my mind. They looked funny to me: all different sizes, shapes, ages and backgrounds. Who would have ever thought that these guys would make such an efficient team, eh? That thought gave me the strength to smile as I gave them my last wave.

I never saw them again.

When I was going up the stairs to board my plane, I felt like Superman carrying a ton of kryptonite on his shoulders. My confidence had disappeared, to be replaced by a deep and depressing sense of loneliness. I walked like a zombie behind my fellow passengers and onto the plane. My feet dragged but I could no longer feel my body. The world around me slowed as I relived all my most painful experiences. The more those images accelerated, the more I wanted to just go back in time and start all over again. The only thing I could do was to start a new movie, a new life. Wonderful music was accompanying my memories, and it was not the *Rocky* soundtrack but a piece by Verdi called 'Va, pensiero', also known as the 'Chorus of the Hebrew Slaves'. The song's theme was of exiled slaves singing about their homeland. I felt I had a lot in common with those beautiful and sad notes as I was now going into an exile of my own. Unlike my life, this is a magnificent piece of work, without flaw.

When the plane finally took off, I watched Naples getting smaller and smaller. I could not help wondering why a place of such beauty was home to so much evil. I was now crying gently, with my head leaning against the window and my hands held together. A young woman, sitting next to me, asked me if I was OK. I just nodded.

She asked: 'What is your name, pretty boy?'

Ignoring the crass and unwelcome compliment, I started to reply, 'I am the P...' but I stopped just in time.

I then gave my real Christian name.

The Prince was gone. I would never be called Prince again in my life and I would never introduce myself with my old nickname to anyone. The 'Prince' died when the plane took off, to be replaced by just a young boy, going to a foreign country on his own where he knew nobody and luckily nobody knew him.

EPILOGUE

I followed the whole affair through the newspapers in my newly adopted country. Even though the Captain had already told me about the Butcher's spectacular arrest, it was still glorious to read about it in sensational detail.

The senior FBI figure took control of the operation. He coordinated an international team that, simultaneously, raided several gangsters' and drug lords' homes on both sides of the Atlantic. More than 350 agents of the Italian Special Police Force raided and arrested the Butcher, confiscating more than 40 million euros of art alone. In Italy alone, more than 700 criminals were sentenced as a result. The government had to build a special bunker for their trials to take place. The young Italian magistrate was busy indicting many senior political figures. The whole thing erupted into 'Tangentopoli', which literally means the 'City of bribes': it was a series of criminal processes against politicians at all levels of power.

I recognised several of the FBI guys from my 'seminars' being pictured like heroes, giving interviews to the media and receiving medals and accolades of all sorts. I could not help wondering if they thought of me while receiving their honours.

When I read once more of the Butcher's arrest, I was not only proud for me but also for my boys. We had managed to achieve the impossible. I felt like the general of the battle of Thermopylae, in which 300 Spartans had kept the Persians from invading Europe in 480 BC. The unfortunate thing, though, like I was told by the FBI agent, is that history would not remember us.

I did play an important role bringing down a world of corruption and a criminal empire but, on reflection, I actually made it worse. Out of the ashes of the destruction left from our mission a new and more violent wave of smaller disparate criminal organisations sprang up. This led to more ruthlessness, more turf wars, more killings, more innocent deaths and more drugs on the streets. Just take a look at Naples now. The Big Boss was assassinated in this bloody process but, so far, nobody has been strong enough to replace him. Not completely. At this rate I doubt anyone will ever emerge with the power to merge them into one large crime organisation ever again.

After the collapse of my sworn enemies, Bulldog and the Christian Democratic Party, new political parties have inevitably replaced them. As none of them are capable of doing their jobs, they spend most of their time bickering with each other and ruining the country in one long slow economic downturn. Bulldog never even went to prison for what he did; he spent the rest of his days in exile in Africa.

Judging purely by the end result, I think my people were better off with the very crooks I helped eliminate. Good or bad, at least they were capable of running the city and keeping some kind of stability. I couldn't have foreseen this outcome and, even if I had, I was compelled on pain of death to carry out my mission, but it's still painful for me to admit that it was so pointless.

One thing is for sure: Italy, once my country, is suffering more now than ever. And so am I.

And to think, all I ever wanted was to re-house my Mum after that earthquake.